# GANGLAND
The Lawyers

# GANGLAND

## The Lawyers

*James Morton*

*Virgin*

First published in Great Britain in 2001 by
Virgin Publishing Ltd
Thames Wharf Studios
Rainville Road
London
W6 9HA

A catalogue record for this book is available from
the British Library.

ISBN 1 85227 941 9

Typeset by Phoenix Photosetting, Chatham, Kent
Printed and bound in Great Britain by
Mackays of Chatham, Chatham, Kent

For my Father, who revered all lawyers

# Contents

# Introduction

Perhaps I should start with a double admission. Firstly, my family included, so it was always said, a dishonest solicitor – or soly-citor as my father insisted on pronouncing the word. Secondly, I was a Gangland Lawyer.

As to the first, he was my grandmother's brother which, I suppose, strictly makes him my great-uncle but uncle sounds more immediate and is less cumbersome. His name was David Milner and I know that he was kept, by my father at any rate, on the same level in the family pantheon as my aunt who inadvertently committed bigamy. According to the legend Uncle David had already been retired from practice for some years before the Second World War, at which time he was pressed into service. There was then some trouble over either a forgery, a fraudulent transaction or the client account; details were vague. In the story which now became specific, Uncle David found himself at the Old Bailey in 1943. Apparently, because details once more became vague, he left my grandmother's house in Blackheath with a small attaché case containing his pyjamas and a toothbrush, fully expecting to be locked up, upon which I suspect his attaché case, pyjamas and toothbrush would have been confiscated. At the time he had a wife, and there was also likely succour from several unoccupied maiden nieces who were living in a nearby house which effectively amounted to a zenana. This did not even include the bigamous one who, together with a gin bottle to whose brothers she had become increasingly attached, could also have been rallied in support. None of them, apparently, travelled with him to watch his fate. By the evening, however, he was back having been given what was regarded by the family as a conditional discharge. 'Silly old fool,' my father would say when he retold the story which he did – to the discomfort of the others – most Christmases shortly before we stood for the national anthem and watched the Queen's speech in reverential silence. 'He should never have been allowed to practise.'

The facts were slightly different. Milner had been admitted in 1889 and had been in practice in High Holborn and Blackheath until his hiccough, which had occurred not in 1943 but four years earlier. He had acted for the Prudential when they lent money on mortgage, and apparently since 1900 had dealt with over 12,500 cases with over £12 million passing through his hands.

He had received between one and three guineas for each transaction. Entitled to put his fees up some 33 per cent during the First World War, he had never done so. In 1938 he was made bankrupt with debts of over £9,000, nearly £7,000 of which were monies he had misappropriated from the Prudential. He claimed to have assets of £48,000, but the Official Receiver's version was that he would be lucky to retrieve £5,000. My uncle's house in Blackheath was apparently something of a junk-shop as he had accepted second-hand wirelesses and other electrical goods in settlement of his fees and as security for loans he made quite improperly.

He appeared at the Old Bailey on 6 December 1939 and was remanded for sentence the next day. His age in *The Times'* story, 'Aged Solicitor's Fraud', was given as 72. He must have then aged overnight because in the report the next day he was two years older – which must have been where the toothbrush story came into play. He was sentenced by Mr Justice Atkinson with the sympathy the courts often show to the elderly middle and upper classes. There had been medical evidence about my uncle's health and this pleased the judge. Pointing out that naughty solicitors usually went to penal servitude, he said that the medical evidence showed that over the years there had been a gradual breakdown in his mental powers. 'I hoped I would get a report of this kind,' said the kindly judge, 'because it enables me to give full effect to your 70 years of honest life.' The first four years apparently did not count. Either that or – with the relief arising from the fact that he received a term of three days, which meant his immediate release – the years had fallen from him.

I wonder who wrote the report. It would have been both appropriate and symmetric if it had been another uncle who took an overdose of the ether to which he was addicted, but in fact Atkinson had merely asked the court medical officer to run the rule over my uncle. Today it is unthinkable that no reports were prepared on his behalf. The family may not have turned up to applaud from the public gallery, but someone put up the money for a King's Counsel to represent him. Poor David had not benefited a penny from his fraud; he had been applying the stolen monies to the accounts of those who were falling behind in their repayments. His counsel, in the hyperbole so often used in mitigation, had told the judge that 'any criminal or quasi-criminal in the City had only to get in touch with Milner, pitch a smooth-tongued story and get almost any sum they liked to ask for'.

The *News of the World* had him as being 'almost tearful' as he was greeted by his grey-haired wife on his release. 'I must get back to work again,' he is reported to have said. Whether this was a genuine comment, an indication of his mental instability thinking he still had a job or a bit of spicc for the readers, I shall never know.

Milner, like all the male members of the family, was physically a large man and my cousin, who himself ended up at 6'5", remembers as a child running beside him as he strode over Blackheath carrying a white handkerchief. In later life at any rate he appears not to have been a particularly adroit businessman, an affliction which culminated in his bankruptcy and which, to a greater or lesser extent, beset almost all the other male members of the family. After he was struck off the roll of solicitors in April 1940 he and his wife moved to Kent where, in a desultory fashion, they kept chickens which apparently gave a whole new meaning to the concept of free-range. The birds laid their eggs in such dense undergrowth that my uncle usually failed to find them before they went bad.

Probably David Milner could not properly be described as a Gangland Lawyer. I don't suppose for a minute that, until his own problem, he ever saw the inside of a police station except to ask for directions. His counsel, however, had the key to his problems and those of many another solicitor who has fallen foul of the courts: he had allowed himself to be used by criminals and quasi-criminals.

Although this book is not about my career or really those whom I encountered, how did I become a Gangland Lawyer? How does anyone? In my case it soon became quite apparent to the solicitor to whom I was articled that I was never going to be of any assistance to him in his conveyancing practice for which I had been hired. At some time or another before I arrived, he had also acquired a Welsh ex-police officer as a clerk, Powell, known as Sandy, who claimed – as did most of them in those days – to have had a trial for the national rugby union side. Quite what he was doing in the firm was never wholly clear. Powell worked in an attic at the top of the building and came and went much as he pleased. A great drinker and a great supporter of Tottenham Hotspur, he could be found drunk on the steps of the town hall on the nights when they had a cup victory. He was never arrested. His former colleagues would bundle him in the back of a police car, take his house keys, open gate and front door, point him in the right direction and give him a shove. The name of the game was to get away before he collapsed on the step and brought the wrath of the fearsome Mrs Powell on their heads. When a former police colleague died – and there seemed to be a minor but continuing epidemic in the years when I knew him – a funeral would take place at the local crematorium and they would all repair to a public house on the North Circular Road. There they would drink for the remainder of the day and evening until, almost out of their minds, at 10 p.m. they would have a minute's silence irrespective of the wishes of the other paying customers who would then be invited to join in the singing of 'Abide With Me'. Sandy would often be missing for several days after the funeral of one of his closer colleagues. When he did return he would have serious difficulty in controlling his shakes sufficiently to write anything.

Within a few days of my qualifying he annexed me to appear for one of his clients. I forget the charge and whether I simply had to agree to a remand, but I must have done well because he had a few more appearances lined up for me the following week. There were a number of reasons. It was cheaper to use me than counsel. I was keen and clients didn't (and don't) mind losing provided a show was put on for them. Better still from his point of view, he didn't have to go into the office that morning but could just meet me in the matron's room at the court where he would have a cup of tea, some toast and cut up touches with his former colleagues.

A few weeks later he arranged a deal through an old colleague under which I would prosecute shoplifting cases for a small supermarket chain. The fee per case was nugatory but as my trainer, manager and promoter he regarded it as good experience. Probably he was taking some sort of kickback. He wasn't overmatching me either, because it was not difficult getting local benches to convict unrepresented and inarticulate women. After a time he ceased to bother to come with me and I was left in the hands of a very pretty Italian store detective with whom I was secretly in love, but I was far too staid and frightened to do anything about it. Over a year we had an almost unblemished record together. She would telephone me in an evening and tell me where the following day's cases were to be heard. I would read the papers the next morning at court. Then one day she rang. Could she come and see me? I presumed it was a difficult case, but when she arrived it was to tell me she had been arrested and was appearing the next morning in the local court. My manager kicked into action and the charge was dropped, but I never saw her again. By then, however, Sandy had found me other cases. I had also achieved a modest local fame. One woman prosecuted by me arrived at the offices the following day to pay a small retainer so that I did not appear against her or her sons of whom there were a goodly number.

In those days legal aid was not readily available. I came across a cutting the other day where a woman was charged with causing grievous bodily harm with intent to injure and had been remanded in custody. She had thrown acid in a man's face. Asked if she had anything to say, she replied, 'Can I have legal aid?' The kindly magistrate replied that she did not need it.

Defendants, except major criminals, did not have their own regular briefs and there was often some court-appointed work if you were in the right place. The local jailers would also point clients in my direction on an informal basis. One asked if the arrangement could be placed on a more formal one so that if he sent me a case I paid him £5, and if it went to Quarter Sessions he would receive a further £7. 10s. I pointed out to him that this was financially, let alone professionally, impractical. I had just defended a murder case which had run a day and a half at the Old Bailey and for which I had been paid £22. He did not seem to mind and continued to send me a steady stream of work. I suspect that when the client went down to the cells to collect his belongings after a successful bail application some money had changed hands.

Then I moved a little nearer towards the bigger time. A man I represented was a successful lorry hijacker. Against police opposition I obtained him bail and he decided I should keep the case. In those days it was possible for a man to be arrested and to appear for a jury trial at Sessions within three weeks. Indeed this character had made four such appearances within the last nine months. I asked him why he wanted to leave his highly successful solicitors. 'Their luck couldn't last,' was his reply. Mine lasted over a year for him until at 4 a.m. one morning shortly before Christmas he was found unloading whisky from someone's lorry in a locked warehouse down the East End. Before that unhappy moment he had pointed a number of his colleagues in my direction.

In the meantime the firm had employed another assistant solicitor, Bryan Gammon, a man with the considerable ability and charm required by both advocates and the conmen they represent and so often resemble. He was found with his fingers trapped firmly in the till, or rather out of it because he pocketed cash fees which should have been put in that very place. He left summarily but unprosecuted, and was employed by a very smart firm in the West End. Because that firm was much grander than ours, the ensuing and even inevitable default was that much greater and Gammon moved northwards where he received four years imprisonment following yet more fraud. After his release he deteriorated, and he perished when he accidentally – if drunkenly – set fire to his bed and thereby himself in a small hotel in the Notting Hill district of London. He was another lawyer who inspired great affection amongst his clients and, the noted cat-burglar Raymond Jones, who once appeared in the *Guinness Book of Records* for remaining at liberty following escape from a British prison, would speak lovingly of him twenty years after his death. When Gammon left for points west some of his better clients remained with me.

Now my employer had begun to believe that, quite apart from the toll of the problems of the departing Gammon, the increasing presence of large unshaven men reading the *Greyhound Express* and smoking hand-rolled cigarettes in his waiting room was having a deleterious effect on the elderly ladies who had come to make their wills and, he hoped, leave him a small legacy whilst so doing. My clients were banished to sit on the stairs. It was time to leave and I set up on my own account in Holborn.

This book will also recount the exploits, often inextricably linked, of the Gangland Lawyers' clients. Now comes the first problem: how does one define a gang and gangland? Ronnie Kray used to say that gangs were only for young boys. Career criminals prefer the use of the word team. Gangs certainly conjure up the image of the Thompson machine gun, the chopper and the stiletto, the kilo of heroin. In fact a gang of coiners, counterfeiters, smugglers or money-launderers can do just as much, if not rather more, damage to an economy than the violent criminal. I have therefore taken gangland to mean a floating coterie of career criminals. Never fear, there will be a steady diet of the machine gun. In the increasingly politically sensitive world in which we live it is no longer, in England, polite to refer to the criminal lawyer. He, or now very often she, is a lawyer who defends criminals. In America, Gerald Shargel, arguably the No. 1 defence lawyer in New York at the present, points out that he is 'a lawyer for the Mob and not a Mob lawyer'.

Lawyers are no different from other men and women in society. One expects them, possibly because of their education and the calling they have answered, to perform on a higher plane of ethics than say car mechanics or estate agents. The same is true of doctors and clerics, but there is no reason why lawyers, doctors and clerics should not suffer venereal itch or sticky fingers, tiresome wives or importunate boyfriends any less than stock-car-racing promoters or firemen. Indeed their apologists would argue that such is the stress under which members of the legal profession perform – the decisions to be taken which can in certain circumstances mean life or death or certainly long imprisonment amongst its members – that the rate of alcoholism and divorce is far higher than in many another profession which calls for less pressure on its acolytes.

This book then is about those lawyers good and bad, honest and dishonest, self-sacrificing and sometimes evil, who have consistently defended the men and sometimes women who could be described as organised crime figures or career criminals.

It is also about those lawyers who have stepped across the line and taken up crime as a career for themselves, either acting alone or in some cases organising quite a considerable body of troops. Some were, in their own way, heroic figures. James Boswell, himself a lawyer, writing in the days when attendance at public executions was a social event, described the attorney Mr Gibson, who was hanged for forgery, in glowing terms:

> [He] came in a coach with some of his friends and I declare I cannot conceive a more perfect calmness and manly resolution than his behaviour.
>
> The rope was put round his neck and he stood in the most perfect composure, ate a sweet orange and seemed rationally devout during prayers ...
>
> I never saw a man hanged but I thought I could behave better than he did except Mr Gibson, who, I confess, exceeded all that I could ever hope to show of easy and steady resolution.[1]

An American lawyer who has never found the fame he undoubtedly deserves is George Avery who in 1870, when he was 21, was charged with the murder of John Harper of Rowlands, Pike County. He escaped on his way to prison mainly because the sheriff escorting him was drunk. The next day Avery collected his jailer, delivered him to the prison and surrendered himself. Despite overwhelming evidence he was acquitted of the murder. On the day of his acquittal he was charged with burglary and received 18 months. Now his career took off. He read law in the state prison and, on his release, opened an office in Philadelphia. He had his accusers in the burglary case charged with perjury, but when the charges failed he was ordered to pay the costs. When he failed to do that he was again imprisoned. Finally the debt was paid and he returned to Rowlands, Pike County, where it was said 'burglaries were never so numerous'. He then went to Oil City where, with great success, he hung out his shingle. Unfortunately he was convicted of forgery and was sent to the Western penitentiary where he served 4 years 11 months. During that time he fell in love with the jailer's daughter who offered to help him escape. By now he had religion and declined her generous offer. On his release, as is so often the case, the Light faded and he swindled a neighbour out of $100. The neighbour took a shotgun to the erring lawyer who now went to Luzerne County where he fared little better, ending in the Eastern penitentiary. On his release he stole enough to take him to the mining regions of the West. Now his story becomes one of unalloyed success. He opened another law office, speculated and in 1882 struck rich, clearing some $750,000. He married the jailer's daughter and said he was now leading an honest life. He hoped to become a senator.[2]

Some are born to the work. When in March 1938 William Henry Bey Quilliam went to prison, he was really following in the footsteps of his rather more successful father, Sheik Abdulla Quilliam, a Liverpool solicitor said to have been the leader of the Moslem community in Britain. Hardly had William Henry qualified than he went to the offices, only to find his father had fled to Turkey along with the books and much of the client account. His father did eventually return as Henri Marcel Leon, the head of a school of physiology, but wisely he would never acknowledge his former position as Sheik. William Henry was a talented solicitor with a good criminal practice. Unfortunately he began to indulge in dubious business matters and when the net started to close fled to Bulgaria where he was introduced to a farm on which eggs were blown and filled with cocaine. He declined the lucrative opportunity of becoming the business's European and English representative and, instead, continued his fraudulent activities until he received two years at the Old Bailey. Like Gibson in very much more trying circumstances he behaved extremely well. He asked the judge to increase his sentence and release the members of his team, but this was declined. On his release he was likely to have to go to Zurich where he was wanted for a loan scheme swindle.

Sadly, because of the self-imposed if loose parameters, it has been necessary to omit lawyers who have 'gone bent' in other ways. So there can be no room for Herbert Rowse Armstrong, sometime a Major in the Royal Engineers, who on 31 May 1922 garnered the unique distinction in English legal history of being the only solicitor, or barrister for that matter, to be hanged for murder. Given the abolition of the death penalty and the present disinclination of Parliament to restore it, the good Major is likely to retain that record unchallenged for the foreseeable future.

Nor can a place really be found for the Chicago lawyer Warren Lincoln who, in 1925, planted the heads of his wife and brother-in-law in pots on the front porch because he was tired of listening to them gabble. He denied recognition of the heads, saying he had found them in his greenhouse and put them in concrete to preserve the evidence – something any right-minded lawyer would do.

Another who has to be excluded from the pantheon is the once highly thought of English barrister John Averill. Late in his relatively short career he became increasingly odd, declining to stand when the judge entered court and, shortly before his death and after joining a somewhat arcane Eastern sect, he was suspected of stealing a cross from a Catholic church in West London.

They and many others – such as the former President of the Law Society and then current head of discipline for the profession, Sir Benjamin Lake, who was found guilty of fraud and whose brother and partner, George, was suspected of faking his death in Berlin – will have to wait for perhaps another day.[3]

Sadly, there will of course have been a number of omissions of both lawyers and their clients. If those who think they, their relatives, friends or legal representatives qualify for inclusion in any further edition of this slightly chipped gallery, perhaps they will be kind enough to contact me.

I am most grateful to the many people who have helped with tales of their former colleagues or representatives, or who have otherwise contributed to the book. They include Al Alschuler, Tish Armstrong, Albert Aronne, Mickey Bailey, John Baker, Jeremy Beadle, J.P. Bean, Joe Beltrami, Paula Blezard, James Cartwright, John Clitheroe, Dave Critchley, Jonathan Davies, Louis Diamond, Peter Donnelly, Jack Evseroff, James Ferguson, David Fingleton, Jeremy Fordham, Nigel Forsyth, Frank Fraser, Rod Green, Ralph Haemms, William Hellerstein, Brian Hilliard, Ronald Irving, Albert Krieger, James LaRossa, Rita Matharu, Jean Maund, Helen McCormack, Gavin McFarlane, Bill Pizzi, Humphrey Price, Monty Raphael, Nipper Read, Paul Rextrew, Silvia Rice, Laura Rosenberg, Gerald Shargel, Linda White and Richard Whittington-Egan. My thanks are no less due to those who gave advice, help and allowed themselves to be quoted but did not wish to be named.

This is yet another book which could not have been completed without the tireless help and support of Dock Bateson.

1 *The Journals of James Boswell*, pp. 197–8.
2 'Adventurous Avery' in *National Police Gazette* , 27 October 1883.
3 For those who cannot wait for the day they will find the case of the good Major in a number of books and anthologies, including Robin Odell, *Exhumation of a Murder* and, arguing very much in Armstrong's defence, Martin Beales, *Dead not Buried*. For Ian Wood's problems see *The Times*, 22 July 1989. For those of Warren Lincoln, *Thomson's Weekly News*, 7 February 1925, will provide some help. Lake's case was reported in *The Times* and there was correspondence about solicitors defrauding their clients in the subsequent issues *of Solicitors Journal* and *The Law Journal*.

# 1 James Townsend Saward and the First Great Train Robbery

ONE OF THE EARLIEST of modern lawyers turned criminal mastermind was James Townsend Saward. A member of Inner Temple and apparently having a decent practice by day, by night he was a consummate forger, receiver and putter-up of robberies. It is a tribute to Saward's skill and care that he managed to go undetected or even suspected until he was in his late fifties, by which time his career had lasted at least thirty and more probably forty years. His downfall was due as much to his associates as to his own failings.

Described as short, sturdily built, with suave and polished manners, he was called to the Bar in 1840. By then he had also built up a reputation as a man willing to pay a price for a cancelled cheque or better still a blank cheque form. As with so many other successful criminals, he could never be approached direct and could only be contacted by means of a number of cut-outs. It is curious that those who did know him never recognised him from seeing him in court.

Early in his career he worked with Henry Atwell or more likely had Atwell working for him. Shortly before Christmas 1855 Atwell, who went under a number of aliases, executed a safe-breaking in Brick Lane, Spitalfields, at the premises of an ironmonger J.B. Doe and came away with the prize of cancelled and blank cheques on Barclays Bank. Saward was wise enough to realise that it would be dangerous to forge the cheques for more than Doe's account was likely to be able to stand. He therefore went with Atwell to reconnoitre the shop before deciding that only two relatively small sums could be drawn with the blank cheques.

Cut-outs were the name of Saward's game and so through James Anderson, another of his men, a dupe was recruited to cash the cheques. A young man, Draper, had advertised for a job and Anderson (in disguise) interviewed him and then sent him to the bank to cash one of the cheques. It was a success. Draper was told he could not have the job but was given some money for his pains, and a second young man was recruited to cash the second cheque. Saward's gross profit came to the then not inconsiderable sum of £150.

And so, over the years, it went on. One of Saward's best extra-legal clients was the highly talented Edward Agar, a man of some style, independence and indeed honour. It was he who planned and executed the First Great Train Robbery. In 1855 gold bullion from the London–Folkestone train on the South-Eastern Railway which was on its way to pay the troops in the Crimean War was taken from an apparently secure van. Later, when Agar was called to give evidence against his co-conspirators, he denied in cross-examination that he had ever committed forgery with Saward but, drawing a neat line, admitted:

> I have received the proceeds of several forgeries ... The charge I was convicted of was uttering a forged cheque for £700.[1]

The First Great Train Robbery was one of the most successful crimes of that century, or indeed any other. Had the players devoted the same care to their personal relationships, probably there would never have been a prosecution. As it was, a woman was the downfall of Agar and, with him, his associates.

By the time the robbery was put to him as a proposition Agar had made a good deal of money in America and Australia, where he worked amongst other things as a confidence trickster swindling jewellers. It was a good trick. Using, say, the name Wise he would, along with his 'illiterate' manservant, go to a jeweller of the same name and ask to hire a set of plate for a reception. He would choose the dishes required and say he would send to his wife for the money. Unfortunately because of an injury he could not write, and neither could the servant. Would the jeweller be kind enough to write to his wife for him? 'My dearest, I want £200 or whatever you have to hand. Please send with this messenger.' Off would go the footman and Agar would spend a pleasant time chatting with the jeweller about possible relatives they might have in common. When the servant did not return Agar would go looking for him, and when the jeweller returned home his wife would confront him asking why he had sent for such a large sum of money.

In 1853 Agar, aged 38, described as dark-haired and well built, was back in England, living in Shepherd's Bush with a young mistress, Fanny Poland Kay, and £3,000 in Consols.

In fact it was a William Pierce who had the original plan for the robbery. Pierce described himself as a 'sporting gentleman', but if he was he was not a great success. He boasted that he had won over £1,000 on the 1855 St Leger, but the year previous to that triumph he had pawned his boots. Through his gambling he knew Saward, himself keen on (but not much better at) the tables. At one time Pierce had worked as a ticket printer on the South-Eastern Railway until his employers discovered his addiction to the turf. Through drinking with railway clerks in South London public houses Pierce had heard of the gold being shipped abroad in safes to pay the troops in the Crimea. It was not something he could execute himself, but it might be of interest to a professional. He knew Saward had connections abroad who might buy the gold, and that would solve the problem of its disposal. Like many a criminal job the robbery was on offer for some time until Pierce finally put the proposition to Agar, whom he had met through Saward, in King Street in the City.

The problems were considerable. For a start John Chubb, the founder of the safemakers, had introduced a steel curtain at the keyhole and a steel barrel around the groove of the key. This meant that only a single thin pick could be introduced to the lock. Moreover, with a lock of this kind two picks had to be inserted simultaneously. Worse, there were two locks on the safe. Agar liked neither the idea in general nor Pierce in particular. But Pierce kept on to him and, with the promise of at least £12,000 of bullion being on the train, eventually Agar allowed himself to be persuaded. The rewards were great, as was the challenge, but the penalty for failure was transportation for life.

As he began to research the project Agar realised the robbery would have to take place on the train itself, and now Pierce introduced him to William Tester and James Burgess. Burgess was a guard on the South-Eastern railway and Tester had been a station-master at Margate and was now in a senior position at

London Bridge. It was Pierce who had introduced Agar to Fanny Kay and both Burgess and Tester had already enjoyed the young woman's favours. Although at the trial she was portrayed as something of a slatternly and promiscuous drunk, she must have had some charms to attract the worldly Agar.

Through Tester keys were obtained and impressions taken and, after sending down coins of his own on the railway in a trial run, Agar purchased ballast to substitute for the gold. On 15 May 1855 Agar and Pierce boarded the train and Agar broke open the safe supposedly being guarded by Burgess. By the time the train stopped at Reigate, Agar had opened the first safe and a bag of bullion was handed over to Tester. By the time it reached Folkestone, Agar and Pierce had broken another safe and substituted the ballast. Having walked along and collected the carpet-bags from the luggage van in which the gold had been placed, they were back in London on the last train.

Some of the gold coins were disposed of directly but the rest were melted down – and here Saward was a ready purchaser. Agar would later give evidence:

> I first sold two hundred ounces to a man named Saward. I had known him for some years. When I first knew him he had chambers at No. 4, Inner Court, Temple. He was a barrister, I understood; indeed I have seen him pleading in Westminster Hall as a barrister. I first saw him about this business at a public-house near Ball's Pond. He gave three pounds two shillings and sixpence an ounce for the gold and I gave him sixpence or a shilling per ounce commission. After the two hundred ounces I sold him another parcel of five hundred ounces.[2]

Agar had now disposed of approximately a fifth of the gold to Saward.

So far as Pierce, Agar and their accomplices were concerned they had got clean away, and indeed things might have stayed that way had it not been for the complication of the increasingly tiresome Ms Kay. Pierce, sporting gent that he was, invested in a bookmaking business. Tester was about to leave England to take up a position in Sweden with a young bride and he and Burgess had both invested in the stock market. And so did Agar. The thorn which pierced, if one may use that expression, the bosom was Miss Kay. For the moment Agar had tired of her drunkenness and he became involved with Emily Campbell, a prostitute in the employ of a man called William Humphreys.

He lent Humphreys some £235; but when he tired of the 19-year-old Emily and decided that, whatever her faults, he should return to Fanny Kay and his child, it was arranged that he should go and collect the money from Bedford Row. When he got near the house Smith, a bully of Humphreys, approached him and said, 'Bill sent me to tell you not to come in. There's a screw loose.' He handed Agar a bag and told him to run. As he did so Smith began calling out, 'Stop thief!' Agar only got as far as Holborn before he was arrested by Williamson, the great Scotland Yard detective. The bag he carried was found to be full of farthings. Agar was charged with forgery and he appeared at the Old Bailey Sessions in the October.

The evidence against him had been rigged. Smith appeared under a guarantee of indemnity from prosecution. Humphreys gave evidence in support and another dishonest lawyer, a man named Mullens, testified that he had seen Agar outside the bank where the forged cheque had been presented. Agar's alibi that he had been in Shepherd's Bush trying to effect a reconciliation with Fanny Kay was not believed. He received a sentence of transportation.

Even so, to use a term of the Underworld, he remained staunch. He organised his solicitor Wontner, founder of the firm which still bears his name, to invest money for Fanny and the child and to arrange for the income to be paid to Pierce. Agar was to be taken down to Portland to be put in the hulks but, as was the custom, for the moment he was held in Pentonville. From there he was to write a fateful letter which would bring the house of cards crashing down on Pierce and the others. He wrote asking Fanny to buy an atlas so that she could show their child where Agar was; he also wanted her to purchase two small silver cups. When she asked Pierce for the money she was told that Agar had never left him any and the £1 a week he had been giving her was from his own money. She went to see the prison governor, so setting in motion their destruction.

Agar had kept his silence but, when learning of the betrayal of Fanny, he spoke to the railway company's solicitor. He did not ask for a commutation of his sentence; rather that the company would provide Fanny Kay with an allowance for food and lodging and a sum of £25 a year for the child until the age of twenty-one. In return he would give evidence at the Old Bailey. And this he did. Unshaken by cross-examination, he cut a romantic and indeed heroic figure. Because Pierce was not a servant of the company at the time of the robbery he could only be sentenced to two years, something Baron[3] Martin, the presiding judge, bitterly regretted.

> But I do declare that if I stood in that dock to receive sentence, I should feel more degraded to be in your place than in that of either of your associates. ... [Agar] trusted you and gave you £3,000 stock to be invested for the benefit of his child and its mother, together with £600, his share of the produce of this robbery, and the rest of the gold which had not been sold. In all you must have got out of him about £15,000. This you stole and appropriated to your own use. It is a worse offence, I declare, than the act of which you have just been found guilty. I would rather have been concerned in stealing the gold than in the robbery of that wretched woman – call her harlot, if you will – and her child. A greater villain than you are, I believe, does not exist. [A loud burst of applause.]

On 15 January 1857 Tester and Burgess joined Agar in transportation. In the trial Pierce had made much of the fact that the £3,000 was still intact and Fanny Kay was allowed to keep the money.

No doubt Agar could have offered up Saward as well as the others but he did not do so. In fact even if he had thought of it there was no need, for meanwhile Saward had himself come unstuck. His later coups had involved swindling London solicitors by using them as debt collectors and, when the money was paid, by co-conspirators forging the signatures on the receipts. Saward then turned his attentions to out-of-town solicitors, but his partner Hardwicke was arrested in Yarmouth and a letter written by Saward fell into police hands. He went into hiding but was arrested in a public house off Oxford Street.

> 'Mr Hopkins, I have been looking for you,' said Moss the detective.
> 'My name is not Hopkins.'
> 'No, I believe it is not. It is Saward.'

At his committal at Mansion House Court Saward had been cocksure of his ultimate acquittal, but when it came to it he displayed a curiously apathetic attitude to his own trial. Certainly he was lethargic in his defence. The case was called on 5 March 1857 and he, along with James Anderson, pleaded not guilty to four charges of forgery.

Anderson was described as a servant and Saward as a labourer, but the jury was put right about that within minutes of the opening speech for the Crown when Sir Frederick Thesiger regretted, somewhat hypocritically and certainly sanctimoniously:

> ... the prisoner Saward is a barrister having been called to the Bar in 1840 by the Society of the Inner Temple, to which I have the honour to belong; and I need hardly say how gratified I should be if it could be made out that the prisoner is not guilty of the serious offence that is alleged against him.[4]

Only minutes before, the kindly Sir Frederick had been busy opposing Saward's belated application for an adjournment on the grounds that, although he had a brief prepared, he had been unable to retain counsel. If, said Saward, there could be a fifteen-minute adjournment counsel would readily understand the situation and be able to show he was entirely innocent. No, said the Chief Baron. Saward had known perfectly well the previous week when the case was to be heard, and he had had ample opportunity to retain counsel. Saward subsided and said he would leave the matter in the hands of the court. He could not give evidence on his own behalf, but he was entitled to cross-examine witnesses or call witnesses in his own defence as well as to make an unsworn statement. He did nothing and the jury took a bare five minutes to convict both him and Anderson.

It was only on the second day of the trial that Saward, described as presenting 'a very dejected appearance', roused sufficiently to say something. He wanted the case put over until the following session and to have the notes of evidence of some of the witnesses 'to be made such use of as I may be hereafter advised'. When pressed, he said he believed much of the evidence had been inadmissible. When a man is down there is no point in not keeping him on the ground:

> *Chief Baron*: Then the proper course for you to have pursued was to have objected yesterday. I thought the whole of the evidence was admissible.

And later:

> I lament, with respect to you, James Townsend Saward, that you must have been at one period of your life in circumstances far different from those in which the Court has found you involved ... I deeply regret that the ingenuity, skill and talent which has received so perverted and mistaken a direction, has not been

guided by a sense of virtue, and directed to more honourable and useful pursuits. I am called upon to pass sentence upon you and, for the reasons that I have assigned, it is impossible for me to stop short of the utmost limit to which the law permits punishment to proceed.[5]

Both he and Anderson, for whom Sir Frederick had spoken in mitigation saying it was accepted he was Saward's dupe, were sentenced to transportation for life.

Transportation for life did not necessarily mean that, any more than a life sentence means whole life today. It was possible for a convict to obtain early release on what was called a ticket-of-leave, which required the former convict to report to the authorities and generally behave. Failure to do either would result in a return to prison. There is no record that he returned to England and, given his age, it is highly likely he died in Australia. However, his name did live on and, over the years, any forger of quality was either known as Jim the Penman by the popular press or given the accolade of being the greatest in the business since Jim.

The next lawyer to fall foul of the courts in a major case was the extremely dubious Edward Froggatt, who had a practice in Argyll Street off Regent Street and who in 1877 went down along with one third of the officers of the new detective division at Scotland Yard. On this occasion he had played a relatively minor but important part.

The background to the so-called Trial of the Detectives is that of two high-class fraudsmen, William Kurr and Harry Benson, who operated a series of racing scams. Benson, educated in France, had previously run a series of swindles including one which in 1872 saw him in London as the Comte de Montague, Mayor of Chateaudun, supposedly raising money for refugees from the Franco-Prussian war. He extracted £1,000 from the Lord Mayor but was arrested almost immediately. Fearful of a long prison sentence, he set fire to the bedding in his cell and, fearfully crippled, had to be carried into court on the back of a warder to receive his 12-month sentence. On his release he teamed up with William Kurr, the son of a wealthy Scottish baker.

From at least the previous year Detective Sergeant (later promoted Inspector) John Meiklejohn had been taking bribes from Kurr whom he had met by chance in a bar, tipping him off as to the progress of police inquiries in connection with racing frauds. A Chief Inspector George Clarke, a freemason then approaching 60, was also roped in, possibly with the hint of blackmail by Kurr. At the time Clarke was communicating with a man named Walters who had absconded bail and was using him as an informant, and Benson let it be known that a letter sent by Clarke was in their possession. One of Scotland Yard's most able detectives, the multi-lingual Nathaniel Druscovich, was recruited. He had backed a bill for his brother in the sum of £60, a quarter of a year's salary, and could not pay. Kurr kindly lent him the money and he too was hooked. The fourth officer involved, William Palmer, was also recruited through Meiklejohn. The monies they received were considerable. For informing Kurr that a fraud charge could be 'settled', Meiklejohn received £100. Later Druscovich declined £1,000 for not travelling to Scotland to continue inquiries, but on another occasion took £100 and a piece of jewellery for his wife. He was also given a cigar-box containing £200 in gold as a *douceur* for delaying inquiries. Clarke received £150 in gold. For assisting in the changing of certain banknotes, Meiklejohn asked £2,000 from Benson.

The most audacious of the racing swindles was perpetrated on the Comtesse de Goncourt in Paris. She was persuaded to place bets on horses through a commission agent in London and to be sent her winnings by cheques drawn on a non-existent bank. In a matter of weeks she had been swindled out of £10,000.

In the middle 1870s, Froggatt had acted for a high-grade fraudsman named Walters who was a longtime associate of Edwin Murray. In February 1875 Walters and Murray had been arrested for an assault on a man named Berkley but had been discharged. They were then arrested for running the fraudulent Society for Insurance against Losses on the Turf, a charge which Murray stoutly denied when he later came to give evidence against Froggatt. Murray and Walters had been bailed and fled to America where they had worked a land swindle. Walters advertised as an English gentleman wishing to lend money on landed property. When people applied for a loan he would refer them to Murray, posing as a surveyor. In fact it was often, Murray maintained, a matter of Greek meeting Greek, because many of the applicants were out to swindle the so-called English gentleman. They would try to enlist Murray's assistance and he would pretend to help them, taking a bribe on the side. He would then make an unfavourable report and Walters would require

insurance against the loan. The insurance agent was again Murray. He frankly admitted the scheme did not run for very long, but they were making $400 a day. After that they were arrested and acquitted on a charge of smuggling and following that he, Murray, set up a pocket-book swindle.[6]

Murray returned to England in December 1875, where he lived in Leytonstone under the name of Munroe. Walters remained in America.

Froggatt's part was initially as a receiver of forged notes which he tried to sell on. When his colleagues wanted to pay too little he bought one himself. He also acted as a negotiator and indeed he seems to have grown into his part. When Benson, under the name of George Washington Morton, was arrested in Rotterdam it was Froggatt who devised a telegram:

> Find Morton and the two men you have in custody are not those we want. Officer will not be sent over. Liberate them. Letter follows. Carter, Scotland Yard.

This he said would set the cat amongst the pigeons. However, he was hoist with his own cleverness, his mistake being to say that a letter would follow. The Dutch police nearly did let them go, but decided to wait for the letter of confirmation which never came.

One curious coincidence in the case is that Froggatt made an arrangement with a man named Sawyer who had something to do with Middlesex Sessions. Along with Sawyer, Froggatt seems to have planned to get hold of the notes himself. The idea was to persuade Abrahams to drop the case. Kurr, however, did not trust Sawyer and would have nothing to do with the scheme.

Meanwhile outside solicitors pressed Superintendent Frederick Williamson into pushing along the inquiries and, despite the efforts of Meiklejohn and Druscovich to delay matters, Kurr and Benson were arrested.

When Kurr sent for Froggatt and suggested he should take steps to prevent a witness, Flintoff, from making an identification of him, Froggatt offered the man £50. When Flintoff turned him down, he ingeniously tried to have him prosecuted for perjury. It did not help anyone and Froggatt ended in the dock listening to the tale of his misdeeds given by Benson, Kurr and Murray.

Kurr received 10 years' and Benson 15 years' penal servitude. Setting a precedent they now began co-operating with the authorities in return, they hoped, for an early release. On their evidence Meiklejohn, Palmer, Druscovich, Clarke and Froggatt were charged. Clarke was acquitted. The others received two years apiece.

In those days a prisoner was permitted to make a plea in mitigation from the dock in addition to anything his counsel said. Froggatt took full advantage:

> The position in which I am placed is one of utter ruin in every way, brought about by the machinations, as your lordship must know, of these men trying to get me into their toils. If I did exceed my duty as a solicitor, I have been punished most severely and most onerously. My business has been ruined; ever since this charge has been made against me, I have been unable to do anything, and I am for the rest of my life a ruined man, because on this conviction depended my prosperity in every way. I do appeal to you, my lord, not to punish me with severity. I like Palmer have a wife and children, and I shall be utterly ruined. I shall come back from prison penniless. I implore you, my lord, to pass as light a sentence on me as you can.

Sentencing the men Baron Pollock had this to say:

> The spirit and rule of the law in England have been, and I trust always will be, to make a wide distinction between offences committed under either sudden impulse or under the pressure of want or poverty, and offences committed by persons placed in a position of trust.[7]

And a special word for Froggatt, whom he sentenced to two years with hard labour:

> In some senses I can still feel more what a wretched and unfortunate career yours has been. There are no persons who know the duties and vicissitudes of the profession to which you belong but must feel for you in your present position, especially when, as you have yourself said, the necessary consequences of the crime go beyond any sentence the law can pass upon you.

> My God, my lord, do lessen my sentence.

His lordship clearly did not know of Froggatt's earlier misdemeanours, for the former and certainly unfortunate solicitor suffered what is known in the trade as a gate arrest. He had served most of his time in Newgate prison but then on 28

October 1879, just as he was leaving the House of Correction in Coldbath Fields, Clerkenwell, having completed his sentence, he was arrested. This time it was for embezzlement. In 1871 he had managed to induce the then Lord Eustace into marrying a widow of doubtful provenance and, as part of the prize, he had become one of the trustees of the marriage settlement. Lord Eustace had disappeared during the marriage and over the years so had a great deal of the £10,000 marriage settlement. Froggatt at first blamed his previous imprisonment for not being able to produce the trust deeds and then, in time-honoured tradition, claimed that in his absence the responsibility lay with his managing clerk:

> If I had not been in confinement this would not have happened but my clerk has taken away all my papers from my office and I don't know where they are.

Tried at the Old Bailey within months of his release and re-arrest, this time he was sentenced to penal servitude for 7 years. He died in the Lambeth workhouse.[8]

1 All quotations are from George Dilnot (ed.), *The Trial of Jim The Penman*, mainly pp. 37, 55, 68–9 and 123.
2 *Ibid*, p. 55.
3 Title used for a High Court Judge.
4 *Ibid,* pp. 68–9.
5 *Ibid*, p. 123.
6 A pocket-book swindle was a form of lottery in which the winners received no payment.
7 Benson, due to be extradited to Mexico for a fraud over tickets for the opera singer Madame Patti's tour, later committed suicide in the Tombs prison in New York. Meiklejohn was partly rehabilitated; he was employed in obtaining evidence for the Parnell Commission and he died in 1912 shortly after he had appeared in an unsuccessful action against Major Arthur Griffiths.
8 For a full account of the trial of the detectives, see George Dilnot (ed.), *The Trial of the Detectives*; *Thomson's Weekly News*, 24 February 1912. For an account of the subsequent trial of Froggatt see PRO P Com 1 117, *The Times*, 19 December 1879.

# 2 Bill Howe and Abe Hummel, and 'Marm' Mandelbaum and many others

I T IS SAID THAT THE WORD SHYSTER is a corruption of Scheuster, pronounced shoister, an unscrupulous lawyer in the Essex Street court on the Lower East Side in the 1840s. 'Don't let's have these Scheuster practices in this court,' Justice Osborne is alleged to have said. The story has been denounced on the grounds that records show no lawyer of that name on the rolls of the court, but the name has stuck.

Whether it is true or whether Scheuster is an apocryphal character, he could not have lived with the misdeeds of the two great crooked lawyers of late nineteenth-century New York, William F. Howe and his protégé and later partner Abraham Hummel. Howe was the great advocate, unscrupulous in his court appearances but probably far less venal that the more astute and businesslike Hummel who made a practice out of blackmail and dishonesty.[1] It is sometimes said that they were the real brains behind crime in the New York of the period; that may be an exaggeration but certainly not a great one. The roll-call of their clients produces the great names of crime of all hues – General Abe Greenthal's Sheeny mob of thieves; Chester McLaughlin's gang of forgers; the Whyos, the toughest and most political of the street gangs of the time; Joe Douglas, kidnapper of little Charley Ross; Charles O. Brockway whose forgeries of treasury bills were such that the $100 note had for a time to be withdrawn; George Leonidas Leslie, the most accomplished safebreaker of the period. At least 74 brothel-keepers who were rounded up in one of the periodic purity drives of the 1880s named Howe and Hummel as their legal counsel. They also represented the notorious Clafin sisters, swindlers and charlatans who went on to become pillars of London society – one married into the peerage – in their fight against Anthony Comstock and the New York Society for the Suppression of Vice over a magazine they had published libelling friends of the Divine, Beecher Ward. But the *crème de la crème* of their criminal clientele was the celebrated receiver Fredericka 'Marm' Mandelbaum, who was said to pay them a $5,000 annual retainer.

Amongst their regular clients were politicians, judges, jurors, police officers, society men and women, thieves, prostitutes and almost every murderer who could raise the money for their fees. At one time, of 25 murderers in the Tombs prison awaiting trial, 23 were represented by Howe and Hummel, and the pair had what might be described as an interest in one of the others. Howe put it about that he had 'been invited to assist in the defence of Stokes, but for reasons which cannot now be made public' he declined.

In fact it was more than an interest. The murder of Colonel James Fisk by Edward S. Stokes on 6 January 1872 on the steps of the Broadway Central Hotel garnered the most attention since the murder of Lincoln by John Wilkes Booth. Both were rich men. Fisk was the financial wrecker of the Erie Railroad whilst Stokes came from a wealthy Brooklyn family. Business rivals, they had recently been involved in a libel action and both were rivals for the affections of the beautiful actress Josie Mansfield. Although there was substantial evidence of Stokes' guilt, after three trials and a great deal of tampering by (it was said) Howe, Stokes was given a four-year sentence for manslaughter. In fact, the reason why Howe had declined to appear at the trial was the sensible one that there might have been an insuperable conflict of interests. Howe and Hummel had got to the only eye-witness to the shooting. They had paid the man, probably a doctor, a huge sum of money to leave the country with an undertaking never to return or let them know where he had gone.[2]

Howe maintained he was born on 7 July 1828 at Shawmut Street, Boston, the son of the Rev. Samuel Howe MA, and then went to England. He said he attended Kings College, London, and entered the office of George Waugh, the noted barrister. He then moved to the offices of E.H. Seeley. Unfortunately records to support this claim do not exist. He was certainly a witness for the prosecution in the celebrated Stanfield Hall murder in which the feckless James Bloomfield Rush killed his landlord Isaac Jermy, the Recorder of Norfolk, who had threatened to have him evicted. On 28 November 1848 he shot and killed Jermy and his son, wounding Jermy's wife and the maid, who later identified him in court. Howe's part in the trial was confined to producing some mortgage documents.[3]

Another, less generous, version of Howe's life before arrival in New York was that he was a ticket-of-leave man. It is also said that, at times, he spoke with a cockney accent. It is almost certain that Howe had some sort of criminal record in England and when he was sued over his fees in 1874 by a pair of white slavers, William and Adelaide Beaumont, he was asked about his early life. A. Oakey Hall of the Tweed Ring appeared for him and objected to the question on the grounds of its relevance. The objection was sustained, as was a question as to whether he had lost his licence to practise medicine. He was also asked if he was the same William Frederick Howe wanted for murder in England and the same W.F.H. convicted of forgery in Brooklyn a few years earlier. He denied both allegations and, unlike the situation in an English court where the accuser would have been required to offer some proof of the allegation, there is no record of the judge ordering this.

Howe weighed nearly 300 lbs and, in later life, had closely cropped curly white hair and a moustache. Arthur Train, who practised law shortly after Howe's heyday, maintained that his fortune was not in his face but in his clothing:

> He always wore a blue yachting cap, sometimes a navigator's blue coat and white trousers but more often a loudly checked brown suit, with a low-cut vest displaying the starched bosom of a bright pink shirt and a pink collar innocent of tie, in place of which he sported a gigantic diamond stud, with others of equal size adorning his chest. These he changed on occasion to pearls in the afternoon. Diamonds glittered upon his fingers; on his feet were either yachting shoes or dinky patent leathers with cloth uppers; in his lapel a rose or carnation; in his breast pocket a huge silk handkerchief into which he shed, with enormous effect, showers of crocodile tears when defending his clients.[4]

Towards the end of his life Howe was asked about his jewellery:

> When I was a young lawyer it was necessary to show signs of prosperity. All the young lawyers who were getting a good fee wore

diamonds. The size of a lawyer's fees were then somewhat regulated by the size of the diamonds he wore. If I had given up wearing those diamonds the word would have gone all over the city: 'Bill Howe is broke.' I hate those diamonds but, you see, I have to keep wearing them so that people won't think I'm broke.[5]

He was certainly one of the great old-fashioned barnstorming advocates, but he must also have been a considerable lawyer. He was responsible for the successful argument that the draft laws in the American Civil War were unlawful because they discriminated against the poor, and at the time was known as Habeas Corpus Howe because of the number of soldiers he managed to get out of the army on the grounds that they had signed their enlistment papers when drunk.

On another occasion, perhaps with less merit, he argued that his client could not be hanged because the state had passed a Bill ruling that all future executions should be by electrocution. Since this was not yet in force his client must go free.

On the night of 28 October 1888 Harry Carleton, known to his friends as 'Handsome Harry', shot and killed Patrolman James Brennan. He was regarded as the leader of an East Side gang which included his brother-in-law Thomas 'Boss' McKenna, Edward Ahearn and William Burke. Carleton, Ahearn and Burke had had their eyes on a somewhat drunken German waiter, Julius Roesler, or at least his silver-handled umbrella. They had been trying to buy him drinks in Tuckers at Third and 33rd where he had left his umbrella for safe-keeping. When he turned down their offer they followed him home. He had asked the help of Patrolman Brennan and had been told to go on home. As he arrived on his doorstep Carleton and the others reappeared; he called for help, and Brennan answered the call only to be shot in the face at point-blank range by Carleton. To his credit Roesler chased after Carleton who shouted, 'Go back, you Dutch pig or I'll shoot you'; but by this time two other plain-clothes police officers had joined in and arrested him. Ahearn and Burke escaped.

It was just a lucky night for Boss McKenna. He was already in custody on a robbery charge on which the victim, James Scotty, failed to identify him. But it was not a good night for Scotty. Apart from being relieved of his watch, the court took $10 off him the following day for drunkenness.

The next day, unsurprisingly, the press was not at all keen on 'Handsome Harry'. The *New York Herald* described him as having a weak face and vicious lines 'abated by a mustache'. In keeping with the times they gave a list of his previous appearances in court. His first had been at the age of 16 for till tapping, and on 27 November 1882 he had been convicted of robbery at Corcorna's Roost at First and 40th. He had tried to shoot a policeman on this occasion as well, and had received 5 years.

On his arraignment, 'Handsome Harry's Ugly Day', it appeared that drunkenness would be his only defence; but with the arrival of 'Little Abe Hummel and his belligerent partner, the redoubtable William F. Howe' things took a different course. Prosecution counsel ex-Judge Gunning S. Bedford for one was impressed – or was his tongue wedged in cement?

> His counsel, it is usually admitted, stand the first among their peers for unsurpassed ability, great legal acumen and eloquence, which it is indeed difficult to resist. But gentlemen [of the jury] even these high and ennobling attributes of mind must occasionally give way and yield to the majesty of truth.[6]

Whatever is said about the methods of Howe and Hummel, they worked hard for their clients. The junior partner, Joseph Moss, handled the empanelling and challenging of the jury but the great man, Howe, was there himself to challenge the way the trial judge was making him object to each juror one by one rather than waiting until all twelve were in the box. An attempt to get the prosecution to use their thirty challenges failed. Howe's objection was overruled and he asked for an exception to be noted. This was the standard way of setting out an appeal case. In all, by the end of the three-day trial he would have 35 exceptions noted. As for the jurors, 9 of the 18 stood down were excused on the basis that they opposed capital punishment.

The case would seem to have been overwhelming, but Howe was not done for. Drunkenness would no longer be the issue except insofar as it concerned the unfortunate Roesler whom the newspaper reported as saying, when an attempt was made to challenge his recollection, 'Of course I was not sober like dem temperance beople vot drink nodings, but I vas not drunk' (sic).

Now Howe was going for a verdict of murder in the second degree, which did not carry the death penalty. It would be a question of self-defence. New York policemen were noted for their use of the nightstick and Howe was able to show that

Brennan did in fact have two charges of clubbing against him. He claimed that Carleton had only shot the officer after he had been hit, but unfortunately there was only Carleton to support this theory. Despite the initial belief of the police that they would soon have the others in custody they had failed to find them.

The jury was sent out at 7 p.m. on the evening of 14 December and returned in 40 minutes with a guilty verdict.

> Did Carleton quail? No; he stood up with one hand on the desk before him, with one leg crossed carelessly over the other, and his face was as if carved in stone and as if some sculptor had placed two cruel glittering orbs in the spot where the windows of the soul are found.

Sentencing was postponed for a week and now Howe produced one of his great coups, arguing that Carleton could not be sentenced in any way. The previous spring the Assembly, in the Electrical Death Penalty Law, had abolished death by hanging, substituting electrocution. Howe discovered that death by hanging was to be abolished as from 4 June. Prisoners convicted after 4 June were to be kept alive until 1 January 1889 when they could be electrocuted. At least that was the intention. According to Howe:

> He [Carleton] says that Your Honor cannot now pass any sentence of death upon him. He says that the Legislature by its enactment of Chapter 499 of the laws of 1888, a statute passed, approved, and signed by the Governor ...

The judge agreed and, while the prosecution appealed, unsurprisingly panic followed. If Howe was right, then not only had all murderers to be released but also the logical extension was that until 1 January 1889 they could kill with impunity. Chief of Police Thomas Byrnes and the District Attorney released statements assuring the public that measures would be taken to ensure public safety over the Christmas period.

Howe, with Hummel supporting him, was adamant that Carleton could not be punished 'because of the slipshod drafting of the bill' but other lawyers were not convinced. Of course, in practice Howe's reading of the law could not be allowed to stand and the appeal court held that while it was strictly correct, a mere slip of syntax should not allow the guilty to go free.

But Howe and his firm did not give up. Carleton was still alive the following October when his application for retrial was dismissed. Howe now produced affidavits from Ahearn and Burke supporting the clubbing theory. Surely Governor Hill would grant a reprieve? No, Governor Hill would not.

On 5 December 1888 Carleton became the last man to be hanged in the Tombs prison. By now the papers had become less hostile to him. One of his children had died during the year and he was generally accepted to have behaved well throughout his time in the condemned cell. As he walked to the scaffold he was described as having:

... a high retreating head; a long thin face scarred with smallpox, a curling brown mustache and blue eyes. His face looked intelligent and not unkindly.

As for the hanging itself:

If it had been designed particularly to be an argument for the swiftness and painlessness of the old method of inflicting the death penalty it could not have been more effective. Electricity could not have been more humanely expeditious and certain.[7]

Howe had long been a lawyer to the Whyos and he defended Mike McGloin, one of their early leaders who was hanged in the Tombs on 8 March 1883 for the murder of Louis Hanier, a saloon keeper of 26 Street West. Hanier had tried to prevent McGloin making off with the till takings and was killed with a sling-shot. The day after the murder McGloin is said to have remarked, 'A guy ain't tough until he has knocked his man out.'

It was also said that to make McGloin confess he had been subjected to the Third Degree, the interrogation method of which the New York police in general and Thomas Byrnes (who was credited with its creation) in particular were so proud. He had been left overnight near the body of Hanier.

In 1887 Howe defended Danny Driscoll, charged with the murder of a girl named Beezy Garrity. She had been keeping company with both Driscoll, then the leader of the Whyos, and a John McCarthy. In a gunfight between the men, Driscoll accidentally killed her.

Howe had battled long and hard to save him but, when he failed, he seemed to display none of the angst the modern lawyer shares with his unfortunate client. By now he had turned his attention to his feud with the Tombs' warden with whom he had a long-standing quarrel over the smuggling of a knife to Driscoll. Now he accused the warden of bribery and favouritism. Not a word about the unfortunate Driscoll. Instead:

> Lawyer Howe ate walnuts and sipped sherry yesterday while he said that there was proof enough in existence to warrant the instant removal of Warden Walsh from his office.[8]

Six months later he defended Driscoll's successor-in-title, Danny Lyons who, on 5 July 1887, shot Joseph Quinn, the lover of 'Pretty' Kitty McGown, a prostitute in Lyons' stable. With a string of appeals Howe managed to keep the Whyo alive for the better part of a year before the inevitable happened.

The *New York Times* wrote a short tribute to Howe's client, 'Simple Story of Commonplace Life'.

> He knew better than to steal, but he stole and was sent to the reformatory. He stole again and was sent to the penitentiary. He stole again and was sent to State Prison. He murdered and he was hanged.[9]

Howe also ran rudimentary psychiatric defences and, from time to time, appeared in cases which cannot have brought him a penny – except, of course, in terms of helpful publicity. The faithful Abe Hummel saw to it that, when in 1870 Howe defended Jack Reynolds for the murder of William Townsend, the very least the senior partner deserved was a pamphlet devoted to praising his efforts. 'Lawyer Howe had evidently made extensive preparations to prove his client *non compus*.' And, in fairness, he clearly had.

The facts were simple. In the evening of 29 January, Townsend, a small-time shopkeeper, was sitting at home with his young daughters at 192 Hudson Street when Reynolds, who had a few minutes earlier stolen a knife from the shoe repairer who worked next door, came into the basement and sat down saying, 'I'm your brother.' Townsend told him he was not and must leave. The man went outside and when Townsend followed him and placed his hand on his shoulder, he was stabbed in the heart. Passers-by tackled Reynolds and the police were called. The only defence open to Howe was one of insanity.

Those were the days of Lombroso and his assessment of skulls, the shape of which – together with an abundance of pubic hair, or lack of it, in women – would prove or disprove criminality. Reynolds had a depressed left frontal eminence onto which Howe latched in support of his theories. Psychiatry was in its early stages and Howe had the idea of raising the defence that his client had suffered an epileptic fit which resulted in either what he called volitional insanity – which meant he had no control over his will – or impulsive insanity, which meant he could not resist the impulse. To this end he quoted the doctor Trousseau who cited the case of a judge who would leave the bench, urinate on the carpet of his chambers and return to the courtroom without any recollection of what he had just done.

At the end of the case Howe called Reynolds to the witness box to be questioned not by himself or Samuel B. Galvin, who prosecuted, but by the jurors themselves – something they did with enthusiasm but without any success in eliciting more than 'I can't remember' to their questions. No doubt he had been well schooled by his attorneys.

All the books on Howe say that his forte was his closing speech to the jury, and his efforts for Reynolds were a good example of the rhetoric he favoured. Here he is at the beginning:

> ... for some good reason, known only to HIM 'through whom we live and move and have our being' it is left to you by your verdict to say whether this poor wretched animated piece of ruined nature, one certainly of the poorest of God's creatures is, upon testimony, such as has been introduced, to be strangled by the cord of the hangman when an indication is there, defying science ...

It is clear that Howe managed to instil some doubt because the jury retired for over two hours and twice asked if alternative verdicts could be introduced, but the judge's rulings went against him. The next day Reynolds was sentenced to be hanged and Abe Hummel, who went on to write two Broadway plays, set out his stall as an author:

> At this announcement the doors of the court were ordered to be barred to prevent the egress of the vast audience and the condemned man who seemed in no perceptible manner affected by the sentence, was conveyed to an adjoining room and from there thence to the streets, but before gaining the Tombs the crowd again flocked around him and, amidst the hootings and yelling of the gamin, he was lodged in his dark cell on the lower tier of the prison,

moody and dejected, to receive such spiritual comfort as would prepare him for the next world.[10]

Abe Hummel always did have a nice turn of phrase.

Howe had taken on Hummel as an office boy in his offices at the corner of Leonard and Center Street at $2 a week in 1863, where he worked putting coal on the fires. There was still no formal Bar examination; lawyers were attached to other lawyers for their training and simply took over work from their employers. In May 1869 Hummel became his partner, and in 1900 they moved to the New York Life Building on Broadway.

Hummel was also said to have been born in Boston, this time on 27 July 1847 – some say New York – and attended Public School No. 15 on E 5th Street. He was, without doubt, the more astute and venal of the pair, but he maintained standards. When he organised the blackmailing of young men who had so forgotten themselves at the sight of the underwear of chorines that they proposed marriage and wrote confirmatory letters, he would invite round the lawyer acting for the man, where brandy would be drunk, cigars smoked and the lawyer could see the foolish letters destroyed. Nor did he allow one girl more than one bite at the same man. Fees were split equally between the girl and the partnership.

On the credit side of his activities he became an expert on theatrical contracts and the firm's legitimate clients included P.T. Barnum, Sir Henry Irving, John Barrymore and Lillie Langtry. They also represented Olga Nethersole who, when playing the title role in Daudet's *Sappho*, was arrested for publicly demonstrating the embrace known as 'the Nethersole Kiss'. They argued that the actress had given art a new dimension and the court agreed.

But perhaps their greatest extra-judicial triumph was the defeat of Pinkerton agents in spiriting Marm Mandelbaum away from the jurisdiction of the New York courts to safety when it appeared that the great receiver was at last going to take a serious fall.

Marm Mandlebaum, described as a 'bustling Israelite' and 'as adept in her business as the best stockbroker in his', was undoubtedly the Queen of Receivers with her offices at her home at 79 Clinton Street and representatives along the eastern seaboard and Chicago, Mexico and Europe. She had graduated from being a small-time receiver to the queen of criminal society, holding splendid dinners at which her favourite thieves, such as George Leonidas Leslie, the bank robber, sat at her right hand.

She took care never to handle goods at her home. Instead a messenger would call and she would send a trusted representative to examine the stolen articles and report back to her. Her integrity was described as absolute. She also established what was referred to as a Bureau for the Prevention of Conviction and would lend money to those who needed defending, but woe betide those who could not or would not repay her the fees advanced.

There are a number of differing accounts of her betrayal, but it may have been through Lizzie Higgins, for whom Marm Mandelbaum would not provide the services of Howe and Hummel. When she went to prison for 5 years Lizzie squealed.

Mandelbaum was finally entrapped by Detective Frank over some silks coming from a burglary on W 14th. The *grande dame* was not pleased and said to Frank, 'So you are the one who is at the bottom of this, you wretch you.' She had hit him on her arrest and he wanted to prefer an assault charge but was told to wait. On 23 July she was produced in the court in Harlem, much to the protest of Howe who had wanted the case heard in one of the more sympathetic regions of Manhattan.

The courts may not have been sympathetic but the *New York Herald* was:

> When a man who has lost a $50 watch went to the police station and offered '$25 and no questions asked' for its recovery what could be more profitable for the time consumed than for a detective to go to 'Mother Baum' and buy for $15 an identical ticker for which the shrewd woman had paid no more than $10?
>
> To now have to run about among a lot of minor fences in search of stolen property that once could be confidently looked for at the Mandelbaum place will be very annoying to detectives whose habits have become fixed. It is no wonder that Mother Baum had never before been troubled by detectives. Shall a man quarrel with his own bread and butter, particularly when the person who provides it gives him occasionally a new dress for his wife and diamond studs to illuminate his own official front?[11]

In July 1884 a Grand Jury returned a bill against her and her son Julius, along with Herbert Stroub – described as a clerk but possibly an unofficial replacement for the now deceased Herr Mandelbaum. She had trouble raising bail of $100,000 and three sureties were turned down before she was released.

The authorities were right to be wary of letting the woman out of their sight. In December 1884, despite being under watch by Pinkerton agents who rented a house opposite hers, she escaped. Having sent out a servant about the same build and heavily veiled, while the agent was decoyed away she left the house and was driven to New Rochelle, where she boarded a train to Chatham Five Corners and then to Canada. The neighbours who had let out the house for the Pinkertons' use were also providing Marm with information.[12]

When she fled to Canada she took with her jewels said to have been stolen in Troy by two of her best clients, Billy Porter and Mike 'Sheeney Mike' Kurtz.

The next appearance in court was an unmitigated triumph for Howe, aided and abetted by Hummel who passed up Shakespearean quotations for the senior partner to offer as *bon mots* as he looked around the court feigning innocence of the whereabouts of his client.

Meanwhile Marm had been arrested and held in Montreal, from where the New York District Attorney prophesied the speedy return of her and the jewellery. Abe Hummel was immediately despatched north to deal with matters, something he did completely successfully. Marm and the jewellery remained in Canada, and before her death she only once crossed the border when she returned in 1891 for the funeral of her daughter, watching from a distance and catching a train back home. Hummel gave a short interview on that occasion. She died in Hamilton, Ontario, a respected woman, on 27 February 1894. Her body was returned to New York for burial.

It might be supposed that the authorities would at least pick up the $100,000 forfeited bail, but that would be wrong. Hummel had arranged a string of interlocking sales and mortgages so that the poor bondsmen were quite unable to pay the court and, better still, because of the complexity of the deals no further action was taken against them.

Whilst Howe and Hummel were never directly related to the Tweed Ring they did provide invaluable assistance because if on election day a repeat voter – such as the experienced and much-valued Reddy the Blacksmith – was caught, they were there on hand to have him released to vote again before the day was out. Howe had already been behind the scenes at the trial of Richard 'Boss' Croker who was charged with the murder of John McKenna during a fight at the ballot boxes during the 1874 elections. The jury had disagreed during the first trial and Croker never stood trial a second time.

After Croker left for America, politics in New York in the 1870s were dominated by the Ring comprising the eponymous William Marcey 'Boss' Tweed along with Peter Barr, 'Brains' Sweeny and Richard 'Slippery Dick' Connolly and the lawyer 'The Elegant' Abraham Oakey Hall. Born in Albany on 26 July 1826, Hall was the District Attorney for New York City in the 1850s and in 1862 joined the Democratic Party. Together they built and masterminded a political organisation which dominated both city and state politics.

Described as a 'nervous witty little man who delighted New York with his rhetoric of inanities and his absurd pince-nez', Oakey Hall was Mayor from 1868 to 1872. He wrote and acted in some of his own plays, including *Let Me Kiss Him for his Mother*.

It is estimated that the Ring-owned Judge Albert Cardozo was bribed a staggering 200 times by Howe and Hummel to release their clients. When the Tweed Ring was dismantled Cardozo resigned but was never prosecuted. Judges Barnard and McCunn were impeached but not prosecuted either.

When the Ring collapsed Oakey Hall was the only one who stayed to fight. In all he faced one Grand Jury and three trials, and in essence he was charged with misfeasance in public office. He had signed some $6 million of fraudulent vouchers. His defence was that he had only been acting in his ministerial capacity and the real villains were Tweed and Connolly. Hall's law partner, who also appeared as his counsel, did what he could to help him by saying that he never considered Hall had the talents of a businessman.

The final trial began on 22 December 1873 and concluded on Christmas Eve with the judge in poor humour. He had been asked something of a technical question by the jury and, in retaliation, said that if they did not reach a verdict soon he would lock them in their chambers all night. They responded promptly by acquitting Hall.

Immediately after his release he wrote another play, *The Crucible,* described as an artfully contrived drama with a simple plot, the gist of which was that he had never conspired with the Tweed Ring. It was not a success. Opening on 5 December 1875 it ran for only 22 performances. Hall went to England for a time before returning to New York where he resumed his career as a lawyer and journalist. On 25 March 1898, this one-time mocker of organised religion was baptised into the Roman Catholic Church. He died seven months later on 7 October 1898.

On what could be described as the white-collar side of his practice, Howe represented Policy Number organisers who were always keen to ensnare people with spare cash, their own or others. Even the greatest of firms of lawyers were not immune from a spot of defalcation by their employees. On 24 November 1888 James Bethell received 25 years and 4 months for embezzlement whilst a real estate clerk with the fashionable and respected firm of Shipman, Barlow, Laroque and Choate. On arrival at Sing Sing he said, 'This is where I am to be buried.' He was told he could earn nine years' remission. He had spent the money on a Policy game. Philip Goss, who ran the Policy shop, was charged and represented by Howe. The sole witness against him was Bethell and it was apparent that a complex legal game was being played. What Joseph Choate's firm wanted was to retrieve some of the lost monies from the Bank of the State of New York which had handled some of the stolen stock. If Bethell, who 'had been destined to become one of the shining lights of the legal profession of the city', gave evidence against Goss then Howe would have cross-examined him, no doubt discrediting him for the purposes of the civil case. After four adjournments and a good deal of blustering and allegations of prosecution trickery by Howe, the case against Goss was dismissed. At a suitable time it was reinstated. He pleaded not guilty but in a bargain was allowed to change his plea and received a $1,000 fine, which was paid immediately.[13]

What the firm could do was to give the impression that they had judges and city officials in their pockets, and undoubtedly in many cases they did.

The 'vulture-like' Hummel was also the more literate and inventive of the pair. He kept an unconnected telephone in his office and if a client asked whether he knew a judge there would come the reply that he had lunch with him practically every day. Hummel would then reach for the telephone and hold an imaginary conversation arranging a meeting with the named judge:

> By virtue of such an auricular demonstration of intimacy the client would be convinced that his success or liberty was 'in the bag' and that Howe & Hummel were cheap at any retainer they might choose to name.[14]

Some stories were embellished over the years, often to Howe's advantage. One very popular one, recounted by Arthur Train as told to him by Francis Wellman, is of the girl prosecuted for the murder of her lover. At the end of his speech to the jury Howe pushed his long fingernails into her cheeks so that she screamed. He then continued:

> Look, gentlemen! Look into this poor creature's face! Does she look like a guilty woman? No, a thousand times no! Those are the tears of innocence and shame! Send her back to her aged father to comfort his old age. Let him clasp her and press his trembling lips to her hollow eyes! Let him wipe away her tears and bid her sin no more!

The girl in question was Ella Nelson and another version is that she had been hiding her face in her hands when Howe had prised them apart. The language is certainly florid enough for the great man. She had offered to plead to manslaughter, a plea which Wellman, then an assistant district attorney, had rejected. She was wholly acquitted.

Howe's tricks did not always go unnoticed by the judge. On another occasion, with the lawyer on his knees and weeping as he made his final speech, he moved closer to his client and her child. At once the child began to yell and then stopped. Howe wept more. Said Recorder Hackett: 'Mr Howe, you had better give the baby another jab with the pin.'

Howe was a great believer in publicity. Here he is explaining for the benefit of his adoring public how he chased away burglars:

> Yes, I shot at 'em. There were two and I think I hit one of them but he got away. No, I shalln't report it to the police. I've got a revolver in every room and I'm a good shot. I don't object to burglars as clients – they're pretty good clients – but I seriously object to their operating on my house.[15]

His last great case had come some three years previously when in 1897 at the age of 69 he defended Augusta Nack, described as a woman of operatic proportions, in the notorious Nack-Guldensuppe murder. It was a case which he believed he was well on the way to winning until a touch of religious intervention caused him insuperable problems.

The story was one of the usual domestic triangles so loved by the press and public. All participants were good-looking German immigrants. Augusta was a midwife by trade and lived with Herman Nack, the owner of a sausage shop on Tenth

Avenue. He also kept a boarding house, one of whose tenants was Willie Guldensuppe, who sported a still-life tattoo on his chest and was what we would now call a masseur but was then described as a rubber in a Turkish bath. Soon Nack was supplanted in Augusta's affections, and this went well until she fell in love with Martin Thorn, a barber. Willie was not as compliant as Nack and the pair planned to dispose of him.

They leased a cottage in Woodside and one day in May 1897 they killed him. They had left nothing to chance because Thorn was armed with a revolver, rope, dagger, poison, a knife and a bottle of carbolic acid. Willie was shot, stabbed with the poisoned dagger and an attempt was made at decapitation. Augusta Nack then cut up the rubber, putting him in a bathtub and leaving the water running while Thorn took the head to drop in the East River.

Unfortunately for the pair, the water and blood burst the drainpipe outside the cottage and instead of disappearing into the sewage system formed a puddle in the yard in which a duck took a bath. The disappearance of Willie had already been reported and had caused considerable interest, so when the duck waddled home with its feathers covered in blood its owners told the police. It was only a matter of time before two and two were added together.

The defence was a blanket denial. The pair did not know of Willie's life or death nor – until it was proved that they did – had they known each other or rented a cottage. The dissection had been a fine one and there were still a significant number of pieces of the body missing, including the head and the tattoo. For Howe, Willie simply did not exist. He argued that the assembled parts could have come from half a dozen mortuaries and he had a fine time making up a string of names including Gildersleeve, Goldylocks, Gludensup and, since the jury was well educated, about 'a creature as imaginary as Rosencrantz's friend Guildenstern'. Observers regarded him as being well on his way to another spectacular acquittal.

Then unfortunately a local Presbyterian vicar started visiting Augusta Nack in prison and, worse for Howe, brought his simpering, curly-headed four-year-old son with him. According to the story the child climbed on her knee and lispingly asked her in the name of the heavenly and earthly Father to tell the truth. Subsequently Thorn received life imprisonment and she a modest 9 years.

Howe wrote to his partner:

I had the prettiest case, and here is all my work shattered. I can still prove they couldn't identify Willie's body and that it wasn't cut up in the Woodside cottage. Now all my roses are frosted in a night and my grapes withered on the vine.

Always a high liver and a heavy drinker, his health began to fail and, although he continued to defend a number of murder cases including Michael Considine who had been accused of shooting a man in the Metropole Hotel on Broadway,[16] the Nack case was effectively his legal swan song.

As an advocate Hummel was never in Howe's class, which is not to say he did not have his moments. One of the firm's great opponents was humbug in the human form of the vice reformer, Anthony Comstock. Comstock had been dealt an earlier blow as the forces of evil were represented by Howe and Hummel in a vice case in New York, and he lost another brush with Abe over the aggravating spectacle of a *danse du ventre* by three Philadelphian Egyptians, Zora, Fatima and Zelika.

Hummel had argued that the dance was part of an ancient religious ceremony which devout Moslems, such as these girls, were bound by their faith to perform at regular intervals. The second point was that the dance was not as Comstock had said 'a lewd and lascivious contortion of the stomach'. Hummel explained that the stomach was a small sac whose contortions, if any – which was not admitted – could only be seen from inside the body.

The girls gave evidence, swearing on a copy of the Koran which Hummel had thoughtfully provided and, during his speeches when he regularly mentioned Allah, they looked appropriately and 'reverently toward the East, as is the custom with members of their faith'. The case was dismissed and Comstock reprimanded as an interfering busybody.

Continuing to display his literary talents in addition to his work on theatrical law, he wrote *In Danger*, a highly readable book which amounted to in-house advertising and explained the firm's services to clients and potential clients.

Howe died suddenly on 2 September 1902, survived by his third wife, and the effective end of the firm came shortly after his death when Hummel was prosecuted in a suit which lasted for years following his faking of evidence in a divorce case. His efforts to evade the finality of the process were regarded in American legal circles as almost a triumph in themselves. Indeed, even while Travers Jerome was prosecuting him as being a suborner of evidence, the District Attorney was still quite prepared to have Hummel as a witness in the celebrated Stanford White murder trial.[17]

Hummel's downfall, the Morse-Dodge case, is one of almost infinite complexities; but essentially, in June 1901 Charles W. Morse, the dubious Maine financier, had married the divorced wife of Charles Foster Dodge. The late husband had at one time been a conductor on the Southern Railroad, but had fallen further in society so that he was now managing cheap hotels on a fairly irregular basis. The divorce had taken place in New York after a perfectly reputable lawyer, William A. Sweetzer, swore that he had personally served the papers on Dodge who had employed another lawyer, Mortimer A. Ruger, to act for him.

The new marriage was not a success and members of the Morse family, notably 'Uncle Jim' Morse, spent a good deal of time and money – a figure of $60,000 is suggested – with Hummel, trying to dissolve it. Fortunately Ruger had died in the meantime and for the small matter of $5,000 Dodge was persuaded to sign an affidavit saying he had never received the original papers.

In October 1903 Hummel obtained an order requiring Mrs Morse to show why her new marriage should not be declared invalid. At the hearing he produced a Dodge lookalike, named Herpich, and snared Sweetzer into saying to him, 'How do you do, Mr Dodge?' The divorce was annulled. Sweetzer was not pleased and managed to obtain possession of Ruger's papers which showed he had acted for Charles Dodge.

The District Attorney Travers Jerome had long been unsympathetic to Hummel's behaviour and now he tried to use Dodge to impeach his lawyer. Dodge was arrested in Atlanta and brought to New York. Hummel obtained $10,000 from 'Uncle Jim' and bailed out Dodge who then, surprisingly, disappeared. In fact Hummel had sent him off with ample funds to drink and whore himself to death in New Orleans. There then followed something approaching a farce when Jerome's detective traced the drunken Dodge and put him in the hands of the Texas Rangers. Hummel tried one last rearguard action by enlisting an armed posse to free him, but Dodge had been spirited out of Texas before battle could be joined.

On 27 June 1905 Hummel was finally indicted. With his enemy in his pocket, Jerome seems to have been extremely generous and offered Hummel a plea bargain which he declined. Dodge, assisted by a new set of $40 teeth, gave evidence and Hummel sensibly declined to go into the witness box.

He was found guilty on 20 December and the Appellate Court found against him on 10 May 1907. On 16 May his conviction was affirmed and when Judge Edgar M. Cullen, the Chief Judge of the Court of Appeals, declined to give a certificate of reasonable doubt and to stay the proceedings, Hummel took the news well. To conform to prison regulations of the time he had his hair cut and his drooping moustache shaved off. He then gave a party for his friends to which the press was not invited, and on Monday 20 May a crowd gathered in front of his brownstone at 52 E 73rd to see him off. At 4 p.m., escorted by his nephew Abe Kaffenburgh, he surrendered to the warden at Blackwell's Island where he was given cell 23. He was to be allowed daily visitors except on Saturdays and Sundays. Almost immediately there were rumours of his ill-health and he was admitted to the prison hospital. According to the reports he suffered a complete nervous breakdown and his life was despaired of. Would his sentence be remitted so that he could die in peace? That was one of the questions which kept readers buying the papers. He survived and was released on 19 March 1908 after which he left New York, returning only once when his cruise ship landed and he took time out to have a chat with reporters. Over the years it was reported on many occasions that he had died, but in fact he died in his flat in Baker Street, London, on 21 January 1926.[18]

His body was brought back to New York and his funeral was attended by a few elderly lawyers and a young man who, to the interest of the other spectators, took a rose from the coffin, kissed it and threw it on the grave. Later the boy claimed he was Henry D. Hummel, the son of Hummel's long-term liaison with the actress Leila Farrell whom his father had represented in a breach of promise suit against the vaudevillian Nat Goodwin. His claim was good, but although the overall estate was sizeable the New York County part on which Henry had a claim amounted to only some $17,000. He soon returned to his job as a baker's delivery assistant in Portland, Maine.

What happened to members of the firm? Hummel's nephew Abraham Kaffenburgh was disbarred on 7 July 1906 for allowing the business to continue under the name of Howe and Hummel, and also for his part in attempting to smuggle Dodge out of Texas. Another lawyer Benjamin Steinhardt, indicted along with Hummel, was now suffering from *locomotor ataxia* and never stood trial. Because of his illness he survived another potential legal disaster when he was found to have represented both plaintiff and defendant in the same action.[19] An application to disbar Nathaniel Cohen failed and he joined other members of the firm, David May and Isaac Jacobson, in a practice which continued until the 1930s. As for the firm of Howe and Hummel itself, the shingle was taken down in November 1906.

1 Not everyone agrees that Howe was the less dishonest. Richard Rovere describes him as a 'very queer tick indeed. He was a man with a past which he found prudent to conceal ...' *Howe and Hummel*, p.35.
2 Edgar Salinger, letter to *The New Yorker*, 28 December 1946.
3 The night before his execution on 21 April 1849, Rush told the Governor of Norwich Prison that he wanted 'roast pig and plenty of plum sauce' for his dinner. On the scaffold he instructed William Calcraft, the hangman, to 'put the noose a little higher'. A set of Staffordshire flatback figures was made to commemorate the trial. For an account of the case and Howe's small part see the *Notable British Trials* Series. Other accounts include Leonard Gribble, *Famous Judges and their Trials*.
4 Arthur Train, *My Day in Court*, p.27. Howe was not the only flamboyant dresser amongst the New York lawyers of the period. Counsellor Tom Nolan wore a Prince Albert coat with low-cut sateen evening waistcoat, and sported in lieu of a tie a diamond collar button and three jewelled breast pins. The top was an emerald shamrock, in the middle the United States flag in rubies, and at the bottom a flapping American eagle also in rubies.
5 Quoted in 'Decadence of New York's Criminal Bar' in the *New York Times*, 7 September 1902.
6 This and following quotes from the *New York Herald*, 29, 30 October, 10–15 December 1888.
7 *New York Herald*, 10 October, 3,4,6 December 1889.
8 *New York Herald,* 24 January 1888.
9 *New York Times*, 'Met Death Bravely', 22 August 1888.
10 Abraham Hummel, *The Trial and Conviction of Jack Reynolds for the Horrible Murder of William Townsend.*
11 *New York Herald*, 26 July 1884.
12 *Ibid*, 5 December 1884. Howe gave an interview to the paper the next day.
13 *New York Herald*, 11 August 1880.
14 Arthur Train, *My Day in Court*, pp.29–30. Arthur Train also wrote *The Confessions of Artemus Quibble* based on Abe Hummel. It was enormously popular and there sprang up a number of Artemus Quibble clubs, one of which based in Harvard lasted for many years.
15 *New York Tribune*, 23 November 1901.
16 The Metropole, which was near Times Square, was immortalised in Cole Porter's *Ace in the Hole*. 'You can see them every day walking up and down Broadway, they congregate outside the Metropole. There's wise guys and boosters, card sharps and crap shooters and they've all got an ace down in the hole.'
17 On 25 June 1906 Harry Thaw, a millionaire playboy, was accused of killing the architect Stanford White whom he shot dead on the Madison Square Garden roof. He believed that some years previously Thaw had debauched his wife Evelyn, a Gibson girl in the hit show *Floradora*. She was known as 'The Girl on the Red Velvet Swing'. Jerome wanted evidence from Hummel about visits by Evelyn Thaw to his office. See Gerald Langford, *The Murder of Stanford White*.
18 *New York Times*, 24 January 1926.
19 Joseph Auerbach, *The Bar of Other Days*.

# 3 Arthur Newton and 'Chicago May' Sharpe

I N 1893, WHEN ARTHUR JOHN EDWARD NEWTON was at the pinnacle of his career, he received an accolade given to few solicitors when a profile and a cartoon of him appeared in the popular magazine *Vanity Fair*. This was slightly curious. After all, not many solicitors who have been to prison for conspiracy remain on the books of the Law Society, let alone have adulatory articles written about them – certainly not within a matter of three years of their supposed downfall.

Newton, whose family claimed to be descended from Sir Isaac Newton, the scientist remembered for his experiments with apples, had been rather better educated than some solicitors of the time when he qualified in 1884. His father had been an actuary, manager of the Legal and General Assurance Society, and had sent his son to a preparatory school and Cheltenham College where he excelled at football. There had clearly been money in the family, for he served his articles with the fashionable firm of Frere Foster in Lincoln's Inn Fields and became a solicitor.

Once qualified, Newton opened offices opposite the Great Marlborough Street Police Court and within a matter of a few years had one of the three biggest criminal law practices in London. He was regarded as a good advocate who eschewed the bullying tactics of most of his contemporaries.

The *Vanity Fair* cartoon, by the fashionable Spy, shows Newton in a double-breasted waistcoat and wing collar looking rather like Clark Gable as Rhett Butler, and the adulatory article by Jehu Junior which accompanied it had Newton as 'not eloquent but he is lucid; and though he is strong yet he is courteous. He can swim; he had more than once been found guilty of giving a conjuring entertainment. He has the great advantage of good appearance.' As for his peccadillo? It was certainly not more than that '... and then he once got himself into trouble by too zealous defence of an undeserving client'.

In addition to his talents as a swimmer and a conjurer – perhaps the reference is to his having made a witness vanish – throughout his life Arthur Newton consistently sailed close to the wind. The 'undeserving client' of his first slip had been Lord Arthur Somerset and the case the Cleveland Street Brothel Scandal of 1886. Others would follow.[1]

The Cleveland Street Brothel Scandal stemmed from the arrest of certain boys who worked in the Post Office at St Martin's-le-Grand and who supplemented their income by male prostitution. It was thought, at first, that one of the boys had stolen money from the Receiver General's Department and Charles Swinscow was asked how he could have as much as 18 shillings in his possession. Pressed for an explanation he said it had come from his going with men at 19 Cleveland Street. He had, he said, been persuaded by the appropriately named Henry Newlove first to 'behave indecently' together and then to go to the male brothel in Cleveland Street run by Charles Hammond which catered for the nobility. Another boy, Thickbroom, was also involved.

When questioned Newlove said that a visitor to the brothel was Lord Arthur Somerset, a major in The Blues and Extra Equerry to the Prince of Wales. Somerset approached Newton to act for him and the lawyer's part in the affair was to try to get potential witnesses against Somerset out of the country.

It is curious that a young man such as Newton should have come to the notice of the high and the mighty so early in his career. Over the years some solicitors have, for good or bad reasons, come to be the repository of secrets of their social betters. Sir George Lewis was one and, a half century later, Arnold Goodman – the fashionable adviser to the mighty during Harold Wilson's regime – was another. Just how Newton achieved his position is not clear but he was definitely a man with whom to be reckoned and, to a great extent at this stage in his career, trusted. Early on in the inquiry when it became apparent that it would be a far-ranging one he had gone to see the Assistant Director of Public Prosecutions, Hamilton Cuffe, to warn him that if Somerset were to be prosecuted another name would appear: that of Prince Albert Victor, known as Eddy, the eldest son of the Prince of Wales and grandson of Queen Victoria. It may be that Newton was exercising a spot of blackmail on behalf of his client – later in his career there were suggestions that he was not averse to the same for financial reasons. There may have been nothing in the suggestion, but it was sufficient for Cuffe to inform Sir Augustus Stephenson, and so on up the chain to Lord Salisbury, the Prime Minister.

Newton failed in the attempt to send the boys abroad even though he had offered substantial terms – £50 cash, a new suit of clothes and £1 a week to run for three years, as well as their passage to Australia. What he was able to do was to warn Somerset that a warrant for his arrest was imminent. His Lordship left for France the next day and although he returned on 30 September 1889 to attend the funeral of his grandmother his stay was short-lived. He left again on 18 October never to return, dying in Hyères, in the South of France, on 26 May 1926.

As for the boys, Newlove received four months with hard labour in the House of Correction and Swincow and Thickbroom were dismissed from the Post Office. Hammond, who owned the Cleveland Street brothel, fled to Seattle.

Summonses were issued against Newton, his clerk Frederick Taylorson and a translator, Adolphe de Gallo. It is curious why they were ever laid, but there was a general feeling amongst the public and the police that people in high places had been allowed to get away with things. Newton was to be the sacrificial lamb and, it must be said, he acted as such.

Submissions that there was no case to answer failed at the magistrate's court when Vaughan, the stipendiary magistrate, committed them for trial. All this cost money and now Newton was looking around for help. Lord Arthur's father, the Duke of Beaufort, contributed £1,000; he had been asked for £3,100. Others did likewise.

Since it was thought that it would be better if the case was tried before a High Court judge, an application was made for it to be moved from the Old Bailey to the High Court. On 31 January 1890 leave was granted. At this stage it is probable that few thought anything more than a bind-over would be handed down to Newton. De Gallo had already gone from the proceedings when the Grand Jury refused to indict him. Taylorson, meanwhile, was causing trouble. He refused to listen to his and Newton's counsel, the great and formidable Sir Charles Russell QC, who wished him to plead guilty. The following exchange is recorded:

'Damn it, sir, do as I tell you,' shouted the great man.
'Damn it, sir, I will not plead Guilty.'

And Taylorson was as good as his word. The trial opened on 16 May 1890 in the Queen's Bench Division. With Taylorson still remaining adamant that he would plead not guilty the charges against him were dropped, which shows that sometimes at least the client has the better judgement.

This left Newton to face the court in the form of Mr Justice Cave, a man with considerable experience in bankruptcy but little in criminal law. Russell had persuaded the prosecution to drop five of the charges in return for a plea of guilty to the sixth, a general count of perverting the course of justice. It was all intended to be a low-key affair. He had been told that 'a persuasive rather than a hostile attitude towards the authorities would result in the matter not being too deeply gone into'.[2] His mitigation was therefore of a young man who had acted over-zealously to prevent his client being subjected to blackmail. At that moment there were still few who thought that anything worse than a bind-over would be forthcoming. The first warning sign was when Cave adjourned the hearing until Tuesday 20 May. Russell asked if he would like an affidavit from Newton verifying the facts and the judge ominously said he did not unless there was additional matter.

When Cave passed sentence on 20 May he made it quite clear that he did not think Newton had been acting from these altruistic motives when he had tried to get the boys out of the country on behalf of wealthy clients:

Your offence has been committed for the purpose of securing the absence of these persons from England in the interests of wealthy clients and to impose a fine, therefore, would only in all probability result in their paying the fine for you. I must, therefore, pass a sentence of imprisonment.

Newton was sent to prison for six weeks. In a sense he was fortunate, in that Cave did not add the words 'with hard labour'. Then, as now, leading counsel did not necessarily hang about to see the results of their labours and Arthur Jelf, who was tidying things up for the absent Charles Russell, asked that Newton be treated as a first-class misdemeanant which meant he would have books, newspapers and food sent in, be allowed to wear his own clothes and generally have none too uncomfortable a life. Jelf then supported this by way of medical evidence, but Cave was clearly unhappy about things and ruled that 'the matter must be in abeyance and at present I see no reason for departing from the ordinary course'.

Neither was Newton happy with his confinement in Holloway, then a male prison. As an ordinary convict he had to wear the rough arrow-marked clothing and was deprived of reading materials. He complained about depression and he complained about diarrhoea. As a result he was given 24 ounces of white bread and two extra pints of cocoa a day. His work was repairing clothes.

In the month and a half while he remained in Holloway he submitted two petitions. The first asked that his sentence be reduced on health grounds; his wife was expecting a child and as a fully fledged convict he could hear no news of her confinement. The second was once more that he be deemed a first-class misdemeanant so that he could continue to exercise control over his practice.

In fact his brother lawyers thought he was being badly treated and 250 firms including the great Lewis and Lewis signed a petition to this effect. However, nothing would shift Cave and after Newton had been in Holloway a fortnight he reviewed the medical evidence, saying that:

the prognostications of injury to his health have not been verified and there seems no reason to apprehend any serious effect upon his medical and physical condition.

Unless Newton's condition deteriorated Cave would not change his mind. He was proved right. During his stay Newton actually added 2lbs to the 160lbs he weighed when he went to Holloway. On his release he tried once more to tap the Duke of Beaufort and was once more rejected, something about which he felt extremely bitter. All was not bad news however. He had already learned that the Law Society was not disposed to take any action against him. His brother solicitors' hard work on his behalf in his absence had had the desired effect.

Nor had the quality of his work suffered by his absence. In 1894 he was representing the Duchess of Marlborough over her lost jewels and posting a reward, having taken over the case from Sir George Lewis.[3] The next year he acted for Alfred Taylor, the co-defendant of Oscar Wilde, and three years after that for the disreputable Count Esterhazy in a successful libel action against the *Observer* when he was awarded £500. Within four years, such was his success and reputation that he joined the gallery of legal luminaries to be featured in *Vanity Fair*.

By the turn of the century Newton had one of the three great criminal practices in London. The others were owned by the very fashionable Sir George Lewis and Freke Palmer, who shared with Newton the principal criminal cases of the time. Newton's was, however, the closest to the Underworld. His clients now ranged from the louche to the criminal, from the music-hall star Marie Lloyd through dukes and duchesses to chorus girls and adventuresses, from actors to the talented but dishonest American jockey, Tod Sloan, and mostly he did what he could for all of them. He had the reputation as a great fixer with the ability to charge £100 for a telephone call which removed the wart from a client's back.

> ... a man of the most agreeable presence and a great favourite with the fair sex, he was in constant demand for supper and luncheon parties in the West End of London. The ladies of the theatrical profession made him their legal adviser, with the result that he began to spend a good deal more money than he could earn.[4]

At least according to his clerk he did not encourage litigation:

> My dear sir, going to law is like going to war: you can never be quite certain of the outcome and even the victor usually loses more than he wins.

Newton had long represented Chicago May Sharpe, one of the many American men and women who came to London about that period to work as pickpockets, hotel thieves, safebreakers and at the badger game. She thought reasonably well of him:

> He was a smart man, charged good-sized fees and knew the ropes. The last thing he said to me, when I went off to do my long-bit, was, 'May, don't complain about anything, or they will land you in Broadmoor.' He represented both big and little criminals and fixed his fees according to his clients' ability to pay.[5]

When in 1907 she and Charles Smith shot and wounded their robber associate, Eddie Guerin, near Russell Square underground station it was again to Newton that Sharpe turned for her defence. He could seemingly be used as a conduit pipe for messages. In a letter intercepted by the authorities in Holloway prison she wrote to her current boyfriend Baby Thompson, 'You can hear all from Arthur Newton.'[6]

A perusal of the Metropolitan Police files for the period will show the number of serious cases in which Newton appeared. He acted for the international white slavers led by Aldo Antonious Celli (alias Carvelli, Shanks, Cortini, Ferrari and Leonora) who had been recruiting girls from Belgium to be taken to New Zealand but who had stopped off in London, so earning Celli and his partner Alexander Nicolini six months' hard labour and the infinitely more tiresome deportation.[7]

In 1911 Newton was suspended by the Law Society for his conduct following the defence of Harvey Hawley Crippen for the murder of his wife, the music-hall actress Belle Elmore. Although this was not the aspect of the case into which the Law Society specifically inquired, he had instructed himself on behalf of the dentist accused of poisoning his wife and leaving her body in the cellar of their North London home while he fled to America with his girlfriend Ethel Le Neve. Newton had telegraphed Crippen, now under arrest on the *Megantic*:

> Your friends desire me to defend you and will pay all necessary expenses. Will undertake your defence, but you must promise to keep absolute silence and answer no questions and do not resist extradition. Reply confirming. Arthur Newton.

The friends in question seem to have amounted to one. Newton said in the *Daily Mail*:

> I was on the eve of starting a short holiday when an old business friend of Dr Crippen came to my office yesterday and asked if I would undertake his defence, promising to do all he could to supply the necessary expenses for him.[8]

The newspaper took a rather more robust line, suggesting that the friend was 'that prince of quacks Eddie Marr, alias "Professor" Keith-Harvey alias "Professor" Elmer Shirley, alias W.S. Hamilton, obesity specialist', and that the meeting did not take place in Newton's office but that the solicitor had gone out to shake down Marr who put up £100.

While Crippen and Ethel Le Neve were still on the liner bringing them back to England, Newton was hard at work. A number of newspapers had speculated on the cause of death and the efficacy of poison and Newton had been quick to apply for *rules nisi* for alleged contempt, resulting in fines of up to £200 on the offending papers and costs for himself.

Initially Ethel Le Neve had instructed a separate solicitor, but she soon found herself being looked after by Newton. Later, to her fortune, she left Newton and instructed Hopwood and Sons who briefed 'the cleverest man in the kingdom', F.E. Smith, later Lord Birkenhead. She was acquitted of being an accessory after the murder.

Said Mr Justice Darling when Newton later appeared before him:

> Crippen was not defended as he should have been. [His case] was conducted very largely for the purpose of making 'copy' for the newspapers.

The brief for Crippen's defence was first offered to Marshall Hall. His clerk, A.E. Bowker, who had accepted the brief for the great man from Newton in the sensational Robert Wood, Camden Town murder,[9] regarded Newton as being utterly unscrupulous and so wanted money with the brief, the standard procedure for dealing with solicitors known not to be good payers.

> We discussed terms but when he said he was not prepared to pay any of the fees until the case was over, I became suspicious and insisted on a cheque with the brief. We haggled for a time, for I wanted the case badly. The defence of Crippen offered just the sort of challenge that would spur Marshall Hall to one of his great efforts of advocacy; but I continued to demand a cheque and would not budge.
>
> Newton then banged out of chambers shouting. He walked up the Middle Temple Lane ... furious at his failure to obtain the services of Marshall Hall. Three doors up the lane from Temple Gardens he saw the name of Alfred Tobin, and stopped. Newton knew quite well that Tobin was not within miles of being a leading criminal silk. Newton's temper, however, had got the better of his judgement, and ten minutes after leaving me he had arranged for Tobin to lead for the defence of Crippen.[10]

According to Newton's clerk, Henchy, his master was held in high regard by Marshall Hall who, commenting on a particularly meticulously drawn set of instructions, remarked, 'Confound it, Newton. This isn't a dashed brief, it's a verdict.'

Newton also rather tricked his unfortunate expert witness into giving evidence. One of the points of the case was the identification of the body of Belle Elmore, something done through an appendix scar. At a bridge party Dr Turnbull had been prevailed upon to examine the piece of skin which he originally said was a fold rather than a scar. He had been promised, he said, that he would not be asked to give evidence. Travers Humphreys commented:

> Little did that unsuspecting scientist know the man he was dealing with when he made that statement to Mr Arthur Newton ... What Arthur Newton wanted he usually got, by fair means or otherwise.[11]

By the time of the Crippen trial Newton was 50, with a taste for the finest Havana cigars and a penchant for wearing dove-grey gloves which he ordered by the gross from a glove-maker in Jermyn Street. Asked about the gloves he commented, 'But in our profession it is so difficult to keep one's hands clean.'

According to W.E. Henchy, his managing clerk, Newton had angled for Crippen as a high-profile money-spinner which would enable him to pay off his racing debts. A heavy gambler relying largely and foolishly on the tips given to him by Tod Sloan, Newton was also a serious money-borrower. How much money he made from the trial will probably not be known. Crippen mentioned £12,000 for an appeal – the money to be put up by Professor Munyon of Philadelphia, Crippen's old employer – but it does not appear that sum was ever forthcoming.

Newton certainly sold the exclusive rights to anything Crippen had to say after the trial, and Crippen thought he was to receive £500 for his memoirs from the *New York American*. Newton had also obtained £1,000 for Crippen to undertake a two-month lecture tour of the States in the event of an acquittal. He invested some of Crippen's money, which the man had hoped to leave to Ethel Le Neve but, sadly, the Charing Cross Bank failed on the day he stood trial. It owed £2,500,000 to depositors and had failed through a fraudulent land speculation in Canada.

What really riled the Law Society, however, was the deal Newton made over the sale of Crippen's confession. It was then common practice in a sensational murder – when there was no legal aid available except representation under the Poor Persons' Defence Act – for a newspaper to pay the defence costs. The *quid pro quo* was that the defendant would give an exclusive story to the funding paper with, in the event of a conviction, a death-cell confession to be published usually on the Sunday after his execution. In this instance Newton appears to have slightly changed the standard practice.

The *Evening Times*, a paper which had a circulation rarely exceeding 100,000, suddenly sold nearly a million copies. The reason was its headline:

CRIPPEN HANGED TO-DAY AT PENTONVILLE

–

HOW HE MURDERED BELLE ELMORE AND MADE AWAY WITH
THE BODY

–

HIS FULL CONFESSION

–

THE POISON WAS ADMINISTERED IN INDIGESTION TABLETS

Unusually the story was in the third person and it was explained that Dr Crippen had made a confession before he died to a friend who was unable to keep the awful secret any longer and was now telling all to the newspaper.

In fact, a few days before Crippen's execution on 23 November a man had called at the offices of the *Evening Times* and told the editor, Charles Watney, that Crippen had confessed to Arthur Newton who was prepared to sell the story for £1,000. Newton met Arthur Findon, the newspaper's advertising manager, and agreed to sell the story for £500 to be paid in gold sovereigns. He would dictate the story but he would in no way be connected to it. On the evening of 22 November when the paper put out posters advertising the scoop of next day Newton panicked, fearing that the Law Society might have learned of the events. When he said he would not go ahead, Watney threatened to publish an account of the deal.

Newton, now in an extreme bind, agreed to dictate the confession to a friend who would deliver the story to Findon's flat. At 3 a.m. on the morning of the execution the friend arrived and, in turn, dictated the story before throwing the script on the fire from which part was rescued after he had left.

The writer Edgar Wallace, at that time the paper's racing correspondent, was prevailed upon to add a certain amount of human interest and wrote the paragraphs which would bring retribution on the paper's head:

The statement printed below is Crippen's own statement. It bears in every line the stamp of authenticity. It is unnecessary to say that no journal – even the least responsible of journals – would print this confession of Crippen's without unimpeachable authority. That authority we possess.[12]

The rival newspapers applied to Newton and the prison governor for confirmation of the authenticity of the confession and received emphatic denials from both sides. The *Evening Times* when challenged to produce proof could not do so, and it was not helped by Newton's ambiguous statement:

It is not within any man's right to throw doubt on the confession. So far as I am personally concerned, I can say nothing about the confession. I personally knew of no confession, and beyond this I cannot discuss the matter.

This was the beginning of the end for the paper. A solicitor was consulted and advised the directors to publish the whole story, setting out Newton's part, but the decision was taken that the *Evening Times* would live down the problem and that to set out Newton's machinations would ruin him. The paper survived a few months, Newton for only a little longer.

He had also been treating with the extremely dangerous Horatio Bottomley, the fraudulent editor of *John Bull*.[13] Bottomley had put up £50 and probably very much more towards the defence, plus a further £150 towards an appeal. Two days before Crippen was executed Newton had visited him in the death cell and, as the Committee of the Law Society found:

in abuse of the privilege thus extended to him, aided and abetted one Horatio Bottomley, the editor of *John Bull*, to disseminate in that publication false information in the form of a letter purporting to have been written by Crippen from prison, although, as the respondent well knew, no such letter in fact existed, and had further published or permitted to be published through the medium of *John Bull* and the *Daily Chronicle* other false statements relating to the same matter, well knowing them to be false, whereby the public might be deceived.

The Committee reported that Newton had been found guilty of professional misconduct and on 12 July 1911 he was suspended from practice for 12 months from 25 July and ordered to pay the costs of the inquiry and hearing.

All was not well at Marlborough Street Court in the years before the First World War. Its jurisdiction was the area of Soho which then as now abounded with clubs which were in effect disorderly houses and gambling clubs. The Metropolitan Police Commissioner received a series of complaints that his detectives were shaking down the club owners, in return for which they were either left alone or were warned of imminent raids. The clerks at the court were also suspected of leaking documents to club owners, and there was more than a little suspicion that solicitors were doing the same. One disappeared and the second was caught in a raid on a particularly low-class gambling den. This left a couple of other firms and the temporarily restored Mr Newton, but now his mind was on bigger things.

In 1913 he was charged, along with Berkeley Bennett, with conspiracy to defraud a young and rich pigeon, Thorsch. A third conspirator, Count Festetics – who was certainly Hungarian, probably not a Count and who most likely devised the operation – was never found, but the trio cleared around £9,500 profit from the unfortunate Austrian.

In 1911 Festetics had been introduced to Bennett who boasted of his friendship with the proprietor of the *New York Herald*, Gordon Bennett. In turn Festetics introduced Thorsch to Berkeley Bennett, who now claimed to be a near relative of the millionaire. Thorsch was charmed by the manners of Bennett and seduced by his purported connections, as well he might be. The man had received considerable training in good behaviour since, in his earlier life, he had been a shopwalker.

Now Bennett mentioned that there was the opportunity of purchasing forests in Canada suitable for making pulp. Indeed he had 60,000 acres and held an option on another 40,000 at a very favourable price. Thorsch bought 25,000 acres and went into partnership with the Count for a further block. In fact Bennett had no land, although he later bought 3,500 acres for a sum of £3,900, around half the price he had originally quoted as a bargain basement offer. Newton, acting for all parties, banked the cheques.

Bennett went to Canada, ostensibly to pick out the best acreage for his partners, and returned to throw a party at the Café Royal when he announced that the value of land was rising further. Out came the Count's cheque-book and Thorsch's was not far behind. This time he paid over £5,000.

It was unfortunate that Thorsch then met a man who did know Gordon Bennett well and on meeting Berkeley Bennett nailed him as an impostor immediately. Thorsch instructed his own solicitor who, in turn, instructed an inquiry agent. In due course the Director of Public Prosecutions was approached. Warrants were issued for the arrest of the three men but there seems to have been a leak; either that or the Count had extremely good antennae. He left England never to be seen again.

Newton defended himself and Travers Humphreys, who prosecuted, thought that, although he might have been better off with one of the silks he had instructed over the years, the defence was well thought out:

> ... it was, as I thought at the time, an attractive one and certainly had the merit of affording, if accepted, a complete answer to the charge.[14]

Of Newton himself he wrote that he had:

> ... a charming manner and considerable gifts of advocacy based upon an extensive knowledge of the world rather than a knowledge of law.

Newton maintained that he and his friends were entitled to make a profit from Thorsch provided that Thorsch had not himself made a loss. He wanted to call witnesses to show that the land Thorsch now had was worth more than he had paid for it. Why, he argued, should they let Thorsch, whom they had known for only a short time, have the land at cost price? However, the trial judge Mr Justice Ridley would not allow witnesses to be called. It was not a case of speculating as to the future growth of Canada, simply whether the money the defendants had admittedly pocketed was a legitimate profit. At the time of the purported purchase Bennett had no land to sell.

After the conviction of both men, Newton was late in putting in his application for leave to appeal. In fact, probably this was just as well because prior to 1967 the Court of Criminal Appeal could and did increase sentences they thought were too lenient. Both Newton and his counsel had seen which way the wind was blowing when he applied for leave to appeal out of time, and Lord Darling remarked dangerously that if leave to appeal was not given then the sentence could not be increased.

*Counsel*: I apprehend your Lordship will not do that.
*Darling*: You must not do so.

The sentences of 3 years penal servitude and 18 months imprisonment he had passed on Newton and Bennett respectively stood. If anything, remarked Lord Darling, the judge at the trial had erred on the side of leniency.

Curiously Humphreys thought of the solicitor:

> For my part I never looked upon him as the author of the fraud in which he became involved. I would go so far as to say that if the originator of that scheme could have been brought to justice it might have been possible to leave out of the indictment the name of Arthur Newton ...[15]

With time off for good behaviour Newton was released early from Parkhurst on the Isle of Wight, where he had been the prison librarian and general legal adviser to the convicts. This time the Law Society did strike him off the Rolls. He became a private detective and also a marriage broker, negotiating settlements between those who were rich but had no social status and those who had but were penniless.

Game to the last, shortly before his death on 3 October 1930 at 71a Ebury Street, Chelsea, he was fined for his involvement in a gambling club in the West End. He was then 70. He had often said:

> If I had to put a tombstone on a buried friendship I would not mark it R.I.P.; I should just have it inscribed I.O.U.

But it did not appear on his.

1 There have been any number of detailed accounts of the case including H. Montgomery Hyde, *The Cleveland Street Scandal*, and Theo Aronson, *Prince Eddy and the Homosexual Underworld.*
2 PRO CLAS 12 May 1890.
3 *The Times*, 28 May 1894.
4 S.T.Felstead, *Sir Richard Muir*, p.175.
5 May Churchill Sharpe, *Chicago May*, p.132.
6 PRO Crim 1 108/2. See also James Morton, *Gangland 2*.
7 See for example PRO MEPO 3 197.
8 *Daily Mail*, 3 August 1910.
9 Robert Wood was charged with the murder of Phyllis Dimmock, a prostitute, who was found with her throat cut in her lodgings in Camden Town. Wood was suspected because a picture of a rising sun said to represent a public house frequented by him and Dimmock, drawn by him, was found at the lodgings and he had asked another prostitute, Ruby Young, to provide him with an alibi. Instead she went to a journalist who informed the police. The evidence against him was strong but Wood made a good impression in the witness box. There was also some resentment against Ruby Young. He was the first person to be acquitted after the accused was given the right to give evidence under the Criminal Evidence Act 1898. Generally it is thought that Wood, who later went to Australia, was fortunate, but there were two other viable suspects.

In 1903 Newton also acted for Samuel Dougal, the Moat Farm murderer. Dougal seduced and killed a 55-year-old spinster, Camille Holland, to obtain her fortune. Her body was not discovered for four years. Condemned to death, he changed his story and said the gun with which she had been shot went off accidentally. He was hanged on 14 July 1903, finally confessing his guilt. There are numerous accounts of both cases and both are in the series *Notable British Trials*.

10  A.E. Bowker, *A Lifetime with the Law,* pp.23–4.

11  Douglas C. Browne, *Sir Travers Humphreys*, p.76.

12  *Evening Times*, 23 November 1910.

13  Bottomley himself went to prison in March 1922 when he was jailed for 7 years for fraudulent conversion. He had probably cleared over £600,000 from the swindle.

14  Travers Humphreys, *A Book of Trials*, p.140.

15  *Ibid,* p.138.

# 4 Clarence Darrow and Earl Rogers

VEN THE GREATEST LAWYERS can find themselves in professional difficulties. Clarence Darrow was one of them. The little localised difficulty which left him fighting for his professional life came relatively late in his career when he travelled to California in 1911 to defend the McNamara brothers, James and John. Heavily involved in the labour union movement, both had been charged with the bombing on 30 September 1910 of the Times Building in Ink Alley, Los Angeles. In the subsequent explosion twenty people died; four as they missed a safety-net into which they tried to jump from the burning building.

Darrow's record as a defence lawyer stands with the greatest. He too was heavily involved with the labour movement. He had defended, amongst others, anarchists charged with the 1886 Haymarket Riot in Chicago and Eugene V. Debs, head of the American Railway Union, charged with contempt of court in 1894. At the turn of the century he defended miners in the Pennsylvania coal strike of 1902.[1] Five years later he successfully defended William 'Big Bill' Haywood, head of the Industrial Workers of the World (the Wobblies), who in 1907 had been charged with the assassination of the former governor of Idaho.

Darrow did not really wish to appear in the McNamara trial. At the time he was a sick man and was tiring of the rigours of court work. However, partly through his fee and partly through a suggestion that if he declined the brief he would be regarded as a traitor to the labour movement, he was pressed into service. The money put at his disposal by the Unions was the equivalent of $3 million today, with his fee being the equivalent of $500,000. He was also to be allowed to select his co-counsel and to set the trial strategy. It soon became clear to Darrow that the case was hopeless; the evidence against the brothers was overwhelming.

One great difference between American and British trials is that in the United States there is pre-trial examination of the jury as to their beliefs, so that the jurors potentially most antagonistic to prosecution or defence may be eliminated. Some prefer to phrase it the other way and say it is so that the jurors potentially most favourable to the prosecution or defence may be selected. To this end, if the money is available in an important trial, inquiry agents are used to research the background of potential jurors.

On 6 October 1911 Darrow's principal investigator, Bert Franklin, approached a juror named Bain and, finding he was in financial straits, offered him $4,000 to acquit the McNamaras. The next month, it was increasingly apparent to Darrow that there was no defence likely to succeed, and now it was a question of trying to save James McNamara, who had actually planted the bomb, from the gallows. Darrow was about to try to strike a plea bargain when Franklin approached a second man. Unfortunately this time he picked quite the wrong man in Lockwood, who was himself a former deputy sheriff and a friend of the District Attorney. Lockwood reported matters and it was arranged that he should receive his bribe at 9 a.m. on 28 November at the corner of Los Angeles Street and Third. Unfortunately not only were the police watching but Darrow was in the area. Franklin was arrested.

As for the trial of the McNamaras, Darrow encountered difficulties. James was by no means unhappy to face the gallows and so become a martyr to the Union cause. Eventually on 1 December 1911 Darrow persuaded the brothers of their perilous situation and, to what was described as pandemonium in court, he announced they would be changing their pleas to guilty. Four days later James received life imprisonment and John was sentenced to 15 years.

Darrow's actions are a good example of a lawyer doing what he can for the client rather than for the cause. However, now he was no longer a hero to the working class but regarded as their betrayer. On 29 January 1912 Franklin, who by this time had pleaded guilty to attempted bribery, gave evidence to a Grand Jury implicating Darrow. That afternoon Darrow was arrested on a charge of jury tampering.

It is curious, in retrospect, that the prosecution elected to proceed first with the Bain case – possibly because it was the first in time. In England the cases would have been heard together so that the prosecution could have obtained the maximum amount of prejudice from the evidence of one charge against the other. In California the cases had been severed.

Darrow, with one ear to the saying that a lawyer who acts for himself has a fool for a client, retained to appear with him the enormously talented and enormously flawed Angeleno lawyer, Earl Rogers, who by this time was well over the hill and drinking heavily. How they interacted and who actually did the work depends upon whose account of the proceedings you read.[2]

According to Darrow's biographer, Irving Stone, initially Rogers was keen to share the chairs with Darrow:

> I've been slipping somewhat and I need Darrow almost as much as he needs me. Selecting me to defend the nation's acknowledged premier criminal lawyer will eventually place me in Darrow's class.

The relationship between the hard-living Rogers and the austere Darrow was not an easy one, particularly as Rogers seemed to believe in the prosecution's case and the pair quarrelled over tactics. Nor did their wives have a rapport. When Mrs Rogers invited the Darrows for dinner, Ruby Darrow wore darned cotton gloves, something Mrs Rogers regarded as putting on a show of poverty. As for Darrow himself, she said:

> He always had a hangdog look. He was one of the dirtiest men I ever saw; his nails were dirty; his ears were dirty.

For a time Rogers seems to have carried the case, with Darrow slumped in inertia. At the end of the day Rogers would accuse his client of presenting a picture of guilt, but when Darrow did eventually rise from his torpor and begin to take a more positive interest in his case this did not suit the flamboyant Rogers who disappeared from the court for two days on a drinking binge. Nor was the question of fees satisfactorily resolved. According to Adele Rogers:

Earl never got any part of his fee from Darrow except maybe running expenses. They were always pleading poverty, right on the verge of starvation. It got so I couldn't pay our bills at the stores.

And from the other wife, Ruby Darrow:

Earl Rogers came to us every morning and blackmailed us. If we didn't give him money he said he wouldn't go into court.

But every morning 'Clarence would dig deep down into his pocket for a roll of bills' and then he and Rogers would walk arm-in-arm into court, a picture of total unity.

Eventually, it was agreed that the closing speech should be divided between them, with Darrow having the last word. In their different ways the speeches of both men were quite brilliant. Rogers spoke first and it was reported that he 'moved his audience to tears and laughter at will'. Commenting on Darrow's known meanness and the fact that a plea bargain was being negotiated, he asked:

Do you think Darrow would throw $4,000 to the birds when he had the McNamara case practically settled? When he lets go of a dollar it squeals. It is a mental, moral, physical impossibility for him to do it.

He went on to ask, again rhetorically:

Will you tell me how any sane, sensible man who knows anything about the law business – and this defendant has been in it for 35 years – could make himself go to a detective and say to him: just buy all the jurors you want. I put my whole life, my reputation, I put everything I have into your hands. I trust you absolutely. I never knew you until two or three months ago and I don't know much about you now. But there you are. Go to it.

It was the sort of closing speech of which great trial lawyers are made. Darrow's speech, which lasted a day and a half, was even greater. To the horror of the prosecution he not only moved the jury to tears, the judge cried as well. On the verdict of 'not guilty' Judge Hutton commented:

Now the case is ended, I consider it entirely proper for me to congratulate Mr Darrow on his acquittal. I know that millions of hallelujahs will go up through the length and breadth of the land.

That left the Bain case. Now Darrow was in more difficulties. Both Rogers and his principal assistant, Horace Appel, withdrew from the trial, leaving the up-and-coming Jerry Giesler to assist Darrow who now effectively defended himself. He could not argue that there was no point in bribing Bain because there was *every* point. At the time when Franklin handed over the money the McNamara brothers were still intent on contesting everything. In March 1913 the jury was deadlocked, with 8 out of the 12 wanting to convict Darrow. A plea bargain was struck. The District Attorney agreed not to re-try the case; Darrow, for his part, promised never to practise law in California again. It was not the great man's finest hour.

In hindsight it is easy to at least see Rogers' viewpoint. If Darrow was taking only one-sixth of the $3 million of today, where was the rest going? Surely not just to Franklin's researches.[3]

Rogers was one of the great and dishonest advocates who functioned in an era when judges were not as strict with the lawyers who appeared before them. Regarded as having a far sharper and more resourceful brain than Darrow, it was said of him that when he was sober – which was for perhaps a third of his waking hours – he was almost impossible to beat.

> Rogers was tall, magnificently proportioned with a full head of graying hair, roguishly handsome features, beautifully expressive eyes and a stirring voice. A dandy who dressed in the height of fashion, Earl Rogers had all the requirements of a matinée idol.
>
> He used his penetrating brain mostly for antisocial purposes. There was no client too venal for him to lavish his inexhaustible gifts upon.
>
> In the days before legal ethics were solidly established Rogers brought fits of apoplexy upon judges and prosecutors by the manner in which he juggled testimony, stole or switched incriminating exhibits, engaged in torrential acts of passion, anger, ecstasy, hysteria, to confuse the issue, divert the attention of the jury and jim up the prosecutor's case.[4]

Others describe him as tall, thin, pallid, built like a wedge, with jet-black hair, a man who used perfume and a lorgnette for effect.

He had been a reporter in his early days and on his admission to the California Bar in 1897 he was employed by Telfair Creighton. When he came in drunk after a long session which followed his successful defence of a busty blonde, Creighton threw him out.

Rogers was thought to be one of the lawyers who would always have one juror bribed in murder cases and he was certainly capable of disposing of unwanted witnesses on a temporary basis. He was, however, well versed in the rudimentaries of forensic evidence and, unlike his admirer Bill Fallon, actually prepared cases thoroughly.

Much of his life out of court was spent avoiding his debtors and Jerry Giesler obtained a job with him when he had been working as a debt collector. Rogers was avoiding payment on a set of law books and Giesler went to the office. He later recalled: 'His office was trained to smell bill collectors the way bird dogs smell bob whites.'

Giesler did not collect the payment but he saw Rogers and said he wished to clerk him. He was eventually taken on and enjoyed enormous personal success.

One client Rogers lost to the gallows was towards the end of his career. Charles Bundy choked a delivery boy, dragged him into bushes and killed him with a baseball bat before robbing him of $20 with which he bought his girlfriend a present when she arrived that evening from Los Angeles, in the hope that she would consent to sexual intercourse with him. Bundy was 17 and the case told heavily on Rogers. It was his firm belief that, in a murder case, the defendant must give evidence, otherwise there was no hope of an acquittal. He did not put Bundy – whom he regarded as insane – in the witness box and when the jury returned a verdict of guilty blamed himself. He argued the case in front of the California Supreme Court but he was unable to persuade them to commute the death penalty.

He obtained a happier result for Gabrielle D'Arley who killed Leonard Troop, her pimp boyfriend, at the moment when he was buying a ring for another girl whose father had died and left her a hardware store. D'Arley had been working in a crib and had picked a sailor's pocket for the money to buy her a ring. Instead Troop was spending the money on this other girl. Rogers followed his precept and called her. His daughter recalls her father in the case as '... not real. He was giving a performance. His heart was not in it.' The jury acquitted Gabrielle and she was taken out of the brothel and later married a man in Arizona. As for Rogers, the journalists who watched the trial noticed that this was the first time they had seen him under the influence in court.

The story is that Rogers' final collapse, never far away, began when a witness said he didn't find him frightening, merely amusing, and the jury laughed. Rogers walked out of court and when he could not be persuaded to return his partners resigned and the firm dissolved. The loyal Jerry Giesler remained with him.

His penultimate appearance was for a boy who was alleged to have damaged his eyesight in order to avoid the draft. He went to a nurse who scouted for an optometrist who supplied glasses that weakened rather than strengthened the eyesight for the wealthy who wished to avoid call-up. Rogers convinced the jury that it was not the boy's fault he had picked such an incompetent.

But by now he was on his last legs as an advocate. His final appearance was for Harold Denman, an 18-year-old soldier accused of killing Philip Metz, a Los Angeles grocer, in a robbery. The DA demanded the death penalty as an example to soldiers and the boy was convicted.

From then on it was downhill. Rogers' family tried to have him committed but, acting for himself in what must have been one of his greatest defences, he sweet-talked his daughter Adele out of it in the witness box. He did indeed go as a voluntary patient to Norwalk Hospital where one of the other patients was his former assistant on the Darrow trial, lawyer Horace Appel. Rogers said that every morning Appel would give him a cheque for $1 million, and the real reason he did not take it was that he had found out Appel's bank account was 'slightly overdrawn'. On his release there was talk of his setting up again, but within hours he was found paralytically drunk in Chinatown. Invited to represent the film star Fatty Arbuckle in his trials over the death of Virginia Rappe, he had the sense not to accept. On 23 February 1922 he died in a flophouse hotel. The stories vary. One is that he borrowed a quarter from the clerk to buy a drink and died in the lobby with the clerk saying what a powerful drink it must have been. Another is that he had been in the habit of giving advice to a young lawyer who used to visit him. When the lawyer called that day he could get no reply and the door was broken down; there inside the room was the dead Rogers.

Of him, Jerry Giesler said:

It has been written about Rogers that he was something of a charlatan and that his chief vocation in life was cheating the gallows of its legitimate prey. No man was ever more generously endowed with legal brains than Rogers. No man ever gave more of himself fighting for his clients. In fact he gave so lavishly it burned him out and he died at an early age. To steal a phrase from Vachel Lindsay, 'His valour wore out his soul in the service of men.'[5]

1 Probably his most famous cases, however, were the 1924 trial of Nathan Leopold and Richard Loeb who kidnapped and killed the son of a friend and, the next year, that of John T. Scopes in the Tennessee Monkey trial accused of teaching the theory of evolution. The trial was made into a film *Inherit the Wind* with Spencer Tracy as Darrow. He also appeared for Henry Sweet, a black Detroit doctor who had used force against a white mob trying to evict his family from a white neighbourhood. Born in 1857, Darrow died in 1938 in Chicago.

2 For the Darrow version see Irving Stone, *Clarence Darrow for the Defense*; for the Rogers account see Adela Rogers St Johns, *Final Verdict*.

3 See Irving Stone, *Clarence Darrow for the Defense*, Chapter IX.

4 *Ibid*, p.313.

5 Giesler went on to become one of the great West Coast lawyers, numbering amongst his clients Bugsy Siegel, Errol Flynn and the young Cheryl Crane who shot her mother Lana Turner's lover Johnny Stompanato, as well as Marilyn Monroe in her divorce suit against Joe DiMaggio. For an account of his cases see John Roeburt, *Get Me Giesler*.

# 5 Bill Fallon and Arnold Rothstein

ONE OF THE GREATEST of rogue lawyers of the New York pre- and early Prohibition era was William Joseph Fallon who continued and refined – perhaps coarsened is the better word – the practices of Abe Hummel. Unlike Howe and Hummel, however, he flourished not for nearly half a century but for a bare six years. And unlike the pair, who were described as their own bosses and vultures at that, Fallon was a peacock and the mouthpiece of the gangster Arnold Rothstein.

Fallon, born on 23 January 1886 in a house next to the Church of St Mary the Virgin on W 47th, graduated from Fordham in 1906 and after a short spell in practice in White Plains he worked for a time in the District Attorney's office. During his time as a deputy district attorney he prosecuted the much admired prison governor Thomas Osbourne, who earlier had spent a week as a prison inmate himself learning the conditions at first hand.[1] Osbourne was charged with being absent from duty, admitting four people to death row where the corrupt police officer Charlie Becker was awaiting execution for the murder of Herman Rosenthal and, worst of all, what at the time was called a 'lavender' allegation, committing gross immorality with at least five inmates to one of whom he was alleged to have said, 'You are a good-looking boy. If I were a girl I would fall in love with you.' The case against Osbourne was stopped by the trial judge but he was a ruined man. Fallon admitted later, 'I turned a prosecution into a persecution.'

After he left the District Attorney's office he worked in the Bronx and then in partnership with Edward J. Glennon until, on 12 January 1918, he joined Eugene F. McGee on Broadway where within a short time he became known as 'the great mouthpiece for the Grand Dukes of Racketland'. He was certainly the mouthpiece of Arnold Rothstein, who for the next six years not only provided work for the partnership but actually funded it.

Fallon probably made his name in his defence of Betty Inch, who had been on the stage as Betty Brewster, and who was now charged with blackmail. He put her on the stand to show her splendid ankles to the jurors, and in both the trial and re-trial obtained a hung jury. It was an early example of what would become one of his trademarks – that, in apparently hopeless murder cases, he could achieve a hung jury. His technique was a mixture of badgering prosecutors and judges and confusing the prosecution's witnesses. If this was not thought to be sufficient, he bribed jurors. The whole of his closing speech would be addressed to a single juror whom he had often bought in the court lift. Even in these delicate negotiations he cheated: his practice was to pay half in advance and to decline to pay the other half on the basis that the losing party could hardly complain.

Another reason for Fallon's success lay in the fact that many of the cases against his clients never came to court because he had taken the precaution of paying the arresting officer. He also purchased the services of the staff of District Attorneys to ensure that evidence disappeared.

On one occasion, during a recess Fallon had the prosecutor summoned to the telephone where a female voice informed him of his wife's infidelity. The man had taken his briefcase with him and, stunned by the news, he left the case – and with it the court papers – in the kiosk. When he remembered it he found the case had disappeared. Fallon demanded the trial be continued and without the stolen evidence he won an acquittal.

If Howe had a repertoire of jury tricks, Fallon extended the range sometimes almost legitimately. On one occasion, when defending a Russian for arson and attempted fraud on insurance companies, much of the case depended on discrediting the evidence of a fire officer who said he had smelled kerosene on wet rags. Fallon produced a number of bottles and asked the witness to sniff them in turn and say which was water and which kerosene. When the man said all five were kerosene, Fallon drank from the fifth bottle saying that to him it seemed like water and the jurors should take the bottle into the jury room and taste it for themselves. If it tasted of kerosene, then they should convict. If it tasted of water, they should acquit. They acquitted. The fireman, after sniffing kerosene from four bottles, still had the fumes in his nostrils when he sniffed the water in the fifth.

Arnold Rothstein, born in 1882 and son of 'Abe the Just', a highly respected mediator, was one of the new breed of Jewish Underworld figures who had a very thick finger in the crime pie. His father had a fine reputation as being both pious and even-handed, but unfortunately his privately educated son did not inherit these qualities. He was a gambler through and through, often pawning his father's valuables in the morning to get a stake and redeeming them with his winnings before nightfall and the return of his parent. He soon came to the attentions of Big Tim Sullivan who asked him to manage the gaming at the Metropole on 43rd St. From then on Rothstein scarcely took a backward glance as he moved ever upwards in demi-monde society. He was able to attract high rollers to the tables and, no slouch himself, is said to have taken $250,000 from Percival H. Hill of the American Tobacco Company in one night's play. A friend of Herman Rosenthal, it was he who led the change in character of the Tenderloin, removing and at the same time alienating much of the non-Jewish element. Having opened his own gambling house in 1913, he played a marathon billiards match with a Philadelphia pool shark, Jack Conway. After 36 hours Rothstein defeated Conway and, feted by the papers, he was now a made 'sportsman'.[2] Unfortunately his influence was a malign one; he often used the former bantam-weight champion Abe Attell as his fixer.

He was always open to financing an illegal operation, for which his fee was 90 per cent, and for muscle he used first 'Little Augie' Orgen and then after his death, Louis Lepke. When bootlegging was at its height he backed not only 'Legs' Diamond but also Waxey Gordon, Owney 'The Killer' Madden, Frank Costello, Frank Erickson and Meyer Lansky.

In the 1919 World Series it was Rothstein who persuaded eight players of the Chicago White Sox to lose against the infinitely inferior Boston side. The Black Sox scandal, as it became known, reached such a height that Rothstein was called to give evidence in Chicago before a Grand Jury. Fallon appeared for Abe Attell, the paymaster for the operation, and it was he who masterminded Rothstein's appearance in Chicago before the Grand Jury, persuading him to surrender voluntarily and advising him to say nothing, pleading the Fifth Amendment, a technique common in New York but then unknown in the mid-West. In court, on Fallon's advice, Rothstein played the injured innocent and the Jury declined to indict him.

The players themselves were not so lucky. As an example to others they were banned for life from major league baseball. The incident has thrown up one memorable story. As 'Shoeless' Joe Jackson left the inquiry a child approached him and, according to folklore, asked plaintively, 'Say it isn't so, Joe.' The great man, named because he once played an innings on a wet field in his socks, replied, 'I'm afraid it is, kid.'[3]

Rothstein was also involved when Julius 'Nicky' Arnstein, husband of singer Fanny Brice, was charged with mail bond robberies on Wall Street.[4] Over some 18 months $500 million of bonds were stolen from banks and brokerage houses. The *modus operandi* was for the messenger taking the bonds to another finance house to be beaten and robbed on the way. Finally, on 6 February 1920, a small-time thief named Joe Gluck was arrested and as part of a deal told all. The messengers were, he said, paid to take their beatings and hand over the bonds. The man behind the enterprise was a Mr Arnold. However, when it came to it he picked out Nicky Arnstein instead of the great man.

Arnstein was by no means an innocent. A handsome man, he had a conviction for fraud and had already been involved with the Gondorf brothers in a wire-tapping case. He was known as what was then called a deep-sea diver, a card-sharp on ocean-going liners. When the Assistant Chief Inspector John L. Sullivan commented to one of Arnstein's potential victims that he should surely know he was about to be fleeced, he received the reply, 'Of course I know but he's better company than the honest men on board this ship.'

For a time Arnstein fared well in Fallon's hands. For some two years he was on the run until Fallon could arrange that instead of being arrested he surrender to the police. There followed a game of hide-and-seek in which Fallon's partner, McGee, led police officers around the East Coast and the mid-West for a fortnight before it was safe for Arnstein to give himself up. Whether by accident or design, Fallon drove him through a police parade on Broadway to surrender at the precinct.

Unfortunately Fallon by this time had become besotted with the actress Gertrude Vanderbilt. He had seen her on Broadway some two years previously, but met her when he went with Arnstein to appear before the Supreme Court in Washington. Arnstein knew her and she happened to be appearing in the capital in a review. In good Fallon tradition, Arnstein's first trial had ended with a hung jury and it was intended that Fallon should conduct the re-trial. For a period Gertrude Vanderbilt was a major influence for the good over Fallon and successfully weaned him away from Rothstein. The result was a disaster for Arnstein. Now he was left with Eugene McGee to represent him. There is no doubt that McGee had a far superior knowledge of the law, but he lacked Fallon's charisma and his touch with a jury. Arnstein was convicted at the re-trial.

Rothstein does not appear to have been that perturbed by the temporary defection of Fallon. He provided the pair with the money to set up a new office and told Fallon, who was coming off one of his periodic binges, to get a new shirt and a haircut. One condition of Rothstein financing the reconstituted firm was that Fallon should give up drink and should not draw more than $250 a week. It was a lost cause. The night the partnership's articles were signed, Fallon borrowed against them and was off on a spree. Soon he had worked out that he could draw his money in advance and within a matter of weeks was drawing his salary for July of the following year.

Nor does Fanny Brice seem to have held things against the lawyer. She named her second child after him. As for Arnstein, divorced by Brice, on his release he drifted to California where he became a small-time gambler at the Hollywood Park and Santa Anita racetracks. Asked about the case, he declined to comment on Rothstein's involvement but said, 'Someone had to take the fall and it was me.'

When he was defending former District Attorney Charles B. Andrews of Saratoga County for receiving protection money from Jules Finer, Rothstein was again in the background. Fallon, still keen not only on actresses and the nightlife in general but drink in particular, was continually late for court and was reprimanded by the judge. He then bribed a bellboy at the judge's hotel to call him half an hour late, and when the judge arrived in court he found Fallon ostentatiously looking at his watch.

Another of Fallon's regular clients was also a Rothstein associate – Robert Arthur Tourbillon, better known as Dapper

Dan Collins or, because of his initials rather than his behaviour, Ratsy, and partner of 'Count' Victor Lustig, who not only sold the Eiffel Tower twice for scrap but also was foolish enough to sell Al Capone a money-making machine.

Behind every front conman there must be a partner working in a seemingly subordinate role – a secretary-cum-chauffeur, a valet, one who interrupts meetings at crucial moments with telegrams (in the days when there were such things) and messages. Someone whom the mark can question to establish the credentials of his master; someone to call his master from the room to take a telephone call from which he will never return. Behind Victor Lustig was Dapper Dan Collins.

Not that Collins was not an artist in his own right. Born in Atlanta, Georgia, in 1880, he first worked in a circus riding a bicycle down a tunnel into a cage full of what were described as 'wistful' lions. He came to New York at the turn of the century and with his undoubted charm and a head of blond hair, it was easy for him to fleece women. It was said of him that he would meet a girl at 9 p.m., by ten past he would have his hand in hers and by ten past nine the next morning he would have her pocketbook in his hand.

Although he teamed up with Lustig in the Eiffel Tower swindles and on some of the money-box tricks, he was also a leader in his own right and perfected a little wrinkle on the badger game. The simple version which has been worked over the centuries worldwide involves a woman taking a man to her room, then when he is almost completely undressed and she is partly clothed, in bursts her uncle/father/brother/probation officer etc. The role played will depend upon the apparent age of the girl. Money is then extorted from the man to assuage the husband's feelings or, if the girl is seemingly young, to pay for a period in a hospital to allow her to recover from her terrible experience.

Collins' wrinkle was that it was he who was the apparent victim and not the woman whom he had selected to pay for his next suit of clothes. His victim was not simply a half-drunken man who had been picked up in a bar and set up for the trick but was part of a longish term of seduction. However, once in the room, seemingly the 'police' directed their attention more to him than to the woman, claiming that he had transported a woman across a state line to commit a felony. This was in breach of the so-called Mann Act which, although intended to stamp out prostitution, was regularly used over the years against adulterous couples including the English music-hall star Marie Lloyd and her jockey husband Bernard Dillon, the architect Frank Lloyd Wright and Charles Chaplin.

To protect the woman, always upper class and married, Collins was the one who initially handed over his wallet to avoid arrest and prosecution. The problem was that there was insufficient in it to meet their demands, whereupon the woman could be relied on to ante-up her furs, jewellery and cash.

Meanwhile, in 1923 Fallon was in serious trouble over a charge that he had bribed a juror in a bucket-shop case. By now the firm was known ironically as The Broadway & 42nd Street Bar Association. More dangerously, Fallon had also fallen foul of William Randolph Hearst and the tycoon's New York *American*. The allegation was that he had bribed a juror in a stock market swindle case; he had offered the man $5,000, half down but, true to form, had retained the second half. Fallon failed to appear for his trial on 3 June 1924 and for a few weeks was shuttled from apartment to apartment by Gertrude Vanderbilt. Finally she was followed by the police and he was arrested at 586 Academy Street on 14 June. Bail was now set at $35,000.

Fallon's defence was an all-out attack on Hearst whom he maintained was persecuting him for discovering, in Mexico, birth certificates showing the magnate had fathered twins by his long-time actress companion Marian Davies. On the witness stand he patted his breast pocket to indicate that he had them on him, ready to produce if required. Successful efforts by the prosecution to suppress the references were ineffective, and they certainly were not going to take the chance of having the certificates produced. The damage had been done; including a time-out for dinner the jury acquitted Fallon in under five hours. He is said to have thanked the jury individually and then turned to Hearst's reporter, Nat Ferber, who had been instrumental in providing the case against him, saying, 'Nat, I promise you I'll never bribe another juror.'[5]

But he probably did so during the three years before he died of heart disease coupled with alcoholism. Certainly his own case did not diminish respect for him. When the former boxer Norman Selby, known as Kid McCoy, was charged with the murder in Los Angeles of Mrs T. Morse in the August following Fallon's acquittal, the great man was asked to undertake the defence for a fee of $100,000.[6] In the end he refused, saying he was now concentrating on civil rather than criminal cases, but the trial seems to have closely followed the scenario of those he did conduct. The trial itself ran throughout November and December 1924 and in mid-December the judge had counsel in his chambers issuing stern warnings about an approach made to a Mr Appfel, one of the jurors, who was finally allowed to remain on the case. At the end of the month the jurors debated for what was then a record 78 hours, with the three women holding out against the murder charge for the nine-times-married Selby. One of them, Marie V. Hunt, for much of that time demanded an absolute acquittal. Finally they returned a verdict of manslaughter and the downcast Selby received a sentence of 1–10 years.

Fallon did little criminal work during his remaining years at the Bar but he remained behind the scenes, advising and plotting, never more so than when Rothstein associate 'Dandy' Phil Kastel was the beneficiary of another hung jury. Counsel of record for Kastel included Joe Shalleck, a one-time associate of Fallon.[7]

Any pretence of fidelity to his wife, the long-suffering Agnes, having long evaporated in a haze of alcohol and underwear, Fallon was distraught when Gertrude Vanderbilt went abroad in the summer of 1925. That year he was seriously ill at his father's home. In the August of the next year one mistress caught him half-naked in a room in the Hotel Belleclaire with another. He saw she was about to throw something and got between the woman and his current amour. For his pains he received the acid in his face, but he made a complete recovery.

Fallon died at 11 a.m. on 29 April 1927 in his apartment at the Hotel Oxford, 205 W 85th. A few days earlier he had been taken ill while defending during a probate action. Following his funeral on Broadway which was attended by thousands, he was buried at Calvary cemetery in Queens.

In 1929 Gertrude Vanderbilt failed in an action to assume control of Fallon's estate, having claimed she had loaned him in excess of $35,000. In 1933 she met the journalist Ferber at a party in Chicago, and asked him to help write her autobiography. When Ferber read the manuscript he told her that the real stuff would be about the Hearst birth certificates. She told him they had never existed and it had been a total bluff by Fallon.[8]

During his twelve years as a defender at the Bar Fallon is thought to have appeared in around a hundred murder cases, winning some sixty of them and securing comparatively light sentences for the defendants in the others.

Both Arnold Rothstein and Dapper Dan Collins survived him – the former only barely. Now a millionaire several times over, in 1928 Rothstein went to pieces, developing a hand palsy and eye twitch and slurring his words, but not through alcohol. He had had a poor year from investments and loans and the police suddenly started to make inroads into his empire, raiding his gambling establishments. His horses began to lose and he lost over $130,000 at Belmont Park racetrack in Queens. On 8–9 September he played in a two-day poker game with several West Coast gamblers in a room in the Park Central Hotel in New York and lost over $320,000. He declined to pay, saying he would settle in a day or so because he did not have that amount of cash on him. Later that night he was heard to claim in Lindy's, the popular Broadway restaurant, that the game had been fixed.

On 4 November 1928 at about 10 p.m., he received a telephone call at Lindy's: one of the players in the game, George F. 'Hump' McManus, wished to see him. Rothstein was found by a lift attendant three-quarters of an hour later near the lifts at the Park Central Hotel. Asked by the police who had shot him, he replied, 'Never mind. Get me a taxi.' He never recovered.

In 1929 Collins was sentenced to five years over a swindle in which a New Jersey farmer was relieved of $30,000. On his release he announced that he had retired and was now to lead a sedentary life. But he did not, making several further appearances in courts over the years.

In June 1939 Collins appeared before the courts for the last time. He had been posing as an immigration officer, extorting $200 from Helen Modzelewski, the wife of an illegal Jewish immigrant. Unfortunately he went back for more and she called the police. On his arrest he was described as once again being his usual dapper self with the neat grey spats he always wore and a stylish grey hat over his now iron-grey hair, but after his conviction when he appeared for sentencing he was nearly 60 years old and was showing his age. As a fourth-time offender he was entitled to expect a lengthy sentence and, despite the relatively little money he had obtained, he received one of 15–30 years. 'I've been around but today I'm just an old reprobate,' he told reporters before his sentence, and afterwards remarked, 'The only way I'll ever come out again is feet first.' He died in Attica prison in upstate New York in 1951. No one attended his burial service.[9]

Of Rothstein, his sponsor, protector and client, Fallon had this to say: '[He] is a man who dwells in doorways. A mouse standing in a doorway, waiting for his cheese.' He was rather more generous to Collins. Asked why he associated with him, he replied, 'Because he is a philosopher as well as the Chesterfield of crime.' Of himself and his excessive drinking and womanising: 'I have only my own life to waste.' Of Fallon, his former partner, Eugene McGee – who incidentally was supported financially by Rothstein until the shooting – commented, 'He lived as if he were afraid the light would go out any minute and he wouldn't have another quarter to put into the meter.'[10]

But by the time Fallon died there was a new and very bright star in the firmament of gangland lawyers. His name was Samuel Leibowitz.

1 See Thomas Mott Osbourne, *Within These Walls*. At the end of September 1913 Osbourne, who was the chairman of a State Commission on Prison Reform, decided to spend a week as Tom Brown, a prisoner at Auburn, so that he knew from his own experience what the conditions were like. His actions were known to the Warden and the staff and also to the prisoners themselves whom he implored to regard him as one of them. He asked to be treated as any other prisoner. In sociological terms, he was an overt observer. It might have been even more interesting had he been a covert one. In the first few pages he describes one of the prisoners, the Chaplain's assistant, as 'very nice-looking'.

2 Leo Katcher, *The Big Bank Roll*, pp.53–6.

3 Rothstein appears as Meyer Wolfsheim in F. Scott Fitzgerald's *The Great Gatsby*.

4 While Fanny Brice was waiting outside court for the verdict she went to a speakeasy and parked her new Cadillac on Broadway. When she left she found the car had disappeared. She was told to call the police but informed the owner of the speakeasy that she was under the personal protection of Rothstein. The car was returned intact within half an hour and with a full tank of petrol by the violent gang leader Monk Eastman, who apologised profusely saying that had he known the car belonged to a friend of A.R. the mistake would never have happened. See Leo Katcher, *The Big Bank Roll*.

5 See Nat Ferber, *I Found Out*.

6 Fallon's biggest fee was said to be $125,000 in 1922. He had received $25,000 in $1,000 notes as an advance and blew them on a Broadway spree.

7 'Dandy' Philip Kastel earned his nickname because of the quality and style of his clothing. Born in 1886, he fled to Canada during the First World War to avoid the draft. He was a long-time associate of Rothstein, and after his death teamed up with Frank Costello, moving operations to gaming machines in New Orleans. He died in the Hotel Roosevelt in that city on 16 August 1962; he was found with a bullet in his head and a gun next to his body. He had been in ill-health for some time and was being attended by nurses around the clock. The inquest verdict was one of suicide.

8 See Nat Ferber, *I Found Out* (p.231) and also David Nasaw, *The Chief* (pp.337–40) in which he quotes a friend of Marion Davies saying, 'If she'd had a child by Hearst she'd have worn it round her neck.' In any event that summer Hearst was sufficiently disturbed by the allegations that he kept Davies on the West Coast. These allegations constantly surfaced throughout their lives.

Gertrude Vanderbilt, born in 1900 and said to be distantly related to the celebrated family, went on the stage at the age of 14 and three years later married her booking agent Joseph Pincus. The peak of her career came when she took over the lead from Ina Clarke in a Broadway production. She retired from the stage but shortly before her death in 1960 she announced she was to play in summer stock in Michael Arlen's *The Green Hat.*

9 For US Department of Justice records on Collins and Victor Lustig see FOIPA No. 906430.

10 See Leo Katchel, *The Big Bankroll,* p.168.

# **6** William Cooper Hobbs and Edmund O'Connor

S TRICTLY SPEAKING WILLIAM COOPER HOBBS was not qualified as a solicitor, at best being only what was then called a managing clerk. In accounts of the celebrated Mr 'A' case he is, however, usually referred to as a solicitor and in any event he ran, without any supervision whatsoever, the firm of Appleton and Co. in Portugal Street just behind the Law Courts. He was without doubt one of the most venal of lawyers of his own and many another generation. The solicitor William Charles Crocker, who clashed with him for thirty years, described him as 'a cunning and wholly unscrupulous scoundrel with notoriety and penal servitude as his ultimate destiny'.[1]

Shortly after the First World War he had been what was known in the trade as an ambulance chaser, acting for plaintiffs injured or at least involved in road accidents. He had himself been involved in an accident and he bolstered his claim by remaining in bed unable to move. Damages would be enormous. Unfortunately for him he met his match in W.J. Emmens, the claims investigator for the National Bus Company involved in the accident. Emmens managed to chat up Hobbs' housekeeper and began walking out with her and buying her dinners. Eventually she let slip that Hobbs had a young female relative of whom he was fond. A plan was devised whereby a telegram was sent to Hobbs to the effect that the relative, Millie, was seriously ill and was calling for him. Hobbs fell into the trap and leaving his sick-bed made for a train. He had been photographed running along the road and, as he reached Marylebone Station, he was met by Crocker, acting for the insurance company. Crocker recalls that he put on a great show of surprise, saying how pleased he was that Hobbs was now out of bed. Hobbs quickly realised he had been had, but the action continued and he was awarded rather less than had been paid into court, which meant he was liable for the insurance company's costs. Apparently he took his defeat in reasonably good part, telling Crocker that he had the best claims man in England. Crocker believed that the only touch of human kindness Hobbs ever exhibited had been towards Millie.

Throughout his career Hobbs made a speciality of latching onto and blackmailing homosexuals. Crocker recalled meeting him one day when Hobbs was defending the owner of a male brothel and, rather naïvely, asked whether there was any money in this kind of work. Hobbs replied, *'Money*? There's money to burn – money to burn.' He then took out a packet of letters from his drawer and continued, 'All from men of good standing and rich clients of the prisoner *begging* to be allowed to help him.' Crocker thought that Hobbs as a blackmailer was supreme: 'He had no more compunction than a rattlesnake and was insatiable.'

One of his great friends was the homosexual theatrical wig-maker William Berry 'Willie' Clarkson, who had a shop in Wardour Street, and it was from a flat over these premises that many of the men would be bled dry by Hobbs.

Hobbs first came to public light, or at least to the dock on his own behalf, in 1925 when, in a brilliant working of the badger game, he masterminded the blackmailing of Sir Hari Singh, then the nephew of the Maharajah of Kashmir, to the tune of £300,000. It was a classic example of the game, played this time not as a short-con but as a long one. Indeed it was a well laid-out, long-term plan which, but for greed amongst certain members of the winning side, would have been a total success.[2]

Sir Hari Singh, the 'Mr A' of the case, was the nephew and the heir-presumptive Prince of the Maharajah of Jammu and Kashmir, one of the wealthiest potentates in India at the time. At the age of 27 Singh had been sent to gain a little worldly experience and he was placed in the care of an ADC Captain C.W.A. Arthur, an Irishman and ex-Indian Army officer. Singh's wife was left behind in Kashmir and financial arrangements for the trip were on a lavish scale. The pigeon was ripe for plucking.

Singh was greatly in demand and Captain Arthur was required to obtain a box at the Victory Ball to be held at the Albert Hall on the first anniversary of the Armistice of 1918. It was a ball to have considerable repercussions because it was there that the dope dealer, Brilliant Chang, first stepped into the limelight. The actress Billie Carlton died from an overdose and her partner for the night, Reggie de Veuille, was prosecuted for manslaughter. Chang was believed, but never proved, to have supplied the drugs.[3]

Captain Arthur begged to be excused attendance at the ball and Sir Hari went with his Indian secretary. However, the captain had done his work well. He had booked two adjacent boxes, the second on behalf of a Florence Maud Robinson, the wife of a butcher turned bookmaker, a vivacious blonde if somewhat older than the Prince. It was thought that she was a particular type who might attract the young man. Mrs Robinson went with a Mrs Bevan, another handsome woman. The atmosphere was relaxed and visits were paid by the parties to each other's boxes. Drinks at the Savoy followed and Mrs Robinson went off home to Chapel Street where she and her husband lived in precarious style. The next day she was presented to the Prince and this time Captain Arthur was present and the soon–to-be-cuckolded Mr Robinson strictly absent. Within a short time she and the Prince became lovers. It worked well because Mrs Bevan took up with the Prince's secretary and the quartet went to the Hotel St James et d'Albany in the rue St Honoré in Paris for Christmas. At least the Prince was being allowed a short run for his money ...

Christmas night produced the well tried and tested scene. Mrs Robinson was in bed with the Prince when, in the early hours of Boxing Day, there was a knock on the door and, instead of it being a solicitous Mrs Bevan, there was a man. Accounts of what was said and by whom vary, but it is clear that the Prince was under the impression that the man was the wronged Mr Robinson who now had the evidence to divorce his erring wife. In those days, substantial damages could be awarded against a co-respondent.

'Mr Robinson' was in fact a Montagu Noel Newton, who in some reports was said to be a solicitor but who is most kindly described as an adventurer. In 1908 he had been sentenced to 20 months hard labour after having obtained and duplicated the notepaper of Sir George Lewis, the fashionable solicitor. He had then written to various people suggesting they send money to a young woman, Violet Fraser, who was also involved but whom Sir George declined to prosecute. Newton had been defended by his namesake, the dishonest Arthur Newton. Later he would make claims that Newton had left him unrepresented, but an inspection of the Sessions files showed this was not the case and that the future Director of Public Prosecutions, Sir Archibald Bodkin, had appeared for him.

Mrs Robinson knew Montague Newton very well indeed but somehow failed to make this clear to the panic-stricken young man. After all, she had arranged to give Newton a signal from the bedroom when the Prince visited her at Chapel Street so that he and Hobbs' clerk could save themselves the expense of Paris, but for no clear reason this part of the plot had failed and Newton's reward was a few nights in the cold. She left Paris that morning to catch the packet to Dover.

Sir Hari now turned to Captain Arthur.

What never became clear was exactly how the Captain had made the acquaintance of the other conspirators. This cannot have been wholly by chance. Now, for the moment, he was all sympathy. There were all kinds of problems: the India Office would certainly be displeased; the Prince might also be disinherited by the Maharajah; a public scandal must be avoided. Had poor Sir Hari thought for a moment he would have realised that the Maharajah, who ruled a country where polygamy was the norm, was unlikely to have cared at all. But the essence of a good badger game is to instil utter panic in the victim. Sir Hari agreed with the sensible advice of Captain Arthur that Robinson must be bought off – and bought off he would be in the form of two cheques each in the sum of £150,000. There were two cheques because the Prince's funds would not meet the full £300,000 without accommodation by the bankers. On neither of them was the payee named. Certainly there would be no problem with the first £150,000. When he and the Prince left Paris, Arthur had the cheques in his pocket.

Mr Robinson was now told of his wife's infidelity and went to see Hobbs to start divorce proceedings. The clerk had already been busy, had paid in one of the £150,000 cheques at the Midland Bank's Kingsway branch in the name of Charles Robinson and had withdrawn the whole sum. Now he told the genuine Robinson that he could settle the affair for £20,000, later raised to £25,000, of which Hobbs would take £4,000 for his legal fees. Hobbs, Newton and Arthur divided the rest equitably. Mr Robinson kindly handed over most of his £21,000 to his wife, while Newton took £10,000 from her by force.

That still left the other £150,000 cheque to be cashed. At some point Sir Hari came to his senses and consulted his own lawyers, the fashionable Lewis & Lewis. The cheque was stopped. The Prince went back to India where Newton, unwilling to let well alone, pursued him. The Prince's wife had now died and he had withdrawn into mourning. Newton, now thinking of valour and discretion, returned to England. Most people might have thought that the pigeon had shed enough feathers and the conspirators should be content. Newton certainly was. He had a matchbox lacquered in which was placed a razorblade which he presented to Hobbs. The significance of the gift came out in the trial when very discreetly medical evidence was called to show that oriental gentlemen liked surplus pubic hair removed.

Mr Robinson was not so pleased. Somehow he discovered that the pickings had been £150,000 and he took the view that he had been swindled out of £129,000. In 1924 he sued the Midland Bank. The case was heard by Lord Darling, coming out of retirement for the occasion, and Hobbs gave evidence on subpoena. He had suffered misfortunes in the meantime. On the night before he was due to appear in court his office had been burgled and the relevant papers stolen. Moreover he found it difficult to stand while giving evidence. When he complained that he was in pain the public gallery began to laugh and he furiously turned on them saying, 'What's the good of you laughing, you baboons there?' It was he, rather than they, who was rebuked by Darling. Nor did he get much sympathy when he told the court how he had been robbed by a Russian seaman on a cross-Channel ferry in 1920. Rather to Darling's dismay, Hobbs told how the man had been prosecuted at the Old Bailey and he had retrieved his money.

Newton, who had risked coming back from France for a fee of £3,000 paid by the Bank, helpfully told the court that both the Robinsons had been in the plot from the beginning. He had known Hobbs for years and had introduced him to membership of the Eccentric Club, that odd establishment where all the clocks work backwards. No, it was not correct that he, Newton, had been expelled from the Club. He had also done some extra-legal work for Hobbs who had wanted 'a little bit of a fire in Wardour Street'. A deal of his money had gone in a coffee speculation, but he had then won something in the region of

£17,300 from Arthur playing Slippery Sam.[4] Arthur had tried to get some more money from Hobbs, who declined to pay, and he had then sued Newton for money lent. Newton had settled the matter for £1,000.

When he came to sum up to the jury, the witty judge had his usual fun at the expense of the players. 'I do not know the religion of this man, but this was Mrs Robinson's way of keeping the Christian Festival of Christmas.' The actual verdict was a series of specific answers to complicated questions, but in essence Robinson lost his claim. The jury thought it had had enough and asked for exemption from future service. But the judge disagreed:

> I don't think so. It takes rather longer than this for that to happen; and it has not been one of the dullest cases for you.

Darling at any rate had enjoyed himself.

The week-end before Darling summed up, both Hobbs and Arthur fled for the Continent. Arthur made it to France where he subsequently received 13 months because part of the conspiracy had taken place on French soil. Hobbs had employed a double, with make-up and wig by Clarkson, to sit in the Law Courts and so dupe the police. But this did him little good, for he was arrested at Gravesend as he was about to board a Dutch ship for Rotterdam. At the time he was in the company of another swindler, Bob Morison, and between them they had £1,250. Having explained that he was not fleeing the country but simply going to take the waters at Baden-Baden, he was returned to London where the Bow Street magistrate remanded him in custody and he appeared before Mr Justice Avory on 2 March 1925 in a trial which lasted nine days. Hobbs was then 60 and pictures show him as a dapper, if corpulent, little man with a white beard.

Sir Travers Humphreys prosecuted and told the court that he would much prefer to have had Newton, with his conviction for forgery, in the dock alongside Hobbs, but there was no way to prove the conspiracy without him as a witness. He said that Hobbs specialised in libel and that in these and other dubious cases he obtained confidential information which he sold on – in essence doing really what Hummel had done a quarter of a century earlier in New York. Hobbs' defence was that he had been acting in good faith throughout, but it was not one which appealed to the jury and he was fortunate to receive only two years. As for the others, both Mrs Robinson and Mrs Bevan disappeared. They seem to have been arrested in Nice and were thought to have been making their way East. Perhaps they eventually did. The former butcher Mr Robinson died in the 1950s. Montague Newton flourished in a roguish way for some time, dying abroad. When Kashmir became a republic Sir Hari, by then the Maharajah, went into exile with much of his considerable fortune.

As for Captain Arthur, he did not lie down and bear the lash lightly. He found a champion in the *Empire News* – or they found a good story in him because his version of his life and the events which led to his imprisonment appeared at the end of 1925.

This recounted that in essence he was a dupe, not guilty of robbing Sir Hari any more than the readers who had already given him their sympathy. He had met Sir Hari through shooting expeditions and although after the War he had intended to settle his own neglected (but unspecified) affairs, he was prevailed on to accompany the young man and his staff of twelve to Europe.

As for the Victory Ball, Sir Hari had decided to go only at the last moment and it was quite by chance that they found themselves in the box next to Mrs Robinson. She, Arthur could vouch, was the only affair Sir Hari had during his visit. She was about 30 and 'He delighted in the company of wit; beauty was a secondary consideration in his selection of feminine company.' Which doesn't sound very flattering to Mrs Robinson. Sir Hari went to the ball dressed as a toreador and he, Arthur, as a Rajah. He didn't actually see Mrs Robinson that night; it was in fact a few days later that he came to the apartments and to his surprise found her there, pressing Sir Hari to have luncheon in Chapel Street where outstandingly good Indian food was served to the Prince's delight.

He knew nothing of any affair and it was only by chance that the parties met again in Paris when the ladies were *en route* to the Cote d'Azur. He and Sir Hari were staying at the Hotel Brighton and the ladies (whom Sir Hari's aide met on the boulevards) were at the St James. There had been a long Christmas party. Arthur had gone off on his own and meeting with chums had gone to bed about 6 a.m., only to be woken an hour and a half later to find Newton protesting the loss of his honour. He had gone straight to see the Prince and Mrs R. She had been keeping up appearances, saying, 'Oh, my brute of a husband.' The Prince seems to have been sanguine, remarking, 'Well, after all, Maudie, he is your husband.'

It was correct that the contrite Prince had urged him to do what he could to make amends, and he had left for London with the cheques and a letter which contained a full admission, apologies and a statement that 'he would do everything in his power to redeem his error'.

Back in England, Arthur saw Robinson, his own solicitors and then Hobbs. Why he did not leave his solicitors to sort things out he never makes clear, but Hobbs started off asking for half a million which Arthur skilfully negotiated down. By now the Prince had consulted Lewis & Lewis but, poor fool that he was, seems to have dismissed the suggestion that Arthur was in the plot because they left for the Somme together before he departed for India, with Arthur returning to Paris where Hobbs came to visit him. They had decided to repay some of the money and wanted Arthur to act as agent, but he pointed out that he was no longer in the employ of the Prince.

Now the story took a more sinister turn. It seems that Hobbs had found out about Arthur's involvement with a woman 'Vera'. According to Arthur, Hobbs began to blackmail him into opening an account and paying in what amounted to his share to be forwarded to the Prince, but this never quite seems to have been done. Nevertheless, Christmas next year found Arthur back in India managing some of the horses the Prince had bought.

If Arthur is to be believed, Hobbs' cunning knew no bounds. During the Prince's stay in London a private detective presented his credentials to Sir Hari who employed him. Imagine Arthur's surprise to discover that the man, apparently sent by Scotland Yard – and who seems to have behaved impeccably – was Hobbs' agent.[5] Arthur died in Paris soon after his memoirs were published.

Back in the real world, while Hobbs was in prison various newspapers, including the Liverpool *Evening Express* and the Nottingham *Journal,* published highly coloured accounts of his career. These involved race-gangs, providing a passport office for criminals, and fleecing young men including the millionaire store-owner Peter Robinson's son from whom Hobbs and his cronies had extracted £650,000. The papers also said he had conned another innocent, this time the son of a Canadian millionaire, as well as running a crooked gambling den in Paris.

Hobbs, so it was alleged by the papers, was the son of a barge-owner. He became a clerk to a solicitor who specialised in the defence of Underworld characters and thereby learned his trade. He had, said the articles, met Appleby on a train in 1895 and, joining him, from that moment his future had been assured. As for his moneylending business, he had eventually turned the tables on a one-time employer who had ended as Hobbs' clerk. With money earned from that he became an accountant in the City. His great ambition in life had been election to the Putney Conservative Club but, sadly, it was never realised: he was blackballed. Nevertheless he had some compensation; he was a member of the Putney Bowls Club. He was given to wearing a diamond tie-pin in the form of the letters ER; when asked its origin, he would modestly explain that it 'was a present from the King for a service I was able to render'. In fact it came from a young man's estate which Hobbs was administering.

It was certainly true that Hobbs had been involved in the defence of John George Wenzel, who was caught in a robbery at Dalston by Detective Joyce along with Henry Selner and Frederick Reuman who had tried to arrest him. He had opened fire, killing the police officer. Wenzel claimed that the gun had gone off accidentally and he should only have been convicted of manslaughter. He was hanged in a double execution with James Taylor, a 60-year-old army pensioner who had beaten his wife to death with a mangle-roller while drunk. Hobbs also claimed that he had been invited by an unnamed lady to defend the murderer Neville Cream, but that he had been so overworked he had been obliged to decline. This may, of course, have been one of his many exaggerations.

Once he was released Hobbs issued a total of 23 writs for libel. His solicitors were the Chancery Lane firm, Edmund O'Connor & Co., and they instructed the elderly Irishman Serjeant Sullivan to appear for Hobbs in what many would regard as blackmailing actions. Some seven of the newspapers settled by paying damages but would not issue an apology, something with which Hobbs found he could live. However, Tinling, the proprietor of the *Evening Express*, was made of sterner stuff and declined to pay. Oswald Hickson, the celebrated libel firm, acted for him and they instructed Norman Birkett.

In the witness box in front of a very hostile Lord Hewart, then the Lord Chief Justice, Hobbs gave an account of his life. The newspaper, much to Serjeant Sullivan's fury, had not pleaded justification – in other words maintaining the story was true – but had already conceded that it was rubbish. All that was left was whether Hobbs, as a convicted blackmailer, could be libelled whatever was said about him.

Hobbs' version of affairs was slightly different, as might be expected. He had begun his career as a hard-working barristers' clerk in 1879 and had married six years later; he had three children. In 1878 he had in fact been the clerk to a solicitor whose practice had been acquired by Appleton, for whom he had worked for a time. He was also a registered moneylender with an office in Bedford Street.

In 1915 Appleton had asked him back to undertake some urgent business, employing him at £6 per week, and when Appleton died two years later Hobbs had been left half the bank account and a half-share in the practice. Indeed Appleton had been 'more than a brother' to him. A Charles T. Wilkinson bought the Appleton business and retained Hobbs as his principal managing clerk, paying him half fees on work introduced. As for being a receiver of stolen property, he denied that; and as for being in cahoots with a racecourse gang, well, he had visited a racecourse perhaps six times in his whole life.

The newspaper's story may have been incorrect but there was, without doubt, at least a grain of truth behind the fleecing allegations. Hobbs admitted he knew an Edward Arthur Smith: he had met him and loaned money to him in 1901 and two years later had drawn up a trust and indeed had tried to save him from bankruptcy. The trustees of the Smith settlement had included a 'Blinky' Stevens. Did Hobbs know Stevens was a racecourse tout? No, as far as he knew Stevens was an owner. What about a man named Kemp, known as The Squeaker? No, Hobbs had never heard of him.

As for poor Smith, his bankruptcy committee included most of the players in the blackmail case. On it were Robinson, the aggrieved butcher husband, and Montague Newton; also, of course unbeknown to Hobbs, another member named Morison, in fact Hobbs' travelling companion, was now serving a sentence in Vienna.

He was quite unable to explain how a cheque initially drawn for £6. 6s. 0d. four days before Appleton's death – which would be six shillings for the widow and Hobbs' wages of £6 – had somehow become one of £256. 6s. 0d. He had brought the present action 'to show the world and his children that the stories about him were absolute concoctions and to get damages'.

*Birkett*: I'm glad you added those last words. (Laughter).[6]

Hobbs was made of stern stuff and Serjeant Sullivan perhaps even sterner. Infuriated by his and his client's treatment at the hands of Lord Chief Justice Hewart, he went straight to the Court of Appeal. Eventually Hobbs pocketed a total of £17,000 from his libel actions.

From then on, once again he disappeared from the limelight until in 1938 he was back at the Old Bailey charged with forging the will of his old friend Willie Clarkson, who had died mysteriously and suddenly. This time his former solicitor, Edmund O'Connor, was in the dock with him.

For many years 'Wigs by Clarkson' appeared in theatrical programmes and the firm's founder Willie was regarded generally as a highly respectable, if eccentric man. There is no doubt whatsoever that he was a close associate of Hobbs. Even though he had clearly been involved with Hobbs in blackmailing propositions over the years his judgement was open to question when he appointed him as his executor. But, there again, Clarkson had been a trustee of Hobbs' marriage settlement.

Clarkson died suddenly on 13 October 1934 and was buried in Woking. Sir Bernard Spilsbury carried out a post-mortem and there was no inquest. On the day of his death Henry Clarke, one of his solicitors, went to Lloyds Bank in Covent Garden and found a will dated 1927 made on a printed form, with no residuary legatee. This meant that the balance of Clarkson's estate after payment of debts, tax and specific legacies would go to the Crown. Hobbs was named simply as an executor.

In the November Hobbs instructed Clarke to write to O'Connor, who also had acted for Clarkson, asking whether by chance he had a later will as it was understood that one had been made at his office in 1929. Two clerks searched at length but could not find it until on 10 December, after another short search, O'Connor's brother-in-law, William Enright, discovered it. The second will was dated 24 June 1929 and in it Hobbs was named as both executor and the residuary legatee.

Things were then complicated by the arrival on the scene of a man named Brezinski who claimed there was yet another lost will made in 1931 of which *he* was the residuary legatee. A writ was issued and the action settled on the terms that the legatees of the 1929 will would be paid and the residue divided equally between Hobbs and Brezinski who would formally prove the lost 1931 will. Meanwhile, to an extent, Hobbs was running Clarkson's business.

Given that Clarkson was an eccentric there were still some seriously odd, even inexplicable, things about the 1929 (Hobbs) will. A young man called Ivan Godwin, who would not join the firm for a further nine months, was named as a beneficiary; a man who had been with the firm for many years was wrongly named; and a Mrs Rogers (who had last been employed some thirty years previously) was also named as a beneficiary – the problem being that when she was with the firm it was before her marriage and she had worked in the name of O'Brien.

In the course of the action with Brezinski, two experts – including Guerin, the son of the man who had discovered the Dreyfus forgery – had examined the Hobbs' will and both concluded it was a forgery. They had also seen a letter which purportedly supported the will by saying that Hobbs would be looked after if anything happened to Clarkson. The signature on this letter was certainly genuine but the typescript had been superimposed on a letter to Clarkson's bank asking the state of his accounts. The original words had, said Guerin, been bleached out.

The only genuine words on the will were Clarkson's signature; this had been written on a paper from which other writing had been obliterated by chemicals before the faked will (largely in Hobbs' favour) was superimposed.

Hobbs was arrested at his home on 15 January 1938 and promptly collapsed with a heart attack. He was allowed to remain under police observation until he appeared at Bow Street four days later when he was bailed. A little later his old helpmate Edmund O'Connor was brought over from Dublin. Both men strenuously denied the charge of conspiracy to utter a forged will knowing it to be forged. Meanwhile the newspapers started egging their sheets and on the next remand hearing Laurence Vine for Hobbs told the court that there had been rumours in the press about an exhumation, something which greatly alarmed his client. 'There is nothing sensational in this case; it is merely an ordinary case affecting a will,' said Hobbs' counsel.

Generally speaking there is not a great deal of point in forging a will unless the demise of the testator is imminent. But Hobbs had shown in the 'Mr A' case that he was quite prepared to stay in for the long haul, and this may have been the situation with Clarkson. In any event the rumours died away. However, Sir George Lewis, the well-respected solicitor who dealt with the legal aspects of Clarkson's fires on behalf of the insurance companies, said that Spilsbury had told him privately that a sudden fright could have played a big part in Clarkson's death.[7]

What emerged at the trial was a little more about Clarkson's eccentricities which ranged from washing his own handkerchiefs and socks to avoid laundry bills, through using a variety of signatures, to sending Godwin a postcard of a black child in a bath after he had been employed a bare nine months. Godwin described himself as a 'sort of personal servant' to Clarkson.

More importantly, it also came out that Clarkson was a great one for making false insurance claims regarding fires. Indeed one of them had been the Montague-Newton-Hobbs arranged fire mentioned in passing in the 'Mr A' trial. The prosecution suggested that O'Connor had been drawn into the plot by Hobbs because he was in debt and Hobbs would guarantee his bank account.

In the witness box Hobbs gave a picture of his activities over the years. Now he said he had known Clarkson since 1886 and had been a solicitors' accountant. This enabled him to deal with Clarkson's tax, private affairs and claims against him. They had travelled abroad together.

O'Connor, who had defended himself at the police court hearings, was apparently none too pleased with Hobbs when he gave evidence. The overdraft guaranteed by Hobbs having been secured by life policies, Hobbs had paid off the overdraft and sold the life policies for a profit. He, too, had been friendly with Clarkson, prosecuting thieving staff on his behalf and going to boxing tournaments with him. What neither could do was overcome the scientific evidence.

Serjeant Sullivan, who appeared for O'Connor, thought that his client was innocent:

> He was not a criminal but like so many of my race he was addicted to the habit of periodic bouts of intemperance, leaving in truth complete blanks in his memory in which, however, could be inscribed a convincing but entirely false recollection of events that

he was convinced had happened and in which he had taken part. Hobbs had made him absolutely certain that on that day and date he had witnessed that document as Clarkson's will in the presence of Clarkson, Mitchell and Hobbs. Now it was certainly an interest of Hobbs not to be present at the making of the document if he could help. But he had to be present because he had to get into my client's impaired mind the details of all the circumstances connected with the event. Nobody else could do it.[8]

J.D. Casswell KC, appearing for Hobbs, put forward an emotional plea: 'Let Hobbs, an old and sick man obviously tottering to his end, spend the rest of his days in peace.' The jury would have none of it and in short order both Hobbs and O'Connor were convicted. O'Connor, it now transpired, had been struck off as a solicitor for professional misconduct in 1937. In his earlier and, for him, happier days he had defended a number of notable criminals including Frederick Guy Browne in the celebrated shooting of PC Gutteridge.[9]

O'Connor, a Kerryman of immense geniality, had been regarded as one of the great solicitor-advocates and it was said of him that had he gone to the Bar he would have been a second Marshall Hall.[10] Perhaps his best personal defence was when he appeared for William Podmore at the inquest on Vivian Messiter. In 1928 Podmore had applied for a job after answering an advertisement for a salesman at the Wolf's Head Oil Company in Southampton under the alias of William Thomas. Once installed, he began to write up fictitious invoices and collect the commission on them. Confronted by a company representative, Messiter, he killed him with a hammer and hid the body behind boxes in a garage. The decaying corpse was found on 10 January 1928 and letters from Podmore connected him to the crime. It was O'Connor's skill which prevented the inquest jury returning a verdict of murder and naming his client, as was their right in those days. Podmore was jailed for 6 months for an earlier fraud in Manchester and then on his release he collected another 6 months for robbery. Arrested for the Messiter murder on 17 December, this time much of the evidence against him was so-called cell confessions made to other prisoners. At the committal proceedings O'Connor produced a stunt worthy of Marshall Hall. His client was a man of only 5'3" and he challenged one of the doctors to try to move 'the body' of Messiter, a much bigger man and played for the day by one of Podmore's friends. All the doctor succeeded in doing was to rip the buttons off the 'body's' shirt. O'Connor also made inroads into the jail witnesses' testimony but the evidence was overwhelming and, rejecting the petition for a reprieve, the Home Secretary said he had not a scintilla of doubt about the verdict. O'Connor was indefatigable – either that or he was off gambling – because he was reported to be in Paris looking for a so-called mystery enemy of Messiter when his client was hanged on 22 April 1930 still protesting his innocence.[11]

O'Connor failed to attend his bankruptcy examination and fled to Ireland in June 1936, where he was living in desperately poor circumstances under the name of Moran. In fact he was in such a bad way that when Chief Inspector Leonard Burt went to Dublin to retrieve him O'Connor had literally only the suit he stood up in, a razor, shaving stick and a florin. When he brought him back to London Burt bought O'Connor a shirt and tie rather than have him appear in such a derelict condition in front of a magistrate he had known in better times.

He ascribed his fall to being in the hands of the money-lenders, for he was a great gambler and was said to leave his offices for weeks on end to play the tables on the Continent. One can imagine how Hobbs might well have turned the screws on him. William Crocker, who had been investigating fires at Clarkson's premises on behalf of insurance companies, begged O'Connor to turn against Hobbs, but he would not do so. Now O'Connor asked for four offences of fraudulent conversion to be taken into consideration, which would mean a concurrent sentence, something the Recorder of London Sir Gerald Dodson declined to do. He adjourned the case overnight for sentence and the next day Hobbs made an impassioned plea designed to save his funds. He was not, he assured the court, the wealthy man he had been described to be. 'Punish me if you like but don't take my money.' He was also in poor health, but the kindly judge ordered him to pay up to £500 towards the costs of the prosecution and as for the rest: 'Your health will be safeguarded as far as possible where you are going.'

O'Connor behaved very much better. Hobbs, knowing his former friend was penniless, had declined to assist in financing his defence. 'The idea of betraying even a rat like Hobbs being repugnant to him, he decided to fight it out to the bitter and inevitable end. There was more good than bad in poor Ned's make-up.'[12]

Hobbs received 5 years and O'Connor a total of 7 years. Hobbs must have been tougher than was thought; he survived his sentence and continued his harassment of newspapers, threatening authors and editors with libel actions until his death in June 1945.

Elderly solicitors who came before the courts in their dotage seem to have been plentiful. Ten years before Hobbs' death, Charles Sharman, regarded as his protégé, had died following his own five-year sentence. A seemingly respectable West Ham solicitor whose advocacy was much admired, Sharman had for many years been a receiver of stolen bonds. He may also have organised the theft of mailbags from the railways. Certainly he spent his summer vacation peddling the bonds in Europe and America.[13] In 1926, the year after Hobbs first fell from grace, so too did Henry Barnes Hunt, known to the newspapers as 'The Spider', and then in his seventies. In fact Hunt had had a slip or two previously.

Like Hobbs, he does not seem to have been formally qualified but took up practice in the 1880s when he met with a drunken and impoverished solicitor called Cooper. He advanced him money on a cunningly worded promissory note and so obtained his practice. Over the years he did the same to at least three other solicitors. In 1915 he trapped another solicitor and this time received three months' imprisonment; the solicitor was struck off by the Law Society. Undaunted, on his release Hunt set himself up in Southampton Row under the name of Johnson & Co., and when that was discovered merely changed the name of the practice. At the time of his arrest he had set up in yet another practice with a solicitor named Steele Wilson to whom he paid £5 a week for the use of his office. In July 1925 he was sentenced to 12 months imprisonment for carrying on business as a solicitor, but evaded arrest until January 1926. The unfortunate Steele Wilson and yet another solicitor were struck off the Rolls for allowing Hunt to use their names.

For a time Hunt ran a gang of horse copers who would buy (or steal) and then patch up broken-down animals and rent them out on a daily basis. The unfortunate hirers would often find themselves in the courts charged with causing the animal unnecessary suffering. If they avoided this then, when the horse was returned, the gang would strip off the bandages and claim that the animal had been injured during the day's hire. In a more or less legal form of blackmail Hunt would then commence county court proceedings, invariably settling the case out of court. He also ran an ambulance-chasing practice, settling cases for rather more than he told the clients and pocketing the difference. Earlier he had been acquitted on a charge of stealing jewellery from his mistress. In February 1926 he received 18 months' imprisonment. Had it not been for his age, the Recorder said he would have sentenced him to penal servitude.[14]

1  William Charles Crocker, *Far from Humdrum*, p.92.
2  For accounts of the case see *Notable British Trials*; *The Trial of Mr 'A'*; C.E. Bechhofer Roberts, *The Mr A Case*; William Charles Crocker, *Far from Humdrum*; Lord Darling, *Lord Darling and His Famous Trials*, and Douglas G. Browne, *Sir Travers Humphreys*. A novel based on the case is A.E.W.Mason, *They Wouldn't be Chessmen*.
3  For an account of the case and the subsequent career of Brilliant Chang, see James Morton, *East End Gangland*.
4  Slippery Sam was regarded as a superior version of Blind Hookey in which a number of cards, not less than four, were dealt to each player. Betting was blind and then the bottom card was turned over. Ties paid the dealer. Hoyle regarded the game as no guarantee whatsoever against a prearranged fraud. As for Slippery Sam, the players could see their cards and Hoyle took the view that, common to no other gambling game, a player using common-sense lines would have the best of it. *Hoyle's Games*, pp.161–4.
5  'Captain Arthur's Own Story' in *Empire News*, 22, 29 November, 6, 13, 20 December 1925, 3, 10, 17 January 1926.
6  *Hobbs v Tinling*; *The Times*, 5,6,7 December 1928; (1929) 2 KB 1CA; see also A.S. Sullivan, *The Last Serjeant*, Chapter 33.
7  John Juxon, *Lewis and Lewis*. Born in 1856, Sir George Lewis came from a family of solicitors who specialised in criminal law and practised at Ely Place, EC1. As the years went by he weaned the practice away from crime, leaving the field clear to Humphreys & Morgan, Wontners and of course Arthur Newton. He acted for many members of the aristocracy and the peak of his career came when he advised the Prince of Wales over the Tranby-Croft baccarat scandal. For an account of the case see John Welcome, *Cheating at Cards*. Lewis died in 1909.
8  A.S. Sullivan, *The Last Serjeant*, pp.309–10.
9  On 27 September 1927 PC Gutteridge was found shot dead on a road between Romford and Ongar. A particular feature of the case was that he had been shot through both eyes, the belief in some circles being that the pupils reflect the last thing a dying person sees and the imprint would have been of his murderer. Four months later Browne was arrested, at a garage he ran, for stealing a car, and a Webley revolver was found with ammunition of the type which had killed the officer. Kennedy was arrested in Liverpool and blamed his employer. Both were hanged at Wandsworth on 31 May 1928. Curiously, Browne was regarded as rather the better type of the two. He did not smoke or drink and was devoted to his wife. To the end he maintained his innocence. For one of many accounts of the case see Gordon Honeycombe, *The Murders of the Black Museum 1870–1970*. Others whom O'Connor represented included in 1921 Freddie Ford, the counterfeiter who remained an influence in the West End until well after the Second World War.
10  Bernard O'Donnell, 'Hobbs and O'Connor' in *Empire News*, 3 April 1925.
11  See *Empire News*, 19 January 1930.
12  See William Charles Crocker, *Far From Humdrum*, pp.195–8.
13  For an account of his career, see James Morton, *East End Gangland*.
14  *The Times*, 7, 14 February; 25, 26, 27 March 1926; *Empire News*, 28 February 1926.

# 7  Sam Leibowitz

'SAM LEIBOWITZ,' says the doyen of Brooklyn criminal lawyers, 77-year-old Albert Aronne, admiringly, 'he knew all the tricks because he had done them himself. He was in jail. Him and his investigator over some sort of mess with Chilli Acuna but he beat the case. He knew it from both sides.'[1] When it came to it Leibowitz was never actually in jail, but he had certainly been indicted with conspiracy and subornation of perjury.

Samuel Leibowitz was born in Romania in 1893 and came to the United States at the age of four. He wanted to be an engineer but his father, who owned a small store after at one time pushing a hand-cart, insisted that if his son were to go to college he should study law.

When Leibowitz qualified in 1916 he first worked for Jewish lawyers who, when he asked for a $1 rise from his $15 a week salary, tried to get him to agree to 50c. He then joined Michael McGoldrick, an Irish lawyer, at the princely sum of $35. His first criminal case was a court-appointed brief defending Harry Patterson, a burglar who had seen better days. He was accused of breaking into a saloon, had made a confession and was found with a skeleton key on him. The Third Degree method of obtaining a confession was then popular and persuading the jury to disregard it presented no great problem to Leibowitz. As for the skeleton key, he challenged the court to allow the jury to test the key in the saloon lock. The prosecution objected, the court agreed it would be a waste of time and the jury, deprived of its bit of entertainment, promptly acquitted. In fact it was a calculated risk that the prosecution had not done its homework. Leibowitz had tried the key in every courtroom door and had found it opened them all.

In 1919 with savings of $260 he bought himself furniture and law books and opened an office at 50 Court Street, Brooklyn. His first client was a pickpocket, aggrieved at an allegation that he had botched an attempted theft when the victim felt his hand in his pocket. According to the story, the man claimed that he had not even tried. He paid Leibowitz with a $100 bill. After he left Leibowitz could not find the bill and he and his secretary were hunting for it when the client returned bringing the note, correctly pointing out that 'no one ever feels my mitt in their kick'. The case was won, possibly not on those grounds, at Coney Island Magistrates' Court and Leibowitz was up and running. His name was now passed round the inmates of Raymond Street jail as a likely man.

Sam didn't know that the Underworld scouts courtrooms, as the major leagues scout the minors, for promising talent ...[2]

There is an unkind, if apposite, maxim that hard work is no substitute for talent but, in a lawyer, hard work can go a very long way. Leibowitz would always admit that in his case his success was based upon hours of preparation; that and a very astute knowledge of human failings. One of his firm beliefs was that eye-witness testimony was not reliable, and years later when he lectured at legal seminars he would ask Camel smokers whether the man on the packet was leading the camel or sitting on its back. In a typical result, almost half those questioned would give one answer and half the other, with only a few saying correctly that there was no man on the packet.

By 1925 Leibowitz was acting for the then top Italian, Frankie Yale, and his young henchman Al Capone. There had been a long-running struggle in New York between the Irish gang known as the White Hand Gang and Frankie Yale's Italian blackhanders – a spill-over from the original Black Hand extortionists – for control of the waterfront around the Red Hook section of Brooklyn. It came to a head when Dinny Meehan, the leader of the White Handers, was shot dead while in bed with his wife on 30 March 1920. His killer had been hired from Cleveland by Yale for a fee of $10,000. In time the control of the White Handers passed to Richard 'Peg Leg' Lonergan, so called because he had lost his leg in a railway accident, who fought a long rearguard action against the up-and-coming Albert

Anastasia, Joe Adonis and Vince Mangano. After two years of all-out war, in January 1925 Frankie Yale brokered a deal under which Lonergan's men would take control of Furman Street and Greenpoint Piers and, in return, give up claims to Green docks. It took five months for Lonergan to realise he had by far the worst of the bargain; the docks under his control had much less traffic than those run by the Italians. A further six months of all-out war followed, with some twenty-six deaths on the Irish side compared with a modest eight Italian casualties.

On Christmas Day Lonergan led the last charge of the White Handers, a raid on Yale's traditional Christmas party at the Adonis Social Club. Yale – well prepared because the planned raid had been leaked by one of Lonergan's men – had wished to cancel the party but had been persuaded that such a move would be interpreted as a sign of weakness. Instead, with Capone in town, he, Albert Anselmi and John Scalesi were recruited as firepower.

Late in the evening Lonergan limped into the club and called to two Irish girls dancing with Italians that they should 'get back to white men'. As he limped off the dance floor the lights went out and he and three of his men were machine-gunned to death. In all nine were arrested, including Capone who told the police that he had been visiting his mother and was helping out at the club as a doorman. Leibowitz was sent for and he represented members of both factions. Now his task was that of a juggler keeping all plates spinning at the same time.

Or, as his biographer Fred Pasley put it, explaining as he does one of the problems a gangland lawyer faces:

> Our lawyer Blondin must negotiate his tightrope with his entire load intact, for if but a single passenger tumbled off (into police hands) the whole nine were lost.

Our Blondin was fortunate in that he was able to interview James Hart, a survivor of the shooting, who was found by a passing patrolman some three blocks from the club wounded in the thigh and legs. It was on him that the prosecution would rely for an identification leading to a conviction. In the end it appeared, unsurprisingly, that not only had Hart not seen Capone and the others, he had not even been in the club that night. He must have been injured about the same time by bullets fired from a passing car whose driver and passengers he had not been fortunate enough to see either. Capone and the others were released on bonds from $5,000 to $10,000 and on 31 December 1925 Judge Francis McCloskey dismissed the charges. A party was held at which Leibowitz was, perhaps unwisely, the guest of honour.

He moved offices to the Brooklyn Chamber of Commerce Building and then to 225 Broadway in Manhattan. Now he would act for many of the top Mob men. Capone moved back to Chicago and neighbouring Cicero from where he rarely ventured professionally. It would be another 15 years before the lawyer would be called on to act for him again.

Leibowitz's clientele included such luminaries of the period as 'Pittsburgh' Phil Strauss, Bugsy Goldstein and Bugsy Siegel, as well as Vincent 'Mad Dog' Coll when the latter was charged with the killing of five-year-old Michael Vengali in a gang shoot-out.

Leibowitz did not have the problem of the more parochial English gang lawyer in that his clients apparently did not mind his appearing for rival enterprises and in 1931 he defended McColl, an Irish gangster from the Hell's Kitchen area of Manhattan. His defence was a work of art.

The prosecution's case was that McColl had machine-gunned and missed Anthony Trombino of the Dutch Schultz organisation. Instead he had hit five small children, including Vengali who had died. The principal witness was George Brecht, a self-proclaimed salesman of Eskimo Pies, a popular type of ice cream, who happened to be walking along 107 St E at the fatal moment.

During a luncheon adjournment, with Brecht still on the witness stand, Leibowitz took the opportunity of purchasing a number of ice creams which he generously distributed amongst jurors, the prosecuting attorneys and the judge. He then asked Brecht questions the answers to which any self-respecting ice-cream salesman should have known – a description of the wrapper and how ice creams are kept cold in July. Brecht had not heard that, on the thermos flask principle, ice creams keep themselves cold. From there it was only a question or two before Brecht admitted his convictions and that from the age of 19 he had been a professional 'surprise' witness, saying, 'That's the man.' Coll was freed on a directed verdict of acquittal. It was as a result of the killing of Vengali that Coll received his sobriquet 'Mad Dog'.

Leibowitz's fee had been acquired in a way unusual even for those difficult times. Coll had kidnapped an aide to another rival, Owney Madden, ransoming the man for a modest $30,000.[3] But the next year Coll pushed his luck too far when he telephoned Madden from a telephone booth in a drug store threatening to kill him unless money was paid. He spoke for too long; the call was traced and Coll was shot to death. Although he had a Tommy-gun with him, standard dresswear for an afternoon out in New York, he was cramped in the booth and unable to raise it in time. His killers, almost certainly the brothers Abe and Bo Weinberg, were never found. Meanwhile Leibowitz moved serenely upwards.

Leibowitz had also represented the 'Canary who could not fly', Abe 'Kid Twist' Reles. Now in 1940 Reles was charged with robbery, possession of narcotics and six charges linked to murder. He feared, probably correctly, that some of those arrested with him might endeavour to arrange a deal by informing on him and, so to speak, he had the first drop on them. The police were able to clear up some forty-nine killings in Brooklyn alone and he named Frank Abbandando and Charlie Workman in the killing of Dutch Schultz. His evidence was largely responsible for the conviction of his superiors, Louis Lepke and Mendy Weiss.

According to Reles the murder of Schultz had been mishandled. Workman had come out of the restaurant after the shooting and found that Weiss and the third man, Piggy, had gone, along with the getaway car, and he began to run back to his New York flat. He later complained to his superiors about this desertion by Weiss and Piggy. Weiss said that Piggy had simply panicked and driven off. He was cleared of blame as it was felt that Workman had, to an extent, been the author of his own misfortunes by going back to rob the dying Schultz. Piggy, found dead some weeks later, was not so fortunate. He had been taken to Brownsville, where he had been tortured and shot; his body had then been set alight.

For a year Reles was, like Dixie Davis, held in protective custody. It was thought that he might have tuberculosis and he was hidden out in Harbour Hospital under the name of Albert Smith from 1 to 9 November 1941. Then his safe home became the sixth floor of the Half Moon Hotel, Coney Island, in Brooklyn, where he was kept under constant surveillance by six uniformed police officers. It was from there that he was brought to the New York courts to give his evidence.

Then on 12 November 1941 Reles, while guarded by the police, fell to his death from the Half Moon Hotel, landing on the pavement. One of the more ingenious explanations of his death is that he was playing a practical joke, climbing out of the window on knotted bedsheets and then running back upstairs to frighten the guards outside his room. Another is that he committed suicide; to do this he must have lowered himself to the third floor and then jumped, but as his body was found twenty feet out into the street this seems unlikely. However, the Grand Jury was perfectly happy, finding that:

> [Reles] met his death whilst trying to escape by means of a knotted sheet attached to a radiator in his room. We find that Reles did not meet with foul play and that he did not die by suicide. It would be sheer speculation to attempt to disarm [sic] his motive for wanting to escape.

There is little doubt that it was a gangland hit. While in the previous months Reles had been giving evidence against relatively minor members of Murder Inc., now he was due to testify against Albert Anastasia who was on trial for the killing of a Union leader. After Reles' death the case against Anastasia was dropped and although it was re-opened in 1951 no progress was made. Reles was also due to give evidence against Bugsy Siegel, but those charges were also dropped. Lucky Luciano would later say that the killing had been done by police officers who had thrown Reles from his room, and that the contract price had been $50,000. Later still Meyer Lansky said the fee paid had been $100,000.

Meanwhile Leibowitz was tiring of his gang practice and was seeking a judgeship. He had been offered and declined the enormous sum of $250,000 to appear for Louis Lepke when he was duped into giving himself up by the gossip columnist Walter Winchell and the head of the FBI, J. Edgar Hoover. Lepke had thought that he would be charged only with a narcotics offence and not handed over to Hoover, but he was mistaken. As he got into the car with Winchell there was Hoover. He was sentenced to 14 years on the narcotics charge and a 39-to-life on extortion and racketeering charges. Later he would be executed for the contract murder of a Brooklyn candy storeowner, Joe Rosen, who had dared to think of going to the District Attorney when Lepke forced him out of business.[4]

The story goes that Leibowitz and his wife were going to see a Cary Grant film when three men arrived and began pouring dollar bills onto the dining room table. They told Leibowitz it was his if he would undertake Lepke's defence. He declined, saying he was late for the cinema and telling them there were any number of well-qualified people who would act for the gangster.

It was repercussions from the Seabury inquiry which cost Leibowitz the $100,000 fee on offer to defend Capone on his income tax charges. He went to Chicago, advised the great man and then returned to New York to face his own difficulties.

Samuel Seabury began his inquiry at the request of the Appellate Division of the court investigating the alteration of records, sale of judgeships and harassment of innocent women as well as a long-running conspiracy between police, judges, lawyers and bail bondsmen to shake down prostitutes. Later in March 1931 he commenced an inquiry into the competence of the District Attorney Thomas Crain. Despite making severe criticisms he recommended the man stay in office. He was then approached to investigate the City government. During the investigation Sheriff Thomas Farley admitted to having a 'wonderful tin box' and Mayor Walker to receiving 'beneficences' from his friends. Walker resigned when a dismissal hearing was in progress.[5]

Leibowitz's troubles stemmed from one of the witnesses, Chile 'Mapocha' Acuna, immortalised in a limerick as The Human Spitoona. He and a number of others with equally engaging names, such as Meyer Slutsky, worked with Vice Squad officers shaking down women in the citywide conspiracy. When Acuna gave evidence to the Commission he said that his job was framing women in vice raids, which produced him something in the region of $150 a week. There were a number of genuine raids to be made on real houses of prostitution, but when times were slack the Vice Squad would make sporadic raids particularly on the Negro section of Harlem, arresting women at random.

There was, however, a third method of keeping up arrests and income and this was where Acuna excelled. His job was to pass marked money to innocent women.

At the Seabury inquiry he was first asked to identify any officers with whom he had worked and, passing through the room, he named 28 present. He then went on to discuss the *modus operandi*, which basically was a version of the badger game. He and the officers of the day with whom he was working would generally eat at 1 p.m. and 9 p.m. and, he would then provide a detective with a number of addresses to be raided. In turn he would receive up to $10 in marked bills. Watches were set for this military-style operation, and it would be arranged that Acuna would give one of the bills to a girl just before the officers broke in to make the arrests. There followed a little *commedia del arte*. He would be reviled by the officers and in turn protest that the girl was his wife. He would then be taken into another room and there would be pounding on the wall to simulate a beating. In some cases he would be actually roughed up a little to provide verisimilitude. He would then give the officers a fictitious name and be released, while the unfortunate girls were kept in custody. Next day in court the police would say he could not be found.

A variation on the theme included taking a room in a boarding house with a girl and then taking money from the girl and the owner of the house not to make arrests. A third idea was to go to a doctor's waiting room and, despite the nurse's protests, strip off. In came the police and arrested her for prostitution.[6]

And all the time there was a pool of lawyers willing and able to deal with the bail bondsmen and the police and to represent the girls. Some made a tidy living from it. Emmanuel Busch, who represented the celebrated madam Polly Adler, shared his offices with two professional bondsmen. He had about 250 cases a year and grossed some $8,000 annually of which $5,000 came from prostitution cases.[7]

In July 1931 proceedings were taken to disbar vice case lawyers who had given money to John C. Weston, a former prosecutor in the Women's Court. They received a hard time from the court which apparently did not understand their cries that theirs was an honourable part of an honourable profession.[8] Weston, the Assistant District Attorney, does not actually seem to have been qualified; but that did not really matter because Joseph Wolfman, one of the more prominent of the defence lawyers, wasn't qualified either. It had not stopped him from making a touching speech to the court on the celebration of the fifth anniversary on the bench of one of the magistrates.

Weston had been in turn a jewellery salesman, an attendance officer for the Board of Education and then a process server in the District Attorney's office. From this somewhat humble position he started handling cases in the Women's Court and for a period of eight years continued happily without any apparent supervision. According to evidence given to Seabury, he had made reports for the first year but had then stopped 'because they didn't bother to read them'. During his seven years he had helped to obtain the dismissal of some 600 cases. The cost to the defence lawyers was a minimum of $25 a case and often a good deal higher. The largest bribe reported to the Seabury inquiry was $150. In turn the unfortunate client would have paid a far higher figure to the lawyer and the bondsman.

The dismissal of the charge was easy to obtain. The officer could be bribed to fail to substantiate the complaint; Weston would deliberately produce insufficient evidence; alternatively the magistrate could be approached.

Wolfman would get to court about 8 a.m. and wait for police officers, bondsmen and court officials to provide him with his daily diet of cases. After he was retained he would 'approach' the officer and try to 'induce' the complainant to withdraw the case. If that failed, which it apparently did on infrequent occasions, he would then go to the court clerk to see if the magistrate would agree to reduce the charge or throw it out altogether. In return for this favour the clerk received half Wolfman's fee.

The picture of the Ring is complete. The stool pigeon or the officer framed the woman, the officer arrested her, the bondsman bailed her out at an exorbitant charge and usually recommended a lawyer, the lawyer gouged her savings and, either himself or through the bondsman, 'fixed' the arresting officer and the District Attorney.[9]

The Seabury Report, commenting on the arrest and shakedown of the women, said that:

> ... the social and financial status is such to render the charge utterly incredible. She is questioned about her assets, taken to 100 Street Police Station, prevented from using the telephone until she contacts John Steiner, a professional bondsman. He relieves her of her jewellery.

A number of vice officers were arrested and charged in connection with the Ring. Most were convicted in short order, but two were defended by Leibowitz. The first was Robert E. Murray who was acquitted; but the second trial, that of Patrolman Peter Brown, was the more interesting and showed Leibowitz at his best.

One woman convicted was Rita Antonina, who had been arrested by Brown for soliciting and had received two days in prison. She never forgot the slight and when the Seabury Commission began its investigations she contacted them. A buxom French Canadian whose relations were all prominent and respected citizens in Canada, she said she was happily married and a good woman. She claimed that Brown had burst into her room when she was fully clothed, twisted her arm, and tried to force her on the bed just in time for two other officers to arrest her.

Brown's version was that he had been checking out vice haunts in Lower Manhattan, had seen Rita Antonina leaning out of a window and had made an arrangement to return the next afternoon for a fee of $5. She had been lying on the bed wearing only a thin dress; she had then taken it off after he had given her the marked bill. When the police burst in she had taken the marked $5, torn it into pieces and flushed it down the lavatory. In turn Brown had no hefty bank account and did not drink or gamble. Leibowitz thought that if the allegation were true it was likely there would have been more incidents to investigate, and that there would have been money stored away.

When interviewed Brown remarked in passing to his lawyer that he couldn't believe anyone would have an affair with the woman because of a seven-inch appendix scar on her belly. Asked why he had not mentioned this before when he gave evidence at the magistrates' court, he replied that no one had asked him. Leibowitz told him not to mention the scar unless James Wallace, the Assistant District Attorney, asked him about it in cross-examination. Leibowitz was convinced that Wallace would know of the scar. At the end of the cross-examination Wallace turned as if to sit down and then asked if anything else stood out in Brown's memory. It was then that the policeman mentioned the scar as running down to the groin. Asked again why he hadn't mentioned it before, Brown once more replied that no one had asked him. Rita Antonina was recalled to the witness stand and admitted, somewhat shamefacedly, that she did have such a scar.

Leibowitz described the technique as 'spotlighting' – providing a single piece of evidence on which the jury could focus to the exclusion of everything else. Asked what would have happened if Wallace had not risen to the concealed bait and asked the question, he said he would have raised it himself on redirect but, of course, it had been far better for the Assistant D.A. to do it.

It was while he was appearing for other police officers during departmental disciplinary proceedings that he fell foul of Acuna. Leibowitz produced a witness, described in his biography as 'out of a clear blue sky', Eva Esperanza Mackay, who had been Acuna's girlfriend and workhorse. She had by now fallen out with him, for Acuna not only sent clients to competitors but also failed to use his influence sufficiently to prevent her acquiring five convictions for prostitution. It was he who had introduced her to prostitution in the first place and he took a dollar from each sale she made. Acuna was completely destroyed and left the room making threats against Leibowitz.

The pair clearly patched things up because they were soon back, along with a reporter, before the Brooklyn District Attorney, William F.X. Geoghan. Now she said Acuna had never been her procurer and the only reason she had given evidence was that Leibowitz had put her up to it.

> Leibowitz wrote out all the questions he wanted me to answer as a witness against Acuna, and I studied them in his office. He wouldn't let me take them away with me.[10]

Geoghan put the girl before a Grand Jury and, on 29 September 1931, Leibowitz's counter-attack was swift:

> This entire story, coming from a five times convicted prostitute, is an outrageous lie and a foul conspiracy. At the proper time, under the proper circumstances, the absolute falsity of the statement will be demonstrated. Those behind this despicable plot will suffer the full consequences.

He waived his immunity and went before the Grand Jury who nevertheless returned an indictment of conspiracy and subordination. In January 1932 County Judge George W. Martin dismissed the indictment saying:

> To charge any person with a crime, whether the charge be false or true, is a grave matter. The type and character of the witnesses produced to sustain these indictments, and their admitted associations and experiences, do not entitle them to very much credence.

But Geoghan would not accept Martin's ruling and appealed to the State Supreme Court. Theirs was a curious ruling: in July

1932 they dismissed the conspiracy indictment but reinstated the subornation of perjury. But this did not matter because on 22 June Acuna had died of a brain tumour and without him Geoghan was stymied. He moved for the dismissal of the remaining indictment and County Judge Algernon I. Nova agreed, saying:

Lawyers who for years and years build up a good reputation will never be safe if it is our law that an unscrupulous client can walk in and say, 'The lawyer told me to say that.' To ruin and stain a lawyer's reputation, ruin his family life, take away his right to practice upon the word alone, so to speak, of an admitted disreputable prostitute, is carrying it a bit too far.[11]

But, even 70 years on, the incident is remembered not wholly in Leibowitz's favour.

Most lawyers who represent gangland or Mob figures are keen to point out that these are not the whole of their clientele, and Leibowitz is remembered not only for the 144 people he saved from the electric chair – he lost only one to it – but rightly for his long and courageous defence of the Scottsboro Boys accused of the rape of two white women in Alabama.

On 25 March 1931, in one of America's worst cases, nine young black men were accused of the rape of two white women in a box car on a railroad between Tennessee and Alabama. They had certainly been in a fight with some white boys, one of whom was thrown from the train and went to the local sheriff. At the station at Paint Rock the nine black youths were arrested and accused of the rape of Victoria Price and Ruby Bates – charges which, at the time, carried the death penalty. There was neither medical evidence of rape nor were the girls distressed. They were portrayed as injured Southern petals when they were, at best, semi-amateur prostitutes. They were in effect forced to lie because in the manners of the time they could not admit consorting freely with one black let alone nine. Had they done so they would have faced vagrancy charges themselves. The boys' first trial was a farce. The trial judge assigned all the county's lawyers to the defence of the youths, but six of the seven withdrew. Eight of the nine boys were convicted and the ninth, thirteen-year-old Roy Wright, was spared when only seven out of the twelve jurors voted for the death penalty. An appeal was allowed and re-trial ordered.

Leibowitz, at considerable personal risk – at the time a pamphlet 'Kill the Jew from New York' was being circulated – undertook their defence with exactly the same result. The Attorney General, Thomas E. Knight jnr., prosecuted in an entirely unbiased way, suggesting the jury should, 'Show them that Alabama justice cannot be bought with Jew money from New York.' By now Ruby Bates accepted that she had lied and neither she nor Victoria Price had been raped; their story had been concocted to avoid the charges of vagrancy. But her confession did the boys no good and Leibowitz was obliged to return to the Supreme Court, which move brought another series of trials and the declaration that blacks must be allowed to serve on juries. Eventually Leibowitz withdrew from the case when it became apparent that the boys were being used as political pawns.[12]

Leibowitz was also involved at the end of the case of Bruno Hauptmann, convicted of the murder of the Lindbergh baby, 20-month-old Charlie, on 1 March 1932. He was brought into the case with a view to mounting an appeal but, after seeing Hauptmann for some hours, he became convinced that the man was guilty. Seeking a reprieve, Leibowitz then argued with Governor Hoffman – who had the power of commutation of the death sentence – that it was worth confronting Hauptmann with his own son just before he was due to take the walk to the electric chair. Leibowitz believed that this form of the Third Degree would work; he was convinced that at the sight of his child in these distressing conditions, Hauptmann would then crack and both name his accomplices and tell what had actually happened. If he did, then he should be reprieved. In the end Hoffman would not agree and Hauptmann died still maintaining his innocence.[13]

On 6 January 1941 Leibowitz was inducted as a judge of the Supreme Court in Brooklyn. He had been elected with a vote of over 400,000, the largest then recorded. One of the dangers of appointing a defence lawyer to the bench is that he may be over-sympathetic to the associates of his former clients, and it was feared that, given Leibowitz's background of defence work, he would turn out to be soft on crime and criminals. One deputy stipendiary magistrate in London justified those fears when he allowed out on bail a man with a substantial criminal record who was charged with murder. It may or may not have damaged the criminal justice system; it certainly damaged his embryonic judicial career, for he was never invited to sit again.

In Leibowitz's case the fears were totally misplaced and nothing was further from the case. He became a real poacher turned gamekeeper. Brooklyn lawyer Jacob Evseroff remembers Leibowitz well:

> I was a protégé of Leibowitz when I was assistant DA for ten years. I was his blue-eyed boy. He was the most overpowering, overwhelming, autocratic jurist who ever sat on a bench. He was a 1950s incarnation of Judge Roy Bean.[14]

Another judge of the time who barely survived his association with a gangster was Thomas A. Aurelio, who in 1943 faced a challenge to his appointment when his connection with Frank Costello came to light in a wire-tap. It was extremely bad luck on Aurelio that this should happen, because the tap was a random one designed to find some information about the murdered journalist Carlo Tresca.[15]

Tresca was killed at about 9.30 p.m. on 11 January 1943 when a black car pulled up as he was crossing Fifth Avenue with a friend. A man jumped out and Tresca was shot in the mouth. When little progress had been made by the following August a tap was authorised and, on the morning after the Democratic Party nominated Aurelio for the position of Justice of the Supreme Court, the lawyer was heard to say:

> *Aurelio*: Good morning, Francesco. How are you? And thanks for everything.
> *C*: Congratulations. It went over perfect. When I tell you everything is in the bag, you can rest assured.
> *A*: It was perfect. Arthur Klein did the nominating; first me, then Gavagan, then Peck. It was fine.
> *C*: That's fine ... Well we will have to get together, you, your Mrs and myself; and have dinner some night real soon.
> *A*: That would be fine, but right now I want to assure you of my loyalty for all you have done. It's undying.[16]

Now the *New York Times* headlined 'Gangster Backed Aurelio For Bench'.[17]

It should have been the end of Aurelio, but he fought back. He had been admitted to the Bar after the First World War and in 1922 was appointed Assistant District Attorney by the doubtful Mayor Jimmy Walker who subsequently appointed him a judge in 1931. However, with Walker's eclipse he was reappointed in 1935, this time by Walker's nemesis, Fiorello La Guardia, with the following glowing encomium:

> I have reappointed you because I know of your record and have known you as a boy and a law student. You are the kind of career man I want on the bench.

Now Aurelio benefited from the proximity of the 1943 election and defied pressure to stand down, saying that while he accepted making the call he knew nothing about the man's reputation:

> During my brief acquaintance with Mr Costello of approximately six months standing I knew him to be a businessman of good repute, and I definitely disavow any knowledge of his criminal background.

It is difficult to understand how with the most minimal inquiries the judge and former assistant prosecutor could not have discovered that Costello, who had been a bootlegger during Prohibition and a business partner of Arnold Rothstein and Lucky Luciano as well as Huey Long, the Kingfish of Louisiana, was by this time the top Italian racketeer in New York.

Disbarment proceedings were brought against Aurelio and he explained away the reference to 'undying loyalty' by saying, 'That's just the way some Italians express things.' On 30 October 1943 the referee ruled there was insufficient evidence to show that Aurelio was aware of the reputation of Costello. Three days later he won the election by a little under 50,000 votes, defeating the American Labour Party candidate, Matthew M. Levy, who had been fully supported by the Democratic Party.

Just as Leibowitz proved something of a surprise, so did Aurelio. He turned out to be an uncompromising judge, twice rejecting clandestine overtures by Costello who referred to him as a 'lousy ingrate'.

Almost certainly Aurelio knew more about Costello than he cared to admit and had borrowed $7,500 from him. When Costello asked his own lawyer George Wolf, who later wrote the mobster's biography, to collect on the note, Aurelio erupted in some fury saying the debt had been repaid years earlier and, 'Tell that gangster if he ever gets near my court I'll have him thrown in jail and buried there.' It was never disclosed for what purpose the loan had been made.[18]

Aurelio certainly never lifted a finger to try to assist Costello when in 1952 he went to prison for contempt of Senate hearings. Aurelio died in 1973, still sitting at the age of 83. Even his detractors, unlike those of Leibowitz, admitted that he had been an excellent judge.

1 Interview with author, 12 October 2000.

2 F. Pasley, *Not Guilty!*, p. 73.

3 Sometimes lawyers have had to make do with possessions instead of cash fees. When George Marquette shot James W. Cass, a lawman in Denver, and was later captured he gave his .38 Colt revolver to his lawyer. It was later sold on to the millionaire Henry Davidson for his collection. See *New York Times*, 12 December 1924.

4 Lepke was executed on 4 March 1944. It was suggested that he had been about to collaborate with Governor Dewey but had changed his mind, so avoiding reprisals against his family. As for some of the other clients of Leibowitz, Bugsy Siegel went on to open the first hotel casino in Las Vegas where he was shot on 20 July 1947 after having been discovered embezzling Mob funds earmarked for the building. 'Pittsburg' Phil Strauss and 'Bugsy' Goldstein were electrocuted on 12 June 1941 for the murder of gambler Irving 'Puggy' Feinstein. Strauss was suspected of killing at least 28 people; he had been acquitted no fewer than 18 times, though not all acquittals came at the hands of Leibowitz.

A similar story is told about Marshall Hall who received a visit in the 1920s from the London gangleader Darby Sabini, who produced a bundle of £5 notes asking the barrister to defend Alfie Solomon, accused of the murder of Buck Emden. Hall advised Sabini to see his clerk, but took the case and obtained a manslaughter verdict.

5 Jimmy Walker, whose father had been a Tammany Hall boss, was a songwriter before becoming a lawyer. Early in his legal career he defended Louis Kushner, the killer of the New York gangster Kid Dropper. To the delight of the Underworld Walker later went on in 1926 to become the much loved Mayor of New York. Walker, a charismatic man but surrounded by deep-seated corruption, was obliged to resign in 1932 following an investigation into building contracts. He fled to England to avoid his creditors, marrying Betty Compton with whom he had previously had a high-profile affair. They were sued in the English courts and returned to Northport, Long Island, where he bred Irish terriers. Mayor Fiorella LaGuardia was pressured into giving Walker a job and he was appointed to adjudicate labour disputes in the women's garment industry at a salary of $20,000 per annum. He died of a brain clot aged 65 on 18 November 1946.

After the Seabury investigations two magistrates were removed and three forced to resign. Russell T. Sherwood, Mayor Walker's bookkeeper who shared a safebox with him, left the jurisdiction and fled to Mexico City. After the election he was said to have paid $1 million into twenty bank and brokerage accounts. He refused to return even though he forfeited $50,000 property.

6 See New York Supreme Court Appellate Division Ist Department Investigation of the Magistrates' Courts. (The report of Samuel Seabury in five volumes), RS Su 71 AP mc in the New York City Archives, particularly Volume III, pp. 82 *et seq.*

7 Seabury, Volume III, p 84; Docket 2411/1928. Busch paid Weston $50 to have the charge dismissed.

8 See *New York Times*, 22 July 1931. In March 1999 Nigerian born André John-Salakov became the first person in England convicted of passing himself off as a barrister. He was jailed for 30 months after having been found guilty of 19 charges including duping the Charity Commissioners into granting him charitable status and trying to swindle the National Lottery Commission of more than £10 million. He had appeared in over 200 cases and the court was told, 'Many members [of the public] clearly were under the belief that not only was John-Salakov a barrister, but he was

the best barrister that they had ever come across.' *The Guardian*, 27 February 1999; *The Independent*, 20 March 1999. Convictions of men posing as solicitors are rare but not wholly unknown.

9 Seabury, Volume IV, p. 86.

10 F. Pasley, *Not Guilty!*, p. 222.

11 Quoted in F. Pasley, *Not Guilty!*, pp. 224–5. Curiously in Quentin Reynolds' account of the case in *Courtroom*, pp. 348–50, there is no mention of the death of Acuna nor, perhaps more tellingly, that the Supreme Court had reinstated the perjury charge.

12 Four of the boys were released and the other five served lengthy terms until only Haywood Patterson was the last left in jail. On 17 July 1948 he escaped to Canada where he later died of cancer while in prison there awaiting trial for killing a man in a fight in a bar. See James Goodman, *Stories of Scottboro*. Things did not change much over the years in Southern judges' attitudes. William Hellerstein recalls defending in a civil rights case and, 'Every morning me and my colleague would be greeted by the judge, "Here comes my favourite kike lawyers." I'd just say, "Good morning judge." You can't get caught out.'

13 Little Charlie Lindbergh was kidnapped from his room at the family home near Hopewell, New Jersey. A ladder was placed by an open window and the kidnapper(s) made their entry and exit in this way. A ransom of $70,000 was paid on 2 April, but the body of the child was found on 12 May. Richard 'Bruno' Hauptmann was arrested on 19 September after he had tendered a bill recognised as being part of the ransom money. The evidence against him was his possession of $14,000 of the notes. Hauptmann, who had convictions in Germany for robbery, was not well defended. The evidence against him was possession of the money, a voice identification by Lindbergh snr. and the fact that he was a carpenter who could have made part of the ladder. It was also suggested the ransom note was written by him and he made similar spelling mistakes of words such as 'rihgt'. His counsel, Edward Reilly, was drinking heavily and later died of syphilis. Hauptmann was executed on 3 April 1936. Whoever actually did the kidnapping must have been helped by the Lindbergh's maid, Violet Sharpe, who killed herself by drinking crystals of cyanide chloride on 10 June 1932. Since Hauptmann's execution there have been a number of books arguing his innocence or guilt. For the former see Ludovic Kennedy, *The Airman and the Carpenter*. For the latter see Jonathan Goodman, *The Modern Murder Yearbook*. For an account of Leibowitz's involvement see also Quentin Reynolds, *Courtroom*.

14 Interview with author, 12 October 2000.

15 Tresca, the anti-Communist, anti-Fascist editor of the Italian language paper *Il Germa*, had long been a thorn in the flesh of the authorities. Once the lover of Helen Gurley Brown, an early leader of the Industrial Workers of the World, the Wobblies, as might be expected he had taken a close interest in the trial of Sacco and Vanzetti convicted of a pay-roll robbery murder in South Braintree, Mass. on 15 April 1920. The trial had hardly been one of America's finest, with perjured forensic evidence and a judge who openly referred to the defendants as 'dagos' and 'sons of bitches'. The case became a *cause célèbre* for left-wing factions. Sacco was almost certainly guilty, whilst there is considerable doubt about Vanzetti. Both were executed on 23 August 1927. Tresca's killer was almost certainly Carmine Galante acting on a substantial contract commissioned by Vito Genovese, then in self-imposed exile in Italy. Although arrested, Galante was not picked out on an identification parade by Guiseppe Callabi with whom Tresca had been walking.

16 New *York Times*, 29 August 1943, p. 30.

17 *Ibid*, p. 1.

18 George Wolf, *Frank Costello: Prime Minister of the Underworld*. See also Leonard Katz, *Uncle Frank*.

# 8 Vanishing Judges: Joseph Crater and Curtis Chillingworth

ON 6 AUGUST 1930 Judge Joseph Force Crater of the New York Supreme Court simply disappeared off the face of the earth. He left Billy Haas' restaurant at 332 W 45th off Broadway, waved goodbye to a friend, caught a taxi and vanished. He was 40 years old at the time.

He had been educated at Lafayette and obtained a law degree from Columbia before establishing a successful practice and forging political connections as he rose to the presidency of the Cayuga Democratic Club, a major part of the Tammany Hall connection. He was appointed to the Supreme Court by Roosevelt in April 1930 following the resignation of the magistrate Albert H. Vitali. This in turn followed a proven allegation that Vitali had borrowed $19,000 and change from Arnold Rothstein, whose death would dog the administration of Mayor James Walker.

Unfortunately for Crater, earlier in the summer there had been a little localised difficulty when it was discovered that he had been the main speaker at a benefit dinner for a man suspected of buying his appointment to the post of magistrate in the City Traffic Court. In fact Vitali had been even more unfortunate. He had been the guest of honour at a dinner at the Tepecano Democratic Club at the Roman Gardens – other patrons included Cira Terranova, the Artichoke King, who had headed the Camoristas of Brooklyn for over a decade – when a robbery took place. To avoid handing over his jewellery Vitali hid his diamond ring in his trouser pocket and his fellow-magistrate, Michael Delagi, hid one in his shoe. Within two hours of the robbery, in which a detective lost a gun, Vitali had arranged the retrieval and return of all the property. This may have stood him in good stead with his fellow guests, but it demonstrated far too close a link with criminals.

Crater's wife, Stella, who had married him after the judge acted for her in the divorce proceedings against her first husband, had last seen him on 3 August when he returned to New York from their Augusta, Maine, country home. She said he had been intending to return six days later, but when nothing had been heard from him after ten days she despatched their chauffeur to try to find him. He returned with assurances from the judge's friends that all was well with him, though in fact he had vanished at least four days earlier. No one seems to have done very much until, when the judicial term began on 25 August and there was still no sign of him, they organised a search. Even then his disappearance was not reported to the police until 3 September.

As far as could be established, on the day of his disappearance Crater had been in his chambers and had an aide cash two cheques totalling $5,150. Where did he go? What happened to him? And *why* did he go?

Earlier in the evening he had gone to the box office of the Arrow theatre and asked for a ticket for the show *Dancing Partner*. He had been told the show was sold out but to come back for a return. After dinner with lawyer William Klein and a showgirl Sally-Lou Ritz, he said he was going to see *Dancing Partner*; but, in fact, by the time he left them at 9.15 the curtain had already gone up. Someone did collect the return, but the man at the box office could not remember if it was Crater. This of itself was surprising because the judge was distinctive, if not distinguished looking; heavyset, he had a very small head for the size of his body, so resembling a turtle.

At the time New York cab drivers were required to keep records of all starting points and destinations. Despite this and offers of rewards of $5,000 from the City and another $2,500 from the *New York World*, no driver came forward.

There were, of course, numerous sightings. He was working as a tout on a Hollywood racecourse; a beggar in Illinois; 'I didn't pull his whiskers, but I'm pretty sure they were false', said a Chicago housewife; an amnesia victim in the Missouri State Insane Asylum. Other sightings showed him to be a gold prospector in California, a tourist in Italy and, perhaps best of all, as late as 1946 the operator of an Arab only – apart from himself, that is – bingo game in North Africa. There were also numerous confessions, generally by down-and-outs who wanted a whiff of notoriety and the food which would, for a time, accompany it.

Seven years after he disappeared Crater was ruled legally dead and his widow remarried. She had been evicted from their apartment at 40 5th Avenue and had worked as a secretary. On the pronouncement of his death she received $20,561 in insurance monies. The cost of the search had been estimated at $300,000.

But Crater's legend lived on in cartoons and jokes, with one hoaxer suggesting the police raid a Montreal hotel where the good judge could be found in room 761. The raid duly took place, to the surprise of a honeymoon couple.

In 1954 Henry Krauss, a German butcher, said Crater had used his house in Yonkers. Later he had returned home and found the kitchen full of bloodstains. Unfortunately Krauss died and the investigation did not proceed. Then in 1964 the Dutch psychic Gerard Croiset contacted the authorities to say the body could be found in New York, again in the Yonkers. He predicted that there would be an abandoned road, a small pond and three trees on a roadway to the site, with the body lying two and a half feet beneath the surface. This turned out to be the Krauss house and there was considerable excitement when the spot, near Sprain Lake golf course now described by Croiset, was found. The excitement was short-lived when the next day, after his men had turned over 15,000 cubic feet of soil, Sheriff John E. Fry told the press, 'There wasn't even a bone some dog might have buried for future reference.'

As to why the judge disappeared, that was seemingly almost as insoluble as the first question, where? Over a period of months a Grand Jury investigated his disappearance and heard the evidence of hundreds of witnesses, but it produced no solution. For a time there was a flurry of interest when it was announced that a chorine from Atlantic City would give evidence, but nothing came of it. The judge was also known to have had a liking for showgirls and had had a long-standing mistress, Constance Braemer Marcus. Perhaps more importantly, he had been a patron of the Broadway speakeasy Abbey Club also patronised by Legs Diamond and Dutch Schultz.

From time to time life could get quite exciting in the club, and it was there that Schultz fought Charles 'Chink' Sherman who shot him in the shoulder. Sherman was stabbed and clubbed with a chair; when he came out of hospital he vowed vengeance, but in fact he ended dead on a county dump-heap.

Crater's wife firmly believed his death was linked to corruption in the Cayuga Democratic Club; she was convinced he had been murdered because of 'a sinister something that was connected with politics'.[1] It is certainly possible that the cash the judge withdrew on the day of his disappearance was blackmail money, and that he was killed by people he knew at the Abbey Club. They, if no one else, would have easily been able to dispose of a body.

Despite the loyal protestations in his wife's book, Crater almost certainly was involved with at least three women of doubtful reputation. Elaine Dawn, a Ziegfeld girl who had been with him to the club, was one and June Brice, also known as Jean Covell, was another. She disappeared early in the investigation and was in and out of mental hospitals for the rest of her life until she died in 1948. More dangerously he was known to Vivian Gordon, said to have had, 'five hundred sugar-daddies', to be an expert blackmailer, adroit at the badger game and a working friend of Arnold Rothstein.

Then in 1955 Harry Stein made a confession shortly before he was due to die for the killing of Andrew Petrini, a *Reader's Digest* messenger, in a botched $4,000 robbery in New Castle, New York in 1950. It seems that, early in 1929, a man named Joe Lesser was indicted in New York City on first-degree forgery involving some $190,000 real estate mortgages. Crater was then not yet a judge, and he employed 'Chowderhead' Cohen as a private investigator. Cohen was acquainted with two men close to Lesser, and they approached him to see if something could be done. Cohen in turn enlisted Harry Stein and, through Crater connections, Lesser was guaranteed a walkout for $5,000 which was paid over. In February 1929 he was convicted. Stein knew Max 'Boo-Hoo' Hoff in Philadelphia, and a deal was struck that he would arrange the return of the money from the judge. Through Vivian Gordon, Stein knew Crater's every move. He was kidnapped and when he laughed at the suggestion that he should repay the $5,000 he was shot in the back of the head at 2 p.m. on 13 August 1930. His body was put in acid and when it had dissolved sufficiently the remains were tipped into the Passaic River outside Clifton.[2]

In fact the story is not completely improbable, and it harks back again to the Seabury inquiry into the payment by lawyers for appointments as magistrates and the conduct of lawyers, police, bail bondsmen and magistrates in the Women's Court generally. On 22 February 1931 Vivian Gordon was found strangled in Van Cortland Park, with a rope knotted around her throat. According to the newspapers she maintained she had been convicted on false police evidence, had made a complaint about a Bronx lawyer, John A. Radeloff, and was due to give evidence before the Seabury Commission. In fact it would turn out to be much deeper than that.

A fortnight later her daughter, Benita Bischoff – rather unkindly described as 'a plain girl with a dark complexion and black hair'[3] – committed suicide by gassing herself on the kitchen floor, said to be from the shame of the publicity. She had been a member of the local girls' hockey team but when she turned up at the rink the others would not skate with her. She had been living with her father and step-mother for some years but some three years earlier her mother and another man had tried to kidnap her, pulling her into a car. She had barely escaped.

Within four hours of Vivian Gordon's killing, Harold Stein, a man with a reputation as a strangler, was found in possession of her jewellery and coat. In her diary she had noted she had lent him $1,500, but when questioned Stein maintained he had no idea why she should make any entry about him at all. Earlier he had served 10 years in Sing Sing for choking a woman and stealing $250 in 1921.

The lawyer John Radeloff, a cousin to the quality criminal Joseph Radelow, was held as a material witness in $50,000 bail; unable to raise this he remained in custody until it was reduced several weeks later, after which he was charged with extorting $1,000 from a tailor, Joseph Garber.

There may have been no evidence against the lawyer in the murder case, but the prosecution alleged that he was the man who had arranged a contract with Stein to kill Vivian Gordon. He was clearly in up to his elbows. Ms Gordon had invested her ill-gotten gains from the badger game in loans, some of which had been made to Radeloff. In her diary, which was found soon after her death, she wrote:

> Radeloff said Samuel Cohen [Chowderhead] had been in to see him last week. Samuel Cohen is the one who was to have knocked me off last winter.

Another entry reads: 'I believe that Radeloff and Samuel Cohen pulled that jewellery deal alone.' There was also a note that she had seen Radeloff with his wife and had roundly abused him in her presence, something she deeply regretted.

Stein was defended by the great Samuel Leibowitz. The prosecution relied heavily on a taxi driver, Harry Schitten, who said he had been offered $1,000 to chauffeur a seven-passenger hired Cadillac that night. Vivian Gordon was led to believe her role was to relieve a sucker named Greenberg of some $25,000 worth of diamonds. Once lured into the car she was taken to Van Cortland Park in the Bronx and strangled. Far from being a sucker, Greenberg was another player in the game.

Very surprisingly, and to the wrath of the prosecutor, both Greenberg and Stein were acquitted. I.J.P. Adlerman, Chief Assistant District Attorney, described it as the greatest miscarriage of justice that ever took place in Bronx County and moved unsuccessfully to have the jurors' names struck from the jurors' roll as being unfit to serve. The Grand Jury, when it reconvened, announced that it was appalled.[4]

It was Radeloff's lucky year. In the October he was acquitted of extortion and returned to practice; he said he had merely been claiming his fees. Overall Stein was not so fortunate. While in custody he had been identified as the man who, to gain entry to a woman's apartment, posed as a bond salesman and, after chloroforming her, stole her jewellery. For this little escapade he received 25 years. The probation officer's report said of him: 'An alert underworld sophisticate ... suspected of being involved with bootlegging, narcotic peddling, robbery and murder.'[5]

The next year while in prison he was named with Greenberg in an indictment involving counterfeit money.

Crater was not the only judge to disappear in mysterious circumstances. Justice John Lansing, who a century earlier left his New York City Hotel on 12 December 1829 never to be seen again, was another. He had been receiving threats following his jailing of another lawyer, John V.N. Yates, on contempt charges.

For a time it seemed as though the disappearance of Judge W. Lynn Parkinson, who disappeared on 26 October 1959, was an echo of the Crater case. He had been seen standing outside Chicago's Drake Hotel. His hat, umbrella and spectacles were found at different places along the lakefront, the hat some miles away. When he did not appear after several days the FBI were called, but his body was not found for six months when it was discovered in the lake.

Although the inquest jury failed to return reasons for the death it seems that the judge, far from being involved in organised crime and chorus girls, suffered from low blood pressure and was on medication for depression. He had been drinking after court and witnesses had seen him fall to the ground on several occasions. The fact that his property was found in a number of different places was explained by the falls. It was thought the hat had probably been picked up by a passer-by and later discarded, or that it had blown away.

One of the most memorable of the disappearing judge cases was that of Judge Curtis E. 'Chick' Chillingworth of Florida's Fifteenth Judicial Circuit, and his wife, Marjorie, who vanished from their home at Manalapan – some 50 miles from Miami – on 15 June 1955. 'Vanishing' is the correct term in that their bodies were never found, but from the beginning there was little reason to doubt what had happened to them. The twin questions to be answered were why and on whose say-so.

In June 1923, at the age of 26, Chillingworth had been the youngest man appointed to the Florida Circuit Bench. Long regarded as a candidate for Florida's Supreme Court, over the years he had preferred to sit controlling conduct amongst lawyers on the Gold Coast. After builders came to the house the morning after the disappearance and found a broken floodlight in the porch, the alarm had been raised. At first it was thought that the judge might have been kidnapped for ransom or been harmed by criminals who had appeared before him, but nothing came of those leads. Various rewards were posted but again they led nowhere. To an extent the case was written off as a professional job undertaken by out-of-state gangsters.

Meanwhile Municipal Court Judge Joseph Peel practised law in West Palm Beach. Described as debonair and suave and 'an adaptable kind of fellow who could fit in equally well at an American cocktail party or an African tribal dance, even if he hadn't been invited,'[6] he had taken his law degree at Stetson University, Daytona Beach, in December 1949 and gone to work in the law office of the State Senator John R. Beacham. Political connections are usually desirable in American law practices and in May 1950 Peel was appointed a judge *ad litem* of municipal court by the West Palm Beach City Commission. When the regular judge was not sitting this lawyer, barely out of law school, could impose a maximum sentence of $500 or 60 days in prison. When not sitting *ad litem*, for the next nine months Peel was a highly regarded defence lawyer until he accepted an appointment as municipal court prosecutor in March 1951. From there it was a simple step to winning the election for municipal court judge in the 1952 city elections. It was a two-year part-time appointment and he conducted a practice at the same time.

Now he acted for Floyd Albert 'Lucky' Holzapfel in the settlement of a small claim brought by Holzapfel for false arrest by a bail bondsman. It was the beginning of a long friendship, when both were aged 27. Holzapfel had an interesting track record. He had a good war record, and received a Purple Heart before leaving the Army with a 50 per cent disability benefit, and had attended Central State College in Oklahoma City and then Oklahoma City University. After that he had worked in the fingerprint section of the Oklahoma City Police Department. Unfortunately he collected a 60-day sentence for bookmaking while on holiday in Los Angeles and soon after that, back in Oklahoma on New Year's Eve 1946, he was arrested for three armed robberies and received 2–5 years in the state prison. He was pardoned by Governor Roy Turner on the extraordinary condition that he attend the law school at the University, but he claimed that he had been refused admission and drifted to Miami where he worked in a series of jobs including bartender, salesman, carpenter's assistant and gas station attendant.

It was shortly after they became associates that Joe Peel received his first legal reprimand. He had acted for both husband and wife in a divorce suit and, worse, had given the husband a form to send to his wife agreeing not to contest the case and waiving service of any more documents. But the husband had forged her signature. He received 18 months imprisonment and Peel a very public reprimand at the hands of Chillingworth:

> On this record I am thoroughly satisfied that counsel has been guilty of unprofessional conduct ...
> Because of the youth and inexperience of counsel and his frankness in promptly acquainting the court with the facts as soon as a complaint was made, I feel that a public reprimand would be a sufficient disciplinary measure under the circumstances.

No action was taken to remove him from his position as a municipal judge and Peel and Holzapfel set about finding ways to fight the election eight months away. These included the unusual (for a judge anyway) arrangement with *bolito*, a form of Numbers, runners and illegal moonshine sellers that in return for a modest weekly payment they would be tipped off about raids and would have lenient treatment if they were so unfortunate as to be arrested. As with all good businesses this soon expanded and protection for a rather larger moonshine operation run by George David 'Bobby' Lincoln was priced at $750 a month. They also joined with 'Barney' Barnett in two strip clubs and a night club.

When Peel ran for municipal court judge he told voters they could:

> ... rely upon my record of accomplishments as municipal judge during my present administration. I will continue my efficient, fair and impartial administration of justice if re-elected. And if re-elected the people of the city can be assured of continued fair and sincere adjudication of cases appearing in the municipal court.

Either the public had not heard of the collusive divorce or did not care about it. Peel was re-elected.

But it was then that he fell a second time; again in a divorce case, again an old one. It was alleged that he had told a plaintiff that her divorce had been finalised, as a result of which she bigamously remarried. A complaint was made to Judge White on the Circuit Bench and, as was the practice, he conducted a preliminary hearing, suspended Peel and referred the matter to Chillingworth for adjudication. Meanwhile Holzapfel was called before a Grand Jury which was investigating the Numbers racket in West Beach.

Peel's suspension ran out and he formed an association with another lawyer, Harold Gray. It was when Gray discovered that Holzapfel had a criminal record that he insisted he be banned from the office. In December 1956 Gray was taken to the Chi Chi strip club car park by Peel, where he was given a severe beating by Holzapfel. A charge of attempted murder was brought, but Holzapfel was acquitted after producing a surprise witness to say that Gray was the aggressor.

Eighteen months later Peel sold his law practice and announced that he was going into property development near Mexico City. In fact he joined a construction company near Lake Worth. Then in November 1958 the body of a young man was discovered in the Everglades and a forensic examination showed that it had been bound with tape similar to spools found at the Chillingworths' home the day after they disappeared. The body was identified as that of a moonshine runner, Lew Gene Harvey, who had been released on bail in the previous September. He was a known associate of Bobby Lincoln, who in turn was arrested. Harvey's wife told the police that her husband had been offered a job installing air-conditioners in West Palm Beach and that he had noted the man's licence plate number before leaving his home with him. When this was traced to John Lloyd, an alias of Holzapfel, at last the connection was made.

In May 1959 the police, who had been tipped off, watched a break-in at a house in Miami by two men who loaded a truck. It was stopped by the officers and in it, along with Holzapfel, were a hundred Army rifles, machine guns, ammunition and an anti-tank gun.

He received 15 years, but the conviction was overturned on technical grounds. By now the police had managed to put an undercover man into the Holzapfel-Peel set-up and Peel, who was now running an insurance company, asked him if he would kill his former colleague. Lincoln, arrested for his moonshine running, was also beginning to talk, naming Peel and Holzapfel. He was offered immunity if he agreed to give evidence against the former judge. Charges were then brought against Holzapfel for the murder of the Chillingworths, and on his first day in court he explained how it all happened.

Peel had been afraid of the consequences of a second appearance in front of Chillingworth and had asked Holzapfel and Lincoln to kill the judge. They had posed as yachtsmen and knocked on the judge's door with the story that a boat was in trouble and would he call the coastguard. They had taken the judge and his wife out to sea, both had been weighted and thrown overboard. The judge had managed to stay afloat and had been beaten with the butt of a shotgun before he sank. Holzapfel and Lincoln had been paid in dollar bills from the takings of the *bolita*.

Both gave evidence against Peel in a trial for the murder of Judge Chillingworth alone, and the pressmen watching the case believed by 11:1 that the jury would return a verdict without recommending mercy. They were wrong. By a majority the jury recommended mercy, which meant life imprisonment. Holzapfel, for his pains, was sentenced to death. In the second trial for the murder of Marjorie

Chillingworth, in exchange for another life sentence, Peel pleaded *nolo contendere*.

1 See *inter alia* the *New York Times*, 5, 12, 17, 18 September, 12 October 1930, 26, 27 June 1964 and 24 September 1969. With Oscar Fraley, Crater's wife – who died in 1969 – wrote a book on the case, *The Empty Robe*.
2 Camilo Weston Leyca in *American Weekly*, 23 September 1956. Stein was eventually executed on 9 July 1955. He and two others had been convicted and on 6 March 1952 their appeal had been rejected unanimously. Things had temporarily improved for them when the Supreme Court ordered a review of the case on 13 October 1952, but on 15 June 1953 the court upheld the original verdict by a majority of 6:3.

  Gordon was not the only girl to die during the Seabury inquiry. On 9 May 1930 Virginia Brannen, who was due to give evidence, was killed and her body thrown over the wall of a convent in the Yonkers. *Empire News*, 10 May 1930.
3 *New York Times*, 4 March 1931.
4 *New York Times*, 1 and 22 July 1931.
5 *New York Times*, 6 November 1931.
6 See Ernie Hunter, *The Chillingworth Murder Case*, p.12. For another account of the case see Jim Bishop, *The Murder Trial of Judge Peel*.

# 9 Davis and Schultz, George Morton Levy and Costello, O'Hare and Capone

J UST AS THE DISTRICT ATTORNEY TRAVERS JEROME'S real target had not been Abe Hummel but Charles Morse, so, twenty years later, the aim of Thomas Dewey had been focused on James J. Hines, the Tammany District leader, rather than the lawyer Julius Richard 'Dixie' Davis.

Davis, known as the Kid Mouthpiece of the Dutch Schultz mob, had been educated at Belleville High School in New Jersey before working in the Capitol National Bank while attending night classes at the New York Law School. After graduation he worked for the lawyer Lyman E. Warren, then moved on to work for Bondy & Schloss for about eight months before setting up practice on his own at 36 W 44th. Later he took Martin Weintraub into partnership.

Life was a struggle in mid-town Manhattan and he moved his office to 151st Street, opposite the new Twelfth District Magistrates' Court on Washington Heights. Now, after about six months and at a time when almost all the local operators were Afro-Americans, he began to pick up clients who ran Policy or Numbers games in Harlem. Although unlawful, the Policy racket was by no means then run by mobsters but rather by gamblers running an illegal business.[1] A tame lawyer was nevertheless essential to a Policy operation – to be on hand to appear in court and, in conjunction with the bail bondsmen, arrange bail immediately one of the operator's staff was arrested. Davis was just that man.

Bondsmen could bribe the police to draw up the charges in such a loose fashion that the defendant would be discharged at the trial and it was also possible, using political influences, to get to the judges. Additionally they had the award of cases to lawyers in their grasp, and Davis started working at $10 a case for a bondsman who kept $15 of the $25 fee paid by the client. Later, as Davis became more fashionable, he would increase his fees until he was taking 70 per cent. He was soon able to operate without the bondsmen and was taking the better part of $30,000 a year from one Cuban Policy banker, Alexander Pompez.[2]

It was Davis who had the foresight to suggest to George Weinberg, one of the most prominent of the then few white Policy bankers and a very junior partner of the legendary Arthur Flegenheimer (better known as Dutch Schultz), that the golden stream could be diverted into a massive racket. The connection between George Weinberg and Schultz came from George's brother Bo, one of Schultz's chief lieutenants and a man for whom Davis had an unhealthy regard:

> I became very fond of Bo, and when he took his hair down over a bottle of scotch and yarned about his murders it was like reading about the pirates in Treasure Island. Bo had committed more murders than any other man I ever knew, but even when he was drunk there never seemed to be an ounce of malice in him.[3]

In 1931 one of Davis' clients, Jo Ison – the inheritor by default of the empire of Henry Miro, who had been driven out of the rackets by Judge Samuel Seabury – was himself under attack from organised crime figures. Davis suggested that he look to Bo Weinberg for protection, and a weekly fee of $500 was agreed. Two years later Davis, as Schultz's lawyer, had moved to a floor of offices at 1450 Broadway where he was now employing five junior lawyers, and his weekly income from Policy cases alone was $500.

Once Weinberg began operations with Schultz he was able – with the latter's gunpower and connections resulting in some forty murders and six kidnappings – to eliminate the Afro-Americans as employers, converting them into employees, and so consolidate the independent Policy operators into what amounted to a monopoly. Curiously, one of the very few who successfully resisted the physical blandishments was a woman, Stephanie St Clair, known as the Marseilles Tigress.[4]

Arthur Flegenheimer (sometimes spelled with a double 'g') was the son of a German Jew who deserted the family, leaving young Arthur to a life of juvenile crime. Born on 6 August 1902, he grew up in the Bronx where he was a member of the Bergen gang of pickpockets and shoplifters and by the age of 20 had interests in selling beer, slot-machines, beer joints, restaurants, taxi companies and professional boxing, as well as the Numbers racket. In his entire career he acquired only one conviction when, in 1917, he was sentenced to 15 months for burglary.

On his release from prison Flegenheimer announced that henceforth he would be known as Dutch Schultz in tribute to the former leader of the Frog Hollow Gang, and he moved into the benefits of Prohibition.[5] He had his own brewery providing what was regarded as some of the worst beer in the Bronx, as well as an empire built on smuggling whisky from Canada and Europe. Much of his stock he hi-jacked. He went into the slot-machine business with Frank Costello and recruited Jack 'Legs' Diamond and Vincent 'Mad Dog' Coll, from the notorious Hell's Kitchen area, as his enforcers. Diamond was well established by this time and his smaller empire served to swell that of Schultz. Coll, along with his brother Peter, began his career as a beer delivery boy at $150 a week, working his way up through the ranks.

By 1930 Schultz, a much less appealing man than Al Capone, held New York in the same way that Capone did Chicago. His rivals were simply eliminated. He was also regarded as a pathological miser. It was said that:

> You can insult Arthur's girl, even steal her from him; spit in his face and push him around and he'd laugh it off. But don't steal even a dollar that belongs to him. You're dead if you do.[6]

Both Diamond and Coll tried to steal from Schultz. Even by the fairly lax gangland standards Coll had behaved badly. He had wanted a cut of the Schultz cake and with his brother, Pete, had started to lay out the groundwork for a rival business by hi-jacking his leader's beer trucks. He had tried to recruit Vincent Barelli and, when the man refused, shot him and his girlfriend Mary Smith. After he had been arrested for a violation of the Sullivan law, Schultz put up $10,000 bail and Coll rewarded him by jumping it. As a lesson Schultz had Peter Coll murdered. There followed the Schultz-Coll war.

With far less money and fire-power Coll managed to outwit Schultz for some time. Much of his revenue came from kidnapping Schultz's men and allies, particularly those from the Owney Madden gang, and ransoming them. In July 1932 he earned his nickname as he tried to machine-gun Anthony Trebino and other Schultz men on East 107th Street. Instead he killed five-year-old Michael Vengali.

Coll hired Samuel Leibowitz for his defence to the murder charge, and the great lawyer destroyed the principal witness against him: a self proclaimed ice-cream salesman, George Brecht, who in fact was a professional eye-witness. Coll was freed on a directed verdict.

To finance his defence Coll had kidnapped an Owney Madden man whom he ransomed for $30,000. The next year he tried blackmail once too often when he made a call to Madden from a telephone booth in a drugstore during which he threatened to kill him unless money was paid. He was seen making the call and was shot to death in the booth; although he had a tommy-gun with him he was cramped for space and unable to raise it in time. His killers, who were never prosecuted, were almost certainly the brothers Abe and George Weinberg.[7]

With his last rival eliminated, just as Capone controlled the politicians in Cicero so Schultz had his own in New York. It was through his efforts that William Copeland Dodge was returned as District Attorney and the white-haired James T. Hines became the Tammany Hall politician. But his success does not appear to have brought Schultz happiness. He became increasingly paranoid and aggressive, surrounding himself with guards he did not trust and women whom he believed were cheating on him sexually.

In the late afternoon of 2 March 1935 Davis was with Schultz in the Harmony Hotel in Cohoes, near Albany in upstate New York. 'Hotel' seems to have been something of a grand name because it was little more than a cobwebbed, decaying doss-house where Schultz maintained a first-floor suite. Also present was Jules Martin who looked after Schultz's restaurant interests and who was trying to explain where a sum of $70,000 had disappeared to – siphoned off by him from part of the $2 million he had extracted in protection money. Martin was explaining that he had only taken a more modest $20,000. It was then that Schultz shot him.

What I remember mostly now is Martin's moaning. At one moment he was shouting, protesting, arguing with the Dutchman in that loudmouthed way of his; and the next he was moaning, almost screaming, even louder than before. He folded slowly over a chair, and from his mouth the blood dripped to the floor.[8]

There cannot be too many lawyers who have witnessed their clients execute someone in cold blood, and Davis was quite properly horrified. For his part Schultz was apparently quite properly penitent.

'Dick, you must hate me for this,' he told me. For he realized what a horrible thing he had done, shooting down Julie right in front of me. I was not a mobster. I was a lawyer, a member of the Bar in good standing; and he knew there was not supposed to be any rough stuff when I was around.

Schultz sent another helpmate, Lulu Rosenkrantz, to make sure the hotel clerk was kept occupied while Davis left the room. While scurrying along the sidewalk 'right past the window of the room where Martin was', Davis reflected on his position – or, more probably, the ghost writer did so some four years later:

It is very unhealthy to be an eyewitness to a murder when a man like Schultz is the killer. To a man like him the only good witness is a dead witness. As I ran, I kept thinking of the mess I was in and I couldn't help longing for the days when I was just a Kid Mouthpiece, making lots of money as a shyster in the magistrate's court. Those had been the happy days.

Davis, in an effort to exculpate himself and preserve his status as a lawyer, said he left immediately. So far as he was concerned the shooting had occurred simply because Schultz was drunk.

As for the unfortunate Martin, his body, which had additionally been stabbed twelve times, was found the next afternoon on a road outside Troy, wrapped in a blanket. The cover-up was ingenious. Before its removal the body had unfortunately dripped some blood into the cracks of the hotel floor, so to confuse the issue Schultz had Rosenkrantz stand on the spot and another henchman, Danny Dale, hit him on the nose so that it would bleed into the crack. Dale broke Rosenkrantz's nose and a doctor was called to attend to it, so providing a witness to the cause of the bloodstain.

It was quite clear that there was still a mess to be cleared up and, far from Davis going to the police or saying that was the end of his acting for Schultz, he telephoned the politician James Hines who was said to be able to control 5 out of the 25 Tammany Hall votes. Hines could place his supporters in judicial office and pick his own District Attorney. Nevertheless he was in the hole to Schultz to the tune of $1,000 a week and when he was told by Davis to catch the 6.20 train to Albany he caught the 6.20 train to Albany. Davis, the Kid Mouthpiece, had organised things:

> I cultivated Jimmy Hines from the beginning. I soon learned that to run an organised mob you've got to have a politician. You have heard about the suspected link between organized crime and politics. Well, I became the missing link.

Hines was a third-generation politician steeped in Tammany Hall tradition. His grandfather had worked under Boss William Tweed and his father, who was a farrier, had served Richard Croker in the 1890s. In 1907 he was elected alderman of the 11th Assembly district, and in 1913 he became chief clerk of the Board of Aldermen drawing $5000 annually. He served in the First World War and, against advice, ran for borough president; although he lost, he had served notice of his political intentions. Once Prohibition came Hines sold his services to bootleggers and Numbers runners alike. His tariff was stiff and, for example, he charged $500 a month to allow gambling in the back room of a Harlem club. It was only one of many such services. He became a friend of Lucky Luciano and wintered with him in that gangster's home-from-home in Hot Springs, Arkansas. By the 1930s he was earning between $500 and $1,000 a week from Schultz, and after Schultz's death he hooked up with his old friend Luciano and the increasingly powerful Frank Costello.

Whatever Hines accomplished on that occasion in Albany, it was not sufficient to satisfy the local District Attorney because Davis was hauled before a Grand Jury, an experience he passed with such flying colours that Schultz told him, 'There's no one in my mob I can depend on the way I can on you.'

The killing of Martin was not the only time Davis found Schultz in a murderous mood when he believed he had been swindled. He also told the story that once at the Bridgeport, Conn. hideout he awoke to hear voices say that, 'Dickie's got to go. I'll give it to him tonight.' Davis ran from the hotel but, realising there was nowhere to hide, he returned. However, he had a brewery in his own name and he told Schultz that if he was killed the brewery would go to his relative. It was, he said, a strategy to keep himself alive, because the mean Schultz would never allow himself to be cheated out of the brewery. Schultz relented, saying he would then kill Bo instead.

Now Schultz was charged with income tax evasion. Many were wise enough to know how to circumvent this problem, the first requirement being to move the trial out of town. In 1934 Schultz, under the aegis of Davis, surrendered himself to the authorities in upstate New York. The second requirement was to create an atmosphere favourable to the defendant amongst the locals who would be called to jury service. First he paid a PR man $10,000 to set the scene. Then drinks were on the house for children and adults alike and, before the re-trial after the jury had disagreed on a cast-iron case against him, he hired a dance hall for the townsfolk. In 1935 the Dutchman was found not guilty.

Back in town he found that Italian interests had moved in on his rackets. In his absence the so-called crime syndicate had been formed. Its founders were: Frank Costello, mainly interested in gambling; Lucky Luciano, whose specialities were prostitution and, more profitably, drugs; Joseph Doto, also known as Joe Adonis, who had particular interests in labour and political rackets; Bugsy Siegel and Meyer Lansky, the latter then considered along with fellow member Louis Lepke Buchalter as an enforcer rather than financial genius.[9]

Schultz, regarded as becoming increasingly unstable and under threat from Luciano, was not invited to join. Now, in his absence upstate, Luciano and Vito Genovese had taken over a large proportion of the empire and, worse, had seduced his most trusted lieutenant, Abe 'Bo' Weinberg, who disappeared shortly after his former employer's return. It was thought that he had been killed in a Manhattan hotel and his body, encased in cement, had been dropped in the East River. The hotel room had then been re-papered.

Schultz's death followed his announcement that he would kill the Special Prosecutor of Organised Crime, Thomas Dewey, who was in the process of breaking up his slot-machine empires. Lawyers and journalists were regarded as out of bounds in those days and when Schultz put the proposition to Johnny Torrio and Luciano the syndicate refused to sanction it, however inconvenient the talented Michigan lawyer was becoming. Schultz had to go.

He had already been involved in the killing of one police officer, Danny Iamascia, whom Schultz had seen following him on a Manhattan street. His bodyguard, thinking the policeman was a Coll man, had opened fire. Through the machinations of Davis, Schultz was bailed and the charges were later dropped. The death of a police officer could be explained away. To kill a prosecuting lawyer was, however, beyond the pale.

The Dutchman was killed on 23 October 1935 in the Palace Chop House, Newark. With him were his wizard accountant Otto 'Abbadabba' Berman, who had devised an improved way of tampering with Policy Numbers pay-outs and who was opposed to the killing of Dewey, and gunmen Abe Landau and the broken-nosed Lulu Rosenkrantz, who were not. Their killers were Emmanuel 'Mendy' Weiss, Charles 'The Bug' Workman, and a man named Piggy who has never been identified. Workman shot Schultz while he was in the washroom and then killed the others. He then returned to the washroom and took Schultz's money.

All the men died in the hours following the attack. Schultz survived the longest, dying at 8.40 p.m. after making a series of what seemed to be incoherent rambling statements in front of a police stenographer who was hoping he would name his killers. He is reputed to have said, amongst other things, 'Please crack down on the Chinaman's friends and Hitler's commander', 'Mother is the best' and 'Don't let Satan draw you too fast'.

But Dixie Davis survived on the streets for another two years until on 14 July 1937 he was indicted along with George Weinberg as part of a Policy racket conspiracy. By this time the once fashionable Broadway lawyer was hiding with Weinberg and his show-pony girlfriend, Hope Dare, in a cabin in the Adirondacks. Their tormentor was Thomas E. Dewey, and they were in effect hostages for Jimmy Hines. At this stage neither was that worried. All they had to do was to ride out the forthcoming election in November when they believed Grover Whalen would defeat Fiorello LaGuardia in the mayoral election and there would be a more favourable Attorney General in place who would quash the indictment. It was a bad miscalculation.

Davis had already appeared before the Bar Committee in New York and had succeeded in having evidence obtained by a wire-tap excluded. The referee had reported that Davis could be allowed to continue in practice, but the Bar's Appeals' Committee reversed his decision. The trio moved on; Davis and

Hope Dare to Philadelphia and George Weinberg first to Minneapolis, where he tried to set up a Numbers bank before rejoining the others.

On 2 February 1938 the police arrived at the flat. Hope was also charged and Davis, in exchange for her release, agreed to waive extradition to New York. His bail was set at $75,000 which he had no chance of raising. He remained in the Tombs, the prison off Center Street, where George Weinberg suggested that they should turn state's evidence. For a time Davis, according to his version of events, remained staunch. He believed that in law a Policy was not a lottery and he would be discharged on a technicality. On the other hand, he was becoming increasingly annoyed that Hines would not give the nod to people who would put up the bail money. Finally, however, when Hines told Hope Dare he was under no obligation to Davis and Weinberg agreed to turn state's evidence, Davis followed. Hines was arrested and charged.

At first Dewey had Davis – guarded by his assistant George Horan and others from his office – moved from hotel to hotel, a defence against rumours that the Purple Gang from Detroit had been hired to kill both him and Weinberg. Eventually it was decided that a house should be rented on Long Island. It had a staircase which could be lowered and raised, making it in effect a tree-house, and there they lived under guard for the better part of a year. There were certain perks: Hope could and did visit on a daily basis.

Davis wanted to have a fresh suit every other day and a round 180-mile trip was made to keep him happy. He believed one of his family would be taken as a hostage against his giving evidence.

Of Martin's killing Davis told Horan, 'I had never seen a murder before this one. I couldn't sleep for a week.'

> I believed him [said Horan]. He was a cowardly little man, vain as a peacock with the morals of a package thief. But he never lied to us.[10]

As is standard American practice, now that he had him as a witness Dewey coached Davis in the way he should give his evidence:

> 'Of course you realise I want you to tell me everything you can remember but if after trying to recollect a fact you should fail, drop

it there. If you are in any doubt about any fact we will resolve that doubt in Hines' favour.'

Right then I knew I was in the presence of a great guy. That wasn't the way we had prepared witnesses on my side of the fence.[11]

When it came to the great day Davis was pleased with the way in which he gave his evidence:

... it was the easiest testifying I ever did. I had nothing to hide this time. No corners to cut, no fear of contradicting myself. I came through all right even though I was up against a most able cross-examiner.

The newspapers saw a slightly different trial: 'Gang Counsel "Forgets" Knowledge of Law; Rebuked by Court for Unethical Answers'; 'Perjury Before Juries and in Tax Cases Readily Admitted by Schultz's lawyer'. There were also adverse comments on his 'moral regeneration'.[12]

In his evidence Davis described how meetings with Schultz took place at Davis's mother's flat at 898 West End Avenue and how he paid Hines cash 15–20 times. When payments from Schultz slowed down or even failed, he himself supplemented the money from his own pocket.

When it came to it all the good work was to no avail. Dewey asked one question too many about a co-lateral poultry fraud and the judge, Ferdinand Pecora, declared a mistrial. It was six months before the re-trial would take place and, during that time, both Davis and Weinberg – along with another witness, Policy banker 'Big' Henry Schoenhaus – lived under guard in their safe house in Westchester. Then came the news that Louis Cohen (who 20 years earlier had shot Kid Dropper) and Danny Fields had both been killed. Weinberg, suffering from stomach ulcers, believed the reason for this was that Fields was himself assisting the District Attorney and that, at the end of the trial, both of them would be marked men.

Just before he was due to give evidence in the second trial Weinberg killed himself. On 30 January 1939 Joseph Kaitz, who had been assisting Dewey for some three years, left a gun in his coat pocket and at 1.50 p.m. Weinberg shot himself in the head. He died two hours later in hospital. The authorities maintained it was suicide but lawyer George E. Mulry, who practised in Mineola, Long Island, telegrammed Governor Lehman:

> Informed believable source that Weinberg's fingerprints are not on revolver of Dewey hireling. Check. Confiscate revolver for confirmation.

When pressed Mulry would not disclose the name of his informant, but he was correct in saying there were no fingerprints. Dewey, who claimed that this was 'crackpot stuff', maintained that he had run an immediate inquiry and that only one smudged fingerprint had been obtained. In only one instance in the last twenty years had fingerprints been found on a revolver used in a murder or suicide, he maintained. This, apparently, was because of the checked grip on the gun. Mulry clearly had good information and retaliated by saying that there were no powder deposits on Weinberg's hands, but he was fighting a losing cause.

> Davis could not understand it (the death of George) saying, 'Why did he do it?' This was the pitiful side of Davis – he never fully realised the enormity of his crimes. Could you tell such a man that dead men have a way of perching on a murderer's shoulders?[13]

At first the news was kept from the jury, but later Weinberg's evidence from the first trial was read to them and, according to reports, they tired after the first hundred pages of a total four hundred.

This time Hines was convicted in short order. He went to Sing Sing in 1939, where he worked in the prison greenhouse before being paroled on 1 September 1944 on condition that he did not engage in politics of any kind. He died in March 1957. Davis was given a year's imprisonment which he had effectively served.

> So that's my story. By the time you read this I will be free again, facing the world.
>
> But I won't be alone. Hope [Dare] will be with me. We are going to be starting out from behind the eight ball. Please wish us good fortune.[14]

They married and, like so many others, went West to start a new life. For a time they did enjoy some good fortune but they were divorced in 1944. However, they had prospered financially. By the time Hope Dare filed for a division of property they owned an ice-cream plant, a home in Hollywood and a chain of malted milk shops.

There were good reasons for Weinberg to have killed himself – his health, his fears for his safety as a stool-pigeon and the possibility that he would be seriously investigated in connection with the murder of Schultz himself. Fearing, no doubt, that one of his star witnesses might be spooked, Dewey had persuaded the District Attorney not to interview him on the subject until after his evidence against Hines had been completed. Why should anyone wish to kill Weinberg? It would depend upon the side for which a participant was really playing. One rather far-fetched theory is that it was feared that Weinberg might be about to change his testimony, which might have ruined the prosecution's case.

Whatever the answer, Weinberg was buried in a ceremony attended by two dozen people in Queens. The press was not welcome and one mourner smashed a photographer's camera before he was dragged away. Davis was not present to see his old friend put to rest.[15]

As for Dewey, his subsequent career is a curious story. Initially a hero for his disposal of Lucky Luciano and others, he rather fell from grace. His prosecution of Luciano made Dewey a celebrity and set him on the road which led nearly to the White House but, in retrospect, it appears to have been a fairly shabby affair with a string of witnesses mostly addicted to drugs testifying against Luciano and, according to Leonard Katz, ready to say anything for their next fix.[16]

Charles 'Lucky' Luciano, a small man with delicately shaped hands and feet, was born in poverty near Palermo in 1897, coming to New York in 1906. It was at school that he put together his first protection racket, defending – after first beating them – young Jewish boys at a penny a day. From there on it was a short step to being a leading member of the Five Points youth gang and then on to peddling drugs. The Harrison Act of 1914 had effectively ended the legal opium-based medicine trade – marijuana would not be made illegal for nearly twenty years – and there was now a black market. He was arrested in 1916 and he now served a year in prison. He would claim that he never touched drugs again, but in fact he was caught selling morphine in 1923 when the police found both that drug and heroin in his home. He escaped arrest by informing on a dealer at nearby 163 Mulberry Street where there was a trunk full of narcotics.

By the 1930s Luciano had effectively become one of the great *capo di capos* in American crime. Operating from the Waldorf-

Astoria, where he kept a suite under the name of Charles Rose, and the Claridge Hotel as well as a small office on Broadway, it was said there was no gambling enterprise, no dock racket, no Garment District extortion racket conducted without Luciano's authority and cut. There is no doubt whatsoever of his pre-eminent position after the assassination of Schultz but, as that former leader had found Thomas Dewey to be a trial and tribulation, so did Luciano whose Achilles heel was trafficking in women. In 1935 he was charged with compelling prostitutes, a trial in which he was defended by George Morton Levy.

Levy, the son of immigrant parents whose father was the proprietor of a small Long Island hotel, began his working life as an office boy in the law firm of Rosen & Eno on Park Row, Manhattan. He was another talented advocate who seems, particularly in his earlier career, to have been completely unbusinesslike so far as accounting was concerned. His lack of financial records would almost cause his downfall in front of the Kefauver Committee when he would be accused of associating with gangsters.

He began his career as a qualified lawyer in Freeport in 1912, mixing law with real estate and prospering at neither. One of Levy's first criminal cases was the defence of Judge Corydon Norton who sat as a justice in Hempstead and was accused of embezzling some $20,000 in motoring fines over a five-year period. He had, he maintained, been accounting properly; cashing a cheque, putting the money in an envelope and sending it to the state treasurer. He had never received an acknowledgement but, he claimed, he had continued to post the money in cash. One of the problems he faced was that with other non-motoring fines he mailed a cheque to the town treasurer.

On the plus side was his good character. There was no evidence of heavy drinking or an expensive mistress. He lived in modest circumstances with his wife and family and his docket showed the fines he had imposed. There was no suggestion that he had been falsifying his accounts. Simply, the money had disappeared.

Levy was helped by a representative from the state treasurer's office who was extremely hostile and personally offensive to him. When the judge intervened to protect Levy the witness turned on him. By the end of the case Levy had, with the unwitting help of the witness, made it appear that Judge Norton was the victim.[17]

The jury acquitted Norton and, curiously, some months later the state treasurer committed suicide. Levy recalled:

> I was pretty cocky about it and then the state treasurer committed suicide. That was a shock to me. I had thought I was being clever in handling that treasury assistant and now the thought suddenly struck me that he might have been stalling and answering in that shifty way because he knew the state treasurer was guilty ... Deep down I hadn't a bit of confidence in Norton's story, and now there was a very good chance that it might have been true all along. It taught me two things I've never forgotten: (a) never be too cocksure about anything and (b) conduct every defence as if you believed your client's word implicitly. It's the only ethical thing to do in any event, and if you don't you may end up being a dope.[18]

Over the years Levy successfully defended in a number of murder cases, often involving women who were thought to have disposed of erring husbands and lovers. His practice expanded and he equally successfully defended figures on the edge of organised crime including Dubert L. Armstrong and James Brown for harbouring repeating voters in the highly charged Nassau County election of 1929. Then on a Friday in 1936 he was invited by Moses Polakoff, the lawyer for Lucky Luciano, to defend him in a trial which began the following Monday. Before he accepted this high-profile case he consulted his then partners, Leo Fishel and Elvin Edwards. Fishel asked:

> Are you a lawyer or aren't you a lawyer? We're a firm specialising in trial work, and this is a trial like any other trial. I don't care who is the defendant.

Edwards was out of town and Morton Levy wanted his opinion as well. Fishel undertook to obtain it, saying that it had better be the correct one or he would have his resignation on his desk on Monday morning.[19]

> However, this was a case in which the theory of guilt by association would eventually do Levy a great deal of harm. He charged Luciano his standard fee of $2,500 with a $500 daily retainer.

According to Harry J. Anslinger, former United States Commissioner of Narcotics, Luciano had used the tried and tested method of the pimp in recruiting his stable. He took out young working-class girls, waitresses, manicurists, shop-girls, and gave them a good time before making them pay for their release from their drab existences. He also made them pay for the heroin to which he had introduced them, turning them over to his subordinates. By 1935 it was estimated that he was taking a cut of the earnings of 5,000 prostitutes nationwide.[20]

His downfall came when it grew apparent that the same bondsmen and lawyers were representing the prostitutes, who all told the same story when they were arrested – usually that they were poor girls from out of New York who had been visiting a friend. Fines were paid by the bondsmen and in the background was the shadowy figure of the disbarred lawyer Abe Karp. The trail led through Ralph Liguori, a known pimp, Benny Spiller, a loan shark, and a financier, Tommy 'The Bull' Pennochio, to David Bertillo, a man known to have contacts with Luciano.

On 1 February 1936 a raid was made on brothels across New York, collecting over 100 prostitutes, pimps and madams along with Liguori, Pennochio and Bertillo. Luciano sensibly absented himself to Hot Springs, Arkansas, a town with Mob connections and an administration known to be sympathetic to such as himself. He was seen there walking with Herbert Akers, the Chief of Detectives, and arrested by Federal Agents. Bailed in the sum of $5,000 by Owney Madden, he was rearrested and lodged, with all possible comforts, in the local prison from where he mounted a long fight against extradition. His undoing was to offer the Arkansas State Attorney $50,000 to let him remain in the state. He was promptly returned to New York where he posted bail, this time in the sum of $350,000.[21]

For some long time in the trial there was no mention of him but the overall picture of the degradation of life as a prostitute – earning $25 a week for servicing dozens of men daily in what amounted to a slaughterhouse – had its effect on the jury. Then came evidence linking Luciano from 'Cokey' Flo Brown, who told how Levy's client said of the women, 'First you got to sit on them. Then you got to step on them. Talking won't do no good. You got to put the screws on.' Another witness, Nancy Presser, told how she had fallen from being the mistress of such figures as Dutch Schultz and Joe Adonis to working in a $2 crib in Harlem. She had, she said, been befriended by Luciano and had spent nights talking with him – no sex – at his Waldorf Astoria suite.

Levy did a fine job with the material in his possession. For example, Presser was unable to describe Luciano's suite accurately, explain how no one saw her arrive or leave or even to say whereabouts in New York the hotel was positioned.

Indeed it is said that of a poll of journalists attending the trial, 13 were for an acquittal and one for a conviction. Perhaps the public indignation which accompanies large-scale pimping, rather than the quality of the evidence, was sufficient to convict Luciano and his subordinates on 62 counts. He was sent to Dannemora, then known as the Siberia of the North, a maximum-security prison in upstate New York, near the Canadian border, to serve a sentence of 30–60 years. As was standard practice Levy handed over the appeal to Martin Conboy, a leading Catholic layman who never attracted the stigma which attached to Levy for his defence. From then on, however, Levy would always be referred to as Luciano's lawyer.

After the trial it was only right that the witnesses should be rehabilitated, and both Brown and Presser went to Europe for that purpose. Over the years Luciano's lawyers obtained statements that they had given false evidence and that they had been coached by the prosecution, but the Court of Appeal, as is so often the case, would have nothing of the recantation.[22]

Perhaps Dewey's crowning triumph was his prosecution of Louis Lepke Buchalter and his subsequent refusal to do a deal with the gangster who – in return for a commutation of the death sentence imposed for his murder of garment district trucker Joe Rosen – wanted to implicate Sidney Hillman, then president of the Amalgamated Clothing Workers and one of President Franklin D. Roosevelt's senior labour advisers. Dewey's ethical stance was hailed by the right-wing press. In 1944 he stood unsuccessfully as Republican candidate against Roosevelt.

Dewey's image suffered as the years went by. He refused to appear before the Kefauver Crime Commission, citing ill-health. The Committee had wanted to question him about Luciano's pardon and why gambling had been allowed to flourish in Saratoga where Meyer Lansky was said to have operated unmolested. It is sometimes suggested that he had convicted Lucky Luciano on perjured evidence and had commuted his sentence because he feared exposure. He had then spent taxpayers' money on a cover-up. In *Reminiscence*, Charles Poletti suggests that Dewey took pay-offs from Luciano.

Unfortunately in the 1960s Dewey became a stockholder in Mary Carter Paints which had interests in Luciano's old friend Meyer Lansky's gambling resorts in the Bahamas. The connection was exposed in the *Wall Street Journal* and won that year's Pulitzer prize. It was said of Dewey 'From racketbuster to racketbacker'. He died in 1971.

Clearly all was not well in the prosecutorial ranks in the 1930s and 1940s. For example, just how successful were the efforts of former judge William O'Dwyer, the Brooklyn District Attorney, in clearing up organised crime in the first years of the War? An internal note on the work of the Kings County District Attorney from F.L. Strong, dated 21 October 1941, lists the cases against the various defendants and then adds:

> Outside of his work on the murder rings O'Dwyer appears to have accomplished little in prosecuting rackets.
> In addition to the Murder Ring and union extortioners, the only rackets referred to in O'Dwyer's annual report for 1940 are card swindling, shylocking around the Navy Yard and dealing in stolen cars. So far as I am aware, no action by him against any other rackets has been reported in the papers.[23]

And just where did O'Dwyer stand in relation to those he prosecuted? Clearly something was wrong in the Brooklyn District Attorney's office, but it was never satisfactorily established just where the blame lay. When in the 1950s efforts were made to interview O'Dwyer on the subject of the death of Abe Reles, who had dived out of a window of a building where he was being guarded by police before he testified against Albert Anastasia, O'Dwyer wrote declining to return for questioning but said he would be happy to be interviewed in Mexico.

Immediately after the death of Reles the case against Anastasia died as well. Moreover, the 'wanted' cards for Anastasia, 'Dandy' Jack Parisi and Tony Romeo, wanted on yet another killing, had been removed from the files of the Police Investigation Bureau.[24] A 1945 Grand Jury was never quite able to get to the truth, but it would seem that they were removed on the authority of the Chief Clerk, James Moran. Had Moran not been well over 6' and weighing 200 lbs, it would have been possible to call him a shadowy figure. O'Dwyer had been a magistrate in 1929 and Moran had been his clerk. As O'Dwyer progressed through the judicial and political ranks so Moran came with him. Decisions in respect of cases to go before the Grand Jury or to be discontinued were taken by this unqualified man.

When O'Dwyer became Mayor after a bitter fight with Fiorello LaGuardia, Moran was appointed First Deputy Fire Commissioner at a salary of $10,000. Just before O'Dwyer, whose mayordom had not been a success, resigned and became the Ambassador to Mexico, he appointed Moran to be City Water Supply Commissioner at the improved salary of $15,000 a year for life. In O'Dwyer's time as Mayor, political decisions of any significance had to be filtered through Moran. Unfortunately he did not last in office long enough to collect his $15,000. There was evidence that he had leaned on gamblers, demanding cash contributions to help O'Dwyer's 1948 mayoralty campaign, and in June 1951 he was convicted of perjury regarding his relations with Numbers operator Louis Webber. He resigned.[25]

The 1945 Grand Jury fairly laced into O'Dwyer:

William O'Dwyer testified that his chief concern and paramount object was a conviction for murder of Anastasia, because Anastasia was the leader and most prominent gangster in the Brooklyn Underworld; that not a single murder in organized crime was committed in Brooklyn without Anastasia's permission and approval.

We find every case against Anastasia was abandoned, neglected or pigeonholed.

We find that William O'Dwyer as District Attorney ... failed and neglected to complete a single prosecution against Anastasia.[26]

Dixie Davis recounts a conversation Hines had with Edward P. Mulrooney, the former Police Commissioner. Mulrooney asked Hines why he dealt with an Underworld character and Hines replied:

'Ed, you know we need those fellows on election day and we can't forget them between elections.' There it was, out of Jimmy's own mouth, the alliance between the underworld and politics.[27]

And essential partners were their respective lawyers.

Meanwhile Frank Costello had continued to flourish. In 1934, however, with the unwelcome attentions of Dewey and LaGuardia, Costello was forced to move his centre of operations from New York to Louisiana. Determined to loosen the grip Costello and his gaming machines held on New Yorkers' purse strings, in a dramatic and well-publicised move LaGuardia seized and destroyed a large number of the machines which belonged to his one-time supporter. Costello moved down South invited, so the story goes, by the Kingfish, Huey Long, Governor of Louisiana, to finance his welfare programme. In the way in which history is always being revised this account is now challenged.[28]

In the standard and generally accepted version of events, in the spring of 1935 around 1,000 slot-machines had been installed in downtown New Orleans. They were under the day-to-day control of Dandy Phil Kastel. A Costello-Kastel firm, the Pelican Novelty Company, was formed as a holding company. It had two functions. Incorporated under a charter which devoted some of the profits to charity, it could benefit from certain Louisiana tax and other laws, and secondly, with Meyer Lansky's brother Jake and Kastel as officers, neither Costello nor the Kingfish needed to appear on the notepaper. According to one source Long's take was $20,000 a month, stashed in a tin box in the Roosevelt Hotel, New Orleans.[29]

With the assassination of Long on 8 September 1935 there was need for a re-think. Fortunately Costello and Kastel had bought powerful friends amongst prominent New Orleans businessmen. Business went on as before, except there were now different hands receiving the winnings from the machines.

It is perhaps even more difficult to believe that George Morton Levy did not know all this and a great deal more about Costello and his reputation when he involved him in the security for the Roosevelt Raceway trotting track. In 1932 Levy had been involved with greyhound racing on the Mineola Fair Grounds in Nassau County. He had persuaded the courts – the idea was not his own but was based on a Florida decision – that the option to purchase a winning dog was not a bet. The option was $2, and if it won or was placed the punter could exercise the option and buy the dog at a fixed price. If he did not exercise the option it would be repurchased at the figures on the tote board by the grandstand. Those who asked to place a bet instead of purchasing an option at the window were excluded from the track. Litigation conducted between Levy for the track and the District Attorney ran until 1937, when a Bill to legalise dog-racing was vetoed by the Governor. Morton Levy then turned his attention to harness racing, or trotting as we know it.

It was not until after the Second World War and relaxation in fuel restrictions that evening harness racing took off in a big way, and one problem it faced immediately was the presence of organised crime in the form of illegal bookmakers. Ben

Downing, a Quaker in his early seventies and the Commissioner for Harness Racing, was responsible for the tracks in New York City. He became convinced that bookmakers were operating at the Roosevelt track, and no amount of persuasion by Morton Levy could change his mind. Told that there were 75 police on duty who had not been able to find a single illegal bookmaker, he replied that this was because the police and the bookmakers were in league together. He hired special agents of his own and when they reported that bookmakers were indeed working the grounds he told Morton Levy that he would refuse to issue a licence to the Roosevelt Raceway. It was then that Levy proposed he should employ Frank Costello. According to Morton Levy's partner, Downing said he had never heard of the man and Levy enthused:

> According to the newspapers Costello has tremendous influence with all the bookmakers in New York. If that's true he knows them and might be able to scare the bookmakers away.[30]

There was never any attempt to conceal Costello's participation and he was paid $15,000 a year. The cheques went through the books and apparently this satisfied Downing. Levy maintained that there were no bookmakers to be frightened away and the whole exercise was a purely cosmetic one for the benefit of the Commissioner.

Those with a cynical turn of mind might argue first, what was an upstanding lawyer like Levy doing hiring the leading gangster in New York? By the time Levy appointed Costello as Bookmaker-finder General the papers had covered the Aurelio scandal; the *New York Times* had carried a story that he was one of the financiers of the drug trade and Joe Valachi, the Mafia supergrass, had told the McClellan Committee in 1948 that Costello had warned that anyone dealing with drugs would have to face a Family trial. Costello may genuinely have been against drugs but he was also genuinely the top *mafioso* of the period. Morton Levy's explanation of how little he knew of him simply does not stand any sort of scrutiny.

That apart, cynics might also argue that the payments were being extorted by Costello. In a way it is as if the Jockey Club had hired the Krays to look after Newmarket. A third explanation offered by Leonard Katz is that Costello was being paid for his potential political influence. Harness tracks could be closed down almost at the whim of the state's legislature and

Costello had many state legislators on his books. It is inconceivable that Levy did not know this.[31] But, for the time being, everyone including the Commissioner was happy. Costello declared his $15,000 in his 1949 tax returns.

In 1950 the books of the Roosevelt Raceway were examined by the Treasury Department and given a clean bill of health. By now, however, Costello's activities were garnering greater attention and the Treasury Department's report was passed to the fledgling Special Committee to Investigate Organised Crime in Interstate Commerce. Over a period of months the Committee travelled to the major cities in the United States, calling witnesses to give evidence before them. On 12 March 1951 George Morton Levy was to be the first witness in New York; the Committee wanted to question him about his relationship with Costello.

Levy first realised something was seriously wrong when he asked if his appearance could be adjourned and was told certainly, the Committee would wait until he was ready, but he would still be the first witness.

Basically, so far as Levy was concerned, the Commission wished to inquire into four things. First, that he had been a golf-playing friend of Costello and Frank Erickson; secondly, that he had hired James Watson, Erickson's son-in-law, to work in connection with Levy's racing interests; thirdly, that he had hired Steve Moro at Costello's request also to work at the Raceway; and finally the question of the $60,000 paid to Costello over a four-year period. Erickson, described as a bookmaker, had taken over the gambling interests of Arnold Rothstein, for whom he had worked, when Rothstein was shot in 1928. Throughout his life he was the corporate face of crime.

Levy acknowledged that he knew Erickson and particularly Costello who had played golf at Lakefield, Fresh Meadow and Pomonock with him. In fact his friendship with Costello went back to 1931 when Levy's son, young George, had been in a motorcar accident and became paralysed from the waist down. Morton Levy was in difficulties over paying the hospital bills until, apparently as a simple gesture of friendship, Costello – without being asked – passed him $2,500 in Lindy's restaurant on Broadway which eased his financial troubles. Levy had repaid the money six weeks later. From then on Levy considered himself to be in Costello's moral debt.

The questioning of Levy by Senator Charles Tobey of New Hampshire concentrated particularly on the $60,000, with the additional problem of a $7,000 survey fee paid to Watson. Moro had apparently merely used Costello's name to apply for a change of job at the Raceway. In retrospect it is apparent that the questioning was a fishing and blackening expedition rather than the Committee having anything substantial with which to back up their beliefs. Finally Levy delivered his best thrust:

> *Levy*: Well, I would really like to have you express your idea of what you think the payment to Costello was for, and give me an opportunity to reply.
> *Tobey*: Perhaps I will, before we get through.

But he never did.

Two further points arose. First, there had been a tap on Costello's telephone and, according to the transcript, he had been heard asking Levy to get him admittance to the Raceway and Levy had called Costello 'Boss'. There was also a reference to 'jeopardising the bookmakers'. Despite lengthy running around in circles it was never clear that the tape had been transcribed properly. The reference to admission to the track referred to the Pinkerton Detective Agency's policy of refusing admission to anyone they considered to be undesirable, coupled with their refusal to be liable for any law suit which might follow. The 'boss' might have been Costello referring to Levy as boss and asking, if he was, why he could not get his friend entrance. Levy suggested that jeopardising the bookmakers was a mistranscription and that it should be 'jeopardised by bookmakers'. The second and more important question was a loan of $10,000 made to the track in 1942. Levy offered to look up his records, but the Committee took the view that he was prevaricating. In fact he had forgotten that he had borrowed the money from his mother. Affidavits were submitted and the Committee grudgingly withdrew its allegations and apologised for any injustice Levy might have suffered.

> It is apparent ... that you did a very inadequate job in presenting your side of the controversy to the committee when you appeared before us in New York. You assumed that many things were known that were not known. Some inferences and accusations were made which were unanswered.[32]

Later in the inquiry when questioned by Senator Charles Tobey, Costello adopted a robust attitude to the question of the

$60,000. He said he knew nothing about harness racing either at Roosevelt or any other racetrack. Indeed the approach from Morton Levy came out of the blue.

> *Tobey*: Well, you were paid sixty thousand dollars a year: is that right?
> *Costello*: That's right.
> *Tobey*: But you did take sixty thousand dollars for doing nothing?
> *Costello*: That's right I did.
> *Tobey*: Isn't that kind of synonymous with taking candy from a child?
> *Costello*: No. I know a lot of lawyers that get a fifty thousand dollars fee that's only worth fifteen hundred dollars.
> *Tobey*: We aren't talking about lawyers.
> *Costello*: Then why talk about me?

Following the Kefauver Committee's hearings, trotting scandals were now big newspaper stories and Levy's position was not helped by the killing of Tommy Lewis (labour czar at the Yonkers track) by Snakes Ryan in an apartment house on E 191st. It did not matter that the shooting was in relation to building service welfare funds rather than racketeering at the track where Lewis controlled the pari-mutuel clerks and other employees.

Matters were made worse by an article in *Life* magazine, 'The Great Trotting Scandal', in which Levy was named as the Mr Big of harness racing and brought up his association with Luciano, Costello and Erickson as well as his ingenious defence of the purchase options at the Mineola track.[33] The Moreland Commission into harness racing followed and questioned the Roosevelt Raceway's relationship with Bill De Koning, the labour czar of Long Island. De Koning had a bar and grill from which he ran the Mule Club; $6 a week was charged to members for a party and membership of the Club was compulsory for all union members at the Roosevelt track. Levy gave evidence that he had repeatedly tried to stop this neat form of extortion. In response to complaints about Levy's profit-sharing arrangement with the track, he agreed to give up his agreement and work only as legal counsel to the track. Additionally the Raceway gave up its shares in a company designed to buy Yonkers and so provide a trotting monopoly for Roosevelt.

Morton Levy's obituary in the *New York Times* suggests that over the years people forgot his association with Costello and in any event forgave it. He became the Grand Old Man of Trotting and was inducted into the Hall of Fame of the Trotter at Goshen in July 1967. He died at the age of 89 on 19 July 1977. When asked about his representation of Luciano he would reply, 'It's not who you represent. It's how you represent them.'

After the appeals of Luciano had been rejected the lawyer who had instructed Levy, Moses Polakoff, turned to working for his client behind the scenes.[34] Luciano had what, in other circumstances, might be called a 'good war'. In 1943 at the request of the US Navy he was transferred from the maximum security prison Dannemora to Great Meadows penitentiary; he was seemingly helping in the preparation of the invasion of Sicily. A decade later Estes Kefauver tended to doubt the value of the help and questioned exactly what deal had been made with Luciano, who had clearly expected his freedom:

> During the War there was a lot of hocus-pocus about allegedly valuable services that Luciano, then a convict, was supposed to have furnished the military authorities in connection with plans for the invasion of his native Sicily. We dug into this and obtained a number of conflicting stories.
>
> One story which we heard from Moses Polakoff, attorney for Meyer Lansky, was that Naval Intelligence had sought out Luciano's aid and had asked Polakoff to be the intermediary.
>
> However, that version did not totally conform with the recollection of Federal Narcotics Agent, George White. His version was that he had been approached on Luciano's behalf by a drug smuggler, Augusto Del Grazio, who claimed he was acting on behalf of two lawyers, and also by Frank Costello who was heading the Free Luciano movement. Del Grazio had said that Luciano had many contacts in the Underworld and was a principal member of the Mafia. The deal was that Luciano would use his Mafia contacts in Sicily to assist undercover American agents.[35]

There is also a story that Luciano benefited from the burning of the French liner SS *Normandie,* orchestrated by 'Tough' Tony Anastasio, Albert's brother.[36] It is said that this was to demonstrate how the Mafia controlled the docks. Concessions were demanded, one of which was the transfer of Luciano from Dannemora. Although the story is thought to be apocryphal there was no more arson on the New York docks.[37]

Over the years a number of stories have grown from legend to gospel. One is that Luciano was secretly released in 1943 and sent to Sicily to accompany the invasion. Luciano spotters have him in the village of Gela where the Seventh Army established its headquarters. He is suggested to have been a member of the tank crew which picked up the local *capo*, Don Calo. The reality is probably that he was not in Sicily until after the War when he was definitely in Palermo with Don Calo discussing the formation of the Sicilian Separatist Party. Officially his sentence had been commuted and he had been deported from the United States in 1946, with a condition that he did not return to the Americas.

His send-off from New York had been in grand style. With Frank Costello and Meyer Lansky on the dock to wave him farewell, he boarded the *Laura Keane* on 10 February and sailed for Naples. He then moved to Rome where he took a suite in the Quirinale Hotel.

Within the year Luciano had also obtained a passport and in February 1947 he headed for Cuba from where he conducted drug-dealing and prostitution, justifying the latter on the basis that he was not using Sicilian women and non-Sicilian women were only half-human. From the island he controlled the Mafia, approving the killing of Bugsy Siegel who had been found skimming the take at the Flamingo Hotel in Las Vegas built with Mob money. Political pressure, however, subsequently forced Luciano out of Cuba and back to Italy where he lived in Naples, carrying on his business with Costello and Lansky at long range and threatening to write his memoirs.

Back in Italy he was, according to the interviews he gave to magazines such as *Life,* leading a respectable and indeed quiet life. On 26 January 1962 Luciano died at Naples' Capodicino airport, having gone there to meet the producer of a potential film of his life. The official reason for his death was a heart-attack, but it is thought that his coffee may have been poisoned. It was known that the narcotics division of Interpol was actively interested in him and there were fears that he might co-operate with them.[38] His body was flown back to America and buried in St John's Cemetery, New York.

His lawyer, Moses Polakoff, was born on the Lower East Side of Manhattan on 24 March 1896, and on qualifying worked as an Assistant US Attorney before setting up his own practice in 1925. He represented numerous Underworld figures and in 1957 he won an action against the *New York World-Telegram* which had accused him of associating with crime figures. Undoubtedly he did have one major crime figure as a friend, and that was Mafia financier Meyer Lansky.

Unlike Levy, Polakoff was never obliged to appear personally before the Kefauver Committee. Lansky had refused to let him appear at the first hearing because of the smears to which mobsters' lawyers were being subjected, but on a subsequent appearance Polakoff had angry clashes with Tobey of which he undoubtedly had the better and during one of which he set out the lawyer's creed:

> *Tobey*: You were counsel for Luciano.
> *Polakoff*: I was.
> *Tobey*: How did you become counsel for such a dirty rat as that? Aren't there some ethics in the legal profession?
> *Polakoff*: I don't want to get into any controversy with you about that subject at the present time but under our Constitution, every person is entitled to his day in court whether he is innocent or not. When the day comes that a person becomes beyond the pale of justice, that means our liberty is gone. Minorities and undesirables and persons with bad reputations are more entitled to the protection of the law than are the so-called honourable people. I don't have to apologize to you—
> *Tobey*: I didn't ask you to.
> *Polakoff*: —or anyone else for whom I represent.
> *Tobey*: I look upon you in amazement.
> *Polakoff*: I look upon you in amazement, a Senator of the United States, for making such a statement.[39]

He died in 1993 at the age of 97.

At the same time as George Morton Levy was having trouble with greyhound and harness tracks in New York so was another lawyer, Eddie O'Hare, this time in Chicago. While Levy could be said to be more or less in control of the situation, however much Costello was acting on the sidelines, there is no doubt that there was only one boss in Chicago and it was not O'Hare.

Edward O'Hare originated from St Louis and formed a partnership with Oliver P. Smith who in 1909 invented the mechanical hare used in greyhound racing. Smith filed patent application papers and from the end of the First World War, despite the illegality of betting on dog-racing, the owners of greyhound tracks paid a percentage to O'Hare and Smith, who died in 1927. By then the sport had taken off, with lawyers around the country devising schemes that could bring betting within the law. O'Hare bought the patent rights from Smith's widow.

O'Hare was a fine athlete who rode, swam and played golf as well as boxing in his youth. Unlike many lawyers he neither drank nor smoked. He married young and had two daughters and a boy 'Butch' whom he idolised.

However, he was not known as 'Artful Eddie' for nothing. Even during Prohibition liquor was on sale legally for medical reasons and at the outset, against a $100,000 bond, a liquor wholesaler George Remus was allowed to store whisky in the same building as O'Hare had a law office. In 1923 all the whisky had gone from the warehouse onto the streets of Chicago and New York. Remus laid charges against a total of 23 men, including O'Hare who was sent to prison for a year and fined $500. It appears that O'Hare had promised to make good Remus' loss but failed to do so. The conviction was overturned on appeal when Remus withdrew his evidence after O'Hare started making reparation, including passing over a share of his racing interests.

Greyhound racing, wherever in the world it has been run, has been the victim of abuse and trickery – or at least the dogs have. One of the simpler ways in the days when there were few if any security controls at a track was to feed seven out of the eight dogs meat, or to give them a long exercise before the race. To paraphrase W.C. Fields, greyhound racing was not a sport of chance the way it was played in America in the 1920s. It was ideal for racketeers.

O'Hare opened the Madison Kennel Club in Madison, Illinois, and operated with great success until a series of police raids closed him down. Meanwhile Al Capone had his own Hawthorne Kennel Club in Cook County, kept open with the aid of Judge Harry Fisher whose lawyer brother Louis acted for the owners of the track. In a daring move O'Hare opened a track, the Lawndale Kennel Club, next to the Hawthorne Club, letting it be known that if there was any interference he would refuse to allow the use of his mechanical hare at rival tracks. Al Capone proposed a merger of interests and O'Hare agreed. For a time he operated as both legal counsel and manager, and by the time Judge Fisher was overruled by the Illinois Supreme Court and the tracks were closed O'Hare was sufficiently well thought of to be operating tracks in Florida (in 1931 the first state to allow greyhound racing) and Massachusetts.

Nevertheless O'Hare affected to dislike the men with whom he dealt:

> You can make money through business associations with gangsters and you run no risk if you don't associate personally with them. Keep it on a business basis and there's nothing to fear.[40]

O'Hare had one weakness, however – his son, Butch, for whom he was prepared to do literally anything. He believed that if he informed on the financial aspects of the Capone organisation it would assist his son in his naval career, and to this end he was prepared to take any risks. Through a mutual friend, John Rogers of the *St Louis Post-Dispatch,* he was introduced to Frank Wilson, the tax inspector who, with his boss Elmer Irey, eventually brought down Capone. Later O'Hare would warn Wilson that a contract was out on his life, with gunmen imported from New York.

By 1931 it was apparent – from information mainly provided by O'Hare and a former bookkeeper at the tracks, Leslie Shumway, who had been traced to Florida – that the tax of $32,000 on Capone's 1924 income of $120,000 had never been paid. It was, of course, only a fraction of his real earnings, but it was the most that could be proved. Capone's offer to repay $400,000 in tax, interest and penalties was rejected. For a time he played ducks and drakes with the courts, suggesting that he was unfit to travel from Florida, but he was unable to delay matters endlessly. Efforts to bribe the jury were thwarted after O'Hare passed on more information to Wilson and, with no way to reach the judge, James J.H. Wilkerson, Capone received the maximum sentence – a $50,000 fine, costs of $30,000 and 11 years' imprisonment. Via Cook County prison and Atlanta he was sent to Alcatraz in San Francisco harbour. Humiliatingly, on Capone's arrival with the others, the warden telegraphed the Attorney General: FIFTY THREE CRATES FURNITURE FROM ATLANTA RECEIVED IN GOOD CONDITION INSTALLED NO BREAKAGES.

Eight years later, the Capone days behind him, O'Hare had become president of the Sportsman's Park racetrack in Stickney, the developer of greyhound tracks in three states, a real estate investor as well as the owner of an insurance company and advertising agents. He seems genuinely to have detested his pay-masters for, despite Wilson's warning that police officers were quite likely to betray him, he continued to inform on Capone's successors, and indeed others, to both the state and county police.

Capone was due to be released on 19 November 1939 and for some time prior to this O'Hare had been what might be called *distrait*. The reason for this was that, as Wilson had warned, Capone had learned of O'Hare's betrayal and revenge was bound to follow.

In the afternoon of 8 November O'Hare was killed while driving along Ogden Avenue from his office at Sportsman's Park. Two men fired at him from a passing car, hitting him in the head and neck. Amongst the objects found in his possession were some religious artefacts, a watch from his mistress, Sue Granata, whose brother was in the state legislature, inscribed *Amor Sempiternus*, and a note in Italian: *Mari, Oh Mari, quanto tempo io penso per te. Fammi passar una notte insieme con te.* (Mary, Mary, how much I think of you. Can I spend a night together with you.)

There was also a verse cut from a magazine:

The clock of life is wound but once
And no man has the power
To tell just when the hands will stop
At late or early hour.
Now is the only time you own.
Live, love, toil with a will.
Place no faith in time.
For the clock may soon be still.

There was also a note from George Woltz asking O'Hare to call a Mr Bennett who wanted to know about an ex-bootlegger and bankrobber Clyde N. Nimerick. Both Woltz and Bennett were FBI agents in Chicago. The note was signed 'Toni' – Antoinette M. Cavaretta, O'Hare's confidential secretary, who later married the mobster Frank Nitti.[41]

He would probably have thought his sacrifice for his son well worthwhile, for Butch O'Hare received the Congressional Medal of Honor from President Roosevelt for 'one of the most daring single combat flights in the history of aviation'. On 20 February 1942 Butch O'Hare had brought down five Japanese twin-engined bombers, disabling a sixth over the Pacific. He was also given a parade in Chicago. Surprisingly he returned to the Pacific and was shot down on 26 November 1943; his body was never recovered. It was suggested that his continued heroics were in some way designed to expiate the guilt he felt for his father's behaviour. In 1949 Chicago's International Airport was named after him.

1  J.R.'Dixie' Davis, 'Things I couldn't Tell till Now' in *Collier's*, 29 July 1939, p.37. The Policy or Numbers racket is essentially an illegal lottery. The player picks three numbers from 000 to 999. The real odds are 900–1 but the pay off is 600–1. The

winning numbers are decided by, say, the last three numbers of the closing price of the New York stock market, or race winners at a track. In fact they can be manipulated, and were by Dutch Schultz's financial wizard, Otto 'Abbadabba' Berman. Winning players are expected to give a percentage to the man who sells them the ticket. Davis continued his story in *Collier's*, 22 and 29 July and 5, 12, 19 August 1939.

2 Pompez was himself the son of a lawyer and initially ran a Policy bank out of a cigar store he owned. Later he owned the semi-pro negro Manhattan baseball team, the Cuban Stars. In 1932 he was coerced into the Schultz combine and he too gave evidence against Jimmy Hines in return for which he received a suspended sentence. See Rufus Schatzberg, *Black Organized Crime in Harlem: 1920–1930*, pp.115–16; Thomas E. Dewey, *Twenty Against the World*.

3 *Collier's*, 29 July 1939.

4 Samuel Mitgang, *The Man Who Rode the Tiger*, p.204.

5 The feared Lower East Side Frog Hollow Gang were essentially white slavers. They were broken up in 1913 when three of their leaders received a total of 42 years.

6 H.A. Danforth and J.D. Horan, *The D.A.'s Man*, p.65.

7 Robert Leibowitz, *The Defender: The Life and Career of Samuel S. Leibowitz 1893–1933*; Quentin Reynolds, *Courtroom, The Story of Samuel S. Leibowitz*.

8 J.R. Dixie Davis in *Collier's*, 22 July 1939.

9 Journalist Martin Mooney may be credited with the first information on the organisation when he wrote of a meeting of 'the executives of Crime, Incorporated' in a New York hotel. Although he named no names he said the meeting was graced by at least three important local and national politicians. *Crime Incorporated*, p.38.

10 H.A. Danforth and J.D. Horan, *The D.A.'s Man*, p.66.

11 *Collier's*, 26 August 1939.

12 *New York Times*, 2 September 1938.

13 H.A. Danforth and J.D. Horan, *The D.A.'s Man*, p.105.

14 *Collier's*, 26 August 1939.

15 See *New York Times*, 30, 31 January and 1 February 1939.

16 L. Katz, *Uncle Frank*, p.96.

17 To be able to portray the defendant convincingly as the injured party is a lawyer's trick which, if worked properly, can be highly successful. Judge Jeremy Fordham recalls as a very young barrister watching William Hemming, by no means the greatest of advocates of his time, do this brilliantly in the case of a police officer accused of bribery. It was a case which involved Ronnie Kray and 'Hemming was always sneering "this man Kray", and "the man Kray" so it eventually appeared that it was not his client who was actually in the dock.'

18 Martin W. Littleton, *My Partner-In-Law*, p.34.

19 *Ibid*, p.117.

20 Harry Anslinger, *The Murderers*, p.103. Richard Hammer in *The Playboy History of Organised Crime* suggests a lesser figure of 1,000 prostitutes, but an annual turnover of $12 million.

21 In the 1920s and 1930s Hot Springs was known in criminal argot as The Vapour City or, more rarely, Bubbles. It was one of a number of towns to which criminals could travel and remain in some safety. David W. Maurer, *Language of the Underworld*, pp.120–21.

22 Poletti was chief adviser to the upright but politically naïve Governor Lehman. In *The Last Testament of Lucky Luciano*, the gangster maintained that he had paid $90,000 to the Dewey political campaign as the price for his freedom.

23 In addition to Murder, Inc. there was a smaller ring of killers known as the Larney Mob headed by the Ludkowitz brothers and including a Rose Pantiel.

24 Tony Romeo's body was found on 1 July 1942 in Delaware. He had been one of Anastasia's right-hand men.

25 In the New York City Municipal Archives there are copies of the evidence given to the Grand Jury by O'Dwyer, Moran, Turkus and Police Sergeant Elwood Divvers,

who said that Moran had authorised him to remove the 'wanted' notices. Divvers had been second-in-command of the guards who were asleep outside the room when Reles met his death. See also Burton B. Turkus and Sid Feder, *Murder, Inc.*, pp.336–9.

26 Notes and memoranda relating to O'Dwyer and others as well as copies of the evidence to the Grand Jury can be found in Boxes 1-10 3049/22 in the New York Municipal Archives. For a fuller account of the death of Reles and the cases of Luciano and Anastasia see James Morton, *Gangland International*.

27 *Collier's*, 26 August 1939.

28 T. Harry Williams, *Huey Long*, p 886. Senator Huey Long was shot to death on 8 September 1935 as he was attending a special session of the Louisiana House of Representatives in Baton Rouge. Depending on one's viewpoint he was regarded as either the most-loved or most-hated man in the state. One of his ideas was a tax on the wealthy, and a redistribution so that each family received seed money of $5,000. A man of enormous sexual appetites, he had long-standing contacts with the Underworld. His programme of building superhighways and leisure spas almost bankrupted the state, and there was considerable dissent to his policies in Louisiana where people were beginning to appreciate Franklin D. Roosevelt's Square Deal policy aimed at getting the country out of the Depression.

Long had five bodyguards with him when Dr Carl Weiss stepped from behind a pillar in the Capitol building and shot him with a .32 automatic. Weiss was himself shot an astounding 61 times. The motive for the killing is not clear, although it is known that Weiss and his family hated Long. A second theory is that he was accidentally shot by his own guards. Long was buried in the Capitol grounds; Weiss in an unknown grave. For a fictionalised account of Long see Robert Penn Warren, *All the King's Men*.

29 Leonard Katz quoting Peter Hand in *Uncle Frank*, p.101.

30 Martin Littleton, *My Partner-In-Law*, p.192.

31 Leonard Katz, *Uncle Frank*, p.170.

32 Letter from Estes Kefauver to George Morton Levy, 11 July 1952.

33 Ernest Havemann, 'The Great Trotting Scandal' in *Life*, 16 November 1953.

The Moreland Commission also found that applicants for licences at the Yonkers track had to obtain approval from Dutch Schultz's old friend Jimmy Hines, who was far from being retired.

34 For a full account see Rodney Campbell, *The Luciano Project: The Secret Wartime Collaboration of the Mafia and the US Navy*.

35 Estes Kefauver, *Crime in America*; Harry J. Anslinger, *The Murderers*, pp.103 *et seq.*

36 This was the family name. Albert is said to have changed the 'o' to an 'a' to spare his mother shame.

37 As with so many aspects of Mafia life and legend, supporters and detractors of the theory can be found in number. For example J. Robert Nash appears both to credit and discredit the story in *World Encyclopaedia of Crime*, pp.31 and 254. Carl Sifakis promulgates it in *The Mafia File*, p.14. There is a long and detailed analysis of the various versions of the causes of the fire in John Maxtone-Grahame's *The Only Way to Cross*, pp 361–92.

38 Norman Lewis, *The Honoured Society*, p.222–3.

39 Testimony of Meyer Lansky, October 1950. Kefauver, Part 7, pp.157–8.

40 Quoted in John Kobler, *The Life and World of Al Capone*, p.226.

41 Nitti may have controlled the Chicago Mob or merely have been a front man for the more talented Paul 'The Waiter' Ricca. On 19 March 1943 Nitti, who suffered from claustrophobia, committed suicide on a railway line rather than face a prison sentence over charges of extortion from the motion picture industry.

# 10 Chippy Patterson

O NE OF THE MANY LAWYERS who found himself before a Grand Jury and whose career ended as Davis's began was the aristocratic and totally eccentric Philadelphian Christopher Stuart Patterson jnr., known to his upper-class friends as Chiffy and to his Underworld clientele as Chippy. During a career which ran for 30 years from 1903, he defended 401 men and women on murder charges, winning outright acquittals for 171. Only eight went to the electric chair.

Patterson's relationship with the Underworld was curious to say the least, although he seems to have acted in a wholly quixotic, Pied Piper way rather than involving himself in their machinations for personal gain. One example from late in his career comes when on 11 May 1928 Agnes Curry – the widow of executed bank robber Joe Curry – and Edward J. Regan popped into the City Hall, Philadelphia, to obtain a marriage licence. She gave her occupation as a domestic and the bridegroom as secretary. A disgruntled police officer commented that the only domestic work the bride did was to polish guns, while the only secretarial work her new husband performed was to sign confessions. The nuptials themselves took place that day at the Cardinal's Chapel in the Rectory at Eighteenth and Race Streets and were performed by a Father Hooey.

One curious fact about the wedding was that at the time both were wanted on a charge of armed robbery, and the most curious was that Patterson gave away the bride. With the Father staying behind, the wedding party then left the Rectory in

Regan's armoured car and on Thompson Street Regan saw a huge Mack which he believed belonged to a rival, Max Hassel. He asked Patterson to take his new bride home while he stole the truckload of alcohol.[1]

Patterson was raised in the Philadelphian equivalent of the Cabots and Lodges of Boston and soon rebelled against his environment. Born in 1875, the son of a lawyer who would eventually cut him out of his will, Patterson began to drink at the age of 15 and he developed an equal taste for the louche. One of his early interests was in a fighting bird, Caligula, which he would inject with the illegal stimulant Colafra. By the time he was a freshman at Penn he had become an out-of-control drinker. At the age of 22 he finished law school and in the Spring of 1903 defended his first murder case – that of a black man, Aline Mason, accused of shooting a fellow card-player. The jury acquitted him of murder, returning a verdict of involuntary manslaughter. Unfortunately, to celebrate his success Patterson began to drink, finally showing at up his brother's engagement party. He was then not seen again for three days.

Years later one of the Mason jurymen, himself in need of a lawyer, sought out Patterson. They had acquitted, he recalled, because Patterson had so palpably believed his client: 'If a man like you believed this poor coloured man's story, what right had we to question it?'

His success with Mason had not gone unremarked and he was taken up by an elderly trial lawyer, S. Morris Waln, who found him a week after the party. Waln offered him a temporary accommodation on the basis that he would defend three abortionist clients – Elizabeth Ashmead, her son, Howard, and a Dr Matthew McVicars. If the trial in every sense of the word was a success, then there might be a more formal arrangement between the lawyers.

The good Dr McVicars said that the girl, Annie Spencer, had died from pneumonia. The prosecution knew otherwise. Using one of the classic methods of trial lawyers, Patterson shifted the emphasis of the case to a defence of the dead girl's morals. Fortunately the full facts were not before the jury, because the pretty housemaid had been unsure which of three potential fathers was actually the parent. Patterson's reasoning was simple. If they convicted the defendants the jury would be saying that the unrepresented and dead Annie Spencer had been 'a bad girl'. If they acquitted, her reputation remained intact. The jury acquitted in less than an hour.[2]

Unfortunately, after purchasing a gift for every member of his family, Patterson spent the remainder of his $2,000 fee in the Brighton Hotel in Atlantic City with a girl from the chorus of *The Black Crook* which was playing the Broad Street Theatre. Over the next months, when sober, he appeared for the clients of Waln and some other lawyers but there was no question of anything more than *ad hoc* cases. For a start, while he bathed daily he tended to go unshaven and had taken to wearing shirts with frayed cuffs and unpressed suits. Nor was it exactly clear where he was living; the best guess was one of the brothels in town.

He was called out in the middle of the night shortly before Christmas 1904 to assist Celia Stone, the proprietress of three 'legitimate' brothels or parlour houses on and near Franklin Street, when the *Public Ledger* began an all-out war on white slavery. Parlour houses, of which there were between 40 and 50 and whose occupants totalled rather less than 1,000 at a time, were a long-standing Philadelphian institution catering for Society clients and providing an evening entertainment as well as prostitution for those able to pay the prices. This left a considerable number of slum brothels where girls, mostly between 15 and 18, were expected to service 50 clients a night. Patterson advised Madam Stone to close for business until he was able to discover just what was in the air. Through his contacts he learned that the war was to be waged against the slum brothels and not establishments such as hers, and he then spent a happy Christmas on the premises.

During the clean-up of the slum brothels Patterson and Mrs Stone took over the welfare of one Polish girl aged 15. They gave $1,000 to Patterson's sister, Eleanor, who removed the child to a private hospital and later sent her back to her family in Poland. Eleanor was only too pleased to have had contact with her brother, but unfortunately the next family reunion was not in such happy circumstances. He attended the Benedict's Ball in Horticultural Hall where the receiving line of the cream of Philadelphian Society was headed by Mrs Alexander Brinton Coxe. Unfortunately the two ladies he brought with him were inmates of one of Mrs Stone's parlour houses. Perhaps fortunately, he blacked out and was taken to a private room at the Lying-In Hospital where his sister had taken the Polish girl a fortnight previously. He committed himself to the Pennsylvania Hospital for Mental Diseases and, after he was released 30 months later, he never drank again. He opened an office at 1523 Chestnut Street and began a practice in criminal law. His biographer Arthur Lewis describes his clientele:

> Word got around City Hall and magistrates' courts that the lawyer who not only didn't give a damn whether he collected a fee but could actually be counted upon for a small hand-out, was back in business. Within a few weeks his two-room suite was jammed to overflowing with clients of all sexes and colours: men, women, homosexuals, whites, and every shade of black and yellow – the latter compliments of Norrie Vaux, whose hospital, Lying-In, was adjacent to Chinatown.[3]

Such spare time as he had was largely devoted to the pursuit of tall, well-developed women, often prostitutes or chorus girls. In 1908, for example, Lucia Cooper, his *inamorata* of the moment, was appearing at the Casino Burlesque billed as 'Six Feet of Golden Dynamite – 44 × 30 × 36'.

One of his long-standing clients was the talented confidence trickster George Flatico, whose abilities extended to selling non-existent property to the actress Miriam Hopkins. His more usual lines of business included arranging bets on horse-races the results of which were already known, shoplifting, being a fake telegram boy, and the badger game.[4] He sent Patterson a painting for one of his marriages. The painting was signed 'Vincent' and the accompanying note said that Flatico had found it in a dreary corner of a Chicago gallery 'where it will never be missed'.

Patterson's way of life and his own inclination largely estranged him from his family. He also flitted in and out of associations with lawyers in the City who were never able to harness his talents. He did, however, found the Patterson Athletic Club designed to assist the families of prisoners and recently released men, as well as providing a cemetery with room for 150 graves near the New Cathedral Cemetery on Nicetown Lane for the burial of penniless ex-convicts. The Athletic Club, which held no meetings and had no clubhouse, was also used as a device by judges who wished to parole prisoners but could only do so to a sponsor. The prisoners would be paroled to the Athletic Club until a proper sponsor could be found.

Rarely had he sufficient funds to pay his small staff's wages on time or to obtain transcripts which would have enabled him to appeal decisions on behalf of his clients. One temporary solution was provided in 1919 by the Nelson brothers, three

South Philadelphia thieves who were serving sentences of 2 to 5 years. They rented a house and installed Patterson along with their wives and a housekeeper who was to allow Patterson $2 a day. The rent and other expenses were provided by a bank cheque on the first of the month. The arrangement suited everyone. The brothers had the satisfaction of knowing that if their wives were misbehaving it was at least with only one man. They were paroled with the help of Patterson just in time to reap the benefits of Prohibition.

Patterson walked the very thin dividing line between acting for and socialising with clients and participating in their activities, or helping to plan them as did the New York lawyer, Bill Fallon. During the early days of Prohibition while Patterson was living in the Hotel Stenton, a Wilfred Carpentier called on him as an emissary from the Owney Madden gang. They knew that Mickey Duffy was serving a sentence and Madden wanted to know if he needed any temporary help in controlling unruly elements who might take advantage of his absence. Fallon had suggested the approach be made through Patterson, who sent him on his way. Later Duffy and Max 'Boo-Hoo' Hoff, who had by then taken over control of Philadelphia and South Jersey, would offer Patterson an annual retainer of $250,000 if he would handle only their work. He declined.[5]

By 1921 Patterson had left the Hotel Stenton and was staying in the Evans, which was described as Philadelphia's 'best coloured hotel'. He had been invited to stay there rent-free by the manager following the successful defence of a close relative. That year he successfully represented a series of defendants in capital cases, and for the last pair received the sum of $15,000. With the money he moved out of the Evans and into a flat with Virginia Wendell. He also had some money to spare to have a brief romance with the actress Jeanne Eagels, then playing Sadie Thompson in *Rain*. Miss Wendell was not pleased and after Jeanne Eagels had left for Broadway, when she and Patterson were dining in the Bellevue she pressed her cigarette into the palm of his hand and held it there.

> Mr Patterson didn't say a word. You could smell the flesh burn, but he never moved his arm, and you could see the sweat pouring off his forehead. Finally, it seemed like an hour, although I guess it wasn't more than a minute, the woman lifted the cigarette from Mr Patterson's palm, put it to her lips, took another puff, then squashed it on an ash tray.[6]

It was not the only time that Patterson had trouble over cigarettes, although this time it was more to do with his predilection for mixing socially with his clients. One girl Kitty O'Connor, to whom a Philadelphia big-league killer Harry Burton thought she belonged, was making a play for Patterson getting him to light her cigarette. Burton shouted in temper that if he lit it he would blow out Patterson's brains. Unfazed, the lawyer took the cigarette from his mouth, lit the girl's cigarette with it and returned his own to his mouth. He then told Burton to apologise and, according to eye-witnesses, at that Burton began to cry.

Patterson was clearly fond of the Curry family and he expended endless energy in defending Joe Curry and three others when on 4 May 1926 they robbed the Olney bank of $80,000, all of which was recovered in a moment, shooting a policeman during their attempted getaway. A fifth man was thought to be Burton, who was shot in a gangland execution on 8 May. His failure to save the men from the electric chair weighed heavily on Patterson, but the death-cell admissions which he took from two of the others, Juliano and Bentley, exculpated Matt Overnack who had been convicted of complicity in another bank robbery.

By now Patterson had again been evicted from his offices and although his downward physical spiral was inexorable, his record of acquittals in murder cases continued over the years. In 1927 he defended 9 and the following year 21 more. Although most of them were professional criminals and killers, none was executed.

At 2 o'clock in the morning of 9 August 1928 Hughie McLoon, the 26-year-old dwarf former mascot of the Philadelphia Athletics Baseball Club, was shot and killed.[7] He survived long enough to get to Jefferson hospital where Magistrate Edward Carney, for whom McLoon had worked, was one of the first to reach his bedside. Some three years earlier McLoon and the magistrate had raided a private dance at the Ritz-Carlton and confiscated a quantity of alcohol. An effort to padlock the tony hotel had been thwarted by the Mayor but it led to the dismissal of the Director of Public Safety, General Smedley D. Butler. Now Carney would try unavailingly to get the names of the killers from two others who had been with McLoon.

His death was probably due to his inability to keep his mouth closed to the secrets he learned while mixing with the city's bootleggers and killers. Since his time with Carney he had gone down in the world. For a time he had been the ring announcer at boxing promotions, carrying cards almost as big as himself, and in theory managed some fighters. At the time of his death he was almost penniless, scraping a living running a café-cabaret which had been raided by Prohibition agents on 21 July. It may well be that McLoon was deciding that being a snitch was more profitable than being a café owner.

Four days later his tiny casket was surrounded by 200 white lilies in the form of a heart. Max 'Boo-Hoo' Hoff had sent a touching card with his tribute: 'We miss you already little fellow.' It is virtually certain that McLoon was killed on Hoff's orders, and McLoon's killers almost certainly included Daniel O'Leary who was himself shot on 15 August. Two days later a Grand Jury inquiry, before which Patterson would be asked to appear and explain his 'association' with known gangsters, was announced by Judge Edwin O. Lewis. This followed an almost unprecedented 14 killings on Philadelphian streets. Lewis said that as recently as the previous day he had heard death threats to Carney, but the magistrate would have none of it. They clashed at City Hall where the Grand Jury was being sworn:

> Well, I've heard that before and it doesn't mean a thing to me. I heard it away back before General Butler was Director of Public Safety. I have been around City Hall for 28 years and my life is an open book. All I've got to say is that whoever shoots at me better shoot straight.[8]

Patterson gave evidence voluntarily on 10 November. He was questioned for three hours in closed session and afterwards Rupert Raezor, one of the stenographers, said the jury had found 'Mr Patterson's contact with mobsters to be maintained strictly on the basis of a lawyer-client relationship'. He added, however, that the jury had been troubled by Patterson's consistent victories in court which had made additional murders more likely. Presumably in Philadelphia at the time, arranging weddings for fugitive suspects was regarded as a normal lawyer-client relationship. Either that or no one mentioned the Curry-Regan marriage to the jury.

In 1930 Patterson won six acquittals and five manslaughter and second-degree murder verdicts for his 11 clients. His last great defence came in June that year when he represented Pete Valenti, a burglar and dope dealer, released on parole after serving only two years of a 10–20 year sentence for armed robbery. Now Valenti was accused of a grocery store robbery-murder on South Street on 9 April. From the viewpoint of the prosecution, it was a relatively simple case. Valenti and a friend, Vincent Minotti, neither of whom was wearing a mask, held up a grocery store and, without warning, Valenti shot the owner. Both Minotti and Valenti accused the other of firing the fatal shot, but the prosecution regarded Minotti's version as the more reliable and he gave evidence for the State.

Unexpectedly, Patterson made no objection when the prosecution introduced Valenti's record in evidence. Instead he waited until his closing speech to the jury when he laid the blame for the killing at the feet of the judge who had paroled Valenti:

> Valenti is no good. His record proves it. If Society releases this type of man it deserves just what it gets. Damn the law for this, but don't damn the prisoner.

The jury agreed, working on the curious thinking that if Valenti had not been paroled he would not have been able to commit the murder. Instead of the electric chair he was sentenced to separate and solitary confinement for the remainder of his natural life.[9]

In increasing ill-health and poverty, Patterson continued to defend throughout 1932 when his record in death penalty cases was one acquittal and three second-degree verdicts. He no longer had an office or staff; his office had become his coat which was carried by a self-appointed valet. He wore fishing boots in court and 'a disreputable cap instead of a hat'. Such money as he had he spent on doctors for his latest girlfriend, Genevieve, who had contracted tuberculosis. He lived in Missions where rooms were five cents and meals ten, or slept on park benches. In July he was asked to represent two black defendants and obtained voluntary manslaughter verdicts. It was his last case. His court-ordered $500 fee was spent on his girlfriend's medical care. Now he begged and borrowed money from friends to send her back to her home in Englefield for treatment. He collapsed and died on 17 February 1933.

> In the legal world his passing means the death of a brilliant attorney who could and would defend anyone at the bar of justice regardless of their financial circumstances.

In the Underworld his passing means the departure of a friend who never turned its denizens down but who strove with the best that was in him to help them 'beat a rap'.

To the Society in which he was born he was an outcast ... But to the Underworld he was the man who stood between them and the law, who made their cause his own, who fought their battles for them ...[10]

1 Philadelphia *Evening Bulletin*, 12 May 1928. Sadly, Agnes Curry seems to have been another of those Black Widows who permeate criminal history and whose husbands and boyfriends come to premature ends. Regan was killed in an ambush on 30 June 1932.
2 The Ashmeads and Dr McVicars chanced their arm again. On 30 March 1904, with the headline 'Fifty Infants Burned Alive in Heater', the Philadelphia *Press* disclosed that they were running a baby farm. Patterson represented them at the preliminary hearing but not at the trial in January 1905 when McVicars was acquitted after the prosecution offered no evidence. Mrs Ashmead had been convicted in the previous October and now she received three years. This time McVicars seems to have learned his lesson. But Mrs Ashmead had not, and in August 1909 she was charged with operating another baby farm in New Hampshire.
3 Arthur H. Lewis, *The Worlds of Chippy Patterson*, p.106.
4 Flatico can be found operating as late as the 1950s when he served a 215-day sentence in Boston for working a version of the badger game. He was then 65.
5 Max 'Boo-Hoo' Hoff was, at the time, the undisputed King of Philadelphian bootlegging. An associate of Al Capone, he supported Capone's championship of Moses Annenberg in running the racing wire service which became an empire. The 1927 killings were part of a power struggle in which Hoff faced a challenge from his rivals, the Hain brothers. Control passed via Harry Stromberg, better known as Waxie Gordon, to the Italians. Hoff, then penniless, committed suicide in 1941. As for Carpentier, he went about the saloons boasting that Madden would be coming to take control. On 21 May 1919 he was shot and killed by Albert 'Reds' Murphy, one of Patterson's long-standing clients. He was acquitted in February 1920 but was himself killed on 4 October that year. Mickey Duffy, still in the Eastern Penitentiary, sent a floral tribute in the form of a harp. Duffy was himself killed in Atlantic City in 1931.
6 John Wickas, waiter at the Bellevue, quoted by Arthur H. Lewis in *The Worlds of Chippy Patterson*, p.223.
7 In fact although he was always known as the former mascot his stay had been one of only two years. He had taken over in 1915 after the death of the previous dwarf, Louis VanZelt, but moved to another minor league club in 1917.
8 Philadelphia *Inquirer*, 18 August 1928.
9 It is pleasant to be able to relate that Valenti was released in the late 1940s. He married and had three children. He was thought of as a reliable and trustworthy employee, who eventually became foreman of a small printing works.
10 Dorothy Ann Harrison in the Philadelphia *Record*, 18 February 1933. See also 'Chippy Patterson is claimed by Death: Kin in 400 and Down-and-out clients mourn' in Philadelphia *Inquirer*, 18 February 1933.

# 11 Louis Piquett and John Dillinger

EVEN LAWYERS most devoted to their clients' interests rarely arrange the changing of their fingerprints; but Louis Piquett did that, not only for John Dillinger but also for the ferocious Homer Van Meter. A fashion followed by the Barkers, it did none of them any good, certainly not Piquett.

Despite a considerable body of evidence dating back to the turn of the century that burning the skin on the tips of fingers did not, long-term or even medium-term, change the basic characteristics of fingerprints, the news had not percolated to the American Mid-West in the 1930s. Or, if it had, it was disbelieved or ignored. It may well be that fire didn't work but there was always some doctor, very often one struck off for performing abortions, who had a patent remedy. Once Dillinger had escaped from Crown Point jail in 1934 Piquett had one lined up for him.

John Dillinger, born in 1903 in Moorstown, Indiana, was perhaps the superstar of them all. A member of a youth gang called the Dirty Dozen, he majored in crime only after a short stint in the Navy from which he simply absented himself. In 1924 he and an older and more experienced man, the web-fingered Ed Singleton, tried to rob a local grocer, B.F. Morgan. There is some evidence that Dillinger had been drinking. Certainly the grocer knew him and identified him. Dillinger, told by his father that things would go better if he pleaded guilty and that he didn't need a lawyer, drew a sentence of 10–20 years, the statutory minimum. Singleton did not confess and received only two years. In his memoirs, the lawyer G. Russell Giradin argues that this savage sentence soured the youth.[1] However, this rather overlooks the fact that Dillinger's father had already bailed him out from a number of previous thefts and assaults, and he also had something of a history of enjoying forced sex.

While in prison, first in the Indiana State Reformatory and then in Michigan City, Dillinger met the men he would ultimately lead – John 'Red' Hamilton, Homer Van Meter, Charlie Makley and – the captain of the band at the time – Harry Pierpont.[2] Dillinger appears to have had only one flaw in the eyes of these men – he took an 'old lady' prison lover. In all other respects, such as trustworthiness and ability to help others, he seems to have been exemplary. He was released in 1933 following a petition in which some 200 people from Mooresville, including B.F. Morgan, joined. When given the news he promised his new friends that he would work towards their escape. He returned home only to find that his stepmother, to whom he was devoted, had died hours earlier. He then began a series of small-time robberies to finance his promise.

On 26 September 1933, after an abortive attempt when guns thrown into the prison were handed to the authorities, Pierpont and nine other prisoners armed with a smuggled gun took hostages and escaped. Dillinger, on the other hand, suspected by Captain Matt Leach of many of the bank robberies, was arrested in Dayton, Ohio.

On 12 October Dillinger was sprung from jail in Lima, Ohio, but in the attack the sheriff, Jess Sarber, was killed. Now the Pierpont Mob became the Dillinger Mob. The renaming was due to Leach who spent that part of his career in hopeless pursuit of Dillinger. He hoped that by renaming the Pierpont Gang he would engender rivalry between the two leaders. But Pierpont did not mind at all; he was quite satisfied that Dillinger had kept his promise and had stage-managed his escape.

Despite his enormous fame, Dillinger survived for only a limited period. During his first run the gang undertook between 10–20 robberies – many were falsely attributed to them, and the members never actually admitted which were which. He, along with Evelyn ' Billy' Frechette, a girl who had been on the raid to release him in Lima, as well as Pierpont, Makley and Russell Clark, was arrested in Tuscon in January 1934. The men were taken back to Ohio and charged with the murder of Sarber.

Their arrival in Ohio was a triumph of publicity: 85 officers met the plane and Dillinger was lodged in the escape-proof prison in Crown Point.

It was now that he met Louis Piquett, the extremely dubious Chicago lawyer whose name Dillinger pronounced Pick-Watt. Piquett had been born in Wisconsin and, after taking the eighth grade at school, went to California. Little about him bears too close scrutiny. He had become involved in politics in the old 21st Ward and in the 1915 Chicago mayoral election he proposed that officials should lock up the store where the votes had been lodged and have dinner before the count began. While they ate, Piquett, who had a spare key, arranged for a friend to change the ballot box. The result in a pro-Democrat ward was a sweep for William Hale Thompson, the Republican candidate, by a 9:1 majority.

Thompson appointed him chief clerk in the office of Harry B. Miller and Piquett began reading law at night. He never attended a university but when Thompson began a second term of office Piquett received a licence to practise in 1918. Two years later he took over from Miller as Chicago's prosecutor. In 1922 he was indicted in the schoolboard scandal for alleged grafts on coal contracts, but the charges were dismissed and the next year he resigned when the Democrats came to power. He then set up in private practice at 228 North la Salle.

A handsome man with a mop of prematurely white hair and a good courtroom presence, he was regarded as someone whose actions ranged between the dubious and the fraudulent. One of his self fund-raising schemes nominally involved his promoting the Order of St Francis. In fact it involved a down payment of 10 dollars and a dollar a month membership fee. He had signed up nearly 400 Franciscans before the scam was exposed by Cardinal Mundelein.

When a major crime takes place there are inevitably a number of lawyers who circle the case and the defendant hoping to obtain instructions. Piquett was recommended by Meyer Bogue who regularly visited the Piquett offices and had been a fairly close prison acquaintance of Dillinger. Bogue thought he could arrange for his representation. Piquett was apparently ecstatic at the prospect: 'If I land that, it will make me the most famous lawyer in the United States.' And from that cornucopia would flow major fees. Arthur O'Leary, his clerk-cum-investigator, also knew the right people through whom to approach Dillinger and one of Piquett's cards was sent along a chain to him.[3] Piquett and O'Leary made their way to Crown Point where, to their dismay, they found a number of other lawyers also thinking they might be instructed.[4] These included Joseph Ryan, a one-armed lawyer instructed by Dillinger's father. Faced with this, Piquett could do little but sit on the sidelines as a committed observer and hope something went wrong. It did.

The fact that Dillinger did not have Piquett on his books already is a comment on the isolation of the man from mainstream organised crime. Piquett was certainly well known in Chicago for he had already defended Leo V. Brothers, accused of killing the newspaperman Alfred 'Jake' Lingle.

Lingle, a police reporter for the *Chicago Tribune*, was murdered on 9 June 1930. It was an unusual killing, breaking the gangster code of the period that journalists and prosecutors – perhaps on the tramcar principal that there would be another one by in five minutes – should not be touched. Known as a courageous reporter who had waged a fearless war against the Underworld, Lingle had left the *Tribune* offices saying that he intended to try to get a story about what was left of the Moran gang. Seen a short time later heading down Randolph to catch a train to the racetrack, he stopped to buy a racing paper and then headed towards the tunnel to the station. A well-dressed young man walked behind him and shot Lingle through the head.

There was an immediate outcry. He was named as a 'first line soldier' in the fight against crime and rewards of over $50,000 were posted by his paper and local groups. But things were not quite the way they seemed. It transpired that through his police connections he had the ability to award beer-selling and gambling rights. Also he had influence in the appointments in the police force, and was into demanding money from brothel-keepers. Unfortunately someone was unkind enough to leak the news that at the time of his death he was wearing a diamond-studded belt given him by Al Capone. His stock slumped and the *Tribune* was reduced to writing articles denouncing other newspaper reporters, notably Julius Rosenheim of the rival *Chicago Daily News* who had been shot to death a few months previously. He, too, had been blackmailing brothel-keepers.

Months later, Brothers, who was considered a small-time hoodlum and who was then living at Lake Crest Drive apartments, was unearthed by a former criminal and former

Pinkerton detective, Jack Hagan. On 21 December Brothers was arrested and charged with Lingle's murder. [5]

Although Piquett claimed that he was taking the case out of the goodness of his heart and 'If Leo Brothers had any money he would have big lawyers here. He came to me broke', Brothers was expensively defended with a battery of five counsel which Piquett led. The evidence against Brothers was not strong, with half the fourteen identifying witnesses putting him as the killer and the other half not. Later many, including the Chicago Crime Commission, believed that Brothers had been framed. It appears he was a man without previous convictions, and he claimed he had no Mob connections. Piquett was at his most flamboyant. During his closing speech he repeatedly clashed with the prosecution and judge, not least over Brothers' indigence. Other rallying calls included, 'Think of that sweet mother. [The white-haired Mrs Brothers.] Do you want to send the electric current through her heart on a record of false conspiracy' [Struck out], and, 'Is it a prosecution by the state's attorney or the Chicago *Tribune*? This is the most gigantic frame-up since the crucifixion of Christ'. [Struck out.] The next day he was back on the subject of the crucifixion as well as reciting the *Star Spangled Banner* and commenting on the assassination of Julius Caesar.

The jury retired for a lengthy 27 hours and came back with a verdict which spared Brothers from the electric chair. Apparently on a first ballot the voting had been 7–5 for an acquittal but, as an analysis of the evidence was made, support for Brothers had dwindled until only juror Philip Hagerman held out, refusing to take any part in the discussion save to repeat his belief in Brothers' innocence.

Brothers received 14 years. 'I can do that standing on my head,' he is said to have announced after the verdict. Over the years there have been persistent suggestions that he was not the killer at all but had been paid to take the rap. Released after 8 years, he returned to St Louis where he was acquitted of the murder charge of service car driver John De Blasi, on which he had been awaiting trial before his arrest, and became a partner in various Mob enterprises such as taxi and loan companies. He died in 1951 without disclosing who had paid him either for the contract or for going to prison. [6]

Ryan did not have a happy time at the Crown Point hearing for Dillinger and was probably out of his depth in the proceedings altogether. Worse, he spoke in a low voice which made it difficult not only for the judge but hard for his client to hear. Dillinger called for Piquett and, apparently, told him he had some tens of thousands of dollars hidden in northern Wisconsin. If Piquett would take the case the fee could come from that.

Anyone who has practised criminal law will have heard such stories. The basic tenet of a criminal law practice is that a bottom should not leave a chair without cash on the table or a cheque which has been cleared in the bank. Nevertheless, in a case which carries major kudos it is difficult to stick to the rule. There is, after all, a great deal of adrenalin which flows through the veins in a high-profile case. Apart from anything else, it is likely to attract other clients. Piquett fell. Given his connections with the Mob it is surprising that he did so. Perhaps he had become too used to regular payments from the friends of Capone.

He worked hard and successfully in early applications to have Dillinger kept at Crown Point jail rather than be sent to Michigan City. Dillinger was delighted and promised him $50,000 for this and future services. By the end Piquett had received only a fraction of the promised sum.

One of the dangers of acting for major gangland figures is that they are often inclined to ask for extra legal favours, which is what happened to the unfortunate Piquett. Dillinger, in Crown Point jail after a legal interview, gave Arthur O'Leary a note to be smuggled to Dillinger's girlfriend, Billy Frechette. Piquett took the note because he was afraid that O'Leary might be searched, and between them they successfully smuggled it out. But far from the 'mushy love note' they had imagined, instead it was a floor plan of Crown Point jail coupled with instructions to 'Red' Hamilton on how the escape should be organised. They discussed burning it, but then realised that Dillinger would eventually learn the note had not been passed over. 'Then,' asked O'Leary of his principal, 'what do you think will happen?' Discretion was the better part of valour and they decided on the course of action of handing over the note, telling her they had read it and explaining how impossible the plan would be to execute.

Once involved for a lamb, Piquett became involved for a sheep and was persuaded that a gun should be smuggled into Crown Point. The idea was probably that of O'Leary. Some suggestions have been made that it was Judge Murray who was paid $6,000 to take the gun in, but these are probably incorrect.[7]

Dillinger escaped on 3 March. He locked up eight deputies and a dozen trusties before escaping with Herbert Youngblood, a black prisoner.[8] They took the car of the lady sheriff, Lillian Holley, and two hostages. Dillinger would never be in prison again. Piquett and Arthur O'Leary, along with Billy Frechette, were in their law office when they heard the news, whereupon Piquett telephoned the prison to obtain confirmation. Drinks were produced and by the time Dillinger telephoned Piquett for instructions on where to go for a safe address, Billy had been sent to lie down in the flat of Esther Anderson who may have been a girlfriend of Piquett but, if not, was still an extremely useful auxiliary. Later Piquett would have severe difficulties in explaining why the three of them were congregated so early and fortuitously in his office.

After a short period of rest and recreation Dillinger put together the Dillinger Mob Mark II. Members included Van Meter, Eddie Green, John Hamilton, and Lester Gillis who wanted to be called 'Big George' Nelson but was to be known as 'Baby Face'.

It is said that Dillinger paid for the defence of Pierpont, Makley and Clark, but that is not strictly accurate. Banks robbed by him paid for the defence, but at least he did send the money to the lawyers. He had cleared $50,000 at the Security National Bank, Sioux Falls, South Dakota, where Nelson killed a police officer. Ten days later they robbed the National Bank in Mason City, Iowa. His financing was unsuccessful; Pierpont and Makley were sentenced to death.

As for Russell Clark, who had a separate trial, the financing of Piquett to join the defence team seems to have been paid for by Clark's girlfriend, Opal Long. Once she heard of the death sentences imposed on Pierpont and Makley, she put down $485 for Piquett to go at once to Lima to conduct the defence.

The fact that her money was not well spent was not the lawyer's fault. Via Esther Anderson, O'Leary sent his employer a note from Dillinger saying that if there was no possibility of saving the men he (Dillinger) would storm the prison. Piquett destroyed the note and contacted Clarence Miller, who was leading the defence team. After seeing Piquett with a woman and recalling he had been with one shortly before the Crown Point break-out, the local authorities then began to think he might be reconnoitring another jail break. He was arrested and imprisoned. He had with him a list of prospective jurors given him by Miller, which was confiscated before his release after an

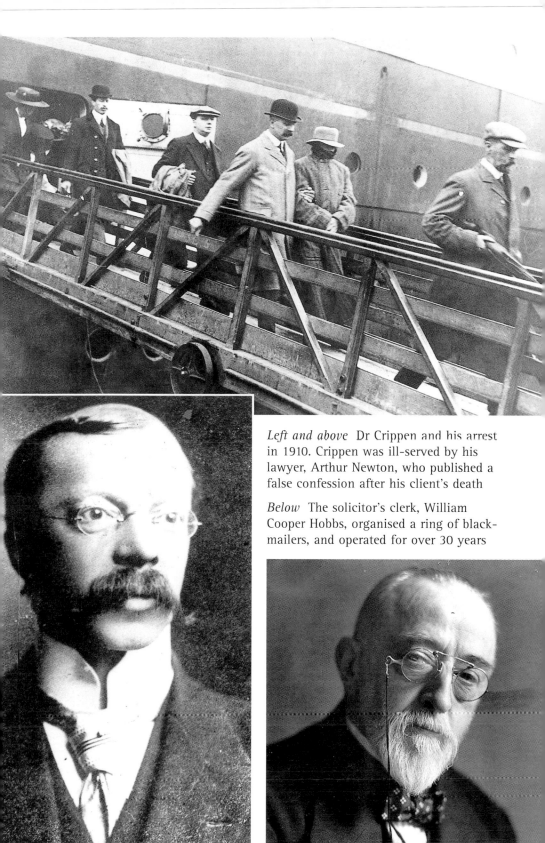

*Left and above* Dr Crippen and his arrest in 1910. Crippen was ill-served by his lawyer, Arthur Newton, who published a false confession after his client's death

*Below* The solicitor's clerk, William Cooper Hobbs, organised a ring of black-mailers, and operated for over 30 years

*Left* John Dillinger (second right) shown here with county prosecutor Robert Estill (centre) and Lillian Holley, the sheriff of Lake Co., Indiana (far left)

*Below* The crooked lawyer Louis Piquett arranged for Dillinger to have his fingerprints changed. Although there have been persistent rumours the body was not that of Dillinger, police took fingerprints to check its identity

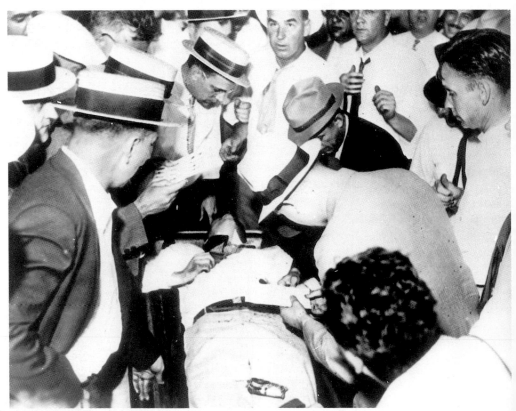

*Above left* (clockwise)
Stephen Ward, Christine
Keeler, Penny Marshall
and Mandy Rice-Davies

*Above right* Billy Rees-
Davies, QC

*Right* Ellis Lincoln, one
of the leading criminal
lawyers of the London
post-war scene, arriving
at the Court of Appeal
for 'Lucky' Gordon's
appeal against his three-
year sentence received
for assaulting former
girlfriend, Christine
Keeler

*Above* News reporters gathered outside Marlborough Street Magistrates' Court, London, 1969

*Left* Attorney Bruce Cutler gesturing broadly beside his client, the reputed Gambino crime boss, John Gotti

*Left* Money laundering lawyer Michael Relton during the Brink's-Mat Gold Trial, 1988

interview with the prosecutor. By 4 p.m. he had obtained another list and was rearrested. Released once more, he was arrested a third time and this time spent a night in jail before being released into the custody of Francis W. Durkin. It was now announced that Piquett was off the case.

His troubles did not end there. A rumour spread that he had offered $50,000 to prison guards to assist in an escape and he was back in jail a second night. It was now as though he was progressing through revolving doors because he was released and in again before Durkin had him bailed once more. This time things were worse. A warrant for his arrest was sent from Indiana, alleging he had participated in the Crown Point break. He caught a taxi and was driven to Fort Wayne where he heard the police were checking hotels. He was driven on to Chicago and safety.[9]

On 9 April, following a tip from an informant, Billy Frechette was caught by Melvin Purvis, the FBI Agent in charge of hunting down Dillinger, as she walked into a restaurant in Chicago. Had the agents held off for a moment they might also have taken Dillinger who was waiting for a signal that everything was clear. He escaped unseen. Piquett was summoned to apply for bail, which was originally set at $200,000 but he argued it down to $60,000. He need not have bothered, for Dillinger was in no position to raise that money. Ms Frechette went to prison to await her trial.

Then on 22 April Dillinger and other members of the gang were caught by the FBI at Little Bohemia Lodge, a summer resort then closed, about 50 miles from Rhinelander, Wisconsin. The choice of hideout was not wholly fortuitous; the owner, Emil Wanatka, was rumoured to have Mob connections, and before the Depression had owned a similarly named establishment on Chicago's North Side.[10] The ensuing battle was a disaster. 'Baby Face' Nelson shot and killed a Special Agent, Carter Baum, and wounded two other law officers. In turn the authorities killed a Civilian Conservation Worker and injured two others, suspecting they were members of the gang. John Hamilton was a casualty on the bandits' side, dying later of his injuries. It is said that he was shot not at the Lodge but later in a roadblock as he and Dillinger drove in the outskirts of St Paul.

What was badly needed was a change of identity and this is where O'Leary and Piquett came in once more.[11] Piquett knew a German immigrant doctor, William Loeser, who at one stage had studied medicine at Kansas and Northwestern universities.[12] Now he had fallen on hard times. His wife had been insane for some fifteen years and the doctor had taken up with the statuesque Anna Patzke. In July 1931 Loeser had received a 3-year sentence following a drug conviction but had been released just over a year later. Breaking the conditions of his parole, he went to Mexico where he had his fingerprints changed and obtained a divorce. He maintained that on his return he married Anna in Kansas City; but a marriage certificate was never produced and, when it suited him, he would admit that while there might have been consummation there had been no regularisation of the union.

Piquett had known the doctor and Anna Patzke for some years, and had acted for them from time to time. When he heard of Dillinger's decision to alter his appearance he went looking for the pair at their apartment at 536 Wrightwood Avenue. Loeser was happy to show the lawyer the results of his own operation and, since he needed some money to get his furniture out of store, offered his services to any interested parties. It was a match made in heaven. His patent remedy was a 'secret' formula of two parts of hydrochloric acid and one of nitro-hydrochloric acid to be used with an alkaloid usually of caustic soda. The pain for the patient was excruciating.

A suitable assistant in the form of Dr Harold Cassidy – at the time on the run from a perjury charge in Illinois – was obtained and a price of $5,000 agreed. This was to be divided fairly. Cassidy would receive $500 and Loeser, Piquett and James J. Probasco, a go-between who had found what could be described as sheltered accommodation for Dillinger at 2509 Crawford Avenue, would split the remainder. The price included minor facial surgery first and then a week later the fingertips. It was during the first operation, which was conducted under a general anaesthetic, that Dillinger's heart stopped beating. He had swallowed his tongue. When he was revived the operation continued under local anaesthetic, punctuated by Dillinger vomiting. Nevertheless the gangster was pleased. He showed his newly lifted face, now minus moles on his forehead and a scar on his lip, to Piquett. His lawyer thought he looked as if he had been in a dogfight.

Nevertheless the formidable Homer Van Meter decided that he also would have a fingerprint removal as well as facial surgery and the unwilling Cassidy was pressed into service again – Piquett persuading him with a mixture of threats and a promise of money up front.

On the more usual legal front, Piquett now went to St Paul to act for Billy Frechette. It was very nearly a wasted journey. Dillinger was in the vicinity and, during the first luncheon break, she walked out of court with the jurors and spectators. She had reached the corridor before she was recognised, and explained that she had merely been going to find some lunch. With his client returned to the court, Piquett made one of his customary fiery speeches:

> Dillinger is the most overestimated, the most overrated man in America. Evelyn Frechette loved Dillinger, and although she knew he was a desperado, she was willing to take a chance with him. We all know where Dillinger belongs, but are we going to punish three people [a doctor and a nurse were charged with her] because they were innocently drawn into this net? Miss Frechette was willing to go the limit with this Public Enemy Number One because she loved him. She did not harbour him under the statute. I appeal to you – give her back her freedom.[13]

The jury deliberated all night and decided not to. Billy and the doctor received two years apiece. The nurse was acquitted.

As has been traditional with all robbers, Dillinger wanted one last big job and then to go to Mexico, but it appears that his abortive trip to Tuscon was as near as he got to the Rio Grande. Piquett did his bit in keeping Dillinger's pursuers on their toes and in the wrong direction by suggesting that he had gone to Europe. Boats were searched in Belfast and Glasgow; there was no sign of Dillinger but in the latter search the authorities were at least rewarded by turning up the German spy Lincoln Trebitsch. By July 1934 Dillinger was still in Chicago where he had taken up with a waitress and prostitute, Polly Hamilton who, as often happens to robbers in hiding, was bleeding him dry.

On 24 July Dillinger, along with Polly Hamilton and Anna Sage – a Romanian-born brothel-keeper – went to the Biograph Theatre in Chicago to see Clark Gable in *Manhattan Melodrama*. Sage, who had owned houses in East Chicago and Gary, Indiana, was facing her third conviction and, along with it, deportation. She had heard the stories that Dillinger, then living as Jimmy Lawrence, was telling Hamilton. Putting two and two together, she went to the FBI agent Melvin Purvis, in charge of the search for Dillinger and other luminaries of the Mid-West, to try to negotiate not only the reward but also a relaxation of the deportation proceedings.

As arranged, that night Sage was wearing red to indicate Dillinger was with her. According to some versions, Purvis called on Dillinger to stop and then the FBI opened fire. Dillinger was hit along with two women passers-by. Hamilton and Sage simply disappeared from the scene and were later taken to Detroit to ensure their silence. Sage received $5,000, half the amount she anticipated. On 29 April 1936 she was deported to Romania where she died in Timisoara in 1947.[14] Thousands queued to see Dillinger's body, dipping pieces of paper and even hems of skirts in the blood.

The death of Dillinger spelled the beginning of serious trouble for Piquett. His telephone was being tapped and through this a number of aiders, abetters and hangers-on including Cassidy were arrested. Piquett, as a lawyer should, heard of it but did little. An attempt had been made to arrest him on a Chicago street, but it aborted when he demanded to see the arrest warrant saying, 'You can murder me here on the street but I'll not go willingly without a warrant.' It is interesting that lawyers who know arrest is imminent so often stand their ground instead of travelling to Mexico or Australia until the immediate fire under them has died down. Is it because they believe in their invincibility, and that just as they have worked the oracle for so long for their clients they will do so one more time for themselves? Perhaps Piquett in particular really did believe no one could touch him.

He was arrested in front of his home on 31 August. The United States Attorney, using the usual rhetoric for such occasions, said, 'We consider this arrest the most important in years.' Asked if he was going to try to cut a deal which would result in his release in a day over a year, he replied, 'Not me. I'm fighting this. My relationship with Dillinger was strictly lawyer and client.' Later he would tell the court, 'I am not a criminal lawyer. I am a criminal law lawyer.'[15]

Bail was set at $50,000, but Piquett was unable to raise it and remained in prison until it was reduced to $20,000. After jury selection, his trial for conspiring with Dillinger, Loeser, Cassidy, O'Leary and the late and lamented Jimmy Probasco (who had meanwhile fallen to his death from the 19th floor of 208 South Clark Street where he was in the care of Federal Agents) opened in Chicago on 10 January 1935. The prosecutor alleged that Piquett had been the mastermind behind Dillinger's escape and the changing of his face and fingerprints. Not so, said Piquett, once more reiterating that his had been a strictly lawyer-client relationship. No, said the prosecution: 'It was of a fugitive with an individual who happens to be practising law.'

Piquett's view was not exactly shared by the motley bunch of co-conspirators who became witnesses – all seeking lesser penalties at his expense – against him.

The principals were Arthur O'Leary, Piquett's former clerk and investigator; Cassidy, described as 'young but his face shows signs of dissipation'; and the 'vinegary' Anna Patzke who wore a brown veil and had once owned a drug store at 1102 Leland Avenue where she met Piquett. She would tell the court that after Loeser had been arrested Piquett offered him $500 and a weekly pension if he would exculpate him by saying his share of the money was for legal fees. She was none too pleased with the lawyer for other reasons. When she had gone with Loeser to Mexico she had left her house in the capable hands of Piquett, only to find on her return that the mortgage had been foreclosed and her furniture put into store. Loeser also gave evidence but, according to the report, he displayed every indication that he was lined up for another long sentence.

Piquett, defying the maxim that the lawyer who acts for himself has a fool for a client, more or less led the team nominally captained by Edwin T. Peifer, taking over much of the cross-examination of witnesses, running his defence along the lines that he was trying to persuade Dillinger to give himself up. He alleged that he had even been negotiating with the judge, William Murray, that in return for a surrender and plea to the murder of a Chicago policeman there would be a sentence of life imprisonment rather than the death penalty. It was something the judge denied.

When Piquett finally gave evidence it was a *tour de force*. He was, he said, the son of a blacksmith. He had gone to California when he left school in the 8th grade, but had returned home to marry 'a little girl from home'. He was still with her and, on cue, Mrs Piquett dutifully began to weep. Having waited tables and tended bar while studying law on the kitchen table at nights, he had become involved in politics in the old 21st Ward and had assisted in the election of Mayor Thompson who appointed him prosecuting attorney. When Thompson began a second term of office Piquett set up in private practice at 228 North la Salle. The more interesting parts of his early political career were omitted.

As to the case itself, he was almost an innocent dupe. It had been the dead Probasco who had approached him when he was visiting a client in prison to ask if Dillinger was trustworthy. It was O'Leary who had thought of the operation. It had been he (Piquett) who wanted Dillinger to surrender, and O'Leary who had counselled the outlaw against it. He had some assistance when Judge William H. Holly told the jury, 'It is not required of a lawyer to surrender his client or to inform law-enforcing agencies of his whereabouts.'

Then during his closing speech to the jury Edwin Peifer collapsed. Ada Martin, a Piquett friend who was described as a trained nurse, ran to his assistance. In fact she was an abortionist in whose racket Piquett worked; his role was to pay off bereaved husbands in botched jobs.

Was the fainting a stunt? No, Peifer had actually suffered a heart attack. Piquett stepped into the breach and made a barnstorming address to the jury:

> I have sent no widows to asylums. I have not stolen from banks nor cheated in receiverships. I am here to be made a horrible example. I am to be sent away for representing a client.

Nevertheless he was not hopeful of an acquittal. Privately he told his wife to say nothing in the event of an adverse verdict but, when it came to it, the jury retired a mere five hours before acquitting him.

'The verdict was one of the greatest surprises that has occurred in Federal Court circles for years,' commented the *Tribune*. 'You are a very lucky man,' said Horace Hagan, waving a finger at Piquett – the only one of 15 defendants in Dillinger cases to obtain a not guilty verdict. But there still remained the indictment for assisting Van Meter.

And then Piquett seems to have made a series of blunders. No transcript of the first trial was obtained and the notes his own stenographers had taken were not written up. He also rather boasted about the hold he claimed to have on Judge Holly and did not endear himself by crowing over the defeated prosecutors. When the new trial began in June 1935, with Brian McMahon leading for the government, Piquett was thoroughly unprepared. He displayed, said the *Tribune*, 'a devil-may-care attitude combined with injured innocence'. He believed that the acquittal on the Dillinger indictment allowed him to argue *autrefois acquit* and to have the indictment quashed. The judge did not agree, saying that Homer Van Meter was not Dillinger and the dates during which the conspiracy was alleged to have occurred were different.

The prosecution had the transcript of the trial and Piquett's answers were lovingly put to him by McMahon as he was reduced to a string of hesitations and 'I can't remembers'. Later he said it was because he feared a prosecution for perjury. Nevertheless at the end he gathered himself for one more speech. Tears ran down his face and, like the long-dead Bill Howe, he delivered part of his address on one knee:

> I am nauseated that the government should take after me. Even the man who killed Lincoln had the right to have an attorney represent him, and so did the men who killed Garfield and McKinley and Cermak. I, too, had a right to represent a criminal.[16]

This time the jury was out only two hours and twenty minutes before returning a guilty verdict. The result did not please Mrs Martin, who had to be pulled away from McMahon.

On 27 June Piquett was sentenced to two years imprisonment and fined $10,000, the maximum penalty, with Judge Sullivan delivering a little homily:

> It is always hard for me to deprive a man of his liberty especially a man who belongs to the same profession as I do and who I have known for fifteen years. I have always found Mr Piquett to be amiable, jovial and a gentleman. But he is too easily led.

On 1 October 1935 Piquett was disbarred by the Illinois Supreme Court. A series of appeals was denied and, a broken man, he surrendered to custody on 4 May 1936. He served some 21 months before being released on 11 January 1938. He then worked, as he had done when studying law, in a series of bars, and in 1945 was found tending bar at Coburn's, 112 South Clark Street. He was never allowed to practise law again. Over the years J. Edgar Hoover preached long and hard about him being a corrupter of the judicial system who kept criminals in business, which ensured that anyone who might have an ounce of sympathy for Piquett knew exactly where he would stand with the powerful head of the FBI. Later, in January 1951, Piquett did receive a Presidential pardon from Harry S. Truman and was making a further attempt to have his licence restored when he died of a heart attack on 12 December that year.[17]

1 Carl Sifakis, *The Encyclopedia of American Crime*, p.207.
2 Pierpont was born to a farming family from Leipsic in Ohio. He had been hit on the head with a baseball bat as a child and subsequently suffered from violent rages. Makley, born in 1889, was a smart talker able to argue his way out of unpromising

situations and an accomplished bank robber. Hamilton was known as 'Three Finger Jack' following a sleighing accident in Sault Ste Marie, Michigan.

3 The elegant and amusing Arthur O'Leary had met Piquett while selling dubious stock in a Pennsylvania lime company and had gone to work for him. His chain to Dillinger seems to have come through another crooked lawyer of the period, Hymie Cohen, the right-hand man of Sonny Sheetz who ruled part of Lake County. Cohen ran gambling and prostitution. Earlier in his career O'Leary had been associated with Lewis W. Mack, disbarred for appropriation of the client account. O'Leary does not seem to have imparted this knowledge to his wife because when later in his career he too was having legal problems she gave Mack $1,000 for her husband's defence which he promptly embezzled.

4 Until the duty solicitor schemes in police stations and at court this was a common practice in England. I recall a major bank robbery in which I was instructed by the wives and families of the suspects. As was the practice I was denied access to the men and I was cooling my heels at about 1 a.m. in a police station in North London hoping to be allowed to see them in the near future when a solicitor, Peter Rusk, appeared. 'I hear there's been a big robbery and some people are in custody,' he told me. 'Yes,' I replied firmly. 'They are all my clients.' Rusk had come from, I believe, Hungary and had a practice near Clerkenwell Magistrates' Court. He had a thick middle-European accent and a penchant for handing out ties to co-defenders, police and court staff alike. He was completely without malice but, in truth, not a man one would want defending you in more than the simplest of cases. There is a story, which may possibly be true, that he once brought his dog into court where the irascible magistrate Tommy Davis was sitting and tied it to the dock. 'Take it out, Mr Rusk,' Davis is alleged to have said. 'I have to listen to you but I don't have to have your dog in court while I do so.' Rusk retired from practice and became a court clerk.

5 For an account of the case and Piquett's summation see the Chicago *Daily Tribune*, for March and particularly 2–12 April 1931. After the case there was a week's review of the investigation and a tribute to Lingle. According to the paper Rosenheim was not a reporter but a blackmailer known as 'The Squawker' who used his contact with the rival *News* to ill-effect. Little is known of Jack Hagan except that he had once been an associate of the Genna brothers and was said to have been a one-time member of Egan's Rats, a St Louis gang. He seems to have cozied up to a Pat Hogan and wheedled the nickname 'Buster' from him. Buster was Leo Bader, alias Leo V. Brothers. Egan's Rats were founded in about 1900 by Jack 'Jellyroll' Egan, principally as strike-breakers. By the 1920s with unions more firmly established, the members turned to safe-breaking and, once Prohibition was announced, entered the game with enthusiasm under the leadership of Dinty Colbeck. The Rats did not really survive the end of the era. Colbeck was shot and the gang split up in the late 1930s. On the anniversary of Lingle's death the Chicago *Daily Tribune* paid $25,000 reward to Hagan.

6 One suggestion is that Capone paid for the jury fixing. If so, what was Brothers doing in the camp of Capone's arch-enemy George Moran? It is also suggested that Moran was displeased with Lingle's political power and his influence over the appointment of Bill Russell as police chief with whom he shared a $100,000 Stock Market account. Another suggestion is that he had been blackmailing a relatively small-time North Side operator, Jack Zuta, and had been scamming money from him under the pretext that he would get back dog-track licences for him. Zuta was briefly questioned over the murder and released. He was next seen in Upper Nemahbun, 25 miles west of Milwaukee where he had gone for the summer and where he was shot on 1 August as he played the mechanical piano at the Lake View Hotel. Legend has it that the machine was playing 'Good for you, Bad for Me', a current smash hit, at the crucial moment. The likely reason for Zuta's death is that it was feared he would co-operate with the police.

A more likely explanation for the killing of Lingle is that he was in a hole. His own tax affairs were not exactly squeaky clean. Lingle could be squeezed by the IRS to give evidence against Capone. In return he might also collect a finder's fee of 10 per cent in the dollar on all money recovered. There is sufficient evidence to show that Capone was prepared to treat tax investigators as his street opponents and not award them the courtesies extended to prosecutors and journalists.

7 See for example G. Russell Giradin, *Dillinger: The Untold Story,* Chapter 7, who does not believe the story and Carl Sifakis, *The Encyclopedia of Crime,* who suggests the meeting between Piquett and Murray took place at the grounds of the Century of Progress in Chicago. It is accepted that there was a meeting between the men; quite when it took place and what was discussed is less clear.

8 Youngblood did not last long on the outside. He was killed on 16 March, shot by police officers in Port Huron, Michigan. Dying, he laid a trail away from Dillinger, saying they had been together the previous day.

9 Clark received a sentence of life imprisonment after the jury had recommended mercy. Charlie Makley was shot to death in another prison escape attempt, this time at the state penitentiary in Colombus, Ohio, on 22 September 1934. On 17 October 1934 Harry Pierpont was electrocuted at the same state penitentiary.

10 At least Wanatka made some money out of the whole affair. He had almost been wiped out in the Depression and the Lodge was his last throw. After the battle it became something of a tourist attraction, and over the years he added various Dillinger artefacts.

11 Perhaps the most famous of gangster's doctors was Joseph Patrick Moran, who was no relation to Bugsy, on whose payroll he appeared for a time. Moran had started life well enough, qualifying with honours from Tufts Medical School. Convicted twice of performing illegal abortions, he then worked as the quasi-resident house physician for Capone.

One version of his death is that in 1934 Fred Barker and Alvin Karpis paid him $1,000 to change their appearances. Moran was drunk and he botched all his work, leaving the men in extreme pain for weeks. When the bandages came off Karpis was even uglier than before and he had merely burned away the top skin on the men's fingers. Moran was taken by Barker and Karpis to Toledo where he was shot and dumped in a lake. Another version of his death is that after the Battle of Little Bohemia in April 1934 he refused to treat John 'Red' Hamilton who died at a Barker-Karpis hideout in Aurora, Illinois. This, together with his unreliability in drink, caused him to be shot after Dillinger's death. There is a story that while in drink he had been boasting in the Casino Club near Toledo where he was last seen that, 'I have you guys in the palms of my hands.' Fred Barker is said to have remarked later, 'Doc will do no more operating. The fishes probably have eat him up by now.'

Now techniques have improved. In February 1997, 68-year-old Dr José Castillo was convicted of harbouring a fugitive and obstructing justice. He had been the confidant of Philadelphia drug lord Richie Ramos whose face he had successfully altered after he disappeared in 1990. He also sliced 50 lbs of fat from his waist and cheeks and turned his fingerprints upside down. Ramos was not found until 1992 when he was offered the chance of 30 years instead of life without parole if he agreed to give evidence against Castillo. Ramos did what he could for his doctor by failing to recognise him in a courtroom identification where the choices were Castillo, a 39-year-old lawyer and a young woman, but the damage had been done.

12 Loeser was also known as Dr Ralph Robeind, and many references to him are in this name.

13 It often suits lawyers to denigrate their clients, downgrading them in the sphere of activities for which they are about to be sentenced. They must, however, be careful to ensure the client understands that this downgrading is not a personal thought but is for the purposes of obtaining bail, reducing a sentence or guaranteeing favourable newspaper coverage, and so does not take offence. When Joseph Tangorra (known as Joey Flowers) and Joseph Truncale appeared with others charged with racketeering in Brooklyn, one of the lawyers commented, 'If these defendants represent a high level of organised crime figures then America is safe.' The lawyer, making assurances doubly sure, spoke to the press on the condition that he was not named. *New York Times*, 29 November 2000.

14 There is a theory that the FBI were duped and it was a small-time gangster genuinely called Jimmy Lawrence who was actually killed. See J. Robert Nash, *Dillinger: Dead or Alive?* In the intervening years Anna Sage had done some travelling. She had been threatened and blackmailed in Romania, had plastic surgery and, for a time, had gone to live in Cairo. See *Empire News*, 1 May 1938. In 1937 Ed Singleton, Dillinger's first partner, fell asleep on a railway track while drunk and was run over by a train.

15 Chicago *Daily Tribune*, 15 January 1935.

16 Chicago *Daily Tribune*, 25 June 1935.

17 Most of the others in the case did really rather well. Arthur O'Leary and Dr Cassidy, who had been in custody awaiting trial, received a year's probation for conspiring to harbour. Loeser received a day in the US Marshal's custody and was returned to Leavenworth to complete his sentence. He disappeared from sight. Cassidy killed himself on 30 July 1946 in Chicago and O'Leary also faded from view, retiring to Dubuque, Iowa. On her release from prison, Billy Frechette, Dillinger's girlfriend, undertook a variety tour, as did his father John Dillinger snr., offering reminiscences of their lover and son respectively. Of Dillinger, Billy said, 'He liked to dance and he liked to hunt ... I think he liked gravy better than anything else. He liked bread and gravy.' She married and surfaced briefly when her husband, a minor criminal, was arrested in Chicago in the 1950s. It is thought Polly Hamilton may have given up the life and married into respectability. For a very full account of Dillinger's career and relationship with Piquett, see C. Russell Giradin with William J. Helmer, *Dillinger*.

# 12 Rosner and Leuci

IN 1973 EDMUND ROSNER fell foul of the New York judicial system when he was convicted of attempting to bribe an agent in the United States Attorney's office for the South District of New York. He was sentenced to five years. Years after he finally went to prison there are still discussions as to whether he was in fact simply the victim of the system rather than a suborner of the police.[1]

Rosner was the only lawyer to go down as a result of the perjured testimony of Bob Leuci, the detective who became known as the Prince of the City. The consensus of opinion is that he was desperately unlucky to be convicted on the evidence produced.

Edmund Rosner and his wife Nancy were both highly successful and expensive lawyers, Nancy being regarded as the brighter. They wore stylish clothes, drove stylish cars and had a high social life. She, the daughter of a Bronx barber, was a graduate of Chicago Law School who was hired by the slightly older Rosner. They became partners and later married. Alan Dershowitz, who conducted the appeals of Rosner, describes her:

> ... an extraordinary lawyer: clever, tough, articulate, prepared and persuasive. She used her exceptional looks to advantage. Her courtroom costumes were all of the same cut: tailored suits with tight skirts; a modest jacket worn partly opened over a low-cut and revealing blouse. She was the picture of sexuality; the effect was as riveting as it was calculated.[2]

In 1966 Rosner opened his own law office specialising in criminal defence work. He did volunteer work for both the Civil Liberties Union and the Congress on Racial Equality. Specialising in heavy drug cases, perhaps his best-known defence (apart from his own) was *Massiah v US* in which a convicted drug-dealer was freed on the grounds that an undercover government agent had extracted statements without the man's lawyer being present.

In 1967 Pedro Hernandez was allegedly seen making a heroin sale in New York. He instructed Rosner that on the day of the indictment he had been in Miami at a CIA-sponsored anti-Castro rally. Travel receipts and hotel reservations were produced to support this along with three witnesses, one a government agent. When this occurred the prosecution was granted an adjournment and on further checking it was found that on the day in question Hernandez, far from being in Miami, had been taking a blood test in New York prior to obtaining a marriage licence.

Hernandez was found guilty and sentenced to 7 years. His witnesses were put before a Grand Jury but declined to answer questions. Hernandez gave Rosner $10,000 for an appeal, which somehow does not seem to have been lodged. He then wrote a letter of complaint to the presiding judge.

Now came offers for him to roll over and give up his lawyer Rosner along with Rosner's investigator, Nicholas DeStefano. When Hernandez went along with the suggestion, Rosner and DeStefano were indicted and Hernandez was released on parole. Rosner hired Maurice Edelbaum, regarded as one of the top criminal defence lawyers of the time and by some as the greatest criminal lawyer they had ever seen. Nancy Rosner took over the practice; together they worked on the defence. To a large extent they were in the dark because they had no indication of what supporting evidence there might be to back Hernandez.

At any rate, that is Dershowitz's interpretation. The version by Robert Daley, former New York City Police Commissioner, is different in almost every way and certainly a darker one. Rosner is described not as a natty dresser with a beautiful wife but as:

> A somewhat overweight young man, with a slightly pockmarked face. His manner was arrogant. In court he strutted, he postured, he was loud – and he carried this performance to such lengths that

his opponents conceived for him a physical distaste as well as a legal one. They called him obnoxious, a man (according to one assistant U.S. attorney) with a detestable face.[3]

The authorities believed that Rosner was the organiser of a string of defences through which, with bribed and perjured evidence, he gained acquittals for major drug-dealers. They believed that Hernandez, along with one of the witnesses, would give evidence against Rosner.

Again it is difficult to determine which version of the events took place. Dershowitz has Hernandez, now out of jail, simply disappearing to Mexico where he remained happily until the statute of limitations against Rosner had run out. Daley again has a more sinister version, with Hernandez disappearing because he was terrified of Rosner and consequently in fear of his life. One of the other witnesses, Gilberto Pulido, was placed in protective custody.

Over the years other lawyers who liked Rosner had warned him about his conduct. William Hellerstein, now Professor of Law at Brooklyn Law School, says, 'I told him years ago, "Eddie, you've got to stop this." He crossed over the line for self-interest. He was a smart fellow but he had no judgement.'[4]

One thing which is certain is that Bob Leuci, who had long been a totally corrupt officer and whose cousin was a captain in the Colombo Family, was sent out to trap Rosner. In February 1971 he had been called to appear before the Knapp Commission established to investigate police corruption in New York and named after the chairman, Whitman Knapp. Routinely called in the hope that he would provide evidence against other narcotics officers, he was interviewed by Nicholas Scoppetta – later to become Commissioner of Investigations for the City of New York – who at an early stage smelled that Leuci was by no means completely wholesome. Eventually a deal was offered: if Leuci would co-operate, then his slate could be wiped clean.

Leuci probably had his own agenda. He was keen to head off any investigation into corrupt policemen, which would inevitably reveal much more of his own participation than he was prepared to admit. What he proposed was that he should expose corruption amongst defence lawyers, assistant district attorneys and judges. It was agreed that he should target what was referred to as the Baxter Street gang, a loose association of criminal defence lawyers, bail bondsmen and minor judiciary around the Baxter Street courthouse. They included DeStefano.

There is no doubt that through DeStefano Leuci did meet Rosner on several occasions. At first it seems the lawyer wanted nothing to do with the blandishments about obtaining evidence. Later, as he was fed incorrect stories that Hernandez was dead and he, Rosner, was favourite for ordering the killing, he succumbed. The Leuci version has Rosner as a much more participating player. Worse, in an effort to save his own skin DeStefano also became a government witness and attended meetings between the Rosners and their new lawyer, Albert Krieger, reporting back to the government on defence strategies in the Hernandez case.[5]

On 24 January 1972 the charges against Rosner in relation to Hernandez were dismissed. Rosner had successfully argued that the government had violated his right to a speedy trial under the Sixth Amendment. Two months later and a few days after the statute of limitations ran out, Hernandez was found in Mexico City. Although he was returned to New York, the judge declined to reinstate the perjury charge against Rosner. Five months after that the New York papers blew Leuci's cover.[6]

Unfortunately for the prosecution, Leuci now decided that he was not going to admit to any crimes, not even the three or four he had admitted to Scoppetta. He was eventually persuaded that these must be admitted – the last was over five years previously – but nothing was said about others which he had, at least partially, let slip.

The trial became a test of credit with Krieger, not holding a full deck of cards, vainly trying to get Leuci to admit more than the three crimes. In turn Leuci presented himself as being an arbiter for those from whom money had been extorted:

> [a] sort of breath of fresh air [whom] they could count on to sit at a mediation or that sort of thing and give them a fair shake.

Robert Morvillo, who led for the prosecution, put it to the jury full square:

> Is Rosner telling the truth or is Detective Leuci, supported by those tape recordings, telling the truth?

The jury thought that Leuci supported by the tapes was. Rosner was convicted on five out of seven charges and sentenced to 5 years' imprisonment. Almost immediately he discovered a number of heroin addicts who alleged they had bought drugs from Leuci, but on a motion for a new trial Judge Bauman ruled their testimony could not be believed and denied it. In England it is expected that counsel who have appeared at a trial will conduct the appeal proceedings, so providing continuity. In America appeal proceedings are invariably conducted by specialists, so now Krieger dropped out. The outspoken Harvard Law Professor Alan Dershowitz[7] took over running a series of investigations and appeals which gradually exposed Leuci as a thoroughly corrupt officer and tried to show that lawyers such as Robert Morvillo had been party to the knowledge of the detective's misconduct. It was an uphill and eventually unsuccessful struggle, although he did succeed in getting Rosner's sentence reduced to one of three years which meant it could be served at Allenwood penitentiary, a white-collar minimum security establishment. In all probability, a 5-year sentence would have been served at Lewisburg where Rosner could have expected a hard time.

As for the players, a highly successful film was made about Leuci. Dershowitz became a successful thriller writer. Some time after the case he represented a client accused of a stock-fraud involving a man named Michael Hellerman, who claimed that Robert Morvillo had assisted him in arranging for the FBI to seize funds following which, through a series of manoeuvres, Hellerman could pay off some pressing loan sharks. Dershowitz raised this in court, confronting a very angry Morvillo. He attributes the later story which appeared in *Village Voice* to the failure of Morvillo obtaining either a federal judgeship or becoming the United States Attorney for the Eastern District. Instead he went into private practice and was appointed chairman of a group 'to investigate charges of unethical conduct by lawyers'.[8]

As for Edmund and Nancy Rosner, the former spent eight months at Allenwood before being released to a halfway house where he worked for a legal publisher. He was disbarred and, despite a series of applications for new trials, so far has not succeeded in having his convictions quashed. 'He was a wonderfully talented lawyer, but his wife was even better,' recalls New York lawyer Gerald Shargel. 'He paid $3,500 to have material he would have got by operation of the law but later. Lawyers are like anyone else. They make mistakes in judgement.'

Nancy Rosner developed her practice of defending major criminals. Like so many lawyers she became involved with one of them. After his conviction had been quashed by a federal district court on a writ of *habeas corpus*, she went off with him to France. The Court of Appeal reversed the lower court's decision and he was called back to prison. Nancy Rosner returned to New York where she started a realty business under her maiden name Packes and the title The Feathered Nest. Recently she sold out of this highly successful enterprise.

1 For differing accounts of the case see Robert Daley, *The Prince of the City*, which argues that Rosner was a long-term corrupt lawyer. For a justification of, and mitigation for, Rosner see Alan M. Dershowitz, *The Best Defense*, in which Rosner is portrayed as very much the victim of governmental machinations.

2 Alan Dershowitz, *The Best Defense*, p.323. See also *Parade*, 22 August 1976.

3 R. Daley, *Prince of the City*, p.92.

4 Conversation with author, 16 October 2000.

5 The affable shaven-headed Krieger, named as 'Dean of the Black Collar Bar', those lawyers whose job it is to defend clients alleged of being *mafiosi*, had a large New York practice before moving to Miami. He returned to New York to take over the defence of John Gotti snr. after Bruce Cutler had been expelled by the court. His clients have included Joe Bonanno, the first of the senior *mafiosi* to write his memoirs. Other paid-up members of BCB are listed as Frank Ragano, James LaRossa and Bruce Cutler. See John Lombardi, 'The Goodfather' in *New York Magazine*, 8 August 1998.

6 *New York Times* and *Daily News*, 15 June 1972.

7 William Hellerstein recalls him: 'Alan is a brilliant lawyer but when they see him judges turn down the temperature many degrees. They don't like being excoriated in print if they don't agree with him. It's very bad ju-ju if you're a lawyer.'

8 Alan Dershowitz, *The Best Defense*, pp.378–9; 'A prosecutor beyond the law? Robert Morvillo: His Informant Raided a Bankrupt Firm' in *Village Voice*.

# 13 Martin Light and the Gambinos

ON 29 JANUARY 1986 MARTIN LIGHT, a New York lawyer then serving a 15-year sentence for possessing slightly under two grams of heroin with intent to distribute, told the President's Commission on Organized Crime what it was like to be a Mob lawyer. Light had grown up in Brooklyn where his grandfather had a Turkish bath frequented by members of Murder Incorporated. He had gone to Brooklyn Law School and, in his last year there, had worked for the District Attorney in King's County. He had wanted to work full-time for the DA, but a prerequisite had been that applicants had to come through the Democratic Party. So he had joined the Democratic Club and within a year the door was opened.

A key phrase of his was 'doing right' and one of the first things he did was to do right by Larry 'Kid Blast' Gallo of the Gallo Family.[1] Young assistant district attorneys often presented cases to a Grand Jury and, when Light was presenting one regarding an extortion racket worked on a painting contractor, Larry Gallo was subpoenaed to attend. Outside the courtroom he came across to Light and explained he was nothing to do with the extortion but that somebody had misguidedly been using his name:

> ... [Gallo] says you know we have nothing to do with this; and he says you know the way we are – you grew up in the neighbourhood; he says if we do something wrong, you just call us on the telephone and we'll come down, you don't even have to come to the house; he

says, but God forbid, if we are innocent and somebody looks to frame us, shame on them; he says you know I have nothing to do with this case; if you are going to put me in the Grand Jury, it's going to be a problem for us, because we can't testify.[2]

It did not take Light long to decide that it would not be fair to put Gallo in front of a Grand Jury and have him go to jail for contempt on 'something he had nothing to do with'. So he said the right thing and excused him.

At the time assistant district attorneys were allowed to supplement their incomes by acting in civil cases such as traffic accident claims – provided that if the case could not be settled, it was handed to another lawyer for the court appearance.[3] He now began to represent friends with whom he had grown up, such as Joe Deserio of the Lucchese Family and Louie Astuto 'Louis Fats' of the Gambinos.[4] When he had papers for signature he would go to the 19th Hole in Brooklyn, which was basically a Lucchese Family hang-out, on one of the days 'when everyone would meet'. His appearances in the 19th Hole did not please the new District Attorney, who forbade him to carry on with his part-time work. He left the District Attorney's office on 5 September 1969 and set up practice as a defence lawyer.

It was then that he had one of those pieces of good fortune which determine the success or failure of a criminal practice. His mother met Sammy Weiss who was part of the Greg Scarpa crew from the Colombo Family, remarked that her son was setting up his shingle and gave him a business card. That night Weiss was arrested together with some associates and Light was asked to represent them. From then on he represented members of all five Families and became particularly close to Greg Scarpa, who had been a made man since the 1950s and who led the support for Alphonse Persico as head of the Colombos when his father, Carmine, was imprisoned.

Scarpa led from the front, shooting at those he perceived to be his and Persico's enemies. He also had a powerful ally in R. Lindley DeVecchio of the FBI, for which organisation he had been an informant for 20 years.[5]

Born on 28 May 1928, Scarpa had joined the Colombo Family through the offices of his brother, Salvatore, who was killed in 1987. He married and had three sons one of whom, Gregory jnr., also joined the Family. He had a good income from loan-sharking, drug-dealing, credit card fraud, a chop-shop and, as befits any good mobster, $250 a week social security and, as does not befit one, as Agent NY 3461 informant's earnings said to total over the years in excess of $150,000.

Scarpa's career with the Bureau dated back to 1962[6] when, on 20 March, he had been arrested outside New York State in the act of committing an armed robbery. It was not his first arrest – he had previously had charges of assault, bookmaking, possession of stolen mail and hi-jacking dismissed. While he was reputed to enjoy killing he was also reputed to dislike the concept of prison even more and, in an arrangement to avoid hard time, he rolled over.

In 1986 Scarpa was trapped in a credit card sting and DeVecchio was obliged to use some of his considerable resources to ensure that his charge was placed on probation and fined. At the time Scarpa was suffering from bleeding ulcers and paid the penalty for something of a racist outlook on life. He did not want blood given to him from the hospital bank in case that came from blacks. Some thirty of his friends and colleagues were therefore corralled into giving blood. It was not all tested, and the blood of one donor who had contracted HIV from an infected steroid needle was used. The infected Scarpa's weight dropped by 75 lbs and much of his stomach had to be removed. He sued the surgeon, Angelito Sebollena, and the Victory Memorial Hospital and, exhausted during the hearing, settled for $320,000 cash to be paid within 24 hours. Later, a woman juror said that they had been prepared to award him millions.[7]

On 18 November 1989 Scarpa and his girlfriend's daughter, Linda, were pulling out of his driveway in their cars when they were ambushed. A van and truck blocked the exit and men in ski-masks opened fire with automatic weapons. Neither was injured. The next year he was involved in a gunfight with Joe Waverley on Avenue U and survived. The month after that he shot Waverley in the stomach. In the August he was arrested on murder and conspiracy charges and because of his illness he was finally given house arrest bail on condition that he wear an electronic anklet.

Unfortunately, on 29 December 1992 Scarpa became involved in a gun battle with Bay Ridge drug-dealers near his Brooklyn home. The electronic bracelet showed that he left home on 82nd Street at 12.01 and drove two blocks to the fight. A bullet hit his nose and shot out his left eye. Incredibly, this man with full-blown AIDS and little stomach walked home, drank a glass of whiskey and drove himself to hospital. The other men were taken to hospital, one with a gunshot wound to the back of his head and the other with wounds in his arms and stomach.[8]

On 6 May 1993 Scarpa pleaded guilty to three murders and to conspiracy to murder. His informant's file with the FBI had once more been closed and he applied, unsuccessfully, to go back on the books. He died in prison on 8 June 1994.

Back in the 1960s and 1970s Martin Light, full of admiration, became Scarpa's mouthpiece:

> Very well-dressed, well-groomed, good-looking, bright, articulate, vicious – I mean he could have dinner with you, and then when it comes time to have dessert he could kill you.
>
> You could see the way everyone answers to him. I mean, he had a club on 13th Avenue and he sits in the chair and everyone comes up to him, and no one ... they don't double-park their car without getting his permission, so to say. In other words, no one does anything without getting his permission.

If anyone in Scarpa's crew was arrested for the run of Mafia problems – shylocking, hi-jacking, gambling, counterfeiting, stolen bonds, narcotics – Light would automatically have the defence. The defendant himself would not have his choice of counsel, nor would he necessarily have access to the papers involved. Scarpa would always be involved in discussions and the defendants expected this:

> Whenever we had cases, he was always in on the discussion – he is very, very bright. He could have been a lawyer probably, or run any big business. But it would be no fun to him.

If a person at a lower level in the organisation had to take a plea to protect his superiors, well that was part and parcel of his life. The Family was more important than the individual:

> Well, it's always the Family that comes first; what's best for the Family is what counts.

As for payment by the underlings, who might or might not be sacrificed for their money, Light would go through a charade with Scarpa over the payment:

> So I would say to him: Does the kid have money, how much can he afford – you know, $10,000? He'd say, 10,000, what are you, crazy?

It's a lot of money because we are going to have to chip in and help him pay it.

So I says, well, you tell me, what do you think is right? He says, all right, you know what, 7,500. I says great, no problem. So he says I'm going to call the kid in and we'll discuss it; I'll tell him – I'll turn to you and say how much do you want, and you'll tell me 10,000, and then I'll tell the kid it's too much money, no way – you got to charge him what you charge me – that way we give the kid some confidence that his boss is looking out for his good, and the boss is on his side.

The cash payments Light reckoned were between 80 and 90 per cent of his fees for a year, of which he accounted to the Revenue for about 30 per cent:

You have to show something; I mean you know, I had a big house and a big car and nice clothes. I had to cover myself up to a certain point.

Scarpa himself did not have to pay for Light's services. Light regarded it as 'smart business'. Nor would Persico, who Light very sensibly would be

glad to represent him for nothing in anything ... out of respect, out of friendship – and they sent a lot of business – we would not charge them at all.

In fact Light and his law partner had a partnership with Carmine Persico in what amounted to a supply company without any supplies. If anything from paper to detergents was required, calls would be made and a deal brokered. They had a third, as did Persico, and the man who was running the business took the remaining third.

In the course of his examination, by design or accident, Light let slip that on one occasion the company had been asked to supply a 55-gallon drum. Pressed, he admitted that he had subsequently obtained an acquittal in a case involving a drum. Carelessly the stomach of the victim had not been lanced and with gases expanding and creating buoyancy the drum floated to the surface of the East River. His client – Billy Cutola of the Colombo Family, who later went on to be a member of the Teamsters Union – had been charged with murder. Afterwards, at a party to celebrate the acquittal:

... we were drinking, we were feeling no pain, we were joking around – that, you know you shot this guy in the head, and according to the medical examiner that, as the person was dying the blood is coming out of the wounds, and as soon as you die the blood stops, so the blood coagulated in the head – and we were talking about it. And I says you think you're so smart, right? He says, well, next time I'll know better, I'll cut his stomach open so the gases could escape and he won't come up.

Just as junior defendants were not made party to decisions taken on their behalf, nor, necessarily, were all defence lawyers in a multi-handed case:

If I was hired as lead lawyer, then I would call the shots; in other words, if it was a six-defendant case and I get the case, I would bring in five lawyers, friends of mine, lawyers similar like myself that could be trusted to do the right thing.

It would be decided who would file motions on behalf of which client and any lawyer who declined to co-operate would find himself dismissed from the case. As for fees, he would keep a third and divide the rest.

If a defendant summoned to appear before a Grand Jury did not obey instructions and decline to answer questions, then Light would report this back to Scarpa. If in a case he chose a lawyer other than Light, then this might be regarded as a sign either that he had committed the crime without letting his captain know or that he might be co-operating with the government. In either case he was not 'doing the right thing' and that had to be reported as well.

Light would be expected to assist in getting witnesses to change their evidence or to leave the jurisdiction. If the witnesses would not co-operate, then they and their families would be threatened, something Light said happened several times a year. It would be his job to get sufficiently long adjournments, possibly by producing false medical certificates, so that the witnesses could be straightened. He would also be required to bribe public officials to see closed court records and, if possible, get into judges. Money laundering was not his forte, but he had assisted in cleaning money through Atlantic City casinos where money would be cashed for chips which themselves would almost immediately be cashed in.

So far as he was concerned, he knew of cases where witnesses were killed, and he regarded it as automatic that if a member of organised crime was found to be co-operating then he would routinely be killed. He certainly should have known of one case because Light himself had been charged with a woman in a bank fraud. He had been acquitted, but she had pleaded guilty and been debriefed by the Drug Enforcement Administration during which she implicated Light. A month later she, her nephew and her eight-year-old son were shot to death.

If a case was lost Light would be required to arrange false witnesses who would impeach witnesses at the original trial. During his 15-year-long career he corrupted police, assistant district attorneys, public officials and, on occasions, judges. He would also be required to make his office available for meetings for crime figures whose conditions of parole included a term that they did not associate with known criminals. One of his clients who used this facility was Carmine Persico on his release from prison:

> If you are on parole and you are seen at a wedding or at a wake or at a restaurant talking to another felon, it's automatic violation. Now, if you come up to the law office, the law office generally is not under surveillance, and if you go to a law office where there is 20 or 30 stories no one knows where you go. And if they do know where you go, he says I went to see my lawyer, and it just so happened that the other person went to see his lawyer or the same lawyer or one of the lawyers in the suite. And you're covered. Legally, they can't violate you if you went to see a lawyer.

Life could also be harsh for lawyers who failed to do the right thing. On one occasion Light's partner failed to notify Lenny Di Maria of the Gambinos, who was then on Riker's Island, that his appeal had been rejected. Di Maria found this out by chance from his cell-mate who had seen it in a law journal and he was not pleased: he had been belittled, lost respect. When he was released he went down to the Ravenite Club, a well-known Mafia hang-out in Little Italy, and told a member that he was going to deal severely with Light whom he held responsible for this loss of face. Light was obliged to get Christy Furnari, a *consiglieri* of the Lucchese Family, to call on one of the West brothers to tell Di Maria that he had better be careful who he was looking to hit because Light was being protected. Until the matter was straightened out Light remained indoors. Other lawyers such as Gino Gallino and Bobby Weisswasser had not been so fortunate and, according to Light, had been killed.

Lawyers were regarded as extraneous and could be beaten or killed, but permission had to be granted unless they were known to have become informers – when they could be killed at once. Light did not regard himself as being at the top level of organised crime lawyers. There were two older and wiser lawyers in New York, he thought, who acted for the bosses and as a result had more respect and looked down on the second division lawyers such as Light himself.

He believed that in New York there were 20–30 lawyers like himself who had been operating for up to three decades. Not surprisingly, there was a network of similar lawyers throughout the States. As for the legitimate lawyers, he accepted that they would not be hired so frequently because they could not provide the required extras.

Towards the end of his evidence Light was asked to account for the decline of the rule of the Jewish gangster such as Siegel, Lansky and Moe Dalitz. The explanation was simple. Successful members of organised crime were setting up their sons as lawyers, businessmen and politicians. Legitimate businesses were being established for them, but their fathers would ensure that their sons had no competition to worry about.[9]

How had he slept at night? Surely he had been in constant fear of either physical harm or denunciation? He accepted that throughout his career as a Mafia lawyer he had been constantly tested to see if he was doing right. He was very careful that he did not act as a bagman when a police officer was being bribed so it could not be suggested that he had pocketed some of the bribe for himself. Instead he would make an introduction for a fee and let the parties work the deal out for themselves. As for betrayal:

> [So] I was protected in my mind, that these people were organised crime people and they just know that they don't talk.

He was correct. Had it not been for his arrest for heroin he believed he would never have been convicted:

> I mean, being an attorney, a well-respected attorney, if the government – when I got arrested, if I didn't have this sample on me, then it would be the word of the witness against mine. And the witness's word would never hold up, from my experience, if I got on the stand – I am a lawyer, I went to this client's house to talk to him and I left and I got arrested. How can I get convicted? The jury would normally believe the lawyer over a witness.

He had put his credo to the test when he was indicted in May 1971. One of his clients, Carmen Santiago, had been arrested the previous September and was currently serving 15 years after being charged with possession of a loaded gun and narcotics at her hotel, the St George in Brooklyn. The prosecution alleged Light had been undertaking a little extra-curricular work by trying to bribe the patrolmen who had arrested her. The case could be sorted out 'whatever it takes; whatever it's worth'. Six days after this approach he met with an unnamed detective whom he recruited to offer one of the patrolmen $5,000. Later he personally offered the man $3,000. The patrolman rejected these blandishments and reported the matter to the District Attorney.[10]

At the trial in 1976 the prosecution had played a tape-recording of the alleged bribe offering, and had used the evidence of both the police officers and the narcotics suspect. Giving evidence, Light had accused the police of stealing $5,000 from his client when he was arrested on the charges. He was acquitted.[11]

Later, in 1981, he and six others were charged by a Brooklyn Federal Grand Jury with defrauding banks and credit-card companies between 1978 and 1980 by using lost and stolen credit cards to ring-up purchases. Light, who once more gave evidence on his own behalf, was the only person to be acquitted.[12]

At his drugs trial he had devised a perjured defence – something which in his penitent state he now naturally regretted, he told the Commission. Even though Light was away, Persico was paying his wife a pension of some $400 a month, something Light expected to cease immediately it was discovered he had been talking to the Commission. In fact it is likely that his wife's income would have ceased irrespective of whether Light had given evidence. In November 1986 Carmine Persico received a sentence of 9 years on racketeering charges. On 13 January 1987 he received a 100-year sentence to run concurrently with his 9 years. He had been convicted of running a commission which controlled labour, loan-sharking, extortion and murder in the concrete industry in New York City. Light, angling for an early parole, had gambled against severe reprisals against himself and his family. As far as can be known his gamble was a successful one.

As for his heroin trial, he was arrested on 14 July after visiting the Brooklyn apartment of an alleged drug-dealer who had agreed to co-operate with the authorities. The meeting was recorded by a machine hidden in an attaché case. According to the evidence he examined two 1.1-lb bags of white powder, complained about the quality of a previous shipment and took four samples – two from a bag of heroin and two from a second bag which contained a substance substituted by the Drug Enforcement Agency. He was arrested as he left the apartment and the samples were found, wrapped in aluminium foil, in his running shorts. After a four-day trial he was acquitted of conspiracy and heroin importation charges but convicted of possessing heroin with intent to distribute. He applied for bail pending sentencing but this was refused, the judge saying that given Light's many contacts in the Underworld he feared that he would use them to 'alleviate his financial crisis'.[13] The week before he had successfully argued that a client should have a re-trial because the jurors had read that he, Light, had been arrested.

In February 1985 Light received the maximum 15 years sentence after a number of his ex-clients told the court that the lawyer had been involved in murder plots, drug-trafficking, robberies and numerous other crimes. The prosecution had submitted a scathing 19-page sentencing letter to the court and Light had contested many of the allegations. As a result a sentencing hearing had been arranged.[14] One former client, Pasquale Senatore, told the court that while he was awaiting trial for armed robbery in 1959 he had been offered $5,000 to kill a woman who lived near Light. He had, he said piously, turned down the offer despite pressure. When he and his partner went on trial he had been told by Light that it would improve his chances if one of the witnesses disappeared. Later when he was told the witness was dead, Light commented, 'There you are, if you had done the same thing with these two other people here, we wouldn't even be on trial.'

Judge Nickerson told Light that his criminal activities were a 'squalid perversion of the lawyer's role', adding that it was the 'court's duty to try to deter those lawyers who might be tempted to act as had the defendant'.

His assessment of himself as not being in the top class was shared by his fellow lawyers. Manhattan lawyer James De Rosa, who over the years has defended his share of the top echelons of crime Family members, thought of him and his downfall as 'Greed, mostly and poor judgement letting himself be caught. He wasn't the quality of Shargel or Cutler. He wasn't a top tier lawyer. At best he was a journeyman.'

He had been represented at his final trial by New York lawyer, Frank A. Lopez, who had himself had a very serious run-in with the authorities over the so-called French Connection case and who came in for serious criticism from the President's Commission in its final report.

In December 1974 a New York State Special Prosecutor had filed an application for an order to show cause why Lopez should not be held in contempt for his failure to answer questions before a Grand Jury investigating the theft of narcotics from the New York City Police Department.

In the late 1960s a huge drug consignment belonging to the French Connection and being sent to America was seized, but unfortunately it subsequently disappeared from safe lockers at the New York Police Department. Lopez was the lawyer for and – alleged the Crime Commission – co-conspirator with Vincent Papa who in 1973 was the target of Grand Jury investigations. Papa was indicted for refusing to answer questions, but before then he had taken the precaution of instructing Lopez to meet with criminal associates and other potential witnesses to monitor and co-ordinate their anticipated Grand Jury evidence. The aim was that Lopez should frustrate the investigation. All the legal fees of those Lopez represented would be paid by Papa.

With Papa in custody Lopez was used to carry messages back and forth, including one to Virgil Alessi who was instructed to carry out a murder. Lopez fulfilled his task. Later he apparently removed cash from the safe deposit of Genevieve Patalano, so thwarting the police who were on their way to seize the contents. He was recorded as saying to his law partner:

> They are going crazy yesterday ... We waited outside the bank until it opened; we ran into the bank vault, pulled the money out, left there just what she said was there and beat it. An hour and a half later they were there with the boys.

Lopez was indicted by the Grand Jury on a total of 24 counts of criminal contempt in the first degree regarding his refusal to answer questions relating to his role in safeguarding Papa's interests. The indictments were dismissed because law enforcement agents had conducted electronic surveillance on him in an unlawful manner.[15]

Kevin Rankin was another in the firing line. This Philadelphia lawyer drew 54 years for his participation in a criminal narcotics conspiracy, but the conviction was overturned in 1986. He had, said the Commission, used his position as a lawyer to suborn perjury, bribe, arrange and participate in a variety of drug-trafficking offences. The Commission considered his case 'if anything, more loathsome than Light's'. He had fabricated a perjured defence in the case of Raymond 'Long John' Martorano and Albert Diadone who were accused of contracting the murder of John McCullough, President of Local 30 of the Roofer's Union, with whom they were locked in battle.

On 16 December 1980 Willard Moran jnr., posing as a flower deliveryman with a poinsettia plant, shot McCullough six times in the head with a .22 revolver on his front doorstep while his wife stood helplessly by him. Diadone and Martorano were given up by Moran, and Rankin paid a prison guard to perjure himself in an affidavit discrediting Moran. Unfortunately the guard was at the time under investigation regarding a drug deal with Rankin and Martorano's son. When questioned by federal agents he admitted his part, went home and killed himself.

However, Rankin had continued to mind the shop for Martorano and was holding strategy meetings designed to limit Martorano's exposure to his heroin and cocaine networks. One meeting was attended by a 'Mob-connected' lawyer from Miami who was a Federal undercover agent. After learning the 'lawyer' had received a $200,000 fee from a coke deal, Rankin advised on how the money could best be placed.

A rather sadder case is that of the Miami-based lawyer Robert Slatko, who was drawn into organised crime because of his serious drug habit. Principally a civil lawyer, he was introduced into organised crime by a major drug trafficker who purchased a Florida bank in order to provide a ready-made high-volume money-laundering service. Slatko was in fact only one of a number of lawyers involved. Law offices were specially designed to frustrate physical and electronic surveillance, and they were used to 'close' drug deals when cash was exchanged for cocaine.

The lawyers were paid in a mixture of cash and cocaine, with additional payments as bonuses. Slatko came unstuck after a major sub-dealer sold drugs to an undercover agent; he had another lawyer draft perjured statements by defence witnesses and schooled them on how to answer questions. A co-operating attorney persuaded the dealer to be represented by a trusted colleague and together they persuaded the dealer to plead guilty. In return the dealer was paid throughout his time in prison.

In one deal Slatko described to the authorities how a well-known member of a Florida-based Family approached a lawyer and explained he had nearly half a million dollars to launder which he wished to place in a hospitable offshore regulatory climate. An aeroplane was arranged to fly the man and the lawyer to the Cayman Islands where the money was successfully deposited in a numbered but untraceable account. The lawyer's payment was half a kilo of cocaine.

Unfortunately the Family member disappeared in mysterious circumstances with over $1 million cash belonging to other members of the crime Family. The lawyer was kidnapped and forced to disclose details of the previous transfer. To save his life he arranged for the repatriation of the money.[16]

After Slatko was convicted and his appeal against a 5-year sentence was refused he committed suicide.

The Commission called for changes in professional standards so that a lawyer should report misconduct whenever he had reason to believe it was taking place, and that suspected attorneys be subjected to aggressive investigation including, where necessary, wire taps.

In fact at the time there were a number of other lawyers who had been similarly tempted if not in quite the extreme way as Light, and the President's Commission's final report had a few harsh words to say about each of them. They included Michael Corio (sometimes Coiro), convicted on 30 November 1989 at the age of 60 on a federal racketeering conspiracy charge of helping drug-dealers conceal their assets. He was also convicted of obstructing justice by advising his clients to lie and withhold information from a Grand Jury investigating a Gambino heroin operation.

His trial had begun seven years after being caught on a bug planted in Angelo Ruggiero's kitchen. Throughout he had been represented by Gerry Shargel and the case had been adjourned on a number of occasions. Now Shargel was involved in another trial and, when Judge Joseph McLaughlin refused any further postponement, he was represented by Bruce Cutler who regularly appeared for John Gotti. On this occasion Cutler did not have a happy time. Early in the trial he had described Corio as having 'an unusual full-service practice'. Cutler has been described as being at his best when he cross-examines informant witnesses, but here the evidence was almost all taped recordings. When he tried to put in evidence 100 pages of transcripts of recordings he wished to play, the judge was less than amused to find the pages were out of sequence.

*Cutler*: Your Honour, maybe I am missing what you are saying ...
*Judge*: You are missing a body of knowledge called the law of evidence ... I suggest you take a course ...

Later Cutler made two short stipulations on behalf of the defence and then during the closing speeches the prosecutor John Gleeson, a very different lawyer from the inexperienced man who had prosecuted Gotti in 1985, continually threw the 'our full-service lawyer' reference in his face.

With the verdict against him and after being released on bail of \$120,000 pending sentence, Corio went with Cutler to the Ravenite Club and into an upstairs room where he met Gotti, Frankie Locascio and Sammy Gravano. Apparently a problem had arisen over the killing of Gotti's former boss, Paul Castellano, shot to death outside Sparkes' Steak House on New York's East Side, and it seemed as though Corio might have to give evidence. He was also asked to see a man he knew in law enforcement to enquire which (if any) Gambino captains might be indicted. He undertook to do this and Gotti was impressed. Gotti estimated a 10-year sentence for Corio, of which he might have to serve 4 years, but by the time the judge and Gleeson had finished he received 15 years. He was then hauled from prison, subpoenaed to give evidence before another Federal Grand Jury investigating the Gambinos. He was repeatedly asked if he had ever attended an upstairs room meeting with Gotti at the Ravenite and his denials earned him a further 27 months for perjury, reduced on appeal to 9 months.

Corio had long ago crossed the line dividing the lawyer and the participant. Caught on tape speaking with Gene Gotti, John's brother, he is heard in the following conversation:

*Gotti*: ... I told you that you're our lawyer – you're not our lawyer, you're one of us as far as we're concerned.
*Corio*: I know it ... and I feel that way.[17]

1 Larry's brother, 'Crazy' Joey Gallo, was one of the first of the major Mafia figures to understand that it was possible to have a relationship with black organised crime figures. He and his brothers were at war with the Profaci Family whose Joe Colombo was shot by the Harlem-based Jerome A. Johnson on 28 June 1971. He lived, brain-damaged, for some seven years. Joey Gallo was shot and killed on 7 April 1972 as he dined in Umberto's Clam House in Little Italy. Control of the Colombo Family passed to Carmine Persico. The brothers' real claim to fame was that they killed Albert Anastasia in the barbershop of the Park Sheraton. They were satirised by Jimmy Breslin in his book and later film, *The Gang That Couldn't Shoot Straight*.

2 All the quotations in this chapter are from the Report of the President's Commission on Organized Crime. To make for continuity I have juxtaposed some of the answers.

3 It was not so very different in England. Many solicitors who worked in the old Metropolitan Police Solicitor's Department had lucrative conveyancing practices to which blind eyes were turned.

4 It is easy to see how associations begin: 'When I was a child my parents lived next door to a Mafia enforcer and I sat next to his son at school. When my father died I was at the funeral parlour when I had a telephone call from the man's son saying he was sorry he was unable to come to the funeral because he was in the state penitentiary. He sent his sister along to pay the family's respects.' Conversation with Chicago lawyer, Stephen Komie, 18 September 2000.

5 There is a long, detailed and entertaining account of Scarpa's career and challenged relationship with DeVecchio by Frederic Dannen, 'The G-Man and the Hit Man' in *The New Yorker*, 16 December 1996.

6 In January 1966 he was recruited to go south to Mississippi to assist in the interrogation of Lawrence Byrd, suspected of setting fire to the grocery store owned by Vernon Dahmer who was to allow his store to be used as a place for blacks to pay poll tax. In the arson attack Dahmer had died and his ten-year-old daughter had been badly burned. The interrogation proceeded satisfactorily. Byrd was snatched outside his television repair shop, taken to swampland and there Scarpa beat him to within an inch of his life. Byrd signed a 22-page confession, received a ten-year sentence and was never the same again. After some trouble Scarpa was paid a $1,500 fee.

   Now he received a good deal of support and protection from an agent, Tony Villano, who used him as a bookie, obtained reward money for him and, when a Drug Enforcement Agent was killed in 1970, went to some lengths to ensure Scarpa was not arrested. Five years later Scarpa was shut down as an agent and not re-opened until five years afterwards when he became DeVecchio's man.

7 Later the surgeon found himself in some more trouble. In 1991 he injected two male patients with Versed, which causes immobility but allows the retention of consciousness. He then had oral sex with them. At the Scarpa trial the judge initially had some difficulty in coping with the situation, telling Scarpa's lawyer, 'Let me get this straight. You're representing a hitman with AIDS against a doctor who sodomizes his patients. Am I on the right page?'

8 The fight had been as a result of a complaint by Joseph, his son by his long-standing mistress Linda Schiro, that he had been treated disrespectfully by the dealers. Joseph himself was later shot in a drug deal.

9 There were a number of fathers in organised crime families whose sons followed in their footsteps. These included Frank Balistrieri who, along with his two lawyer sons Joseph and John, was convicted in Milwaukee on 9 April 1984 of a Hobbs Act extortion over vending machines. Frank Balistrieri received 13 years and his sons 8 each. Disbarred lawyer Carmen Milano, once of the Cleveland Family and who with his elder brother Peter headed the Los Angeles Family in the 1980s, had been disbarred following his handling of fraudulent workers' claims. Again in California in 1974 and for a second time in 1980, Dominick Brooklier was defended by his lawyer son Tony on racketeering charges. See Kim Murphy, 'Not Entrenched like Eastern families', in *Los Angeles Times*, 29 June 1987.

10 *New York Times*, 20 January 1992.

11 *People v Light*, 340–72 (Kings Cty. Sup Ct).

12 *U.S. v Chester*, 81 CR 061.

13 *U.S. v Light*, 84-CR-454S (E.D.N.Y.).

14 This is know as a *Fatico* hearing. In England and Wales more or less the same principle applies. If a defendant admits an offence but disputes the facts, then unless the judge is prepared to accept the defendant's version and sentence him on that basis there must a *Newton* hearing on the facts.

15 See President's Commission, pp.241–8.

16 *Ibid*, pp.239–40.

17 *Ibid*, pp.232–7.

# 14  Ellis Lincoln and Manny Fryde

SOMETIME AFTER HE BECAME Lord Chief Justice in January 1946, Rayner Goddard felt able to say that there were a dozen dishonest criminal lawyers in London and he knew the names of them all. Whether they were all solicitors he never felt able to elaborate. Presumably he included the West End solicitor, Benny Canter, who was one of a number over the years who acted for the Messina brothers – Maltese pimps who controlled vice in the West End for nearly 20 years.

Canter became involved with an officer from the Ghost Squad which had been established at the end of the Second World War to allow officers the freedom to infiltrate criminal organisations. It lasted only a few years because there were fears that the officers were being corrupted by their close association with career criminals.[1] The officer in question was Detective Sergeant Robert Robertson who, while seconded to the Squad, met Morris Page, a hanger-on to the Messinas and their brother-in-law, Tony Micalleff.

Canter and Robertson's downfall came in 1955 when they were involved in the case of a Joseph Grech, charged with housebreaking. Grech seemingly had an unshakable defence. Part of the evidence against him was that the key to the burgled premises had been found on him. Grech maintained that it fitted his own front door and therefore was of no significance. The jury found it was and – from his cell where he was serving three years – Grech unloaded a series of legal bombs.

He had, he said, given Page around £150 to hand to Robertson, who made the key to the burgled premises available so that a locksmith could make a lock to be fitted to Grech's front door. There was to have been a further £150 for Robertson on an acquittal. He also alleged that Robertson had coached Ben Canter about the questions to be put at the trial.

When Robertson, Page and Canter appeared at the Old Bailey charged with conspiracy to pervert the course of justice, Grech unloaded even more bombs. His conviction, he said, had been brought about by the perjured evidence of other officers acting on the instructions of an Inspector Charles Jacobs, attached to West End Central. Jacobs, he maintained, had asked him for £2,000 so that none of his flats or brothels would be raided. After negotiations the terms had been set at £500 down and £30 a week. Canter, said Grech, had been the bagman, taking the £100 to give to Jacobs. According to Grech, Canter came back saying, 'He wants £500.'

When he came to give evidence Canter was in difficulties over his relationship with Micalleff, who had been accepted as a surety in the original case by Robertson:

——Can you imagine any honest policeman agreeing to take Micalleff as a surety for this man Grech?
——That is a difficult question to answer.
——I think it is a simple question. Try to answer it ...
——It depends on the circumstances.

Canter received two years' imprisonment, as did Robertson who for many years continued to protest his innocence, consulting various firms of London solicitors in efforts to have his conviction overturned. The intermediary, Morris Page, went to prison for 15 months.

The first Great Train Robbery may only have required a lawyer to assist in the disposal of some of the gold. The second Great Train Robbery, just over a century later, required very much more active participation.

In the past a number of solicitors have been quite content to leave the running of even quite substantial practices – sometimes in part, sometimes in entirety – in the hands of their managing clerk. They have done this through a combination of reasons – indifference, trust, laziness, dislike of legal practice – and at times it has been to their very considerable cost. John Denis Wheater, who employed the dishonest clerk Brian Field, was one.

Peta Fordham, writing of his trial, described him as having:

> A sad, weak face, with a kind of Edwardian, outdated pomposity.
> The eyes were slightly protuberant and unusually round: the hair,
> always immaculate, looked like a Tussaud production. The mouth
> was invisible beneath a 1910 moustache.

And when he came to give evidence:

> ... as the larynx quivered below the unaggressive chin and the
> hitherto impassive face moved, the pitiful mask, so carefully
> contrived from the front, seemed to slip aside. It was as if a woman,
> face to face with the mirror, had executed a careful make-up, full
> face, but had omitted to see herself in a triple glass. Suddenly, in
> that side aspect, the picture of failure stood out in clear relief. Here
> was no crook, simply a disappointed, not very successful man, who
> had just failed to make the grade all the way along.[2]

Wheater had been educated at Uppingham and awarded the
MBE during the War for his bravery in the Italian campaign. On
the death of his father he had joined the Army Legal Service.
Like so many he had really wished to become a barrister, but the
expense and risk were too much. When he left the service he set
up in practice employing not only Brian Field, whom he had
met in the Army in Japan, but also Brenda Field, his clerk's ex-
wife who acted as secretary and deputy for both Wheater and
her former husband in the affairs of the firm. Now Field was
married to Karen, the ballet-dancer daughter of a German judge.

On the other hand his clerk Brian Field was a good-looking
and highly personable man. He had joined Wheater from the
firm of Probyn Deighton, which then handled a good deal of
heavy criminal work. Jeffrey Gordon, later President of the
London Criminal Courts' Solicitors' Association, remembers
Field being pointed out to him at Inner London Sessions by E.O.
'Cappy' Lane, from the Metropolitan Police Solicitors
Department, as being one to watch in the sense of his becoming
a high-flyer. Field had defended a number of high-class villains,
including Gordon Goody in one of the numerous London
Airport robberies.[3] This one had taken place on 27 November
1962 and netted the tidy sum of £62,000. Goody had been
arrested along with Charlie Wilson, Buster Edwards and Roy
James, all of whom would be involved in the Train Robbery. He
had also passed information on to Goody about potential
country house burglaries. Wheater would appear in court for

Field's clients, although he was not regarded as a great advocate. 'His favourite phrase in mitigation was "He stands at the crossroads." I haven't heard anyone say that for years,' remembers Gordon.

One version of the Train Robbery story is that it was Brian Field who provided the participants with the introduction to a man who had the necessary information. In any event it was he who organised the purchase of Leatherslade Farm, the hideout for the team near Brigedo where the robbery was to take place. He did this with funds from a client named Henry Alexander Field (no relation to Brian) who was facing such diverse charges as buggery, horse-doping and robbery at Stoke. Brian Field obtained a power of attorney in favour of Leonard Field, Henry's younger brother. Wheater borrowed £1,000 from Henry Field's funds, some of the balance being used to buy Leatherslade Farm for £5,500. Leonard Field was to receive £12,000 when the robbery was successful; meanwhile he was told that the property would be used to store stolen cigarettes. Brian Field was to receive a full share of the robbery which took place on 8 August 1963. The pair of them went to view the farm together.

On 16 August two office workers, John Ahern and Nina Hargreaves, walking into the woods near Dorking, saw a briefcase, holdall and camelskin bag. In the briefcase were bundles of £1 notes. They went for the police, and further in the wood a suitcase containing slightly over £100,000 was found. In the camelskin bag, apart from some German currency, was a receipt from the Café Pension Restaurant, Sonnenbichl, Hindelang, made out to Herr and Frau Field. It had not taken long for the police to discover that James and Wheater were the solicitors who had acted in the purchase of Leatherslade Farm and that Field was a clerk in the firm. It was confirmed that Brian Field and his wife had stayed in the *pension*. Seen at his home, he admitted his firm had defended Henry Field and that Lennie Field had come in to ask them to purchase the farm for him.

Meanwhile, the day after the police found the farm Wheater telephoned offering his assistance. He had, he said, purchased the property for Lennie Field, the brother of a client, and he told them that Henry Field lived at 262 Green Lanes, Stoke Newington, which was where the police found Lennie. So far, so good for Wheater. Unfortunately for him when he was confronted with Lennie Field, perhaps out of misguided loyalty to his clerk Brian Field, he went along with his client's story that he had not purchased any farm. Nor was Wheater at all sure that Lennie Field was the man who had come into his office to pay the deposit on the property. The purchase had never actually been completed, but Field had been allowed into possession to begin some building work.

On 15 September Brian Field was arrested and charged with conspiracy to rob the train, Lennie Field having been charged with the same offence the previous day. Wheater was arrested on 17 September at his home in Ashtead, Surrey. As the police were about to search the premises there followed a little conversation with Tommy Butler when he said, 'Don't think I'm being rude, but I would like to search you people first. I don't want anything put on me.' Butler told him he had been listening to too many fairy stories from his clients.

Wheater was acquitted of conspiring to rob the train, but Lennie and Brian Field were convicted. Wheater was convicted of conspiracy to obstruct the course of justice and received three years' imprisonment. The Fields were also convicted of the same conspiracy and received 5 years apiece. Their appeals against conspiracy to rob the train were allowed, but they received no joy from the Court of Appeal when they tried to have their sentences reduced.[4]

Wheater was struck off the Rolls as a solicitor and, after his sentence, went back to the Midlands to assist in running a family business. It might be thought that a moment's hesitation and indecision had done for him, but in fact it was a rather longer period of the non-supervision of his clerk which brought about his downfall. He probably knew a little more about the aftermath of the robbery than was made clear at the trial. He had a client who had approached him regarding the defence of Buster Edwards and Wheater had Edwards' number in his diary. When asked during the trial, the client declined to waive privilege and allow Wheater to say what had passed between them.

Commenting that in many ways Wheater's was the saddest of the cases the judge said:

> There is no evidence that you contributed to your present disastrous position by any profligate manner of living. Indeed your standards seem to have been distinctly lower than your managing clerk Brian Field.

Wheater was paying Field £20 a week and his mortgage. What Field was making on the side was probably double that and more. He was certainly in a position to run a Jaguar motorcar.

Wheater said of himself in the witness box:

> I decided some time ago that I was not cut out to be a solicitor. I think a lot of my clients must have suffered through my carelessness.

In May 1967 the Glasgow hardman 'Scotch Jack' Buggy was killed. He had last been seen in the grandly named Mount Street Bridge Club, which was undoubtedly in Mount Street but where kalooki rather than bridge was the game of choice amongst the patrons. Eventually his body was found bound with baling wire off the coast near Seaford. All kinds of suggestions for the motive were advanced, including involvement with the Mafia and protection rackets. Nipper Read, who had been a junior officer on the Train inquiry, was then serving at West End Central and Field called on him at the station to say that it was common knowledge that Buggy had been in prison with Roy James and had learned that, as with so many others from the Train, his money had been squandered by those to whom he had entrusted it. When Jack Buggy was shot he had been trying to retrieve it on behalf of James and possibly on his own account.[5]

By this time Field was long out of prison. He worked first as a salesman, where his employer described him as 'quite brilliant'. In 1969 he then married a British Airways stewardess and they opened a restaurant in Cornwall. That venture failed, as did the marriage. He then became the overseas exhibitions manager of a publishing company in London and in a local wine bar he met a Welsh girl, Sian Hope. They married and began to develop property.

In April 1979 he and his wife were killed in an accident in which the family of the hairdresser 'Teasy Weasy' Raymond was also involved. They had been driving back from the West Country when their Porsche was crushed by a somersaulting Mercedes. Field had changed his name to Carlton and his real identity was not announced until September 1979. His new wife's family was staggered when, after his death, it learned of his past. Field had wanted to change his appearance and had been advised that merely altering his hairstyle would probably suffice, but he had insisted on a £1,000 facelift. Karen Field, who had remarried a German journalist, said of him, 'He was a very kind man, always patient and understanding.'

Nipper Read recalls him:

Field was a real smoothie and a man of great charm. I had known him when he was defending, and in his professional life he was always extremely straight with me. If he was going to do something he would tell me in advance and not spring it on me in the witness box.[6]

Probably the criminal firm *par excellence* of the 1950s and early 1960s was that of Ellis Lincoln, son of a Southampton solicitor and brother of Fredman Ashe Lincoln who became a barrister. Then in 1966 it all came tumbling down.

That year he was undertaking his twenty-ninth murder case, of which he had lost only two clients to the gallows. His clients had included Lucky Gordon, involved in the Profumo scandal, and three of the Great Train Robbers, as well as Joey Martin who had been convicted of manslaughter after the 1960 shooting of his girlfriend's flatmate. Martin had gone round to the house and, finding his girlfriend away, had gone to bed with her flatmate. Next morning he had been showing her how his Luger pistol worked when he shot her. He was traced after it was discovered that he had left his tie behind. Martin, not defended by Lincoln on this occasion, was convicted of a murder within six months of his release when he took part in an armed robbery at a milk depot in Wood Green during which a milkman who tried to prevent the robbers' escape was killed.

An old London villain recalls:

We all had Lincoln in those days and we seemed to get Not Guilties. He was the one. People talked about Wheater who had that clerk Field but I never heard of him before the Train Robbery.

One former member of the court staff at Marlborough Street where Lincoln used to appear regularly remembers him as:

A plumpish, moustachioed bullshitter. He was all right really, but you had to watch him.

In fact Lincoln had had a chequered start to his career when, in 1940, he was suspended from practice for five years. Now in February 1966 at the Inner London Sessions after a case had come before the court unprepared, his firm was struck off the list of solicitors who could undertake legal aid work there. The circumstances show how different things were from today. The legal aid order had been issued on 1 February and the trial called on 7 February. On 11 February Osmond Martin,

Lincoln's clerk, was hauled before the irascible Reggie Seaton, Chairman of Inner London Sessions, to be told that this was the end of the road as far as legal aid work at that court was concerned. Seaton had removed the firm's name from the list on a previous occasion, but, 'I was prevailed upon to restore it after six months.'

The next week Lincoln made a statement explaining that he had not received the certificate until 3 February. By the time his clerk had an appointment to see the defendant in Ashford remand centre, bail had been granted and with the out-of-court-out-of-mind syndrome which affects clients, the youth had failed to make a visit to Southampton Row an immediate priority. He would be seeking counsel's opinion about the steps he should take to reverse the decision.

He did succeed in getting himself restored, but by now he was under attack on a number of fronts. The next month the firm's former managing clerk, Bertram Hall, who dealt with the conveyancing, was on trial at the Old Bailey for fraud. He blamed Lincoln for his troubles and the jury accepted his story. Meanwhile an application was being made in the Chancery Division to commit Lincoln to prison for his failure to honour undertakings given, he said, by Hall. To add salt to the wound the news of Hall's acquittal came while Lincoln's counsel was reading an affidavit setting out the clerk's alleged defaults. Lincoln squeezed out of that one with an order to transfer a lease to the plaintiffs. In turn they did not press for him to be sent to prison.

On 17 June 1966 he was struck off. He accepted that his book-keeping was not all it might have been, but he complained that the Law Society's penalty was far too severe:

> I feel I should be like my train-robber client Thomas Wisbey. I should sit on a boiler-house roof and protest. I am sincerely hoping that the Lord Chief Justice who is to hear the appeal will appreciate that I am a respectable and reputable person.

When it came to it, however, the Lord Chief Justice was far from impressed. He and the other members of the court accepted there had been no suggestion of fraud and that it was his clerk, Bertram Hall, left largely unsupervised, who had been the cause of much of the problem. Nor had there been any loss to a client because Lincoln had repaid the money from his own pocket. There were bundles of testimonials from counsel, magistrates, clerks and clients.

Unfortunately two years before, in October 1963, the Law Society had warned him over the quality of his book-keeping and that he must ensure the books were kept up to date. The court upheld the ruling of the Disciplinary Committee.

Lincoln had hoped that his son Bryan would take over the firm, but the Law Society ruled that Ellis Lincoln could not work for his own practice and it was sold to Nathan Vengroff for a nominal £225 under what Ellis Lincoln called a special agreement. 'Vengroff was a very odd choice,' recalls a contemporary. 'He was a very nice, very religious Jewish gentleman.'

Some of the details emerged at Lincoln's bankruptcy hearing in December 1968 before Mr Registrar Parbury. His firm had been expanding and gross fees were in excess of £60,000. The idea behind the sale was that Vengroff would apply to the Law Society for approval for Lincoln to work with the firm at a salary of £40 per week. All Lincoln had received was £112 in settlement of an electricity bill. He had gone to work for Vengroff at an office in Cork Street, Piccadilly, until December 1966 when he had literally been handed his cards on a Friday and told not to come back after the weekend. In the following April he began a law consultancy office in Museum Street, Holborn, and passed a substantial amount of his work to the Irish solicitor, the engaging Brendan Quirke.

One barrister recalls Lincoln behaving just like Abe Hummel sixty years earlier and no doubt like many unsung heroes in between:

> I knew him when he was a managing clerk but the customers wouldn't know the difference. They'd have thought he was still the solicitor. He didn't have the usual line with clients about their cases, instead he conveyed the impression that he had a hotline to a network of highly placed policemen and judges all of whom were itching to help. I'd be at the magistrates' court and Ellis would arrive and say, 'I'll give so and so a ring.' He would immediately go and start making calls from the pay phone. I don't know he ever made a connection even but the client was impressed.

In 1971 his application to be restored to the Rolls had been refused. Part of the reason may have been an appearance in a contested civil action in 1967, a spin-off from the troubles brought about by Bertram Hall. Mr Justice Megaw had regarded him 'as a wholly unreliable witness whose evidence was in many ways untrue'. It cannot have helped him.

'He talked to these people as if they were human beings but that's not on – they may be human beings but you can't speak to them as such,' says Louis Diamond, who worked with him for a short period.

Villains regarded him as crooked:

If, say, a Sergeant Smith had your case he'd approach him for you and then tell you how many pounds you had to pull up. He'd act as your go-between.

Some thought he played both sides of the fence:

The other lawyer you could get into was Ellis Lincoln. He was bent but not in the way Patrick [Marrinan] was. With the likes of Lincoln he would take your money and still shop your defence. It was a chance people took. He played it both ways.[7]

A solicitor who appeared in cases with him recalls:

What he would do is pretend he was in a position to bribe an officer not to oppose bail. He would take the money but often he never made any approach at all. If he got bail that was fine, but if he did not he would merely tell the client and his family the officer had gone bent on him. No one was in a position to complain.

Norman Beach of the North London firm Beach and Beach was regarded as another proposition altogether. His clients suffered from the fact that many magistrates actively disliked him, therefore the benefit of any doubt they might have had was not going to them. He was a quirky little man with perhaps more energy than actual ability, who wore a moth-eaten grey-green bowler. He acted in any number of the big criminal trials of the time.

A former member of the court staff at Marlborough Street recalls:

The magistrates thought that if you had him you must be guilty as he was the only man who could bullshit enough to get you off. He was small and ferrety and he used every trick in the book. To get a fair trial at Marlborough Street was very difficult if you had Beach representing you.

One of his contemporaries remembers:

Norman Beach was outrageous. I was at the Old Bailey one lunchtime and there was a terrible hoo-ha. Norman had walked off with the prosecution's papers. He was very apologetic ... picked them up by mistake ... but when you think they were always in a special place ...

Over the years Norman Beach fell foul of both the courts and the Law Society. Unimpressed with the possible identification evidence against his client, he sought to test the ability of the principal witness in one case to recognise the defendant when he was wearing a ginger wig in the dock.

It was a relatively minor case, certainly not one with overtones of gangland. There had been a car accident after which one of those involved, James Austin Owens, was said to have fled the scene. When the police came round he said the previous morning he had lent the car to a man whose name he declined to give. The whole case hinged on identity, and Norman Beach had the bright idea of getting him to wear a wig to court.

Owens, defended by Patrick Marrinam, appeared at the Middlesex Quarter Sessions on 15 November 1956. Beach came in for a great deal of criticism about the case but, in fairness, he had told prosecuting counsel his intentions. If he had really been intending to cheat would he have done that, or was he covering his back?

Many a defendant likes to look his best in court and for his appearance Owens, an Irish labourer, hired a morning suit for the day from Kritz of the Ritz, for which he paid two guineas and a £10 deposit. He was also wearing a wig. He was identified by one witness, but only by the other when a police officer pointed him out.

> *Crowder*: In order that there shall be no mystery about this, tell us why you went to the trouble of borrowing a wig?
> *A*: I was told to wear it.
> *Q*: By whom?
> *A*: By Mr Beach.
> *Q*: Did you know what the object of wearing the wig this morning was?
> *A*: Yes.
> *Q*: What was the object?
> *A*: Because I heard that witnesses were going to identify me.
> *Q*: So you hoped, did you, that by borrowing a wig they would not be able to identify you?
> *A*: It was to put them thinking.

The police maintained that between the accident and the committal proceedings Owens had taken to wearing thick horn-rimmed spectacles and had grown a moustache.

Within the month the police were making inquiries and when Beach wrote to the Commissioner of Police asking him to put a stop to this, he received the rather dusty reply that he had no authority over the police as to how they should conduct criminal investigations or as to whom they should or should not interview.

Six months later on 7 May 1957, Norman Harry Beach was acquitted of aiding and abetting James Austin Owens to attempt to pervert the course of public justice. The jury failed to agree on a count of conspiracy to pervert. Later the Court of Appeal thought that the judge should have told the jury to convict on both or acquit on both. It was one of the troubles of putting a conspiracy on the indictment when there was a substantive offence. Both Beach and Owens were discharged.

Later Beach said, 'I advised my client to do what he did and we did it because we thought it would assist the course of justice.'[8]

His son Martin Beach, himself a solicitor, believes that his father's action, in the days when identification of a defendant in the dock at court was common, was important in proving that in many cases it was the simple fact of being in the dock which caused the identification. 'The wig case was to prove that by changing the person's appearance the witness may have been briefed that this was the guilty person,' he says. 'Rules regarding the identification of defendants have been toughened over the years and a dock identification is now almost worthless.'

Unfortunately for Norman Beach, in 1977 the Disciplinary Tribunal of the Law Society took against his conduct and struck him off the Rolls of Solicitors. This time it was alleged that, in a major porn trial, he had brought a defendant's Uncle Bertie out of the public gallery to sit in the well of the court with solicitors – the better, so the police said, to intimidate witnesses. In January 1979 the Divisional Court upheld the decision. Again Martin Beach believes his father was the victim rather than the transgressor.

Some four years earlier in November 1973 Sir Robert Mark, then the Commissioner of Police for the Metropolis, had given the Dimbleby Lecture in which he took the opportunity to air the subject of dishonest criminal lawyers, something he later elaborated on in his book:

We see the same lawyers producing, off the peg, the same kind of defence for different clients. Prosecution witnesses suddenly and inexplicably change their minds. Defences are concocted far beyond the intellectual capacity of the accused. False alibis are put forward. Extraneous issues, damaging to police credibility, are introduced. All these are the stock in trade of a small minority of criminal lawyers. The truth is that some trials of deliberate crimes for profit – robbery, burglary and so on – involve a sordid, bitter struggle of wits and tactics between the detective and the lawyer ... Let there be no doubt that a minority of criminal lawyers do very well from the proceeds of crime. A reputation for success, achieved by a persistent lack of scruple in the defence of the most disreputable, soon attracts other clients who see little hope of acquittal in any other way. Experienced and respected metropolitan detectives can identify lawyers in criminal practice who are more harmful to society than the clients who they represent.[9]

As a result, the 1970s and early 1980s saw a string of trials, most of which were unsuccessful, in which partners and clerks from firms of solicitors known to have major criminal practices were prosecuted for a variety of offences, often based on evidence given by former clients or supergrasses. One solicitor who did go down was the affable Louis DeMeza who was given a sentence of four years for fraud. He was acquitted of a substantial number of other charges including the theft of some diamonds. Many thought him to be unlucky, and would have preferred to see some others whom they regarded as far more dishonest convicted in his stead.

One of those acquitted was Ben Yahuda, the solicitor brother of barrister Joe Yahuda who during the War had taken over much of the mantle of G.L. Hardy. Ben Yahuda was regarded as one of the less disciplined of practitioners in South West London, with a penchant for leaving his staff to prepare cases while he himself visited the local brothels.

In the days when the addresses of prosecution witnesses appeared on depositions, Yahuda found that he had not adequately prepared a case due to be heard at Inner London Sessions on the Monday. He therefore telephoned them telling them not to attend. When the case was called on the Monday, Joe Yahuda was appearing and faced a wrathful chairman, Reginald Seaton, who demanded an explanation. Yahuda the elder, who always had chutzpah, replied, 'My Lord, on this occasion I was not my brother's keeper.'

Additionally, there was what was known as a 'black book' in which solicitors alleged to be dishonest or untrustworthy were listed. This was a sign for detectives involved in cases with them to exercise extra care.

Of course what happened a good deal of the time was that the officers who actually conducted proceedings in the magistrates' courts didn't know what was or was not admissible evidence.

When they saw their case disintegrating in front of their eyes through their own ignorance it was much easier to blame somebody – judges, magistrates, jurors, solicitors, anyone but themselves. There was mostly no trickery, just a knowledge of the law which no one had bothered to teach the police.

One solicitor recalls seeing his name under a picture on the wall of a City of London police station as someone not to be trusted. 'It was a photograph of someone else,' he remembers. One lawyer who was indisputably not to be trusted was James Latta. Whether the Glasgow-based Latta was merely house counsel or was in fact the leader of the pack is much more difficult to say.

The twin hobbies of James Maxwell Latta, father of three, who had been a sheriff's clerk before he qualified, were collecting antique pistols and mixing with the Underworld. The doyen of Glasgow's criminal lawyers, Joe Beltrami, recalls him well:

> He adored criminals and I discussed the dangers of too close association with him frequently. Many years ago when Ali fought Henry Cooper in the 1960s you couldn't get tickets for love or money and my client Arthur Thompson came to see me and offer me a couple. He also had an invite to a hotel in Piccadilly after the fight. I stopped for a moment and said, 'Who'll be with me?' He said the Kray twins and also Albert Dimes, and he named a few others. I said no offence but it would be wrong for me.
>
> I met Jimmy Latta the same day and he said he'd love to go. Could I ring up Arthur and get him the tickets? That was the attitude of the man. I phoned Thompson and said do me a favour. When Latta phones tell him the seats are gone.
>
> I used to warn him about his continuing to rub shoulders but he wouldn't have the telling. He was not a character young lawyers should follow. He was always swaggering around the court buildings with his arm round his clients. He used to go out drinking with them and I could see he was going to finish up in trouble. He was very anxious to represent them.

He had what Beltrami regarded as a curious way of obtaining clients:

> Many years ago Willie Smith was in custody. Unlike today, a person was sent to the lower court and then to the Sheriff's court but in the meantime stayed in police cells for four days. Jimmy Latta would go to the pubs where the accused's friends were drinking and discuss the case. He said he'd like to help. Smith had been a client of mine for years. Latta went to the police station and spoke to

Willie saying he wanted to represent him. Willie's reply was, 'This isn't an effing breach of the peace job: this is murder. I've already consulted Beltrami.'

For much of the time Latta's interview room was the Hi-Hi, a bar in Gorbals' Caledonia Road where he mixed with the Tallymen, a gang of moneylenders and protection racketeers whose leaders consisted of Frank 'Tarzan' Wilson, Jimmy 'Baby Face' Boyle and John 'Bandit' Rooney to whom he collectively referred as 'my boys'. It was Latta's part to arrange the bribery and, if need be, the threatening of witnesses. And for many years he was a success.

Boyle's father had been a lieutenant of Peter Williamson, the leader of the pre-Second World War Beehive Gang, and Boyle had carried on his father's tradition. He had attended St Bonaventure's School, which held the distinguished record of having eight former pupils serving sentences of life imprisonment during the 1970s. Between 1965 and 1970 he was acquitted of one murder and a second charge was dropped. On two instances potential witnesses had gelignite parcels posted through their letter boxes.

Wilson was a curious character. In appearance he was heavily built, with an ear half torn off and a Y-shaped scar across one cheek. However, he wanted more out of life than being a simple loan shark and spent a good deal of his time in the public library borrowing books on Sicily and the Mafia. In 1959 he had been acquitted of three assaults when the prosecution witnesses refused to give evidence, and in 1966 a jury returned that peculiarly Scottish verdict 'Not Proven' when he was accused of firing a pistol and stabbing a man.

Then on 14 July 1966 came disaster. A pimp, 'Babs' Rooney, had fallen behind on his repayments but still he and his mistress, Sadie Cairney, were celebrating Glasgow fair in Kinning Park when he was stabbed to death over the £7 debt. Boyle and William Wilson, the brother of 'Tarzan', were charged. Wilson was found not guilty of Rooney's murder but received 21 months for theft and assault. Jimmy Boyle received life imprisonment with a recommendation that he serve a minimum of 15 years. At the trial, moved to Edinburgh, Sadie Cairney said she felt in fear of her life and during the hearings a bomb exploded in the home of another witness, the 15-year-old Eddie McGill.

After some years of unavailing effort the police had now managed to convict Jimmy Boyle, and his removal from the streets at last meant that reluctant and frightened witnesses would come forward. Frank Wilson, along with his chauffeur John 'Bandit' Rooney, whom Beltrami defended, and James Latta received a total of 24 years for plotting to have the two men freed. All were found guilty of inducing people to give false evidence at William Wilson and Jimmy Boyle's trial. Passing sentence on Latta, Lord Grant paid this oblique tribute:

> There is no doubt that the administration of justice in Glasgow has been suffering over recent years because witnesses – whether persuaded or intimidated – have failed to give truthful evidence. It has been a crying scandal. Furthermore the tracking down and conviction of the perpetrators, the instigators, is a difficult and in many cases impossible task. I believe we have been bedevilled in Glasgow in the past years, time and again, by acquittals which have resulted in guilty men going free because witnesses have been tampered with, intimidated, and false evidence given. That has been the experience of every judge who has sat here in recent years and of most counsel. You had special responsibilities as a lawyer to ensure that justice was done. But, instead, you allowed yourself to be brought into a conspiracy to achieve the opposite ends and when a member of the legal profession does that, the wheels of justice fail to turn and justice is in danger.[10]

Latta died in the early 1990s.

Many a criminal practice has been built around an unqualified clerk, in the past sometimes a former police officer who may have left the force shortly before an inquiry into his conduct began. The best known of the clerks of the 1960s and 1970s, however, was a former South African solicitor Manny Fryde. He used to be with a firm in Finsbury Square but then he came to an arrangement with a solicitor named Sampson. 'He was Sampsons,' remembers Ralph Haemms, once his clerk and who, after qualifying, has for 25 years run one of London's largest criminal practices with clients ranging from the Krays and their predecessors, the Nash brothers, through the major London families to present-day luminaries such as Dave Courtney. 'Manny never requalified because he didn't need to.'

At the start, Haemms' career was inextricably linked with Fryde. Haemms came to England from Bombay, where he had a B.Sc. at the University, to read for a Master's degree in chemistry. At the time exchange control was extremely strict and he arrived with £4 in his pocket. He had taken the precaution of buying half a bottle of whisky and 200 cigarettes which he intended to sell at a profit. 'I was so embarrassed I gave the whisky away and smoked the cigarettes, which started a habit lasting 20 years.' He went to stay in a Jewish hostel, of which Fryde was a trustee, in Mansell Street, and he was taken on as a clerk in the office at Ludgate Circus. 'I was the office boy, filing clerk, made the tea, emptied the ashtrays, everything.' Fryde was a heavy gambler and Haemms' other duties included placing bets and collecting winnings:

> He never carried less than £5,000 on him. He sent me to one betting shop opposite the Old Bailey and I wasn't to put the money on until the horses were under starter's orders. I didn't know what that meant and by the time I tried to put it on they wouldn't accept it. Fryde went mad. Another time he sent me to the small shop opposite the Law Courts and I handed in the winning ticket. The girl went for the manager and asked who I was from. I said Fryde. He said, 'Here's the money and tell that effing bastard not to come in the shop again.' It was £12,000.

Fryde knew a potentially good clerk when he saw one and Haemms was ambitious. Tiring of sorting files, he said that either he was allowed to look after criminal cases or he would go back to chemical engineering.

> He knew I was ambitious and I'd work 24 hours a day and I did. He was as mean as anything. He never paid me properly. I remember I went down to Seaford to do an ID parade and I missed the last train and I hadn't any money, just the return ticket. I rang him up about 11.30 at night and he wasn't pleased. All he wanted to know was what had happened to the client. I thought he'd at least say go and stay in a hotel and he'd arrange for the bill to be paid, but no. I stayed on the platform all night.

In those days Sampsons, along with Ellis Lincoln, had the cream of the criminal work including the Kray family. Haemms recalls that just before Charlie Wilson, the Great Train Robber, escaped from Winson Green, he managed to telephone the office.

> Manny and I were out and the message he left was that under no circumstances did he want to be produced in London for his appeal.
>
> Fryde certainly had a working arrangement with some senior police officers, including Tommy Butler who headed the investigation into the Train Robbery, but I was too naïve to know what it was. I do know that the day all their photographs were published in the evening papers Charlie Wilson was in our office.

Fryde did impress on Haemms that it was a question of do what I say and not do what I do. He was a great socialiser with the clients, but Haemms was not allowed to do the same: 'At least he advised me not to do what he did – go out drinking with the clients – and I never did.'

As with most clerks and solicitors of the period Fryde was regarded with suspicion by some police officers but, says Haemms, 'Throughout our association he never asked nor expected me to do anything wrong.'

Fryde was a great Zionist, who kept a list of Blackshirts and sympathisers under the carpet in the office waiting room. Once when he went to a witness's house in a murder case and found a swastika painted on the lavatory ceiling, he refused to handle the case further. It took considerable persuasion to convince him that the daub had been put there by a previous tenant and had not been cleaned off.

In 1972 Haemms qualified as a solicitor:

> When I qualified he came into my room, shut the door and offered £5,000 to change my name to his so that it could be on the firm's notepaper. I said, 'I'll do it if you don't mind that your son changes his name to mine.'

The next year Fryde left England, for a time settling in Majorca. Four years later Haemms opened his own practice in Peckham.

Sometimes it is not possible to know for certain the exact circumstances in which lawyers find themselves. When 36-year-old barrister, Shah Mohammed Tafader, was jailed at Isleworth Crown Court for having two Bangladeshi passports on which the photographs and details had been altered, his counsel suggested that the passports might have been used for 'altruistic purposes' rather than for making money.

He had left a bag containing the passports – one in his name and one in the name of Abdul Karim – in the Gulf Air left-luggage in April 1992 because it had been too heavy for carry-on baggage. A month later he returned and inquired about his bag. When he was questioned he was shown the Tafader passport and asked why it had someone else's picture in it. He told officials he could not explain. His home was searched and a bank machine pin number was found. Released on police bail, he fled. After two years he was retrieved from the Continent in 1994. He was, said his counsel, 'a valued member of his community'. He received 12 months.

One of the most popular of solicitors in the North, amongst the criminal classes at any rate, and vice-chairman of York Rugby League Club was bearded Trevor Cox of Clifford Street, York. His practice was listed as one of the biggest recipients of legal aid fees in the country, and his clients were devoted to him.

Yet he had fought a long battle with the police over his conduct of cases. Following a trial at the Hull Crown Court in 1995, he was arrested at his mother's home after the trial judge Recorder Robert Smith had allegedly ordered the police to open an investigation. Four months later it was announced that no further action would be taken, and Cox said he was considering taking action against the Humberside Police:

> In my view there was never any grounds for the original arrest. I believe the police behaved preposterously and I am asking my solicitors to consider suing them.

In 1996/7 his firm was listed as one of those receiving most money from criminal cases paid by the Legal Aid Board. Then in September 1999 his offices were raided by 20 police in riot gear and a member of his staff was arrested in connection with allegations of perverting the course of justice in the trial of Melvyn 'Adie' McLellan – convicted of the Grimsby murder of a drug user, Gregory Dalton, who died of an overdose. The prosecution case was that Dalton had been lured to a flat where he was given a massive overdose, said by the Crown pathologist to be the highest he had ever encountered in his career.

Cox claimed that he and his firm had been co-operating with the police over a two-year period, and there had been no need for the raid which was to collect the remains of a file he said had been offered to them on a number of occasions. [11]

The officer leading the operation is also quoted as saying that the inquiry involved a celebrated case. Indeed it does: it is the case in which a Humberside police officer fathered a child to the chief prosecution witness while the case was in progress. [12]

By now Cox knew he was dying following a recurrence of the bowel cancer he had been fighting for some years: 'It'll never come to trial,' he told a friend.

Says one observer, 'He'd always got good use for a crate of whisky or a couple of hundred quid.' And another:

He was as dodgy as you like. At one time he had an old gangster doing his investigations for him. He had lots and lots of houses he let out. He would hand out £50–£100 to clients. In those days he could afford to bung them. When he was after a drink-drive conviction he had his clients drive him about and they were happy to do it. They absolutely adored him. He was a very, very nice man.

When he died everything was forgiven. A truce was declared so that criminals could attend his funeral without fear of arrest, and the local magistrates closed their courts. When it came to it his estate was insolvent.[13]

Perhaps the best known of the London lawyers who currently act for career criminals is the dapper, cigar-smoking Henry Milner. At one time he practised in partnership in the East End, but in 1978 he commenced an almost boutique practice on his own in Wigmore Street, handling fewer than two dozen rich clients a year. Since then the roll call has included Mickey McAvoy of the 1983 Brink's-Mat robbery, along with two of the alleged receivers (both acquitted) and a considerable number of heavy drug smugglers from London families. He also includes three of the suspects in the Stephen Lawrence murder inquiry amongst his clientele. A long-standing client has been Kenneth Noye, acquitted of the murder of a police officer engaged on surveillance but sentenced to 14 years for handling Brink's-Mat monies, and now serving life for the 'road-rage' murder of Stephen Cameron. As with all defence solicitors he has had his fair share of criticism by the police. 'There's no criminal lawyer worth his salt who hasn't been on the receiving end of that. I ignore it.'[14]

1 For a history of the Squad, see John Gosling, *The Ghost Squad.*
2 Peta Fordham, *The Robbers' Tale,* pp.147–8.
3 An unsuccessful raid, possibly organised by Jack Spot, took place in 1948. Information was passed to the police, who substituted themselves for the night workers who were to be attacked. An earlier and successful one had been organised in March 1936 at the old London Airport at Croydon by Bert Marsh of the Sabini gang, when a quantity of gold was stolen by means of a duplicate key. For an account of the former see Shifty Burke, *Peterman,* and James Morton, *Gangland;* and of the latter see James Morton, *East End Gangland.*
4 *Field, Field and Wheater* (1964) Cr. App. R. 335.
5 One of the men the police wished to interview was Waggy Whitnall, who was in Vienna, and police went there to see him in the presence of his London solicitor, Andrew Keenan. Nothing came of the meeting, but in 1974 Whitnall's uncle Franny Daniels and Abraham Lewis, who had been working in the club, were put on trial at the Central Criminal Court. The evidence against them was largely that of an Australian shoplifter and blackmailer then serving 9 years. He said that he had been in the gaming room on the afternoon of Buggy's death and that Daniels had come in and told everyone to go home. Both Daniels and Lewis were acquitted. For an account of the case see L. Read, *Nipper,* pp.124–9.

6 L. Read, *Nipper,* p.80.
7 Frank Fraser, *Mad Frank*, p.96.
8 PRO Crim 1 2808/9.
9 Sir Robert Mark, *In the Office of Constable*, pp.154–5.
10 See George Forbes, 'The Trial of the Bent Lawyer' in *Scottish Memories*, March 1998.
11 *Yorkshire Evening Press*, 16 September 1999.
12 *Grimsby Evening Telegraph*, 18 September 1999; see also Andrew Anthony, 'Crime and Passion: Sleeping with the Enemy' in *The Observer Review*, 14 September 1997.
13 Nothing should be read in any way as an adverse comment about Cox's former partners, staff, or the solicitor who currently practices as Cox Robertson and Co. in York.
14 Stuart Wavell, 'The Mr Big in criminal briefs' in *The Sunday Times*, 6 September 1998.

# 15 Ronnie Shulman and Billy Rees-Davies

JUST AS THEY DISLIKE the derisory reference 'Old Bailey hacks' bestowed on them by their brothers and sisters who undertake what is seen as more cerebral and undeniably more profitable civil work, London barristers who undertake mainly criminal work would no doubt resent being called Gangland Lawyers. They would point to the so-called cab-rank rule by which a barrister, if available, is obliged to undertake a case irrespective of the merit of the defendant. They would also point to the insulation provided by the two-tier structure of the English legal profession. As a general rule, barristers could not see witnesses or clients except in the presence of a solicitor or clerk. They would also point to what is seen as the quaint practice of prosecuting in the morning and defending in the afternoon.

Nevertheless, once established a great number never did anything but defend cases. Perhaps in some instances outside London it was not wholly their fault, for in the 1960s and 1970s some prosecuting authorities made it a rule that those whom they instructed to prosecute should never appear for the defence. If they did, then it was off the list.

But over the years a number of barristers have behaved in a suspect manner. One went bankrupt a couple of times, another regularly acted in a way which, had it been his client in the dock and not himself, would have resulted in an immediate custodial sentence. Another made an undignified exit to Hong Kong with (it was said) a man from the Customs and Excise running down the tarmac after the plane trying to serve a writ.

One whose work came in by dubious means was William Hemming, the first former police officer to be admitted to the Bar. A thick-set, pipe-smoking man, he modelled his speech on Winston Churchill and he defended almost exclusively. Despite the so-called cab-rank rule he would not generally accept cases on legal aid. Cash in hand, preferably not through the books, was his policy and cases sent to him via police officers would often be marked with a red star – in which case 10 per cent of the brief fee would be sent to the officer. It was an arrangement which suited everybody. He was not generally regarded as a naturally talented advocate but he could be effective. Perhaps his most significant client was the enigmatic Fay Sadler, a number of whose boyfriends led brief but exciting lives. They included Tommy Smithson, who was shot dead after trying to extort money from some recalcitrant Maltese clubowners to pay Hemming to defend her on cheque charges.[1] After returning from court one day Hemming asked his clerk to bring him a cup of tea and died in his chair while it was being brewed.

Perhaps the nearest there has been to 'house counsel' to a criminal in England is Irish-born lawyer Patrick Marrinan, who advised and appeared for Billy Hill and his entourage in the 1950s.

In his younger days Hill had been a relatively unsuccessful thief, although one from a well-regarded family. His sister Maggie was a member of the notorious and long-lasting Forty Thieves, a gang of women shoplifters who looted high-class shops and stores for well over a quarter of a century. At the end of the Second World War Hill teamed up with the Jewish gangleader Jack Comer, better known as Spot, to take over the West End and remove the current incumbents, the White family from King's Cross. After that he and Spot ran the West End for a period of some seven years with no interference from other villains and little from the police. During that time Hill organised two of the greatest of post-war robberies, the Eastcastle Post Office van robbery in 1952 and, two years later, a bullion robbery in Jockey Fields, Holborn. There were no convictions and none of the stolen money, which totalled a massive (for those days) £320,000 plus, was recovered.

The pair fell out for a variety of reasons. Spot had a truly beautiful wife, Rita, to whom he was devoted but who did not get on with Gipsy, Hill's girlfriend. There is every reason to think that Spot, whose real interest was in controlling bookmakers' pitches, was jealous of Hill's coups. Both men had penned their memoirs for rival newspapers and this led to further discontent. Eventually on 11 August 1955 Spot fought Hill's right-hand man Albert Dimes on the corner of Frith Street, Soho. Through the assistance of a dishonest vicar both were acquitted, but the matter did not end there. Spot tried to organise the shooting of Hill and Dimes, and when this failed they retaliated. Frank Fraser along with others slashed Spot badly outside his home near Hyde Park. In the ensuing trial Marrinan defended Bobby Warren, said by many to have not actually taken part in the attack on Spot.

Frank Fraser remembers Marrinan:

> He was a brief who seemed to come from out of nowhere. When I got the three years for the cigarettes no one had even heard of him. But from 1952 onwards his name came into focus. I heard his name time and again while I was away and when I came out from Broadmoor in 1955 he was the predominant figure. I had many drinks with him at Bill's [Hill] flat over at Barnes. He was a good drinker. He'd start with Guinness and go on to Irish whiskey. Then he lost his brief when his phone was tapped and he was slung out of the Bar. It led to the Denning Report on phone taps. I think Marrinan was a rebel. It was the unfairness and corruptness of the legal profession he fought against. Also he got better money from fighting hard for a case. Patrick was intelligent enough to recognise this.

Marrinan's downfall came in June 1957. The previous October he had made a complaint against the police alleging perjury in the case of Blythe, Rossi and Dennis, which he followed up with writs against the officers Tommy Butler and Peter Vibart. Now the Establishment hit back with a vengeance. Without proper instructions and a solicitor in tow, Marrinan had flown to Ireland to see what could be done about Rossi and Blythe who had fled there, and he would pay for it professionally. Fraser recalls:

> Billy Blythe and Battles Rossi had gone over to Ireland after me and they stayed in the same doctor's house. Tommy Butler, the main copper in the Train Robbery, just about kidnapped them over the border into Northern Ireland. They were on the court steps after they were released by the magistrate when he did it. Later in the early Sixties Marrinan was accused of obtaining false passports along with Brown, the man who'd had the Bucket of Blood Club in Brighton and who'd gone to the police about Charlie Ridge and the Brighton detectives.[2]

It was alleged that Marrinan tried to intervene in an identification parade and also to help Rossi and Blythe – who

223

had been temporarily freed by a magistrate – to escape. As a result of the telephone tap on Billy Hill's line, conversations between him and Marrinan were recorded. Disciplinary charges were preferred by the Bar Council that:

> (1) he associated on terms of personal friendship and familiarity with Billy Hill and Albert Dimes and with Robert or Albert Rossi, persons who to his knowledge were of bad and disreputable character ... (3) without being instructed by a solicitor on 29 June he went to Dublin in order to give legal aid and advice to William Patrick Blythe and Robert or Albert Rossi in connection with a charge against them of wounding Jack Comer ... (3)(d) gave advice and assistance to Blythe and Rossi with a view to avoiding their identification at an identification parade; (4) at the Bridewell prison in Dublin attempted to obstruct an officer in the execution of his duties ... (5) [attempted to obstruct officers] by saying to Blythe, 'They are all outside and are going to nick you again. If I were you I should make a dive for it.'

Marrinan wrote to the sub-committee inquiring into his conduct, saying that he had erred in allowing himself to be imposed upon by worthless people, and asked that he be suspended rather than expelled. His plea was to no avail. He appeared before the Disciplinary Committee and unusually the case was heard in public. Solicitor Brendan Quirke remembers as a young man hearing Marrinan plead for his professional life. 'It was very moving.'

Frank Fraser does not remember him as a great advocate:

> If he defended you, he defended you. But he hadn't a good appearance. He had the brain but not the talk. Marrinan had it up there but a very poor speaking voice. In his enthusiasm to do his best he stuttered. A barrister has to have a lot of the actor in him which helps to carry the day. If he gets overheated he loses a lot of the punch and that's what was wrong with him.
>
> On the other hand Marrinan had a razor-sharp mind. My alibi for the slashing of Spot was that I was in the office of a bookmaker who was taking bets over the phone for an evening at a dog meeting. They were called SP offices in those days. Sammy Bellson was to be a witness, along with another man who worked in the office. When Reginald Seaton, who was leading counsel for the Crown, was cross-examining me he asked how many phones there were and what colours they were. I'd been to the office but I'd never worked there and I was in a bit of a quandary. I hadn't squared this with my witnesses at all and whatever I said they was stuck with. They would have to answer correctly and it could be fatal.

I see Patrick looking at me very intently, and instinct told me that I could say whatever I wanted and somehow he would see it was conveyed to my witnesses. It was proved correct. I said there were three phones, one green, one red and one black or whatever. Marrinan stood up, bowed to the judge rather indicating he wished to go to the lavatory. Out he went – security was not the same in those days – and he saw my two witnesses and told them what I said. He came back and looked at me again. It told me he'd done it. Both witnesses gave exactly the same evidence as I had done. Not that it did me any good.

Marrinan returned to Ireland and became a successful solicitor. He died some years ago.

One of the more dapper and able barristers around the Old Bailey in the late 1960s was Ronald Shulman. Married to one of the daughters of the property magnate, Harold Samuels, he had been involved in what would in the language of the times be described as 'an extremely messy divorce'. A slight man with dark wavy hair and a taste for facetious jokes, he could be seen of an evening in fashionable nightclubs. 'He could really start a fight [in court],' says one solicitor admiringly. 'And he usually came out all right.' Shulman was a close friend of the property millionaire Clive Raphael who was killed on 6 March 1970 when his aeroplane (a twin-engined Beagle) plunged into a field in central France killing him, his parents and a woman friend. Shulman's sadness at his friend's death must have been mitigated by the fact that Raphael left him his fortune in a will made two days before his death. His widow, the 21-year-old model Penny Brahms, only received a shilling (5p) together with four photographs of herself in the nude. The shilling was because of Raphael's nickname for her. Her enthusiasm for the will was in direct inverse ratio to the joy Shulman must have felt at his good fortune.

She was right to feel aggrieved and resentful towards the luck of the barrister; though of course, it wasn't luck unless you believe in the phrase that you make your own. The will was a forgery: the result of a conspiracy between Shulman, his one-time mistress and the 51-year-old Eric Henry-Alba-Teran, the Duc d'Antin. There were arrests all round, but Shulman failed to appear at the committal proceedings and fled the country alleging that he had received death threats. He was thought to have gone to Brazil, setting a precedent for the Great Train

Robber Ronnie Biggs, for at the time the extradition treaty with that country had lapsed.

'I went to Brazil twice and I hoped to see him,' says a solicitor, half in jest, who instructed him, 'but we never met up.'

At the trial Peter Bardon, of the Department of Trade and Industry, told the court that he had been called in to assist the French authority's inquiry as to whether the plane had been deliberately blown up. Shulman, when questioned, had asked him whether there was any evidence of sabotage; when he said there was not, 'Shulman seemed surprised.'

In fact it seems not, as many thought, that Shulman had somehow managed to destroy the aeroplane, but that he had taken advantage of the accident by immediately producing the will of a man whom he knew not to have made one.

The girl's counsel said – in the rhetoric of the time, and in fact still fashionable in high-profile cases – that Shulman had 'sold his soul to the devil'. Her part in the conspiracy had been secured by threats of violence and she had typed out the will with one finger after Shulman threatened to smash her head against the wall and kill her if she made a mistake.

She was given a suspended sentence on the day by the kindly Common Serjeant, Mervyn Griffiths-Jones, who accepted that she had been under Shulman's domination. 'If you take my advice you will see no more of this other man and forget this now. You are still young. Go back to your family and start again.' The rather older Duc d'Antin could not urge that he had been dominated by Shulman in quite the same way and he received three years' imprisonment to which was added another year for appropriating Raphael's white Rolls-Royce. He was recommended for deportation after he had served his sentence.

By the time of the trial Penny Brahms had married the gentleman jockey 'Dandy Kim' Caborn-Waterfield, who in 1960 had received 4 years' imprisonment in France for his part in a theft from the safe of film tycoon Jack Warner in Nice.

From time to time there were sightings of the errant Shulman in Brazil, and he was credited, *in absentia*, with the 'Shulman defence' to cocaine smuggling. At Lewes Crown Court so many defendants from South America were claiming that they had thought the drugs they were found to be smuggling were emeralds, that it seemed likely they had been receiving expert English legal advice.

For all that is known, Shulman is still living in Brazil.

Undoubtedly the best-known and probably the most able advocate at the criminal Bar in the 1960s and 1970s was Victor Durand, outwardly calm, beautifully spoken, with a high domed forehead, who betrayed his inner nerves with fingernails which were chewed to the quick. A member of the chambers which produced both Frederick Lawton and Sebag Shaw, he seemed destined to follow them onto the Bench. As a preliminary step in 1959 he was invited to chair an inquiry into rioting at an approved school near Bedford.

His successful defences were legion and one of his greatest triumphs was for Jimmy 'Trunky' Nash – one of the Nash brothers from Islington, precursors to the Krays – whom he defended on a charge of murder at the Pen Club in Spitalfields run by the notorious Fay Sadler. The club was said to have been bought with the proceeds from a robbery at the Parker Pen Company and named as an Underworld joke. At the time it was owned by former boxer Billy Ambrose and Jeremiah Callaghan, a member of another leading family from Walworth. Both were serving 10-year prison sentences but came home on parole at the weekends. The club was frequently raided by the police and, almost as frequently, it changed hands.

Bert Wickstead, later a Commander of the Flying Squad but then a Detective Sergeant, believed that no matter what was on the surface, the real reason behind the incident was that it was part of a West End power struggle, with a chance accident providing an opportunity to establish a new pecking order so taking over from Billy Hill.

In the fight at the club Selwyn Cooney, manager of one of Billy Hill's clubs, was shot. He had been involved in a car accident some time previously with a girlfriend of one of the Nash brothers and there had been a fight over the bill.

Two days after the shooting James Nash surrendered himself at City Road Police Station. He was accompanied by Manny Fryde, then a solicitor's managing clerk from Sampson & Co. In those days, well before the Police and Criminal Evidence Act 1984 with its built-in safeguards for suspects, Fryde had arranged for Nash's surrender on the basis that there would then be no pressure on him to make a verbal or written statement.

According to reports the eye-witnesses, who in the meantime had been subjected to some intimidation, stood up well in giving their evidence, and Wickstead believes the real turning point was Victor Durand QC's final address to the jury: '(it) surpassed anything I have ever heard before or since. It was brilliant, spellbinding stuff.'

The all-male jury took 98 minutes to acquit Nash of Cooney's murder, but at a second trial which began an hour later he was found guilty of causing grievous bodily harm and was sentenced to 5 years' imprisonment.[3]

Durand was suspended in 1961 after he had appeared in a High Court action for a senior police officer but failed to tell the court that his client had been reduced in rank. Initially he was suspended for three years, but on appeal this was reduced to 12 months. He was called to the Bar in 1939 and took silk in 1958. Two years later he appeared for Richard Fleming.[4] The case involved a claim by a press photographer, Alan Meek, for assault and false arrest against Richard Fleming over an incident on Guy Fawkes' night 1958. It was alleged that Durand had advised and pursued a course of conduct intended to deceive the court by creating the false impression that his client, the defendant, still held the rank of chief inspector of police – whereas he had been reduced to the rank of station sergeant for misconduct – when the credit of the parties was likely to be and was in fact a crucial issue.

In June 1961 Alan Meek was granted a new hearing and awarded the costs of the first one. The result in the earlier action, said Mr Justice Holroyd Pearce, had been that Fleming was able to masquerade as a chief inspector of unblemished reputation.

Durand took full responsibility, exonerating his junior and his instructing solicitor who was, in fact, the very experienced 'Cappy' Lane of the Metropolitan Police Solicitors Department. Solicitor Jeffrey Gordon recalls speaking with Lane while he was waiting for the hearing of the next case, another one involving a police officer. Lane told him he had repeatedly said to Durand, 'Victor, why are you doing this?' When Gordon remarked that Lane should have stopped him, Lane replied that Durand was committed to the course of action and it was impossible to sack someone of his standing.

The newspapers reported that his suspension meant the loss of £15,000 or more a year. Durand spent the time gardening and making some improvements to his Sussex home.

The case ruined his chance of becoming a High Court judge, but the lay-off did him no harm so far as the quantity and quality of his work was concerned. Immediately on his return he defended three murder cases in quick succession. The first involved Robert Reed, acquitted of what was known as the Holy Lady killing. It was the first capital murder case in British legal history where two juries disagreed and the prosecution did not offer evidence on the third occasion.

The most famous of the three cases, however, was that of the Brighton nightclub owner, Harvey Holford, when in an apparently hopeless case Durand persuaded the jury that the half-Belgian gun expert who shot and killed his 21-year-old wife Christine was only guilty of manslaughter. She had five bullets in her body and one in her brain. Holford, described as 'The Errol Flynn of the South Coast', was no good in bed, said Christine to her friends, and she had begun a string of affairs including one with barrister Billy Rees-Davies' great friend, John Bloom, the then washing-machine tycoon.

Durand had a number of problems with Holford's defence, the first and possibly the most difficult to resolve being his possession of the gun. He had already been fined £15 for keeping one in his car. What was he doing with another one handy and loaded?

The answer was that this was to protect him against the London gangsters Billy Hill and Albert Dimes. Holford had had an argument with a man named Gillett over the installation of Legalite, a form of roulette, in his club called The Blue Gardenia. According to a letter Holford had written and deposited with a firm of Brighton solicitors – 'To be opened in the event of my death, disappearance, or meeting with any accident that would incapacitate me, or if these events should happen to my wife' – Gillett had apparently hinted that he had connections with Hill and Dimes who would deal with Holford.

There was sympathy for Holford because while in Lewes prison, to which he had been transferred from Brixton, on the night before his trial was due to begin on 4 December 1962 he threw himself from a balcony, fracturing his skull. His fall was broken by a warder. 'The greatest stroke he could have pulled,' admires Frankie Fraser, the long-time friend of both Hill and Dimes who visited Holford in prison and who brokered the gun story. The newspapers were full of his baby, Karen, visiting him. It was reported that his 73-year-old Belgian-born mother, Celeste Holford, had also visited him. 'Mama, hold my hand – tightly,' reported the *Daily Mirror*. And she did. And there was more sympathy for him when Victor Durand, in one of his greatest defences, coaxed the admission from Mrs Holford that she might have encouraged her son to take sexual liberties with her when he was a child. By the end Malcom Morris for the Crown, in his address to the jury, offered Holford a lifeline:

> If you accept as the truth what Holford says was said [about the paternity of Karen] then you will think that was strong provocation.

And strong provocation it turned out to be. His acquittal on the murder charge on Friday 29 March 1963 was well received with the traditional cheers from women in the public gallery. The all-male jury found him guilty only of manslaughter, something with which the judge Mr Justice Streatfield, who had been the trial judge in *Meek v Fleming*, agreed. Holford received four years.

In 1972 Durand took part in one of the more remarkable trials of the period and one which led to a review of the value of identification evidence. In the early hours of 5 November 1972, two gunmen forced their way into the Barn Restaurant, Braintree, Essex. When the owner, Bob Patience, refused to hand over the keys to the safe they shot him, his wife, and daughter Beverley in quick succession. Muriel Patience died later in hospital. George Ince, already charged with a major silver bullion robbery, was identified as one of the gunmen and was charged with the murder.

The trial of Ince at Chelmsford Crown Court took place in May 1973. It was presided over by the unpopular Mr Justice Melford Stevenson, the judge who had tried the Kray twins in their first trial for the murder of Cornell and McVitie and who was not noted for his sympathy towards defendants.

Victor Durand frequently clashed with the judge. Ince continually protested his innocence and was sent down to the cells while Beverley Patience gave her evidence that she identified him as one of the attackers. It was after this that Ince – who had already made an abortive application to change the judge and who, during the trial, had had a telegram sent to the Lord Chancellor asking for Stevenson to be removed – sacked Durand and his junior, Robert Flach. Now he was on his own. Both Durand and Flach remained in court taking no further part, while Ince stayed in the dock with his back to the judge, occasionally interrupting the prosecution witnesses. He offered no defence until he asked whether he could be allowed to take the truth drug. Stevenson said no, but asked if Ince would like his defence counsel reinstated. Ince replied that he would not, and said once more that the judge was both biased and rude.

After a retirement of six hours, at 9.30 p.m. before a tense court the jury returned to say they had failed to agree on a verdict.

Within the week Ince was on trial again, this time before a much more sympathetic judge, Mr Justice Eveleigh. Durand and Flach were back and this time Durand called a crucial witness, a Dolly Gray. Ince had apparently been unwilling for her to appear at the first trial, believing that when (as it must) her real name was given, it would act against him and also that she would suffer reprisals.

Mrs 'Gray' had bravely gone to see her husband, Charlie Kray, in Maidstone prison before she testified. It seems that he did not know she had been seeing Ince before she told him, and this 'Dear John' was a shattering blow to a man serving a 10-year sentence. To his great credit, however, he did not attempt to prevent her giving evidence to the effect that on the night of the murder she had been in bed with Ince.

On 23 May the jury retired for over three hours before they acquitted Ince to wild cheers from the public gallery. Three weeks later a Northerner, John Brook, was found in possession of the murder weapon and was later convicted of the murder of Muriel Patience.

One of Durand's last defences was in the 1986 Cyprus Spy Trial, a consequence of which was the abolition of the right of the defence to challenge jurors without giving a cause. Because the Crown elected to try a number of defendants together, this enabled the defence lawyers to pool their challenges to try to obtain a sympathetic (or at least not hostile) panel. Robin Simpson wanted a young working-class jury; Michael Hill, later Chairman of the Bar's Criminal Committee, wanted an anti-establishment jury but felt they would be better off with a young middle-class jury; Gilbert Grey suggested that if the jury was not too well educated and of too low an intelligence they might take more notice of the judge, therefore the jury should consist of young not unsmart people but no women. Robert Harman thought that since there was such a dichotomy of views they should just take what came, and John Alliott said they couldn't improve on fate. Durand thought that if the jury was young it might be unpatriotic.[5]

The trial also featured one of Durand's most brilliant pieces of advocacy. He was then 78. A number of young aircraftsmen based in Cyprus had been accused of giving away secrets in return for drink and sex. Much of the evidence against them had been obtained by fairly extensive and, said the defence, overbearing interrogation as a result of which many had made statements.

Durand's client, giving evidence, was speaking so fast and so randomly that it was impossible to follow and understand anything of what he was saying. In a momentary pause Durand interposed, 'It may be that there is a little confusion here. Do you think you could elucidate further?' A look of amazement was followed by another long and incomprehensible line of drivel, at the end of which Durand looked up and said, 'I'm much obliged. Now all is clear.' There was a stunned silence followed by a burst of laughter. No one could now believe that Durand's client was capable of stealing the secrets. One of his co-defenders was heard to remark, 'Victor, that is either the worst examination I've ever heard or it is sheer genius, and I know which it is.'[6]

Durand died in 1994 aged 86.

The archetypal Old Bailey defence barrister, whose social and business life spilled over into the more louche drinking and gambling clubs of London and external association with criminals, was however William Rupert Rees-Davies, the son of a former Chief Justice of Hong Kong and known to almost all as the One-Armed Bandit. Also a long-serving Member of Parliament, his career at the Bar was punctuated by rows with judges and suspensions. His social life was happily followed by gossip columnists, not always to his benefit. On his day, he was also one of the most formidable advocates at the Criminal Bar.

A very handsome man in his early years, he had been *Victor Ludorum* of games at Eton and had the distinction of taking the wicket of Donald Bradman when playing for the MCC. During the War, in which he served in the Welsh Guards, he lost his right arm in an accident. Over the years a series of stories developed which he did nothing to correct in terms of the exact details: that he had ignored a warning that he was passing the firing range when practice was in progress, that he had fallen out of a jeep while drunk and – the most colourful if unlikely but not wholly impossible – that the arm had been bitten off in a brothel in Lagos. In fact he had been trapped in a tank crash. Although throughout his life in great pain from the damaged nerve ends, he would allow little if any help in having his tie tied, his fish filleted or his meat cut. He drove appallingly badly in a left-hand-drive car which meant he had to take his hand off the wheel and lean over to change gears. As a result, his car and others near it were often involved in scrapes. Since he would leave minimal time to drive from the Temple to the Old Bailey, he was unlikely to stop if he hit anything. Once, when told he had scraped the side of a car, he replied, 'Nonsense, a gentle caress.'

Rees-Davies was banned from driving for his third offence on 12 September 1983, having been previously banned on 28 August 1975 and in the 1960s. On the first occasion he was unfortunate. He had paid an analyst employed by the police £500 to provide a report showing he was under the limit, but the man had died in the meantime.

However, he was quite capable of using the loss of his arm for his own purposes. Any juror seeing him struggle with a pile of law books – for again he would accept no help – must have been sympathetic. One of his standard lines to them was, 'I'm going to do this case single handed.' And jurors generally loved him.

In many ways he was a throwback to the Edwardian Bar and to Marshall Hall who was one of his heroes. Like Charles Laughton in *Witness for the Prosecution,* he favoured the dramatic late entry. Three or four minutes late, the legal equivalent of the 7th Cavalry would arrive. When he was defending Eva Brindle, the sister of 'Mad' Frankie Fraser, on a charge of conspiracy to pervert the course of justice in an offshoot of the Richardson Torture Trial in 1966, he arrived after the court had been sitting in silence and anticipation for several minutes. He swung straight into continuing the cross-examination of the principal witness. 'Don't you have something to say to me, Mr Rees-Davies?' demanded Judge Rogers. 'Yes. Yer Lordship's clock's wrong. I meant to mention it yesterday but it slipped me mind.' And without taking breath he was on to the attack.

As a result of his old-fashioned beliefs Rees-Davies would often refuse to see a client before the case, certainly if it meant the inconvenience of going to visit him in Brixton prison. He would explain that the great men of the past hadn't done so, and he wasn't going to either. He was not alone in this theory. John Parris recalls being led in two murder cases, in neither of which they saw the accused before the trial. The silk explained to Parris, 'Defending counsel in a murder case should never have a conference with the accused. Otherwise counsel's emotions become entangled with those of the prisoner and he is less able to concentrate on the job.'[7] Billy merely tried to extend this simple but tried and tested philosophy.

If the jury's verdict went against him he would refuse to do the mitigation, leaving it in the hands of an imported and importunate young member of his chambers who had not been present during the trial and would not be paid for his trouble. If he bothered at all, he would explain to the client that after going hammer and tongs at the police for a week, calling them liars and rowing with the judge, it was not seemly that he should start begging for mercy; it was far better for someone else to do so. Unfortunately he did not always impart into his substitute's mind any thoughts as to how the mitigation should proceed.

Billy would be off to his next case, his constituency or, better still, the races or to an auction room, for he had a fine collection of modern paintings. On one occasion his middle-aged instructing solicitor was seen running down Old Bailey to the courts which had been opened opposite the main building. 'No use your hurrying, Mr Halberstam, sir,' said one of the ushers. 'Your counsel left for Sotheby's in a taxi half an hour ago.'

His dislike of mitigating after a trial caused him serious trouble on a number of occasions. In 1964 he did not appear for Colin Herbert-Hall, jailed for 15 years for his part in an £87,000 bank raid; he said he had been attending a speaking engagement at the Conservative women's luncheon club in his constituency at Cliftonville, 35 miles from Maidstone. 'A message that I was required at Maidstone after the luncheon adjournment to make my final speech did not reach me until too late.'[8]

He also failed to appear in October 1970 for the mitigation of Douglas Anthony, who drew 6 years after being found guilty of stealing £28,000 worth of equipment from an engineering firm. He told the court that he had instructed a young barrister from his chambers, James Cartwright, to do it for him. Cartwright maintained he had only been instructed to ask for an adjournment. This time Rees-Davies was reprimanded and ordered to pay up to £210 costs. 'Scandalous,' said the fearsome Judge Edward Clarke QC, docking him his day's fee.[9]

Judge Jeremy Fordham remembers being the junior counsel to Rees-Davies on a number of occasions:

> I never had anything but kindness from him but he was rarely there at the vital moment. I remember in one case in which he led me the main witness was giving evidence and there was no Billy. When he finished his evidence-in-chief people looked at me expectantly. Fortunately the client then collapsed in the dock and by the time they brought him back there was very little of the day left, so I asked a few hesitant questions of the witness to end the session. The next morning there was still no Billy, so I was doing my best when he flung into court spraying papers all over the place

and more or less pushed me aside, beginning, 'Well, Smith, you're a liar, aren't you?'

In another case he made the best reasoned speech in mitigation I ever heard. It required careful analysis and it was the most powerful I ever heard of its kind. It was an intellectual *tour de force*, not emotional just intellectually argued. Billy had a very powerful mind. The trouble was he didn't work at it most of the time.[10]

More serious for Billy, however, was his suspension in 1954 for unprofessional conduct, and a second suspension for a like offence. This time – having promised to take his daughter to the Ascot Gold Cup – he thought he had squared things with his fellow barristers and the judge that there should be nothing to concern him that afternoon, so a spell of Berkshire air would do him good. In fact the case speeded up and Rees-Davies was needed to cross-examine before close of play. The client, asked if he wanted his barrister and not a junior there to cross-examine, said that he did. However, clients were usually happy to excuse his eccentricities. On his day he was regarded as one of the best, if not the best cross-examiner at the Old Bailey:

> If you were found shotgun in hand, photographed in the bank, the loot in a sack at your feet with verbals from here to Manchester, three previous convictions for the same thing and a lunatic story, Billy did not repine. 'Come here to make a documentary with a television company who were held up in the traffic, eh? We'll give it a run.' Often he charmed a jury into believing it was true.[11]

Women were enormously attracted to him. The normally austere judge Melford Stevenson once unbent sufficiently to remark that if Billy had had two hands there would not have been a virgin on the whole of the South-Eastern circuit. In a bank robbery case his co-counsel looked up as a juror was about to be sworn. 'My God, Billy,' he said, 'I've been to bed with her. What shall I do?' Billy looked up and replied, 'Don't worry. I'll do it for you. So have I.' His explanation to the judge was a model. 'My Lord, my learned friend and I think that somewhere, some time in the past, we cannot now recollect where or when, we have met this lady socially. Perhaps it might be better for all if she were to stand down.'

Sometimes his social life counted against him. When he was cross-examining a girl in a brothel-keeping case, he asked, 'Is there a bathroom in your establishment?', only to receive the disdainful reply, 'You of all people dare ask me that question, Mr Rees-Davies.'

In 1958, then aged 42, he was regularly squiring Sevilla Glass Hooper, a 21-year-old model, when he attended a pyjama party. In fact from reports he seems to have been a co-host. When a man arrived in a lounge suit and refused to change, an effort was made to debag him. Suggestions that Rees-Davies had tried to restore law and order were denied by him. He threatened to bring writs for libel but was persuaded not to do so.

He had an enormously quick mind, something which from time to time led him not to read his brief too closely. 'If Mr Smith had been called,' he said to a judge on one of the occasions when he consented to mitigate, 'I would have put his convictions to him one by one and demonstrated him to be the fraudsman he is.' Counsel for the Crown interrupted, 'Mr Smith is a man of completely good character.' Unfazed, without a pause Billy replied, 'In that case he is a very fortunate man indeed.'

At that period of time Judge Rogers, who was seemingly being fed a diet of armed robbery cases to try, must have lost concentration for an instant because he found Rees-Davies addressing the jury in the middle of what was meant to be his cross-examination. 'What are you doing?' he asked. 'Telling the jury to disregard the biased evidence of a biased police officer.' 'That is my function at a later stage.' 'I thought they should be told now. Well, members of the jury you heard His Lordship. Disregard unfair and hostile evidence of biased police officers.'

Outside court Billy could be ruthless. Eating in an Indian restaurant near the Old Bailey and having to share a table, he began to eat the stranger's poppadoms. When told they belonged to the other man he replied, 'Nonsense, any poppadom in my reach is my poppadom.' He was equally ruthless when the charming (if diffident) Wilfrid Fordham left Rees-Davies' chambers at 5 Paper Buildings to set up his own in King's Bench Walk. A law library is essential for any set of chambers, but Rees-Davies was unwilling to see a costly set of the Law Reports disappear without reprisal. He marched over to the new chambers and throughout the day, to the amazement of Fordham, took back the 100-odd-volume set a few at a time.

He could be equally ruthless in court. Defending in a three-handed case in one of the smaller courtrooms at the Old Bailey, he had effectively destroyed the principal prosecution witness. Instead of leaving well alone, one of the other defence counsel stood up to have his say and did it so badly that he was well on the way to rehabilitating the witness. Rees-Davies was outraged. In a stentorian voice, heard all over the court, he called, 'Sit down, cunt.' And the shame-faced barrister did.

In September 1981 an incident occurred for which he might have found himself in jail twenty years later. After a flight from his home in Corfu, he was interviewed by the police over an incident when he was smoking a cigar on an Air Europe flight in the non-smoking section. He then repaired to the back of the aircraft but could not find a seat in the smoking section and so stood in the aisle. This was not allowed either and a stewardess remonstrated again. He later told the *Daily Express*:

> I was carrying a stick because of a slight fault in my left leg. I put the stick down and – most unfortunately – it went down on the stewardess's toe. She was terribly upset and rushed off to make a complaint. It was then that the pilot radioed for the police.[12]

But it was Rees-Davies' association with Stephen Ward which caused him his greatest professional embarrassment. Ward was convicted of living off the immoral earnings of the beautiful club hostess Christine Keeler, who had been careless enough to share her favours with both a Russian diplomat and John Profumo, a minister in Harold Macmillan's cabinet. In the wake of the prosecution of Ward, Lord Denning was invited to conduct an inquiry into the whole affair. From the report, it appears Denning became enchanted with Ms Keeler but was less so with the part Rees-Davies played in the affair.

Before the trial Christine Keeler, not unnaturally, wanted to give her story to the newspapers, and just as naturally Stephen Ward was keen that she should not. As Ward's counsel during a period from 28 January to 6 February 1963, Rees-Davies had acted effectively as a solicitor, interviewing witnesses and endeavouring to negotiate a settlement with a solicitor he had found for her and who had once been his pupil at the Bar. Unfortunately things were not spelled out clearly in the negotiations and when the solicitor said in a telephone conversation that she would accept five he meant £5,000, whereas when Rees-Davies said he was sure that was all right, he thought the sum involved was £500. Rees-Davies loaned Ward £50 and when the £500 came from Lord Astor he repaid himself and gave the rest to Ward's solicitor. But Christine Keeler thought that she had been tricked and instead of settling went ahead and printed. After that it all ended in tears. When

Ward was arrested on the charge of living off immoral earnings, Rees-Davies clearly could not act on his behalf and his solicitor instructed James Burge. Ward took an overdose while the jury was deliberating the evidence against him. The judge had postponed sentence until he was fit to appear, but Ward never recovered.

As a Member of Parliament Rees-Davies was almost automatically entitled to be appointed Queen's Counsel if he so wished but, because of his involvement in the Profumo affair, his preferment was held back for a number of years.

Rees-Davies will be best remembered for the joke made by Judge Alan King-Hamilton when on another occasion he persuaded the judge to allow the artist, Felix Topolski, to sit on the bench with him and sketch the proceedings. Billy then had a nice line in sales of the results, reserving for his own a huge painting of himself surrounded by lesser mortals in what he, if no one else, described as 'The Trial of the Century' – a case in which the remainder of the Richardson gang were being prosecuted for a hugely complex long-firm fraud. It hung in his chambers for many years. *Private Eye* thought that between them they had committed a criminal offence in breach of s 41 Criminal Justice Act 1925; but, if they had, the authorities were not prepared to take any action.[13]

As for the joke, Rees-Davies had been cross-examining a police officer with such vigour that if he had continued in this vein much longer it was clear that an application to allow the prosecution to put his client's character in evidence would be successful. He was also receiving a waterfall of notes from the dock. 'May I have a moment to read this *billet-doux*, My Lord?' he asked. 'Perhaps it's a Billy don't,' replied King-Hamilton in a flash of genuine judicial wit.

It is said of many people that when they died the mould was broken. In the case of Billy Rees-Davies it really was so.

1 For the life, death and aftermath of Tommy Smithson, see James Morton, *Gangland*. Another boyfriend was Jack Rosa from the Elephant and Castle Gang who died in a car crash. He had no licence and his reputed last words were said to have been, 'I wasn't driving.'

2 Frank Fraser, *Mad Frank*, p.92.

3 For accounts of the case see James Morton, *Gangland*; Bert Wickstead, *Gangbuster*.

4 *Meek v Fleming*, 18–20 October 1960.

5 *The Times*, 27 November 1985. Lawyers have always had opposing and entertaining views on who will make a sympathetic juror. For example, Clarence Darrow thought there should be no women from the defence point of view. He also believed that Presbyterians should be avoided, and Baptists were even less desirable. Jews, Unitarians and agnostics should be retained. F. Lee Bailey thought that unless the

defendant had a good military record retired police officers and military men and their wives were undesirable. See R. Hastie *et al*, *Inside the Jury*, which demonstrates that a case can be made for or against almost every potential juror.

6 Louis Blom Cooper, 'Victor Durand' in *The Times*, 13 October 1994.

7 John Parris, *Scapegoat*.

8 *The Times*, 24 December 1964.

9 *Daily Telegraph*, 8 October 1970.

10 Conversation with author, December 2000.

11 'How barrister Billy left his mark' in *The Times*, 21 January 1992.

12 'Flying smoke starts a Billywho' in *Daily Express*, 1 October 1981.

13 *Private Eye*, 12 July 1974.

# 16 Greylord

THE LIST OF LAWYERS disbarred and suspended by the Illinois Supreme Court on 30 November 1994 included Anthony F. Provenzano, who had been sent to prison on charges of mail fraud and possession of cannabis with intent to deliver. There were also a number of judges including Judge Adam Nicholas Stillo and his lawyer nephew, Joseph Theodore Stillo. But the prize striking-off was undoubtedly former Cook County Judge Thomas J. Maloney jnr.

Either on that day or at some other time, it would have certainly included Judge Harry Wilson who in May 1977, holding a bench trial without a jury, had acquitted the fearsome mobster Harry Aleman of murder. Instead, the judge, denying in the teeth of the evidence that he had accepted a bribe, committed suicide at his ranch in Arizona.

Aleman had been acquitted of the killing of Teamsters' Union steward William Logan, but was later sentenced to 30 years on charges of conspiracy.[1] Unfortunately for Wilson the Aleman murder case resurfaced 20 years later when it was discovered that a $10,000 bribe had been paid for the acquittal. Protesting that he had been placed in double jeopardy, Aleman was retried and convicted.

This all resulted from the most spectacular and certainly the most far-reaching of all judge bribing scandals which ran in Chicago throughout the 1970s. The inquiry began in 1964 when it became clear that a ring was operating between lawyers, court officials, police and judges, mainly in traffic cases.

Working in co-operation with the FBI, Chief Criminal Court Judge Richard Fitzgerald and US Attorney Thomas P. Sullivan, it was arranged that a young assistant state prosecutor would wear a microphone and, pretending to be crooked, would do deals first as a prosecutor and later as a defence attorney. The defendants in the cases, which were extended to include phoney robberies and unlawful weapons cases, were undercover FBI agents. Over the years more than 15 judges, four court clerks, 13 police officers and 50 lawyers were convicted in what became known as *Operation Greylord*.[2]

One post-*Greylord* lawyer who was himself a fixer was Robert Cooley, from a family of Chicago police officers. His father, James, appeared six times in *True Detective* and Cooley was himself a police officer until he passed the Bar examination in 1970. In the late 1970s he shared offices with John D'Arco jnr. against whom he later gave the evidence which led to the state senator's conviction for taking bribes.

Never known as a great legal mind, Cooley became a government mole in 1986 when, apparently sick of bribery and corruption and also in hock to the Mob after suffering substantial gambling losses, he simply walked into the US Justice Department and agreed to be wired-up. One of his last cases before his conversion was defending Michael Colella, accused of badly beating Officer Cathy Touhy after she had stopped him for a traffic offence. He claimed he had been so much under the influence of drink that he was not responsible for his actions. Circuit Court Judge Lawrence Passarella, in a decision which led to his resignation, acquitted Colella without explanation, which apparently sickened Cooley.

He went deep undercover because the first successful case with Cooley as a witness was not until September 1991 when a jury convicted the second-ranked Cook County Circuit Court Judge David Shields, along with D'Arco's brother-in-law and law partner Pasquale 'Pat' De Leo, of bribery. In the December down went D'Arco.

The last major figure in the probe to be sent to prison was the former lawyer William Swano who was convicted of bribing two judges in murder cases. In 1991 the one-time public defender had pleaded guilty to racketeering as well as initiating the bribes and a variety of other offences between 1980 and 1986. On 20 June 1995 Swano, who wept more or less continually through the sentencing process, was given four years in prison. In the meantime he had been another star witness in the prosecutions of the former Cook County Circuit Judge Thomas J. Maloney and his bagman Robert McGee. He had paid Maloney to fix the 1981 murder case of Owen Jones, who again had accepted a bench trial and been convicted of manslaughter. He had also tried to give Maloney money on a murder case involving two El Rukn generals, but Maloney had smelled a trap and returned the money.

On another occasion he had, he said, lost a case in which – because the evidence had been considered so weak – Maloney had not been bribed. It was then that he decided that 'to practice in front of Maloney ... we had to pay'.

In April 1993 Maloney and Robert McGee were convicted. Try as their lawyers might to discredit Swano, claiming the cocaine taker and Robert Cooney were 'conmen extraordinaire', there were telephone company records of calls from McGee to Maloney's Chambers to back up the witness along with a record, of which Swano could not have known, which corroborated his evidence.[3] Maloney's conviction also led to a stream of applications for new trials from those who had been convicted in his court.

By 1995 Cooney was part of the federal witness protection programme, receiving a monthly wage of $3,400 and lecturing federal agents from time to time. He was also expected to give evidence in gang trials.

Maloney was back in court in 1999, 5 years into his 15-year sentence. Unrepentant, he was still protesting his innocence when lawyers for two defendants claimed that he had been tougher in the cases of their clients than he should have been, and this was to cover the leniency he showed when he had been bribed.[4]

Disregarding advice not to give evidence and to plead the Fifth Amendment, the 74-year-old judge was in fine form, calling the defence lawyers 'shysters' and suggesting he had been framed, something which may well not help with his Parole Board hearings. He did accept, however, that when he had been a lawyer he had paid small amounts to court clerks to have his cases heard early in the list. 'An entrenched system of gratuities' was how he described it.

In fact Wilson was not the first American judge in modern times to be convicted of taking bribes in murder cases. In February 1985 James McGettrick, a former Cuyahoga County Common Pleas judge, was sentenced to four years and fined $15,000 for taking bribes in separate cases involving Hell's

Angels. He had pleaded No Contest on 16 January to accusations that he had accepted $11,900 in pay-offs, something he had originally described as a 'campaign contribution'. During the trial, evidence was given that the judge had accepted a further $5,000 to fix another murder case. Unfortunately for him, this time the supplier was not an Angel but an undercover federal agent.

The judge had fallen under suspicion when the agent made a chance remark in Heck's Café in Rocky River, McGettrick's home town, about the dismissal of charges in one of the cases as it was going to the jury. The agent had remarked sarcastically, 'We really appreciate what you did for us in the Amato-Chakirelis case.' The judge had dismissed charges of aggravated murder against Richard Amato, and those against Harold Chakirelis were dropped at a later date.

Whether or not the judge was having a burst of the alcoholism for which he was later treated, he appears to have thought that the agent was indeed an Angel and had suggested a further payment for assistance in the case of Hell's Angel Frank Fencl. The agent met him a further four times and the judge came over loud and clear on the tape. He also faced charges of grand theft, accused of bilking the Teamsters Local 436 out of $8,744 in medical benefits.

During the hearings the judge – said by Gerald Gold, his lawyer, to be a very sick man – had walked around the courtroom as if trying to alleviate pain. It was something which cut no ice with the prosecutor, who said the former judge had been seen in a bar on two occasions during the week when he was awaiting sentence. 'He wasn't shuffling and moaning and groaning then,' said Assistant County Prosecutor Edward Walsh who described the judge as a 'bum'.

In fact the judge wasn't putting it on. He died at Ohio State University Hospital on 17 July that year after suffering a heart attack. Before his transfer to the hospital he had been in the medical centre from the date of his arrival in prison; he had terminal prostate cancer.[5]

The next year down went former Justice William C. Brennan who had served on the State Supreme Court in Queens. He received 5 years with an additional 5 years' probation and a fine of $209,000 for bribery. Sentencing him, Judge Weinstein described the 67-year-old Brennan as 'casually corrupt' and 'amiably dishonest'. It was thought that, over the years, he had accepted in the region of $47,000 in bribes, including one involving a reputed organised crime figure charged with attempted murder. The city's Parking Violations Bureau had been the victim of a bribery ring for years.[6]

That case was finally closed when Melvin Lebetkin, a 61-year-old lawyer, was sentenced to two years and fined $250,000 for his role in the scheme. Over the years some $70,000 had been paid to city officials in exchange for lucrative parking contracts. A five-man partnership had obtained the city's first contract to collect overdue fines in 1982, and three years later had been grossing $1 million commission annually. Lebetkin told the judge he had been lured into the partnership by a desire to provide an office job for his wife who was dying of cancer. The Attorney General, however, took the view that he had not been so altruistic and his conduct had been motivated by 'naked greed'. He also claimed at the hearing that Lebetkin had an arrangement with the local Democratic club to steer cases his way, which he would then fix with Brennan. Lebetkin denied the allegation and was never charged.[7]

Back in Chicago it was argued that Cook County Circuit Judge Paul T. Foxgrover was so corrupt that he 'lacked all rationality', and that every sentence and verdict he delivered should be set aside. Frederick F. Cohn argued, 'You can't impose the death penalty when the person – he's a person not a judge – is lacking that degree of rationality.'

In 1992 Foxgrover had pleaded guilty to the theft of $27,500 Circuit Court fines and victim restitution payments over an 18-month period. He served 2 years of a 6-year sentence and was disbarred. In May 1990, during the period of his thefts, he had sentenced Robert L. Fair to be executed for beating his girlfriend and her 11-year-old son to death with a baseball bat in what Cohn referred to as a domestic dispute. The jury had found Fair eligible for the death penalty, and no mitigating circumstances sufficient to preclude the imposition of the said penalty which Foxgrover had then applied. The High Court had affirmed Fair's conviction and sentence on direct appeal. The State had argued that there had been no sufficient link between the Fair case and the judge's corrupt behaviour to justify the reversal of the conviction. The Court should not, it argued, allow appeals where even the slightest taint on the judge would call for a new trial. The 375-lb Cohn was not impressed. 'For them to say this is the slightest taint is for someone to look at me and say I'm slightly overweight.'[8]

On the subject of doubtful judges, it is difficult to know quite how to classify the behaviour of Judge Richard Deacon Jones. The Omaha, Nebraska, judge appeared in February 1998 at a judicial misconduct hearing to answer a 17-point complaint filed by the Nebraska Commission on Judicial Qualifications. When challenged over his conduct he claimed that throwing a lighted firecracker into a colleague's office was nothing more than a misconceived prank. That may be, but the good judge had also sent his colleague a note containing death threats. In court he had set bail for a zillion dollars and on a dozen or more occasions he had described Judge Jane Prochaska to court officials in profane terms. Back out of court, he denied he had touched her inappropriately in or out of an elevator. Nor did he, he said, assault and batter her.[9]

In December 1999 in Allegheny County, Pittsburgh, District Justice Gigi Sullivan waived her right to a preliminary hearing after Donald Geraci, a one-time used-car salesman and restaurant owner and a convicted drug-dealer, gave evidence that in return for legal favours he had supplied her with crack cocaine and prescription drugs over a 30-month period. She had been charged with possession of heroin and cocaine, passing a dud $2,000 cheque, accepting bribes and burglary of Geraci's car lot.

Geraci claimed that Sullivan had reduced bond for a friend of his charged with burglary and had allowed him to sit on the bench with her, as well as tipping him off that the police had warrants to search his home and his restaurant, Café Verona. To facilitate this she had a special code in his pager. It was not all one-way traffic, and Geraci never charged Ms Sullivan for the drugs he supplied between 1996 and 1998. 'That's the kind of relationship we had,' said Geraci.

At their first meeting at his home in Pittsburgh he had, he said, laid out a couple of lines of cocaine, but she had asked for a spoon and a glass of water to inject. 'She drew the cocaine up into the syringe and injected it into her ankle.'

By the time Sullivan waived the preliminary hearing she had completed a drug rehabilitation course. She had also stood for re-election as her six-year term as judge, which carried a salary of $55,000, drew to a close, but had been defeated. 'She's different now than she was then,' said her lawyer Patrick J. Thomassey.

But sadly not that different, for in February 2000 she was fined $300 for stealing clothing from a Value City store in Harrison

Township. Then in September 2000, she was fined $500 and put on probation at Fort Dix after stealing a pair of jeans, a plastic watch and hair colouring from the McGuire Air Force Base. Now she was working on a road crew for a private contractor.[10]

Over the years the British legal system may have suffered from corrupt judges, but they have been corrupt by favouring the Establishment which, in some way, seems to enable us to see them in a rose-coloured light. Certainly no judge in modern times seems to have tried to murder another or been convicted of taking a bribe.[11]

Undoubtedly judges have had favourites amongst the advocates who have appeared before them and, because of the cosy structure of the Bar, if a fellow or former member of Chambers was sitting as a deputy or full-time judge, the barrister could expect a 'sympathetic tribunal' – but that was generally about as far as it went. One possible exception was a former chairman of Inner London Sessions who always and quite properly went out of his way to favour the cases in which his mistress appeared. Indeed, late briefs delivered to her home on the morning of the case would often be accepted by the judge in his dressing-gown.

Some, it is true, have favoured the services of prostitutes over those of their wives, and one stipendiary at an Inner London Magistrates' Court was able to persuade his wife that on the days when he was sitting he was obliged to remain within the jurisdiction of his court, so enabling him to spend his evenings in what could euphemistically be called an hotel in Shaftesbury Avenue. In true British fashion it was regarded as a minor eccentricity, if that, and certainly not a liability.

Generally speaking those judges who have slipped and fallen have done so from an over-fondness for the bottle. Drink-driving has found a handful of them in the dock, but generally a conviction has not until recently required their resignation.

Very few have ended in prison for extra-judicial activities, but those who have fallen by the wayside included a Crown Court judge who was convicted of smuggling.[12] Another was a magistrate from North Tyneside, Thomas Brown, who received 18 months in 1999 for incitement to steal and attempting to handle stolen goods. The judge told him:

> You effectively gave thieves a shopping list of quite expensive items you wanted and you encouraged them to steal them and incited them to steal on your behalf.

Brown had been caught in a trap after shoplifters agreed to act as police informers. He had arranged that they should steal designer clothes and perfume for him and had been filmed after he withdrew £145 from a cash machine to pay for coats and cosmetics worth almost £800.[13]

But compared with those of their transatlantic brethren, these are minor peccadillos.

1 Quoted in *Organized Crime Digest*, 10 May 1989. The case involved a home invasion and burglary ring. Aleman had also been suspected of the killing of Richard Cain, bodyguard to Sam Giancana, the Chicago *mafioso*, and Anthony J. Reitinger, a freelance bookie shot by two masked men in a Northwest Side Chicago restaurant in 1975. Perhaps more importantly Aleman, who was of Mexican descent, was believed to be the Mexican connection to the Mob and was a prime suspect in the murder of Sam Giancana. 'He was a tough guy and he kept his mouth shut,' Jerry Gladden, chief investigator of the Chicago Crime Commission, said of Aleman.

2 Chicago *Sun Times*, 15 December 1999.

3 Chicago *Sun Times*, 12 April 1993.

4 The false appearance of unbiased behaviour has a precedent back in the 1930s when Judge Martin T. Manton was jailed for 19 months for taking some $186,000 in bribes. As part of his cover to make himself look good he had adopted a pro-morality stance, finding James Joyce's *Ulysses* to be obscene. See *US v One Book Called Ulysses by James Joyce*, 5 F Supp 182(SD NY, 6 Dec 1933) and *United States Federal Appeals: Judge Martin T. Manton* 107 F2d 834 (CA2, 1939).

5 See Chicago *Tribune*, 23 April 1984, 8 February and 18 July 1985.

6 *New York Times*, 4 February 1986.

7 *Newsday*, 7 October 1989.

8 *Chicago Daily Law Bulletin*, 27 June 2000; *People v Fair* 159 Ill 2d 51 (1994).

9 *The National Law Journal*, 9 February 1998.

10 'This Week's Winners and Losers' in *New Jersey Law Journal*, 11 September 2000.

11 In the eighteenth century one of the reasons for the appointment of professional or stipendiary magistrates was to eliminate the so-called trading justices amongst the lay magistracy. In the 1960s there were suggestions that a particular judge could be got at but the only name ever given to me was of an Old Bailey judge in the days, 30 years and more ago, when barristers' clerks could sometimes arrange the listing of a case in front of, if not a more favourable judge, then at least a less hostile one. The man whose name was put forward always seemed to me to be one of the most vicious and hostile judges of the time, from whom a defendant could not expect an ounce of sympathy. It may be, which I don't believe, that he was given bribes, but if he was the money was certainly not well spent.

12 Not a judge but another smuggler in this increasingly profitable trade was Glyn Myring of the two-partner firm of solicitors Myring Shah. In 2000 he was sentenced to eight months' imprisonment for defrauding the Customs and Excise of £70,000. Between January and November 1997 the solicitor had made 75 trips to France to purchase cigarettes and alcohol. Initially he had been representing Hamid Zaman who had been arrested for smuggling, but as the investigation developed Myring's part as the driver became clearer.

13 *Daily Telegraph*, 16 January 1999.

# 17 Lawyers for the Mob: Bruce Cutler, Gerry Shargel and John Gotti

O NE OF THE earliest of the recent generations of mouthpieces was Frank Ragano, described elegantly by John Lombardi as a 'human stack of mushroom pizzas who defines the term mob lawyer'.[1]

Ragano was one of the best examples of a lawyer who got too close to his clients and paid the emotional consequences. Over the years, he acted for Santo Trafficante jnr., and later Carlos Marcello and Sam Giancana as well as Gaetano 'Three Fingers' Lucchese. He was born in Tampa on 25 January 1915, the son of an immigrant Sicilian who at one time prevailed on Santo Trafficante snr. to assist him and as a result was sent delivering election leaflets.

Ragano used the GI Bill of Rights to pay his way through the University of Tampa and then Stetson Law School. With a $200 loan from his father he opened a criminal defence practice in the same building as Pat Whittaker, who then acted for the Trafficantes and had promised to put work his way. This was the time of the Kefauver Commission and investigations into *bolito* games, when Tampa was described as the Hellhole of the Gulf Coast.

In May 1954, Santo Trafficante jnr. and his brother Henry were accused of bribery and they and 28 others were arrested on gambling charges. Pat Whittaker referred some of the black low-level runners to Ragano. A Mafia man came and asked Ragano his fee and he said $5,000 per man. This was the first time he had had a case worth over $1,000. Ragano claims that even then he was worried about taking cash, but Whittaker told him all he must do was to ensure he declared it.

Santo jnr. was born on 11 November 1914 and at the age of 16, when his father was running the biggest bootlegging operation on the Gulf Coast, he dropped out of school to run the business with him. The Trafficantes were the first major crime family to acquire a large stake in Havana casinos.

In August 1954 Trafficante snr. died of cancer. By now Ragano was impressed by the multilingual and elegant Trafficante jnr.; he wrote that he regarded an invitation to lunch at Tampa Terrace as a prize: 'The best type of free advertising.' Nevertheless, at least for the purposes of his conscience or for his readers, he maintained he was worried that Trafficante was a *mafioso*. He asked his mentor Whittaker and a relative, and was told not to worry; Trafficante was a gambler and the rest of the stuff about his being Mafia was 'bullshit'. After that he was a regular diner in the Columbia restaurant with Trafficante.

The trial against Trafficante and his brother was a pre-arranged fiasco. It is always desirable to have as many lawyers as possible on your side, and Trafficante had managed to get to the prosecutor who improperly commented in front of the jury that neither of them had given evidence. With Whittaker now drinking heavily, it was to Ragano that the Don turned for his legal work. Trafficante began grooming him, telling him where to have his hair cut, where to buy his shirts and so on. Ragano lapped up the attention and was particularly proud when Trafficante persuaded him to urge L'Unione Italiano in Tampa to call for an investigation into whether the Mafia existed in the city. A Hillsborough County Grand Jury was empanelled and, while it found that organised criminal elements were present, there was no proof of the existence of a secret, important crime group. Ragano had taken a further step away from being an independent lawyer. Beginning in 1955 it was arranged that each autumn, around the time of the World Series, he and his wife would be Trafficante's guests in New York. By now Ragano had completely changed his attitude:

> Even if he was an authentic *mafioso* he was the most charismatic person that I had ever encountered and I admired him.

Ragano's boss had a pragmatic view of evidence:

First of all, if there's no body, the police have a harder time finding out who did it. And number two, some guys do things so bad, you have to punish the families.

This did not mean that they would be physically harmed, but because there was no body there could be no Mass, no burial and, perhaps most important of all, no insurance pay-out.

Soon he was in Cuba with Trafficante (this time without Mrs Ragano), being taken to private sex shows starring a gentleman, known as El Toro or El Supremo, with a penis said to be 14 inches in length – although Ragano does not seem to have measured it. The spectacle, for which El Supremo received the princely sum of $25, lasted half an hour culminating – wrote Ragano, suitably 'shocked to the core' – in oral sex. He seems to have recovered well enough and displayed proper *sang froid* in the face of this unlawyer-like behaviour because three paragraphs later he writes: 'Home movies was a hobby of mine and I thought Superman's performance would make a terrific erotic film ...'

From somewhere, out came the cine camera and Ragano writes that he believes he captured El Supremo on film for the one and only time in his life. Unless, of course, other tourists also had an interest in the cinema.[2]

There were other less tangible benefits from the friendship: as Trafficante's lawyer, Ragano's house was safe from the rash of burglaries taking place in the smart suburbs of Tampa at the time. And other tangible ones as well: Trafficante introduced him to other mobsters, Carlos Marcello of New Orleans, Gaetano 'Three Fingers' Lucchese of New York, and Sam Giancana from Chicago. There was also immediate protection. Gus Zappas, the Teamsters goon who featured in a taxicab war in Indianapolis in the 1950s, threatened to throw a man off a Chicago hotel roof because he had flirted with Ragano's wife.

But there were disadvantages too. In 1966 a photograph was published showing him with Trafficante, Marcello and Jack Wasserman, Marcello's lawyer, along with some minders, enjoying luncheon at the La Stella restaurant in Queens. In the absence of an explanation that he was there as a lawyer pure if not simple, Ragano felt obliged to sue the offending magazine for libel. So did Wasserman. The latter lost on a technicality early in the proceedings, but Ragano went the distance before he also failed. Worse, in the trial Ragano was described as house counsel for the Mob.[3]

It was the beginning of the end of his relationship with Trafficante and at the end of his book Ragano paints a touching picture of the elderly mobster, now riddled with cancer, summoning him to do him the favour of driving him around his lost empire while he confessed his implication in the killing of President Kennedy.

By this time Ragano also felt himself obliged to bite the hands that had fed him so well. Harking back to the libel trial and the reference to him as house counsel, and still maintaining a modicum of self-deception, he wrote:

> I plead guilty to that charge. Without realising it, at that stage of my life, I had become an advocate for the devils who ran the Mafia. Eventually my family and I paid a horrendous price for that moral lapse.

Ragano died in 1985.

The Black-Collar Bar is the name given by writer John Lombardi to a crop of defence lawyers currently defending mobsters, or what is left of them. A senior member is the dapper James LaRossa who spent four years in the District Attorney's office before setting up in private practice in 1965: 'Almost exclusively crime. Any other work was always attached to crime.' From the start he drew clients charged with serious crimes including Paul Castellano, reputed head of the Gambinos, whom he represented in the federal court. After that success he developed a large practice involving organised crime figures:

> Often they are the most fun. They are realistic as opposed to the white-collared chief executive officer charged with tax evasion. They respect counsel. They expect a good hard fight, a well-prepared, well-briefed defence, not a miracle.

There has, he says, never been a hint of a reprisal over a lost case.[4]

In fact it was from a meeting at LaRossa's office that Paul Castellano set off for his fatal meeting at Sparks Steak House at 210 E 46th on 16 December 1985 when, just before 5 p.m., he was shot and killed along with his driver, Tommy Bilotti, before he entered the restaurant. Castellano had been opposed to drug-dealing and had banned the Family from that lucrative field. The effect was destabilising and when Castellano carpeted John Gotti, whose Queens'-based crew was dealing, it was time for the head of the Family's compulsory retirement.

Lawyer Murray Cutler's flamboyant son Bruce became the lawyer to the new head of the Gambinos. It was he who created so many of the headlines and so much controversy about the tactics of defence lawyers over the next decade and a half. Even Cutler's admirers, and they are many, view him with some apprehension:

> He's over enthusiastic. He's apt to see a half-full glass. He genuinely sees good in people. He talks about Gotti as a great family man, good to the Church, good to poor people.[5]

'A lawyer for the mob, not a mob lawyer', reads the headline, and Gerry Shargel agrees. Along with the now less involved Jimmy LaRossa and the reactivated (after a short suspension) Bruce Cutler, he spearheads the lawyers who appear for the real upper echelons of what is described as organised crime.

Shargel grew up in New Brunswick, New Jersey, where his father had a paint and wallpaper store. His mother worked as a secretary at Rutgers University. 'I didn't want to live an obscure life. I wanted to leave a footprint that wouldn't be washed away for a while.' In January 1969 he joined LaRossa (whom he had watched defend) as a student clerk, and by the end of the year he had become an associate. He was made a partner along with Ronald Fischetti five years later. He and Fischetti left in 1976, but their partnership lasted less than three years and each became a sole practitioner.

For much of the time Shargel unusually combined trial and appellate work, and in June 1979 he obtained a re-trial for Anthony 'Tony Pro' Provenzano who had been convicted of murder. The judge having refused to dismiss for cause a juror who knew the prosecutor, the defence had had to use one of its peremptory challenges. He was also receiving clients from Michael Corio (who had also been John Gotti's lawyer), including Jimmy Burke of the Lucchese Family.

In January 1984 Shargel ran into a little local difficulty when he was accused of accepting a paper bag containing $150,000 from the Gambino captain, Roy DeMeo – whose crew was generally used as a killing machine for the Gambinos – to defend a member of his crew, Richard Mastrangelo. On 10 January DeMeo, whose crew was thought to have been involved in up to 200 murders, disappeared and his body was found a week later in the boot of his Cadillac.

Throughout the summer a minor legal battle was waged to have Shargel removed from the defence of Mastrangelo. The argument for the prosecution ran that if DeMeo had paid Shargel's fees on behalf of members of his crew, then these were what is called 'benefactor payments' and could be used to prove the existence of DeMeo's criminal enterprise.

The principal witness was an informer named Freddy DiNome, a protected witness who changed his mind and thought the bag had contained $100,000. Shargel himself maintained that the bag held a mere $2,000 but, since he kept no records deliberately to protect his clients, he was vulnerable. He was, he said, almost always paid in cash by his Mafia clients. Judge Abraham Sofaer finally disqualified him from representing one of the men and also commented unfavourably on Shargel's book-keeping. Anticipating the evidence of Martin Light before the President's Commission two years later, the judge commented:

> By picking a crew member's attorney, in addition to paying him, a crew leader can require him to use an attorney who will ... seek to keep his nominal client from co-operating, or otherwise harming the crew's interests.[6]

Any lingering thought that Shargel might be prosecuted over his involvement, which was never likely, died with DiNome hanging himself in San Antonio, Texas.

In 1988 Shargel represented Jimmy Coonan of the Westies gang from Hell's Kitchen, another whose faulty thinking cost him a sentence of 75 years. He was one more gangster who believed in the flawed maxim, 'No body, no guilty verdict.'

But two years before, in 1986, Shargel had been involved in a defence with Bruce Cutler which would lead to some enmity between him and a young prosecutor, John Gleeson. It arose over the prosecution of a multi-handed RICO case, *US v Dellacroce*, which had been scheduled to feature Neil Dellacroce and John Gotti. Shortly before the hearing Dellacroce died of cancer and so Gotti, now the most famous of the current *mafiosi*, became the leading defendant. John Gleeson had been teamed for the prosecution with Diane Giacalone and the trial was a war from the start. Shargel was also representing Buddy Dellacroce, the drink- and cocaine-addicted son of the deceased Neil. Shortly before the trial began he threw in his hand and in return Giacalone agreed he should have bail. This kindly act did not go rewarded: he disappeared and was later found dead of an overdose. Nevertheless Diane announced that she would prove, by reason of his plea of guilty, evidence of the existence of the Gambino Mafia Family; and, predictably, this produced an uproar. From then on it was a knock-down affair with some of the dirtiest linen thrown about the court. Shargel filed an affidavit to the effect that there had been an agreement that the plea should not be mentioned. The prosecution alleged the affidavit to be false. There was no inquiry into who was correct because the judge ruled the agreement void after Buddy Dellacroce skipped bail.

From then on the trial descended into what the judge himself called a circus. Bruce Cutler was on the top of his form as he called Giacalone a tramp and a slut and then produced Matthew Traynor, a bank robber, self-confessed liar and drug dealer, to say that Giacalone and Gleeson had visited him in prison, found he needed medical treatment and then arranged for him to see a doctor at the centre where Gleeson's wife was a nursing supervisor. Giacalone and Gleeson had decided that it would be impossible to call Traynor, and he eventually became Cutler's witness when he told an increasingly bizarre and demonstrably false tale. He said that Giacalone had decided that he should frame Gotti because she had grown up in an environment where Italian men had called her skinny. Then he went on to say that she was keeping one of her witnesses happy on heroin, and that he wanted to be 'blocked' on valium and codeine which was the medication he was receiving at the centre. He also told the story that he wanted to 'get laid' and that Giacalone had thrown him a pair of her pants and told him to facilitate himself. Later he elaborated, saying she had told him to sniff them and then 'jerk himself off'. In a moment of excruciating detail he said that they had 'smelled like fried scallops'.

Later in the trial an attempt was made to subpoena Gleeson's wife from the medical centre, and although the judge refused to allow it such relations between prosecution and defence as still existed deteriorated even further – if that was possible. In his closing speech Gleeson, referring to an allegation that he had filed a false affidavit to get Traynor medical care, told the jury, 'You should take that accusation and shove it down the throat of defence counsel.'

Gotti and his co-accused were found not guilty on every count. Diane Giacalone left the legal profession shortly afterwards; Gleeson stayed for a return match. It was one of those cases in which the defence lawyers could not take too much credit for the outcome; a juror had been bribed to the tune of $500,000 to ensure not guilty verdicts.[7]

In July 1991, Cutler and Shargel along with John Pollok were ordered from the defence of John Gotti, now charged with racketeering in an indictment which included an allegation of the murder of Castellano. Gleeson was again the prosecutor and Cutler and Shargel had been recorded on tapes at the Ravenite Social Club, said to have been the headquarters of the Family. Some of the references to them made in their absence were less than flattering and some referred to enormous fees paid over. Gotti had been apt to refer to his lawyers as high-priced errand boys whom he called 'Muck and Fuck', alleging also that he had paid money under the table to the tune of $300,000.

Shargel is dismissive of this latter: 'He [Gotti] is the original fisherman story teller,' adding as if for confirmation, 'Sammy Gravanno testified that Gotti is a great exaggerator.'

Gotti was recorded as saying, 'You know and I know that they know that you're taking money under the table.' Shargel was investigated for three years and his records were subpoenaed, but no improprieties were discovered. He remains unrepentant about visiting the Ravenite Club:

> I like to think I have the freedom to go where I want. They are not there to second guess me. Perhaps I should erect a confessional in my office. How dare the government tell me where to go or who to meet. With all the tapes of the Ravenite there was nothing I said to suggest or hint at illegal or unethical behaviour.[8]

The problem arose because if the tapes were played to the jury the lawyers would be in the potentially conflicting position of either having to go into the witness box or having to limit their cross-examination because of effectively giving evidence from the floor of the court. The situation of recusing counsel now crops up much more frequently, and to avoid this a current practice is for lawyers to have a colleague handle the sensitive bits of evidence in which they are personally involved. At the time of the Gotti trial it was a dynamic shift in tactics by the prosecution. Shargel still smarts at the decision of his former law tutor, Judge I. Leo Glasser, to recuse him: 'When Cutler and I were recused we had our asses kicked. I loved that guy [Glasser] but he wasn't kind to me that day.'

There was considerable speculation about who should now handle the case. Names suggested included Barry Slotnick, who had defended that archetypal anti-hero, the subway gunman

Bernard Goetz. Slotnik had been most unhappy about the recusal of Cutler and Shargel:

> It would be my hope that the criminal defence bar would react strongly and if necessary boycott the trial. It seems that this decision gives the government licence to pick and choose what lawyers appear and practise in courts on behalf of the defendant. That's a determination that cannot and should not be made by courts or instigated by the Justice Department.[9]

Other high-profile names suggested included Benjamin Bradfman, Ronald Fischetti, Oscar Goodman (later to become Mayor of Las Vegas)[10] and Shargel's mentor James LaRossa, but when it came to it the veteran Albert Krieger, recommended by LaRossa, came up from Miami and took over the defence or what was left of it. 'The Dean of the Faculty', says Lombardi of Albert Krieger about whom, apart from a suggestion that he looks like Max Schreckt in *Nosferatu*, no one has an unpleasant word. Krieger is very definitely one of the 'good guys' of the American defence Bar. Some of the others are definitely wild children.

Krieger began his life as a criminal lawyer almost by accident when he appeared in the mid-1950s for 'Cockeyed' Willie Rivera, leader of the 111 W Street Viceroys who was then on a drugs charge. Until that time much of his practice had involved arranging plea bargains for lower-level members of the Viceroys on minor charges. Now, with Rivera claiming he had been assaulted by police officer Eddie Egan – celebrated as Popeye Doyle in *The French Connection* – and refusing to bargain, Krieger took the case to trial for a fee of $750. Rivera ended with an acquittal on the felony charge and only a misdemeanour conviction. Krieger says that, 'I began to see the effect a defence lawyer could have.' He appeared in the 1957 trial of Gotti, representing a small-time co-accused, and although he lost the case he handled the appeal himself and won. From then on his mobility was onwards and upwards, but throughout he managed to maintain his independence.

Says one Justice Department lawyer:

> Al may have represented some mob guys, but you don't hear people call him a mob lawyer. He's there at a trial, but he's not in anybody's pocket. He's no *consigliere*. He's completely avoided the reputation.[11]

Krieger then handled the case of the 'Man of Honour', Joseph 'Joe Bananas' Bonanno, who had apparently been kidnapped shortly before he was due to give evidence before a Grand Jury in 1964. No one was convinced by the disappearance, Bonanno was charged with failure to appear and was declared a fugitive.[12] After some years' absence Krieger negotiated a sentence of one year for obstruction of justice.

By the early 1970s Krieger, sated with a diet of drug-smugglers and others, took his family to Miami from where he represented a wider variety of clients including, in 1973, members of the American Indian Movement. They had been charged with federal and state crimes after having taken over a trading post at Wounded Knee, South Dakota, where 83 years earlier more than 200 Sioux including women and children were massacred.

From then on he took half a dozen or so contested cases a year. He did not, he said, like plea bargaining. In 1985 he represented Norman Sanders, Chief Minister of the Turks and Caicos Islands, when he was charged with taking bribes to allow Colombian drug lords to use the islands as a trans-shipment point for cocaine. The evidence against him included a videotape showing him accepting an alleged bribe, pushing so much money into the pockets of his suit that he was unable to cross his legs. In the end Sanders was convicted only of crossing a national border with drug money and received a modest four years.

However, things were not getting any better for Gotti. The news that there was a witness who could place him outside Sparks Steak House shortly before Castellano was shot was bad enough, but there was much worse to come. The underboss, Sammy 'The Bull' Gravano, defected to the prosecution. If convicted, not only did he face 50 years but also the confiscation of his property. He was the man who could unravel and expand on the hours of tapes taken from the bugs in the Ravenite Club. The prosecution was also expected to call on the also-defecting Philadelphian mobster, Crazy Phil Leonetti, to tell the jury what Gotti had told him about the Castellano hit.

In the end Leonetti was not called, but Gravano managed quite well enough. As might be expected, it was suggested that he was giving evidence for his own ends, which of course he undoubtedly was. The agreement he had reached was a maximum term of 20 years and a $250,000 fine. To a certain extent his fate was in his own hands. If he did well, Glasser could give him less than 20 years. If he was found to have lied, he could be prosecuted for any of the crimes he had admitted. What he did was catalogue a seemingly endless number of killings of men for such diverse reasons as cheating, failing to show respect, lying, giving evidence to a Grand Jury and so forth. It was an impressive performance and Krieger, for all his skill, was unable to make much impression on him.

The jury retired on 1 April and were out only a day and a half. They had believed Gravano. Gotti did not wish there to be a media circus on the day he was sentenced, and Krieger and the prosecutor saw the judge who agreed that on 23 June there need be no long speeches in mitigation. Gotti, who received life without the possibility of parole, and a fine of $250,000, was sent to the maximum security prison in Marion, Illinois, then the harshest of all federal prisons. He would have a black and white television, no education classes, be confined to an 8 × 7 ft underground cell, have one hour of exercise daily and two showers a week – he would be taken to the bathing room in chains inside a movable cage. The government, having finally learned that gang leaders rule from their cells, would endeavour to ensure that it was made as difficult for Gotti as possible. At least Cutler would travel to see him.

His conviction was upheld on 8 October 1993. Gotti had claimed that the judge should not have disqualified Cutler but the tapes showed that, as far as the court was concerned, the lawyer was hopelessly compromised. One extract was almost sufficient: 'Go find out what's going on, when the pinch is coming. We're making you an errand boy. High-priced errand boy, Bruce.'

Cutler's troubles were not yet over. On 7 January 1994 he was convicted of criminal contempt of court over remarks made to reporters during the pre-trial hearings. Stating that the lawyer had 'no choice but to obey the court', US District Judge Thomas Platt found him guilty of disregarding three gag orders issued by Glasser. Cutler was not without support; 175 defence lawyers ran a fund-raising social at the Tavern on the Green to pay for his defence. On 10 June he was sentenced to 90 days under house arrest, three years of probation and six months away from the Brooklyn courts. He was also fined $5,000 and ordered to spend 200 hours in community service during each year of his probation, and his practice was suspended for six months in the state's Eastern district. Nevertheless there was some thought that a scapegoat had been made of him. Gangland observer Jerry Capeci wrote, 'If every defence lawyer, prosecutor or other law enforcement official who ever violated a federal court rule were brought up on criminal charges, we'd have to empty the jails.'

Cutler's lawyer, Frederick Hafetz, commented:

> We feel the entire case should never have been brought and feel it will be overturned on appeal. The prosecutor never proved Bruce violated the rules.[13]

But it wasn't overturned.

During his suspension his weight ballooned, but by the time he held a christening party for his son Michael at the Sicilian restaurant Taormina on Mulberry Street in the summer of 1998, weightlifting and exercise had got him back to his normal 210 lbs. His friends thought that with a new relationship he had mellowed. Seemingly in the past were the days when he would describe an indictment weighing 7 lbs as a 'rancid stew made with bad meat and bad potatoes that belongs in the garbage' which he then threw into the court's wastepaper basket, and say of the judge who later held him in contempt, 'Glasser is like the Jews the Nazis used to lead the death camp inmates into the gas chamber.' But it had been a long and often hard road to something approaching conformity.

In July 2000, however, it was an accommodating Cutler who appeared as a witness in an inquiry. His former client the candy czar Gerald Winters, convicted back in 1990 on racketeering charges, wanted a new trial. Cutler had represented Winters, who had been convicted of using baseball bat beatings and arson to further his attempts to build up a door-to-door candy sales empire. Winters maintained that when, during his own trial, it became clear that Gotti was about to be arrested, his lawyer had lost interest in him. He had been sentenced to 34 years' imprisonment.

The case points up the difference between trial practice in America, and England where it is the norm for the defendant to give evidence unless he wants the prosecution and the trial judge to comment adversely about his failure. Winters alleged that he wanted to give evidence but that Cutler had threatened to leave the case if he did.

Cutler told the court that it went against the grain to permit clients to give evidence, saying that he could not recall a single instance in nearly twenty years of criminal defence work when he had allowed his client to do so. In Winters' case:

> I felt very strongly that Gerry testifying would be suicidal. He was so emotionally charged with his own innocence. He would have had a difficult time in the crucible of cross-examination.

As for actually walking out on his client, Cutler would have none of this. ' I would never say that. That's not Bruce Cutler. If he had asked, we would have acceded to his wishes.' Nor would he accept that he cut short the case in order to return to Gotti's defence.[14]

Winters received short shrift from the judge:

> Had Winters testified not only would he not have been exonerated of the charges on which he went down, but he would have been convicted on even more charges ...

And as for Cutler:

> Quite candidly, Mr Cutler would have been deficient had he not used every means at his disposal, short, of course, of actual coercion, to keep Winters off the stand.

Winters believed he would have been acquitted if he had testified. Wrong. [15]

One lawyer who certainly became house counsel or even house minder was Pat V. Stiso, who acted for the Bronx-based drug-dealer, Francisco Maisonet. He was recorded as telling his client 'I'm your eyes and ears' and going on to say that he would be 'the best lawyer I can for you out there'. Unfortunately he went on, so the prosecution said, to do rather more for Maisonet, who allegedly hired hitmen to dispose of his rivals. He was said to have disclosed the identities of informers – something which, although in violation of a court order, must have been extremely useful to Mr Maisonet in his line of work.

The charges dealt a serious blow to Stiso's practice and he was obliged to hand over the cases of 18 defendants to other lawyers. His supporters showed him as a very hard-working, talented man who gave free legal advice to young people and delivered a load of toys to a children's hospital every Christmas. 'He definitely seemed to me like a fighter who was going to get in there and fight for the underdog,' said Juanita Brooks, his trial practice teacher at California Western School of Law.

But the prosecution took a different view. Stiso had represented Maisonet from 1991. Since 1996 his client had been in prison but, it was claimed, had continued his heroin-trafficking operations in the Bronx, grossing a reasonable $100,000 a day.

When Jose Vasquez was hired by Maisonet to kill a rival drug-dealer and Stiso was then hired to defend him, the prosecution alleged that if convicted Vasquez might be able to appeal on the grounds that Stiso had divided loyalties and so had not pursued the case properly. Once Stiso was indicted, the argument against him went that he had a conflicting need to fight the government for his clients and to curry favour on his own behalf. In one case Judge John F. Keenan agreed, telling the defendant that his lawyer was now dealing with the 'same government office that you are dealing with'.[16]

In August 1998 he pleaded guilty, with Mary Jon White – the United States Attorney in Manhattan – saying, 'Lawyers who forsake their professional oath should face punishment under the law as cynical criminals.' Stiso accepted that he had identified the informer to Maisonet and that he had received thousands of dollars, knowing the money was the proceeds of drug-trafficking. He had concealed the money in his office in the Bronx. On 30 March 1999 it was the usual sad story. Choking back tears, the lawyer admitted that he had 'failed to honour my own moral and ethical obligations'.

Sentencing him to slightly under 11 years, of which Stiso could expect to serve 87 months, the judge said that the letters in support from his friends and former colleagues had missed:

> The side of him that allowed him to accept grocery bags of money, tens of thousands of dollars in cash in grocery bags, money that was earned from the sale of heroin.

It had been suggested that Stiso's case was something of a blurring of the line of the ethics of defence lawyers, but Judge Chin would have none of it. 'This case doesn't even come close.'[17]

Another who was found to have seriously blurred the lines, and whom Shargel defended, is Russell Carbone, the New York City lawyer accused in Miami of conspiracy to obstruct justice, along with his paralegal Harry Mejia. Carbone's law practice of defending relatively minor drug-dealers and street-level hoodlums had taken off when he hired Colombian native and former janitor Mejia in the early 1990s. The idea had been to give his office a Hispanic-friendly feeling, and it was an enormous success. Much higher-grade clients had started flocking to Carbone. Now he was defending kidnappers and drug-smugglers, not just street-dealers.

However, life was not always smooth and in 1994 Mejia pleaded no contest and received a conditional discharge for witness tampering in a New York state court. It had been alleged by the prosecution that he had tried to persuade a kidnap victim to fly home – all found – to Colombia.

Two years later Mejia had posted a bond for Julio Caesar Lopez who was accused of smuggling cocaine. The collateral was a New York row house which he had obtained ten days before signing the bond. Unfortunately, Lopez failed to appear and when an investigation into the house took place it was found not only to be in foreclosure but that Mejia had probably acquired the property from a suspect in another narcotics smuggling case. This time the judge commented, 'Mr Mejia ... it seems to me, has dedicated himself in part as a paralegal and perhaps working with others, in basically frustrating the ends of justice.'

That same year the pair's problems surfaced in Miami. In June Carbone took on the defence of Olga Agudelo, accused of smuggling 3 kilograms of heroin from Colombia. That much is certain, but now things become a little less clear. Carbone says he took a modest if unspecified sum on account of his costs and worked hard on the defence. Agudelo says Carbone took $40,000 in cash and she was not given a receipt; much of the time between then and the trial was spent by Carbone chasing the remaining $20,000. She refused advice to plead guilty.

During the trial, which began in December 1996, Carbone argued that Agudelo had been framed by another Colombian drug-dealer, Adolfo Patino. In support of this he called Patino's half-sister, Libia Porras, who told a complicated story. She and Agudelo had a motor-cycle spares business together which was purchased by Patino. He did not want to pay the full price, so he recruited an imprisoned drug-dealer to implicate Agudelo in heroin smuggling on the basis that once in jail she could not try to collect the balance.

Agudelo was convicted and, when asked about the business by a court officer preparing a pre-sentence report, said at once that Carbone and Mejia had met her in the South Beach Holiday Inn and had coached her in her lies. Porras confirmed this, as did her niece Veronica Caicedo. They all gave evidence against their former lawyers.

Shargel did what he could with this unpromising material, suggesting that Porras had made up the tale and that the lawyers were not responsible for checking out the truth of a witness's story. Afterwards he said that, 'Criminal defence lawyers are held in low esteem by the public and I just wonder what role that played in the jury's decision.'[18]

Now things are changing. The latest star of the Gotti jnr. team of lawyers was, amazingly in this old-fashioned macho world, a young Indian woman named Serita Kedia. At first Gotti would not talk to her if he telephoned and found Shargel out, but gradually he came to accept her and was impressed when her arguments led to his obtaining bail. Cutler is impressed with her too: 'She is unflappable, a tireless worker and a real ball of fire.' He believes her future to be limitless.[19]

Shargel is happy with the change in attitude of the clients, saying, 'Bring me a good black Jewish lawyer and I'll hire him.' In fact he may soon think of hanging up his boots. 'Trial law is a young man's game. Seven days a week working long hours is wearing. I still like the fight but it's the training.'

It is not only the lawyers who are thinking of retirement. Many of the major players are now from the ethnic minorities, and while for the moment they may be hiring the top lawyers who have acted for Mob figures for decades – one of Shargel's more recent defences was the trial of gas station mogul, Gurmeet Singh Dhinsa, convicted in 1999 of murder and racketeering – this will soon change as a new generation of lawyers comes to the fore.

Defending mobsters can certainly be tiring. Being the lawyer to the Philadelphia Mafia must have been hard work. In 1992 the Philadelphia Mob's long-standing counsel, Robert Simone, was convicted and received 4 years at a time when the leader, Nicodemo Scarfo, was given a total of 69 years. The RICO indictment had charged Simone with being the unofficial *consigliere* to the Scarfo Family, and it was at one time considering having him become a made member.

On 15 December he was convicted by a federal jury of racketeering and conspiring with Scarfo and former City Council man, Leland Beloff, to extort $1 million from property developer Willard Rouse III. According to the prosecution, he was due to receive 10 per cent of the profits. Two jurors later said they had not believed he was guilty but had been pressured into finding him so and, tired after nine days of deliberations, voted to convict him. They also said they were afraid the judge would not find a hung jury acceptable.

The 59-year-old Simone said that his conviction was the result of a vendetta against him. In previous years he had successfully defended himself on a $1 million federal income tax charge and also a charge of lying to a Grand Jury.

> There is more in this case than Robert Simone at stake here. Maybe
> some day the jury will realise the mistake they made. This is not a
> vendetta against me but against all criminal lawyers who fight the
> good fight.

In September 1994 he lost another attempt to stay out of prison when
the federal appeals court rejected his application for a new trial.

After his release he worked as a paralegal for another firm of
defence lawyers and was successful in his application to the court
that he was not obliged to give his probation officer details of the
criminals with whom he came into contact during his work.

As the leadership of the Philadelphia Mob changed hands, so
lawyers changed with it, and acting for new head John Stanfa
was Salvatore Avena who was alleged to have had personal
links with organised crime. His father John was a Philadelphia
Mob leader murdered in the 1930s and his daughter had
married the son of Salvatore Profaci whose father once led the
Colombo Family. On 16 March 1994, at the age of 67, he was
indicted on three counts. Avena had been taped saying that he
wanted to be a member of the Family and telling Stanfa, as a
demonstration of loyalty, that if he was dissatisfied with the
quality of work he was providing, 'If you want me to put my
brains in the toilet, I'll put my brains in the toilet.' As a result,
said the prosecution, 'Avena is clearly not acting here as a
lawyer, but demonstrating his total fealty to *La Cosa Nostra*.'

The prosecution alleged that he used his office and the lawyer-
client privilege as a shield behind which he could discuss
business with Stanfa. According to tape recordings mostly made
from bugs in Avena's office between 1991 and 1993, Stanfa and
an associate named Sergio Battalia had been overheard
discussing the possible murders of rival Joey Merlino and two
of his family. Of one, Stanfa had said, 'You know what I'll do. I'll
get a knife. I'll cut out his tongue and we'll send it to his wife.'

On 15 May 1996, after nine days of deliberations, Avena was
acquitted of actively engaging in an organised crime enterprise.
The jury was hung over another conspiracy charge and also one
of obstructing the course of justice. The prosecution announced
that it would re-try Avena, but his lawyer Edwin Jacobs said he
doubted it. 'The defence has always said that all he did was his
everyday job of a criminal defence attorney.' He was proved to be
correct. Avena said he was going back to continue his law practice.[20]

In any event, James LaRossa believes that organised crime in
the Italian sense is almost extinct:

We should be spending more time on terrorism and narcotics than a bunch of old men who if you do convict them are more likely to be sent to nursing homes than prison.[21]

1 John Lombardi, 'The Goodfather' in *New York Magazine*, 8 August 1998.
2 Frank Ragano and Selwyn Raab, *Mob Lawyer*, p.45. Part of the Havana nightclub sequence in the film *The Godfather II* is something of a fleeting tribute to this well-endowed man.
3 A number of other lawyers have tried their hand at suing over allegations that they are Mafia-connected. In August 1987 William Bufalino snr. lost an action against *Monthly Detroit* magazine over an allegation in 1981 that he was tied to an upstate New York Family. 'There is no question that membership in an organised crime family and the State Bar of Michigan are incompatible and inconsistent,' said Appeals Judge Nicholas Lambros. *Detroit Free Press*, 25 August 1987. See also Francis Ianni, *A Family Business – Kinship and Social Control in Organised Crime*.
4 Interview with author, October 2000.
5 *Ibid*.
6 For an account of Roy DeMeo's career see Gene Mustain and Jerry Capeci, *Murder Machine*.
7 There is a very full account of the case in John Cummins and Ernest Volkman, *Mobster*, Chapter 8.
8 Conversation with author, 18 November 2000.
9 Anthony DeStefano and Patricia Hurtado, 'Shock Rocks Top Defenders' in *Newsday*, 27 July 1991.
10 Of all American criminal defence lawyers Goodman's client list reads like a roll-call of Mob Honour and included Meyer Lansky and Tony Spilotro. He began to practise in Las Vegas in 1964, when he says of his first case, 'I got lucky – I got sick first, I threw up I was so nervous – but I got lucky and the jury came back with a not guilty.' Las Vegas *Sun*, 19 August 1998.
11 Robert Kunz, 'Krieger's Craft' in *Legal Times*, 14 October 1991.
12 In fact he had genuinely been kidnapped on 21 October 1964 when for good measure his lawyer, William P. Maloney, was shot at. Bonanno was held captive by Steven Magaddino in Buffalo for a year before he was released on condition that he went into exile. He lived in Haiti for a year but then returned to Tucson from where he conducted a war. In 1980 he wrote a self-serving autobiography, *Man of Honour*.
13 Jerry Capeci, 'No Justice in Cutler's Conviction' in the *New York Daily News*, 11 January 1994. For a profile of the lawyer who said of Gotti, 'I was 36 years old, a kid when I met him. But he had faith in me, he trusted me. If that doesn't make you feel good, I don't know what does,' see Jan Hoffman, 'At the office with: Bruce Cutler', in *New York Times*, 7 April 1993. American judges could be quite fearsome in dealing with feisty advocates. On one occasion in New York a judge ordered a lawyer to be handcuffed for an hour for complaining that his case was not being dealt with. At least the judge was kind enough not to bring contempt proceedings.
14 *The Record* (Bergen County, N.J.), 21 July 2000.
15 *Ibid*, 3 August 2000.
16 Benjamin Weiser, 'Legal Advocate or Illegal Conspirator' in *New York Times*, 8 January 1988.
17 *New York Times*, 1 April 1999.
18 *Miami New Times*, 21 October 1999.
19 Jayant Mammen Mathew, 'Mob's Angel' in *The Week*, 15 August 1999.
20 *The Record*, 16 May 1996.
21 Interview with author, October 2000.

# 18 Laundering: Michael Relton and Brink's-Mat

ONE EXTRA-LEGAL ACTIVITY for which lawyers have always been used is changing and laundering money. The days when solicitors obligingly changed money from robberies at 20p in the £1 are, however, long gone. Now, money laundering has become a worldwide business.

On 30 August 1994, 43-year-old Montreal lawyer Joseph Lagana was arrested and charged with 241 counts of having laundered proceeds from drug sales. Charged with him were two other lawyers, Richard Judd and Vincenzo Vecchio, who worked for him. He was said to have conspired since 1993 to ship cocaine to Britain. Lagana had a very much hands-on approach, bringing sacks filled with small bills to the RCMP foreign exchange counter on the corner of Peel Street, Montreal. The other lawyers were not so involved: Judd faced 129 counts and Vecchio a mere 77. The RCMP raids, however, failed to include the man suggested to be the head of the Canadian and Montreal Mafia, Vito Rizzuto, but another former lawyer was also in the frame. Jean-Paul Renaud, also known as Renault, a former fund-raiser for *Les Ballets Jazz de Montreal* who had been disbarred in the 1980s, faced 21 counts. In 1985 he had been sentenced to 14 years after Canada's first clandestine drug laboratory was found at a bungalow in Rosemere.

The raids were the result of a long-running sting by the RCMP begun in 1990 when the exchange house had been set up on the corner of Peel Street and de Maisonneuve Boulevard, and proved so popular that it was continued for four years. It was even thought to have made a profit. The money laundered through the RCMP front was wired into more than 200 bank accounts in Europe, South America and the United States.

When the case came to court in June 1995 Lagana, who pleaded guilty, was described as the brains behind the Cn\$47 million money-laundering operation and the only man in direct contact with Vito Rizzuto. He received 13 years' imprisonment; Judd and Vecchio received 7 and a half years each. The Crown announced that it would appeal and demand a longer sentence for Lagana and Luis Cantieri, said to be his immediate deputy in the scheme, but the suggestion of a longer sentence came to nothing. In August 1997 Lagana was released under new federal regulations which allowed a non-violent criminal serving a first offence to be released after serving one third of his sentence.

Being a money launderer – provided you are not discovered, that is – is no bar to a judicial appointment. When you are found out your life comes apart. Between 1989 and 1991 Robert Flahiff spent a good deal of time commuting to Switzerland on behalf of his then client Paul Larue. Flahiff went to Europe on no fewer than 25 occasions, cleaning \$1.7 million in drug money which came back via Hong Kong, the Cayman Islands, Bermuda and Toronto. A massive effort was made to save him from prison, with his lawyers citing the 'shame and dishonour' he had brought upon his family. At this point in the hearing Judge Flahiff was reported as wiping his eyes. He may also have been reflecting on the cartoon in *La Presse* which pictured the judge at Bordeaux prison where the prisoners are in thrall to the Hell's Angels with a caption, 'Hey! Boys. A judge!' He received three years and resigned from the bench. A small consolation must have been that while he was on 'sick leave' for two years pending the hearing of his case he still drew his Cn\$175,800 salary.

'Lawyer turned Launderer', said *The Times* happily when Westminster-educated solicitor, Michael Relton, was sentenced to 12 years for his part in laundering some of the money from the English Brink's-Mat robbery.[1] At the time Relton's wife, Terri, loyally said that he had been the fall guy after being set up by Gordon John Parry who was then still at large. It must have been some consolation to her that Parry was later brought back from Spain and received 10 years for his pains.

On 26 November 1983 at 6.40 a.m. the biggest of the biggest robberies had taken place when £26 million in gold was lifted from the Brink's-Mat warehouse on the Heathrow trading estate. As in the slightly earlier Security Express robbery which occurred at Easter that year, the guards were threatened – one with castration, others had petrol poured over them, another was coshed for not producing keys sufficiently speedily. The gang drove off with 6,400 bars of gold which had been awaiting delivery to the Middle and Far East. It was clearly a job executed with help from the inside; the premises had been opened with a key and the gang knew the guards' names as well as the workings of the vaults and locks.

It was really only a matter of days before the police latched on to the last guard to arrive that morning – Tony Black – who had missed the robbery because he was ten minutes late for work. Black confessed. Apparently his sister was living with Brian Robinson, one of a number of villains over the years known as 'The Colonel'. Black also identified two more of the team, Tony White and Michael McAvoy.

In December 1984 Robinson and McAvoy received 25 years each. White was acquitted. Later there was said to be £50,000 on offer to free McAvoy and Robinson. Black, who had given evidence for the Crown, was handed a 6-year sentence.

The disposal and laundering of the money presented a problem and much was carried out by a John Perry who recruited Gordon Parry, the client of Michael Relton of Lynn Relton & Co. who practised near the Horseferry Road Magistrates' Court.

Relton was without doubt a shrewd defender in criminal cases. However, he had had a slip-up himself in 1970 when he was suspended for six months for misbehaviour with the client account and had been obliged to make good the deficiency by selling a house.

After that he had made something of a speciality, and certainly a good job, of defending police officers accused of corruption. It is said that of the 30-plus officers he defended only one was convicted. He also had a good number of major villains on his books, and senior police officers believed that information he received from corrupt officers was passed on to other clients. He had defended Parry in 1972 on a drugs trial at Middlesex Crown Court. When his client received three years, Relton continued to act for him while he was in Ford open prison, including arrangements for the purchase of a recording studio in New Cross and a hotel on the Isle of Wight. Now on his release Relton became his business partner. Their joint activities included the popular Brief's Wine Bar opposite Inner London Crown Court in which Relton's clerk, the shadowy Emmanuel 'Ted' Wein, along with three officers who had left the force, also had a share, and which was regarded as so unhealthy that it was placed off limits to serving police officers by Scotland Yard. One of the wine bar's employees was the former bank robber turned supergrass Maurice O'Mahoney who, when charged with yet another post office raid, told the court that much of his work was collecting and laundering money.[2]

There was also a deal turning two houses at Cheltenham Ladies' College into luxury flats. But the pearl in the collection was Dock's Diner Club behind Guy's Hospital where it was alleged that prostitutes were brought in and orgies took place as an inducement to persuade businessmen to participate in their development schemes.[3]

In 1980 Relton's income from his law practice and some small property deals amounted to £147,000. Three years later it totalled £550,000. In 1982 he married barrister's clerk Terri Luff, who had once worked for Ronald Shulman.

In 1984 Relton was approached to launder the Brink's-Mat money and effectively retired from his practice – leaving it in the hands of Emmanuel Wein, who had himself earlier served four years for fraud – to run a property company, Selective Estates. In two years, using the Brink's-Mat money admittedly with the help of the property boom, say the police, Relton turned £7.5 million into a property portfolio worth £18 million, much of it through investments in Docklands.

When the balloon went up and Relton was betrayed by an informer he was fairly safely abroad. But unfortunately he decided to return to complete another property deal and transfer £260,000 to a Jersey-based company. He was arrested and Parry escaped with a police officer clinging to the bonnet of his car.

Initially Relton decided to co-operate with the police, so becoming the first solicitor supergrass. In October 1986 he was charged and remanded on bail with the usual condition that he reside in a suite at a South London police station. His solicitor, John Blackburn Gittings, who would later become Attorney General for Gibraltar, was able to assure the press that Relton was perfectly comfortable. But, unfortunately for the police, security for his family was not firmly in place. Gangland figures wished to know what Relton was saying. Terri Relton had already hired a security company which had traced a microphone to the underside of the kitchen sink. Then came a threat to her life; Relton clammed up and declined to assist further. In the following January, he was brought from the comfortable suite and remanded in custody. Reporting restrictions were lifted so that rumours that he might have become a supergrass could be denied by his lawyers. When he appeared at the Old Bailey in July 1988 he pleaded not guilty.

During the trial Relton said he thought the money had come from Parry's father who owned 26 betting shops:

> I know nothing about the Brink's-Mat robbery and there is no way I could connect Mr Parry with the Brink's-Mat robbery. He was a man of considerable ability and substance ... who came back from adversity and proved himself in business.

Even so, he should have been alarmed when his client was questioned about the robbery in June 1985 at which time his clerk, Wein, had acted for him. Instead of demanding a full explanation from Parry and declining to act further, Relton had disposed of the money by an even more circuitous route, bringing it back from abroad to purchase yet more property.

On his conviction in July 1988 Relton received 12 years' imprisonment and Judge Richard Lowry was able to say:

> Far from serving the community as a lawyer you aspired to live as a parasite. You are not a man who has been led into crime by others. You were grossly dishonest. You were only too keen to mix with persons you knew were linked to organised crime.

The Brink's-Mat laundering trials continued into the 1990s and at one point Detective Chief Superintendent Brian Boyce, giving evidence, said that he suspected Relton's clerk Wein was guilty of corruption.[4] He also named another clerk from a well-known firm and a fashionable solicitor. By the end of the laundering trials several of those convicted early on in the proceedings, such as Relton, had already been released. Civil proceedings took away a considerable part of his fortune, but he was still able to command the table of his choice at the fashionable Quaglino's in Bury Street. He was believed to have business interests in South Africa.

Some time after Relton's release solicitor Ronald Irving, who also had a large criminal practice, met him in Piccadilly:

> When Michael Relton got 12 years I thought that's an eternity. He came out after four or five and I met him quite by chance. I said, 'Michael I thought we'd never see you again. Did you save anything from the shipwreck? He gave a wry smile and said, 'Well, a little.'

In November 1998 the National Crime Intelligence Service put the cat amongst the legal pigeons when it issued a statement that it was targeting six major City firms suspected of money laundering. It went on to say that the companies included household names in the City: 'Well known, allegedly respectable City of London firms.' The article was followed up two days later by another which said the firms under investigation were the tip of the iceberg; the businesses were suspected of acting as fronts for Colombian drug cartels, the Italian Mafia, and criminal gangs in Britain and Eastern Europe.[5]

In fact it was not suggesting that such giants as Clifford Chance or any of the other major international commercial firms were the launderers, rather that some smaller City firms were amongst the top launderers. Whatever the meaning, the Law Society was stung into action. It offered up-to-date guidance on how solicitors should handle strange clients bearing large sums of cash and bankers' drafts for investment, and generally tried to heighten awareness of the dangers of money laundering.

Mike Calvert, head of the Investigation Unit of the Office for the Supervision of Solicitors, the regulatory branch of the Law Society, has no doubt about the vast sums of money washing around and the dangers in which lawyers may find themselves:

> Ecstasy tablets costs between £10 and £15 each and there is an estimated number of half a million taken every weekend which means that half a billion pounds has to be laundered. £500 billion is being laundered annually from this drug alone.
>
> Don't forget that money laundering is not simply money coming from drugs. It's coming from terrorist operations, from people smuggling. In East Europe 15,000 women annually are kidnapped, drugged, used and disposed of by prostitution rings; then there is money to be made from child pornography and from pollutants. The cash generated by all these has to be laundered.

Calvert has evidence that organised crime families have targeted solicitors' firms and have infiltrated some on a long-term basis, ranging from putting book-keepers in place to provide an early-warning system of an accounting investigation to dishonest solicitors who are left as moles for future use.

He believes that while the dangers are greatest for sole practitioners and one- or two-partner firms for whom a sudden cash injection may be the difference between survival and folding, the larger firms are not exempt:

If you have 300 fee earners, statistically at least one has to be significantly bent – probably five or six. There are those who are anxious to please the principal. They meet someone at the golf club who offers several millions pounds' worth of work. 'Shall I cultivate him?' 'Of course.' Then there is the senior partner who has lost his way and the Young Turks are baying at him. He'll be keen to introduce substantial business. They are both targets for the organised criminal.

Calvert also believes the majority are victims rather than professionals themselves, and that there are about 100 firms targeted. They may be innocent dupes at first, but ultimately they will know what they are doing.

The temptations for a solicitor are endless:

He'll think, 'Here's a new client with a large cash business. If I turn him away he'll only go next door.' Travel is a lure. The client says he's thinking of using a number of local firms. Will you be one of them? There's likely to be some travel abroad, possibly at short notice; meetings in Geneva.

Then there is the nature of the transaction. You will receive a sum of money from abroad. It is to be distributed in such and such a way. Now this is blindingly obvious. Why isn't he using a bank? Why am I being privileged enough to do what a High Street bank does ordinarily?

Calvert recalls the case of a solicitor who took instructions from a man who set up a small jewellery business:

He said he had a small legacy to invest. These were the days when it was impossible to do much more than scratch a living as a small jeweller. He started turning over £2,000 a month using the solicitor as a bank, saying that he was arranging the moving of his account from one bank to another, and then it was suddenly £300,000 a month. The jeweller came from a London-based crime family.

As for payment?

There's no sentiment. You'll be paid very well. If you will supply other services the pay will be exemplary, but if you look nervous you won't be paid at all. You may be blackmailed. The best reward will be not to be beaten up outside a nightclub.

Nevertheless, innocents apart, he thinks there are probably twenty firms actively and knowingly involved in money laundering, with twelve operating at any one time:

As with every business there are peaks and troughs. Some weeks there is a greater need than others. When the need is greatest dormant solicitors will be reactivated. They are professional criminals who happen to be solicitors and they will also be operating investment scams and mortgage frauds.

There is also the problem of the struck-off solicitor or dishonest clerk who prey on firms:

Every year ten or a dozen struck-off solicitors come to our notice involved in scams. In 2000 we intervened in 112 firms of solicitors. We reckon that 200 firms will have an actively dishonest solicitor. That's 200 out of 9,000. That's one in 45 that has a significantly dishonest lawyer in it.[6]

The first solicitor to go down for money laundering in England, in a relatively low-profile case, was when Grimsby solicitor Dennis Jebb was found guilty on four counts of money laundering on 16 July 1999 and was sentenced to 18 months' imprisonment.

In June 2000 the Kirby offices of the far higher-profile Liverpudlian solicitor Kevin Dooley of Dooley & Co., who had represented a number of football stars as well as victims of the Hillsborough stadium disaster and the father of the murdered child, Jamie Bulger, were raided by officials of the Office for the Supervision of Solicitors. Documents and client files were seized as the Law Society effectively closed down Dooley's practice. His practising certificate was later restored so that he might work under approved conditions pending an appearance before the Solicitors' Disciplinary Tribunal.

In October, a month after a hearing in which initially reporting restrictions were in place, it appeared that in September Mr Dooley had applied to the High Court challenging the intervention. At that hearing a tale had emerged which the Law Society would say was an example of the dangers in which solicitors can innocently or sometimes more actively find themselves at the hands of fraudsters.

The OSS told Mr Justice Neuberger that it believed Mr Dooley had 'knowingly and dishonestly' been involved in bank instrument frauds and money laundering. It was an example of how a skilled fraudster can put together long-term plans in which the solicitor becomes his tool.

Dooley's client, Silver, had met the lawyer in 1993. Two years later the solicitor was approached by him over a proposed investment by a Mrs Yang and a Mrs Yu through a German company owned by Silver. The idea was that they should invest $500,000 in what was described as a 'leveraged trading programme' which would turn the half million into $100 million. Put in this way, it seems highly reminiscent of the flyers to be seen on telegraph poles in the 1960s offering fly-by-night investment schemes which were only sustainable by the introduction of new capital to pay the dividends. The local Midland Bank manager warned Mr Dooley that he should have nothing to do with the scheme, suggesting a bank instrument might even be forged. The transaction did not proceed and apart from a $25,000 commission to Silver the ladies got their money back. Despite this warning from the bank, Mr Dooley went to Spain to meet Silver and after discussing matters with him decided that he was a man who could be trusted.

In 1996 the OSS carried out a routine inspection of the books of Dooley & Co. After seeing details of the Silver transaction, a letter was written warning that the Office had seen 'numerous examples of this type of transaction and in almost every case they [are] either fraudulent *per se* or part of a larger mechanism designed to facilitate a fraud'.

The lawyer appears to have ignored the OSS's warnings because he did not report back to them when in that same year he was again approached by Silver who was this time acting for a Mr and Mrs Sheppard over a $100,000 investment. Apparently, although Dooley told Silver that the guarantee instrument was worthless, this information was never passed to the Sheppards who lost their money. In fairness there were another half-dozen similar schemes and some were a success. In one case, however, three of Dooley's clients lost $1.4 million and the judge was satisfied that the money had been stolen. Again in 1996, Dooley was involved in the financing of a power plant in Central America. Mr Justice Neuberger said it was clear the scheme was tied up with 'a classic bank fraud'.

Yet again, in 1997 he was sent $3.6 million with instructions to block it in his client account. The funds were then sent to accounts in London, Switzerland, Omagh and Hong Kong. It could have been a money-laundering scheme, alleged the OSS.

Dooley had also allowed Silver to use his offices in Kirby as a business address. He had given a reference for Mrs Silver although he had never met her; and in yet another investment scheme in which he was involved, the name of a dishonest participant was withheld from the honest parties.

For Mr Dooley, it was urged that he had told the National Crime Intelligence Squad of each transaction, had earned little from the deals and had retrieved some money for the clients. He, it was said, 'gradually became mired in a state of suspension of disbelief from which he did not emerge until after the intervention when he was forced to consider, in detail and in aggregate, all the various instruments and their terms'.

Mr Justice Neuberger was not prepared to upset the intervention:

> I accept that, just as there are grounds for suspecting dishonesty, there are grounds for suspecting no dishonesty; stupidity, possibly even incompetence, but not dishonesty.

After the case, Mr Dooley's practising certificate remained suspended by the Law Society pending an appearance before the Solicitors' Disciplinary Tribunal.[7]

Meanwhile Stuart Creggy – once of the Mayfair solicitors Talbot, Creggy – has been fighting a battle in the New York courts as he refuses to hand over in the region of £20 million which the United States authorities claim is laundered drugs money. Creggy declined a request to hand over $31 million from accounts he controls on behalf of 'Spanish Raymond' Marquez, said to have once been the controller of the biggest of New York's Numbers rackets. In 1994 Marquez was fined $1 million after pleading guilty to running illegal gambling.

Creggy, along with his partner Andrew Warren, was arrested in June 1998 but no charges were brought against him. Extradition proceedings have been commenced against Warren. In March 2000 a former member of the US State Department, Jonathan Winer, told the Senate Banking Committee in Washington that the National Crime Squad had uncovered a 'complex international network of shenanigans' involving the lawyers. It is suspected that the money belongs partly to Russian-organised crime figures and partly to the Colombians.[8]

1 *The Times*, 8 July 1988. The American Brink's-Mat Robbery, organised by Joe McGinnis, son of a policeman, had taken place in Boston on 17 January 1950. McGinnis received a sentence of life imprisonment for the raid which netted $2.77 million.

2 O'Mahoney, who in 1974 became the second of the big British supergrasses when informing on a mass of his former colleagues, was acquitted of the robbery in June 1993. He later sued the Metropolitan Police for wrongful arrest and malicious prosecution. The case was settled without an admission of liability.

3 See 'Brink's-Mat; The REAL story at last' in *The Sun*, 8 July 1988.
4 Wein was one of the fairly numerous band of clerks who work, not always honestly, for solicitors undertaking criminal work. After his release from prison he worked for a series of firms before joining Relton.
5 See *The Independent*, 23, 25 November 1998.
6 Interview with author, 3 January 2001.
7 See Paul Lashmar, 'Solicitor denies money laundering and fraud claims' in *The Independent*, 11 October 2000.
8 *Sunday Express*, 23 April 2000.

# 19 Australia: Brian Alexander, Terrence Clark and 'Neddy' Smith

O F ALL THE POLICE FORCES over the years worldwide, the Sydney police of the 1970s and early 1980s must rank amongst the most corrupt. Corrupt police officers always like a bagman to act as the intermediary between themselves and the criminals from whom they are extracting favours, money or both. Brian Alexander was a solicitor's clerk who filled the position admirably.

Alexander was born in Sydney in 1939. His parents separated when he was 10 and he went to live with his father's sister. Although he often referred to himself as a solicitor, he was not qualified and indeed did not do particularly well at St Anne's Marist Brothers School in Bondi. Initially he worked with Philip N. Roach, a solicitor with a practice dealing with lower-level criminals and the prostitutes of the Cross area. During this time he took correspondence courses to qualify as either a solicitor or barrister, but he never completed them. While employed by Roach he became known to – and later became the associate of – not only criminals convicted and not, but also a group of detectives in the New South Wales force.

He worked for Roach for nearly twenty years and then changed firms and joined John Aston who had aspirations for a practice with a higher quality criminal clientele. At the time, Aston had mainly a commercial practice, but was not averse to branching out into taking high-quality criminal cases. This was unusual. Normally a solicitor with a commercial practice would regard anything criminal, with the possible exception of a little high-class fraud, as beneath him. Aston decided to be more all-embracing.

At the time there were three main squads of detectives in Sydney – the Special Breaking Squad, or the 'Breakers' as they were known; the Armed Hold-Up Squad; and the Drug Squad which had only recently been formed. Some members of the first two had been trading with criminals over the years. A major problem for police officers who accept bribes or lean on criminals is that one day, if it suits him or he feels the officer is taking more than his fair share, the criminal may turn. The authorities may well then be prepared to offer him a lesser sentence for informing on the corrupt officer. A cut-out is therefore an extremely welcome addition to the game; he provides some guarantee of fair treatment to the criminal and some degree of protection to the officer. Alexander filled this role admirably. One of the men with whom he dealt was the notorious Neddy Smith.

Neddy Smith, who would later serve a series of life sentences for murder and would be regarded as – if not proved to be – a killing machine, recalled his first meeting with Alexander. Smith had been charged with receiving, something which was not of itself too much of a problem. His difficulty was that he was still on parole for rape. In 1968 he and Robert Arthur Chapman had received 12 years (along with two other men) for raping a young mother after they broke into her home and threatening to drop her baby on its head if she screamed. They also threatened to bomb her house if she reported matters to the police. As Smith remembers:

> He was standing there looking like a combined advert for top brand-name fashions, like Simon Ackerman suits, Yves St Laurent shirts and Gucci shoes. He was decked out to impress, and impress he did. But still there was something missing.[1]

Alexander took some A$3,000 from him to obtain bail on the receiving charge and later came to his aid when Smith fell foul of Roger Caleb Rogerson and the Armed Hold-Up Squad and was charged with shooting with intent to kill and armed robbery.[2] Despite Smith's quite appalling record and the seriousness of the charges, he was given bail and later acquitted of all the counts against him. Alexander later put himself about when Smith was found to have some $39,000 for which he could not account and which the police said came from drug-smuggling. Smith's half-brother had also been arrested and Alexander sold Smith the statements his brother had allegedly made against him.

Smith then allegedly bought the whole of the evidence against him for $4,000, and was asked for $50,000 for the case to be dropped against his wife who was about to be charged. He paid the money but the next day conspiracy charges were preferred. He sent for Alexander who refunded $25,000, saying the rest had gone to two police officers.

However, Alexander was involved not only with Smith but also with some seriously heavy players in international drug-smuggling. They included Terrence John Clark, otherwise known as Alexander James Sinclair, who in his time had a number of lawyers either in his maw or in his bed.

By the age of 30 when Clark was released from his first prison sentence for receiving stolen property, he had a string of minor convictions behind him. Now in July 1974 he turned to drug-dealing. He bought from Christopher Martin Johnstone, known as Mr Asia, who was using seamen from the Straat line of ships to bring cannabis into New Zealand and selling it through a long line of dealers including a heroin addict, Douglas Robert Wilson. Clark was soon making serious money and in early 1975 he decided to go into importing on his own account. He purchased a boat, *Catana*, for transporting drugs from South-East Asia to New Zealand, but before its first run there was a falling out between him and some of his distributors. He then turned his attention to importing Thai sticks using female couriers, but soon realised that value for bulk came from heroin. In October 1975 he and an associate Raymond Burrell were arrested in New Zealand and charged with conspiracy to import. Clark was given bail and absconded to Australia. Burrell, left alone, was acquitted.

Sydney, Australia, was Clark's base of activities for the next two years, but he continued to import cannabis into New Zealand on his new boat *Brigadoon*.

The Mr Asia case, in which Brian Alexander and a number of other lawyers played significant and unhealthy parts, began in New Zealand and effectively ended in England when on 14 October 1979 a naked and handless body was found in an Ecclestone, Lancashire quarry. The face had been mutilated beyond recognition and identification was made only through a Chinese 'long-life' symbol on a pendant around the neck. It was that of drug-dealer Marty Johnstone, one of the founders of the so-called Mr Asia syndicate.

Johnstone, known as Mr Asia, had been an international dealer based in Singapore from 1977 to 1979. At that time it was thought to be his syndicate, but in fact he had been working for Clark and when he was caught skimming money to set up his own syndicate he was killed on Clark's orders.

Clark was born at Gisbourne in New Zealand on 12 November 1944. In August 1962 he was convicted of theft and interfering with a motor vehicle, and in the next nine years was convicted of theft and receiving. He did not go to prison until on 12 March 1971 he was convicted of burglary. Released on 8 July 1974, he began buying cannabis from Marty Johnstone. However, Clark was the mover and shaker. In 1975 he bought the *Catana* to bring drugs out of South-East Asia, and the same year began to import heroin. Now he used a string of names before he metamorphosed into Alexander Sinclair. By the latter half of 1977 he had become a major importer into Sydney with a distribution chain across Australia and was investing with Johnstone. Already there were grandiose plans for a fishing fleet, mining concessions and development in South-East Asia, For the moment his fortune had been invested in restaurants in Sydney, a silver mine in Indonesia and Swiss bank accounts.

In 1976 he had absconded while on bail for drug charges in New Zealand, and in June 1978 he was arrested and charged with possessing an unregistered firearm and receiving. He was fined and extradited to New Zealand to face the earlier charges.

Clark was represented by the Auckland barrister Peter Aldridge Williams, for whom Karen Mary Marie Soich – who had qualified as a barrister but had never held a practising certificate – worked as a clerk. Williams may have got too close to Clark for comfort. Knowing that Williams, a keen sailor, was planning to enter the Sydney-to-Hobart race Clark bought him a set of sails and, on his acquittal, a four-wheel drive as a bonus. He aso received a $30,000 retainer in addition to a like fee. Soich was another matter entirely. She was sent to see Clark in Mount Eden prison and over the weeks became infatuated with him. He was triumphantly acquitted and left court with her for a celebration at a Wellington hotel attended by Williams. From there on it was a life of candy for her. The next year she joined him in Los Angeles where he introduced her to a local pimp and cocaine dealer Benjamin Bennett. She then travelled with him to England where six weeks later on 31 October 1979 they were arrested at the flat Clark had leased at 57 Stafford Court, Kensington.

Soich was charged with having conspired to import and distribute drugs. At the Lancaster Crown Court she made an unsworn statement from the dock, something no longer permissible in English law. It was curiously like the comment made by Neddy Smith's wife some years later. She said that she had been in love with Clark and had no idea of his involvement in drugs.

> ... as far as my own family background is concerned, my father comes home at night and when he comes home, that is it for the day. He sits down and talks with my mother, but he doesn't discuss business with her ever. He leaves that at the business. That was how it was with Terry and I.[3]

Clark had rather more difficulties. He had been charged with murder, as well as conspiracy to import drugs into the United Kingdom and another to supply them. The murder was of his former colleague Johnstone.

Johnstone's end came when he fell foul of a number of the members of the syndicate including the Singapore supplier Jack Choo; he had also been cutting heroin and failing to account. He was persuaded to go to London on the pretext of setting up a Scottish deal and from there drove north with Andrew Maher, who had been designated as his killer. Near Carnforth, Lancashire, Maher asked him to take over the driving and as he got out of the car he was killed with two bullets to the head. His body was then mutilated but Maher, and James Smith who was with him, forgot to remove the pendant. Taken to Ecclestone Depth, the corpse was rolled down the bank into what was believed to be the deepest part of the disused quarry. However, it caught on a ledge and was subsequently found by members of a sub-aqua club who at first thought it was a tailor's dummy.

On 15 July 1981 Clark was found guilty on all counts and sentenced to life imprisonment with an order that he serve at least 20 years. After the judge Mrs Justice Heilbron had been told that he was – give or take a million or two – worth £25 million, he was also ordered to pay £1 million towards the costs of the prosecution. On appeal this was reduced to £175,000.

Clark died in Parkhurst prison on the Isle of Wight in August 1983 following a heart attack. It was said, with no real evidence to back it up, that he had been taking drugs with a view to being transferred to a hospital from which he could escape. The previous month he had promised to name names, reveal sources and expose links with the IRA if his lawyer girlfriend Karen Soich was allowed to practise. On 24 September 1982 members of the Stewart Commission had travelled to the Isle of Wight to see him with his representative, Harry Stevens of Baldwin Mellor & Co., and they put a series of questions to him including an allegation that he had been involved in the killing of Douglas Wilson and his wife Isabel. This is where Alexander had come in. For the record, Clark denied any involvement.

What emerged at the Stewart inquiry was that Alexander was a tried and trusted man on Clark's staff with valuable contacts in the Narcotics Bureau. Witnesses would tell the Commission that if a member of the syndicate was arrested Alexander would be contacted and would not only provide legal representation but would also report back to Clark as to whether they were remaining staunch. On a legitimate income of $32,000 he had earned $130,000 in the year before his death.

On 9 June 1978 Douglas and Isabel Wilson were arrested by the Queensland Police in Brisbane. Although they were never charged they spent some time in providing information on tape with regard to the workings of the Clark organisation. Through Alexander, Clark purchased copies of the tapes for $25,000. On 18 May 1979 their bodies were found in a shallow grave in Danny Street, Rye, Victoria; they had both been shot.

On 25 March 1981 Alexander was arrested and charged with conspiracy with two Federal Narcotics Agents Wayne Brindle and Richard Spencer. The allegation was that the three of them had disclosed confidential information to Terrence John Clark, the leader of the heroin-trafficking syndicate. The case was dismissed at the committal proceedings because the Crown could not prove the source of the leaks beyond doubt. It was, however, the end of Alexander's legal career. Effectively unemployable, he drifted into drink and working in hotels. Neddy Smith was also doing his best to spoil things further for Alexander.[4] Now it was learned that he was likely to give evidence and name names, dates, places and amounts.

On 21 December 1981, shortly after he had been seen drinking with three men in the King's Head Tavern near his offices on Park Street, Alexander disappeared. Two weeks later his car was found abandoned near The Gap at Watson's Bay, a place known for suicides.

According to Smith, however, Alexander was too much of a coward to commit suicide in that way; he heard a story that

Alexander had been driven to the Darling Street wharf in Balmain where, his wrists handcuffed behind his back, he was thrown from a launch with an old gas-stove tied around his body. He was apparently still alive and crying when he went in the water. Smith concludes this moral tale: 'But I had no part in it. That was something I wouldn't wish even on someone like Brian Alexander.'[5]

The early 1990s saw a new role for Smith – that of assistant to justice. He had become an informer and was now the star witness at the hearings conducted by the Independent Commission Against Corruption. Much of his evidence was directed at the solicitor Graham Valentine 'Val' Bellamy, with whom he had had such a working relationship in the past that a Mercedes Benz and a Rolls-Royce which belonged to him had conveniently been registered in the solicitor's name. One incident they shared, according to Smith, was the snatching of a bag containing $60,000, not once but twice in almost as few minutes. Around 3 p.m. on 17 September 1984, a black vinyl bag containing the money withdrawn from a safety deposit box of the Commonwealth Bank in Castlereagh Street was snatched as Mr Bellamy walked through Martin Place. A passer-by – some say it was Mr Bellamy's own father – chased after the thief and retrieved the bag with the help of an off-duty policeman. Sadly, the theft was repeated successfully almost immediately. This time the solicitor was punched in the stomach.

Smith's version of the matter was that the robbery was a put-up job to cover Bellamy's withdrawals from the box on his own account. A fee of $10,000 had been paid to a police officer to help fake a report on the robbery.

Another man who claimed to have worked with Bellamy was a former police officer, Trevor Haken. He claimed that he had been speaking with Bellamy at a police court and had mentioned that the prosecution was going to drop the case against Bellamy's client because a witness had failed to appear. The solicitor, alleged Haken, had seen this as a singular opportunity to make money and had told the client that the police would drop the case for $5,000. The satisfied client drew the money from the bank, which Bellamy and Haken split.

Then there was the question of a tape which appeared to suggest that Bellamy and Smith had chatted about the disposal of some stolen gold coins. He was sure the voice was not his, but he admitted that he knew about some gold coins. Indeed, he had accepted them as part payment of his legal fees.

Poor Bellamy was also accused of faking statements from a number of witnesses, which exculpated Smith in a fight at the City of Sydney RSL Club back in December 1984. He said he had no recollection of them although he presumed he was acting for Smith at the time.

He was not pleased with the ICAC, seeing himself as the only person to be bitten by it. An application for his evidence to be heard partly in private and for his name to be withheld had been refused. He went on television to explain his position, commenting as a sort of trailer for the programme: 'That's the difficulty with being a criminal lawyer. I lost the murder trial; he turned on me.' Curiously he did not seem to hold this ratting against Smith: 'He's a very likeable bloke; a very intelligent bloke. He's lived a very impressive life and he was always good company.'[6]

The ICAC reported in 1994 and recommended that consideration should be given to preferring charges of stealing, perjury and possibly conspiracy to steal against Bellamy. It enjoined the Law Society to consider disciplinary action.

However, Bellamy was not without a sense of humour. At the time applications for the post of the new Commissioner of the ICAC were being considered, and he put his name forward. The firm of head-hunters employed to sift the candidates declined to say whether he had been interviewed, but he did not get the appointment. Shortly afterwards he was served with summonses alleging that he had lied to the ICAC and that he had misappropriated money.

As for Neddy Smith, perhaps he had only himself to blame for his continuing troubles. On 22 January 1955 the *Sun-Herald* published a banner headline: 'I killed Six: Neddy Smith'. Apparently Smith had foolishly been talking to a cellmate who in turn, thinking it might do him some good, had reported the conversations to the authorities. The story about the police killing Brian Alexander had been a blind. The murder, along with five others, was all his own work. It was he who had tied the law clerk to a gas-stove and dumped him overboard – which is presumably how he knew he was crying.

In September 1998 and now suffering from Parkinson's disease, Smith was back in court and convicted of another murder, this time of drug-dealer Harvey Jones. By this time he had recanted his confession and said that his cellmate (known as Green) might have been paid to tell his story through a solicitor enemy of Smith identified as a Mr White. His loyal wife said that all she knew to the detriment of her husband was that he might have been an illegal bookmaker:

> People say I must have been so naïve, but Ned could have been leaving home at eight in the morning, coming home at five and said he was a doctor. I never asked, and he would tell me what I wanted to know.[7]

The Crown decided not to proceed with the prosecution for the murder of Brian Alexander.

In May 1999 Smith appeared in the Glebe Coroner's Court when an inquest was held into the disappearance of male model and cocaine dealer Mark Johnston. What was definitely known was that the last sighting of Johnston had been on 1 September when he called on Val Bellamy to collect $60,000 which the solicitor had been holding for him. Johnston's hired car, a Holden Commodore, was found eight days later at Maroubra after a tip-off by an anonymous woman; there were over 500 grams of cocaine in the car and some loose change. When Bellamy was seen by the police he told them he was constrained by client confidentiality from discussing the matter. However, he also said that Johnston had been to his home and had stayed about 15 minutes before leaving with his money.

Less clear was what had happened to Johnston, whose father Arthur had spoken to Bellamy a week after his son's disappearance. Mark had told his father that he had tried to arrange three meetings with Bellamy to collect his money.

It all came back to those cell conversations. It was alleged that Smith had told his cellmate that he had killed Johnston at the solicitor's request. In the confession he said that he had handcuffed and then garrotted the drug-dealer rather than spoil the carpet by stabbing him in the solicitor's new $3.5 million home at Dover Heights.

Detective Sergeant Neville Smith told the court that he believed Bellamy knew full well what had happened to Johnston, and he found it difficult to accept that the money had been returned to him.

The Deputy State Coroner John Abernethy ruled that Johnston was dead and that he had been killed at Dover Heights. He ordered the papers to be sent to Nicholas Cowdery, the Director of Public Prosecutions.

Arthur Johnston, who had told the court that he believed Bellamy – 'motivated by greed and avarice' – had taken his son's money, said after the hearing that he felt a sense of sorrow for Smith. 'As to Bellamy, however, I feel total repugnance.'[8]

On 5 May 1999 Bellamy, now working as a telephone clerk, was charged with fraud involving nearly three-quarters of a million dollars, including one charge of obtaining $350,000 from Broadway Credit Union.

On 11 October 2000 Bellamy was sentenced to 4 years with at least two to be served. He had pleaded guilty and in mitigation blamed his downfall on Smith. Justice Blanch took the view that he would be at risk from Smith in the prison system, and recommended that on his arrival he be transferred into some kind of protective custody.

1 Neddy Smith, *Catch and Kill Your Own*.
2 For an account of crime and the police in New South Wales after the Second World War, see James Morton, *Gangland International*.
3 See Mr Justice D.G. Stewart, Report of the Royal Commission of Inquiry into Drug Trafficking, 1983, p.106.
4 Mr Justice D.G. Stewart, Report of the Royal Commission of Inquiry into Drug Trafficking, 1983.
5 *Ibid,* p.115.
6 Sydney *Morning Herald*, 16 February 1973.
7 *Daily News* (New Plymouth), 14 September 1998.
8 Sydney *Morning Herald*, 4, 5 May 1999.

# 20 Risk: Judge John Wood and others

IN GENERAL IN THE WESTERN WORLD, lawyers, judges and for that matter journalists – even when they have been on the warpath against organised crime – have benefited from an unwritten rule that they are not deliberately injured or killed. The theory behind this is quite simply that any attack on a judge, prosecuting lawyer or investigative journalist would bring down the wrath of the authorities in triplicate. Nevertheless there is always a lurking fear of reprisal for a job perceived to have been badly handled. One long-standing lawyer says:

> For a long time I represented the Gambinos. Some cases I won, some I didn't. I never had any problem over losing. I was sent to Sicily to see lawyers over there, but I never felt apprehensive. If defendants, irrespective of who they are, see the work is competent and legitimate they won't hold it against you.[1]

Al Alschuler, Wilson Dickinson Professor of Law at the University of Chicago, agrees:

> Defending the boys is much easier for a lawyer. Middle-class guys are freaked out by being indicted. It's all tears and 'save me, save me'. The boys just want to know what you can do for them.[2]

On the other hand another lawyer believes that wannabees might seek revenge:

I represented Gravano before he became affiliated to Gotti, and in 1974 I obtained a Not Guilty for a co-defendant on a murder charge which resulted in the charge being dropped. In a subsequent article about the case my name was left out. I was very grateful. I didn't need the publicity and *animus* might have been generated by Gotti's colleagues. You never know. Gotti has so many hangers-on, who knows whether some nit-wits might try to do something to me for getting that acquittal even though it was years ago.[3]

Clients can take revenge. Ralph Haemms, doyen of lawyers in heavy criminal cases in England, recalls:

I was acting for a 'nobody' charged with possession of counterfeit dollars. I made an application to a judge in chambers for bail and on instructions I drew an affidavit saying he was contesting the case and had not made any admissions written or verbal. I then found he had made three pages of written admissions. I withdrew the application and refused to act for him further. Weeks later I came back from Clerkenwell Magistrates' Court and I was told someone had dropped in a parcel that looked like a bottle of Scotch. I told my clerk if it was he could have it, but he came back white as a sheet and said it was a revolver. I didn't see it or touch it; I just rang up the local police. A very senior officer, whom I knew well, asked me if I had any enemies, clients or police. I said I didn't. It turned out this guy had sent the revolver into the office and had given information that I was going to smuggle it into prison. The little villain got nine months for wasting police time. Later I found out he'd been round trying to find the house where I lived at the time.[4]

More often clients can also seek the opportunity to improve their status with the authorities at the expense of their former lawyers. Albert Alschuler recalls:

Prosecutors were very happy if a scumbag decided to finger his lawyer. If the defendant said I paid you with the diamond ring I stole, then the prosecutor would indict you. It's an occupational hazard for lawyers. It doesn't mean you're guilty.

The culmination of one example of countless client betrayals over the years came when, on 7 March 1995, the San Francisco defence attorney Patrick Hallinan was acquitted of obstruction of justice and drug conspiracy charges. The prosecution claimed that Hallinan had assisted his client, Ciro Mancuso to smuggle huge shipments of marijuana into the United States and had then laundered the proceeds. Hallinan had had a long and profitable career defending Mancuso from 1974 until 1990. In the witness box he said that he believed Mancuso had stopped importing drugs in the 1970s. He testified that Mancuso was 'the most exploitative psychopath' he had ever known.

Mancuso's smuggling operation was indeed a case of large oaks from little acorns. It began in the late 1960s with friends from Tahoe Paradise College, smuggling marijuana and selling it through the college. They then had a small growing farm in Clay County, Kansas, but when this was closed down by the authorities they started to import from Mexico, and later Mancuso teamed up with a Thai exchange student to import an improved variety into San Francisco.

After a period of 12 years in which a case was built against Mancuso, he eventually pleaded guilty to tax evasion and international conspiracy and was allowed to keep $5 million in return for his testimony against Hallinan. In the five-week-long prosecution he was joined by 12 other convicted felons giving evidence against Hallinan. In turn the lawyer called character witnesses including Charles Breyer, the brother of the US Supreme Court Justice Stephen Breyer, San Francisco Sheriff Michael Hennessy and the chairman of the Criminal Justice Standards Committee of the American Bar Association.[5]

Physical protection has generally applied only if lawyers stick strictly to their legal – or in the case of reporters, their journalistic – duties. If they cross over the dividing line between adviser, prosecutor and reporter and enter the world of player, then they become fair game. His avowed intention to dispose of prosecuting attorney Thomas Dewey was a principal reason why Dutch Schultz was gunned down in the Palace Chop House. The reason why Chicago *Tribune* journalist Jake Lingle was shot in the city on 9 June 1930 was not, as originally mooted, because he was exposing racketeering but because he had become a racketeer himself and had not been playing straight. When he died he was wearing a diamond belt-buckle presented to him by Al Capone.

One of the lawyers who became a player rather than an adviser and died as a result was Samuel Rummel, the long-time representative of – and probably the brains behind – Mickey Cohen who, depending upon one's viewpoint, was either himself the Czar of California of the 1940s or a relatively small-time but thoroughly unpleasant mobster.

Cohen was born in 1913 in Brooklyn, the sixth child of Russian Jewish immigrant parents. He took up boxing as a bantamweight and by the age of 19 was running a gang in Cleveland. In 1938 he went to Chicago and then, after some trouble over an assault on a Chicago taxi-driver, he was sent to Los Angeles to look after Bugsy Siegel's gambling interests. After Siegel had been killed, the increasingly wild Cohen became locked in a power struggle with rival Jack Dragna. Over the next few years renewed attempts were made to kill Cohen.

As with Capone, it was the Inland Revenue which finally brought Cohen down. In 1952 he received 4 years' imprisonment, and a further 10–15 in 1962. In prison he did not do well, being attacked by other prisoners almost from the start of his sentence. In his later life he took to religion and, after attending a revival service conducted by the Reverend Billy Graham, invited him to stay, an offer the evangelist accepted. Cohen died in 1976.

One of Cohen's specialities had been the blackmailing of actresses by introducing them to a string of young studs such as Johnny Stompanato – who was killed by Lana Turner's teenage daughter, Cheryl Crane – and then blackmailing them.[6]

But, back on 11 December 1950, Samuel Rummel was shot in the back from about 10 yards in the front yard of his home at 2600 Laurel Canyon Drive. The weapon used was a 12-gauge double-barrelled sawn-off Remington. The gun, left in the crotch of a tree across the driveway from where the lawyer's body was found, was traced back to Riley, Kansas, where it had been stolen as long ago as 1913. Although the police rounded up the usual suspects and more, no one was ever charged with the murder.

Rummel had been far too close to the Normandie Club in Gardena where he had assumed a 40 per cent interest. There had been no professional courtesy in the way he had acquired his stake. Another lawyer, Charles W. Cradick, had been forced by Cohen to take $1,000 and a one per cent for the stake which passed to Rummel. Cradick, who had long been interested in organised gambling, had been involved in a pinball association in Los Angeles County for which he was the attorney. Although he told officers of the Kefauver Commission that he no longer had an interest in organised gambling, they believed he was involved in two other casinos:

*Mr Rice (of the Commission)*: Is Cradick a lawyer?
*Chief Parker*: Yes.
*Mr Rice*: Other lawyers were pushing him around?
*Chief Parker*: We are deeply interested in that connection.

*The Chairman*: Does the bar association do anything out here about lawyers having investments in illegal activities?
*Chief Parker*: Not to my knowledge.

Rummel was also involved in the Guarantee Finance Company, in theory a legitimate loan business but in reality a front for a $6 million bookmaking operation. By December 1951 a Grand Jury was making vigorous attempts to investigate pay-offs to law enforcement officers by the company. Later it would be estimated that the pay-off totalled a little under a quarter of a million dollars.

On 6 December 1951 a highly secret meeting was held attended by the foreman of the Grand Jury, four county officials and two process servers who would serve summonses on potential witnesses for a hearing on 12 December. There were immediate leaks of information because the following day Rummel was busying himself calling meetings to determine a course of defence. Potential witnesses scattered.

On 9 December Rummel himself arranged a secret meeting with Al Guasti, then a captain in the sheriff's office, planning for him to meet that night with Captain Carl Pearson, then head of the local Vice Squad, and his underling Sergeant Lawrence Schaffer. As planned, Rummel picked up Guasti and Pearson and then they collected Schaffer before going to Rummel's office, where Schaffer showed the lawyer confidential files from the sheriff's office dealing with the Guarantee case. It was accepted that apart from the gunman the three police officers were the last to see Rummel alive.

A number of theories for the death were floated, including the suggestions that Rummel was trying to cut a deal or that he might have been making threats to (as the Grand Jury put it) 'someone to move over'. The Grand Jury then indicted Pearson, Guasti and Schaffer.

According to gangster Jimmy Fratianno, the killers of Rummel were Angelo Polizzi and Carlo Licata. He had watched them stake out Rummel's home, but he gave no explanation for the killing.[7]

As the years have gone by the professional courtesy extended to lawyers seems to have become a thing of the past worldwide. In December 1989 the Miami lawyer Gino P. Negretti, then in his seventies, was severely wounded when a car bomb exploded. He had represented many defendants in drug-related cases.

One of gangland's worst nightmares is to find that your own lawyer has been working for the police. In 1993 it was made public that Sidney Leithman – lawyer to the cream of the Montreal Underworld including Frank Cotroni, and Frank Ryan, the head of the West End Gang – was a registered police informer. Frank Cotroni was a controlling part of the Cotroni Family who ran large portions of Montreal crime from the 1940s until the 1990s, and it was estimated that at one time Ryan employed some 300 people in his drug-dealing empire before he was lured to a room in Nittolo's Garden Motel on St Jacques Street, tied to a chair and shot.

Leithman also acted for Ryan's successor, Allan Ross. Leithman's informing was a two-way ticket. He kindly tipped off Ryan that David Singer was about to tell the police all he knew – which was a great deal – about Ross's empire. Ross was eventually convicted in Florida of running a drug enterprise and sentenced to life imprisonment. He was also convicted of the conspiracy to murder Singer charge, but this was quashed on appeal.

Ultimately, Leithman's double game proved fatal for him. From what leaked out, apparently in 1985 he had first given information to the police in a drug investigation into a man who was not his client and was from outside Quebec. The information was good and the man was arrested. Perhaps that wasn't so reprehensible; in fact it helped to preserve the *status quo* in the city. But from then on Leithman really rather spoiled things, since he acted as a coded informant if not a paid one:

> Once you're coded you always stay there. You stay in the system. You don't disappear. You stay there. So, you know, in 1993 I can really honestly tell you that, yeah he was coded at one time.[8]

For a time there was talk of the possibility of upsetting convictions in cases in which Leithman had been involved, but nothing came of it. Montreal lawyer Paul Skolnik wrote to the Solicitor General, Doug Lewis, asking whether Leithman was ever a coded informer; and if so, had he revealed any information about Vincent Lore, a former client convicted in 1991 of a drugs offence and sentenced to life imprisonment? The Solicitor General replied that Leithman was not a coded informant, but many were not satisfied.[9]

Whether or not Leithman was actually on the books, it is probable that word of his poor behaviour had leaked out sometime earlier, because in the early hours of 13 May 1991 he was shot dead at the wheel of his Saab convertible while at the junction of Jean Talon Street and Rockland Road. He had been shot once at a distance of ten metres and then three times at close range. An autopsy showed traces of cocaine in his blood. His killer was never found; nor, officially, was there ever a motive offered for his murder, although it was thought that with a developing cocaine habit the lawyer was becoming a liability. At the time of his death he was being investigated as a co-conspirator in the 1992 Ross case in Florida. It was also believed that the US Government was considering charging him with obstructing the course of justice. Drug-dealers had reported that he had been bribing them not to talk to the police. If he had been charged and had himself rolled over, the potential damage would have been enormous.

Leithman's death was linked to that of a senior RCMP officer, Inspector Savoie, in December 1992. Savoie, who had been second-in-command and then head of the Drug Squad between 1988 and 1992, shot himself in his office just before he was due to be interviewed by internal affairs investigators regarding his contacts with Leithman. When Leithman was shot he had Savoie's telephone number in his pocket, and before his death Savoie told Montreal police that the lawyer had been his informant. It was known that, with no other officers present, Savoie had met with Leithman and Ross in the lawyer's office and at a restaurant on Phillips Square. At the time, Ross was under investigation by the United States Drug Enforcement Administration.

Over the years it was thought that Savoie had received around $200,000 for passing information to the West End Gang. The RCMP were also investigating Jorge Leithe, one of the drug agents, who shortly after Leithman's death resigned and went to live in Portugal. He was believed to have contacts with Leithman and Ines Barbosa, who received 5 years for cocaine dealing. It was thought that he had been leaking information to Colombians and the West End Gang.[10]

At least Leithman was not being paid, unlike some others. For example, in 1992 a Manitoba appeal court judge refused to grant the extradition of an alleged drug-dealer back to California after it was revealed that the man's lawyer in the United States had been feeding information to the authorities in several drug cases. The lawyer had been paid a percentage of assets seized from dealers who had been arrested as a result of his information. He would then represent them after their arrest.

Just as bad – possibly worse – as a criminal finding that his lawyer is leaking information to the authorities, is the member of the prosecution who is leaking secrets to criminals.[11] In 1999 the Crown Prosecution Service found to its horror that Mark Herbert, son of a retired Scotland Yard detective, had sold a list of 33 informers to the notorious London-based Adams family, suspected by the police of drug-running, money laundering and lending.

The prosecution at the Old Bailey claimed that while Herbert had been moonlighting as a bouncer in a South West London nightclub to supplement his £14,000 a year salary, he had been passing information. This included tip-offs about 12 forthcoming arrests, including that of an alleged enforcer for the family; when that man was arrested, there was no sign of evidence at his home and he was acquitted. Herbert had also passed over details of two brothers from South London who were said to be in dispute with the family and to have contracts worth £250,000 on their heads.

In 1988 Herbert had been a junior clerk working on a team investigating the brothers. He had told the jury that he passed the information because he was fearful for his life and that of his fiancée. In fact he had received £1,000 for the information which he had accessed from computers. He was sentenced to 6 years' imprisonment. It was thought that he would be kept in some form of segregated confinement both to protect him and also to prevent him passing on more information that he might have memorised.

One of the more interesting jobs for lawyers has been that of undercover agents as used by the CIA and the FBI. Unsurprisingly few break cover but one who did, or whose cover was broken, was Herb Itkin who was known to the CIA under the code-name Poron and to the FBI as Mr Jerry. He was described by a member of the staff of United States Attorney Robert Morgenthau: '[Itkin is] the most valuable informer the FBI has ever had outside the espionage field. He never lies to us. His information has always been accurate.'

The FBI said of him: 'He is probably the most important informer ever to come to the surface. He knew the younger up-and-coming characters in the Cosa Nostra.'

It is probably also correct that Itkin left a trail of disaster behind him. Born in 1926, the son of working-class Jewish parents, Herbert Itkin was brought up in the Borough Park section of Brooklyn in what was then the middle-class area of 48th Street. His father had a series of small shops and, by accounts, was mild-mannered and ineffectual while his mother was the dominant personality. In 1944 he enlisted in the Army and after VJ Day was sent to Japan with a field hospital unit. On his return with $2,000 savings he bought a luncheonette in Bush terminal, Brooklyn, and put it about that he had been a paratrooper attached to Army Intelligence. The luncheonette, where his parents worked, was not a success. According to one account, his father tripped and knocked his head on the gas tap, turning it on. Itkin told a friend that, when his father did not come home from a Saturday late shift, he went to find him and revived the unconscious man just as the police arrived. In another and more heroic version, protection money was demanded by a Mafia enterprise. His father had resisted their blandishments and his head was held in the gas oven. Itkin had set out in revenge and confronted the leader, who told his henchmen to leave the boy alone because, 'He has spunk.' Whichever version is correct, Itkin snr. did not work in the luncheonette again; he spent some time in hospital and was then divorced.

Meanwhile Itkin jnr. went to law school, working during the day for a local firm, Delson, Levin & Gordon, where his mother now had a position as a book-keeper. He married Diana Kane, one of the firm's secretaries. He qualified in 1953, by which time he had moved to Hicksville, Long Island. He appears to have been worried that his Jewish name would hold him back in his career. Diana Kane recalled:

> Herbie wanted very badly not to marry a Jewish girl. He wanted a shiksa like me. Once he was going to change his name to something less Jewish and I told him, 'Herbie, you can make it wherever you want to go with your real name. Besides, your mother would have a heart attack. You have enough ambition and talent to overcome it.'

It was now that the web of deceit was spun. In 1957, he left Delson's under something of a cloud with complaints having been made to the Bar Association over client poaching. He had, he said, begun his CIA career with a retainer in 1954, the year after his marriage. His version of his recruitment is that it was conducted at the highest level, that of CIA Director Allen

Dulles, who had been impressed with information supplied by Itkin to Senator Joe McCarthy in the early 1950s.

This is not a version which was accepted by federal officials, who place the date as 1962 as a result of a CIA man meeting Itkin by chance in the Madison Avenue offices he rented with other lawyers. Itkin, so the official version goes, was recruited on a part-time unpaid basis because of his contacts in the Caribbean and Asia; the lawyer who had made the introduction became his control. There seems little doubt that his life as a spy was at least a two-way traffic, with Itkin trying to use his CIA connections to further his business interests. The Itkins moved out of Hicksville and into the more fashionable resort of Oyster Bay. Now he was exhibiting signs of mild paranoia. He would eat only from tins opened by himself, and if hot meals were prepared for him they had to be tasted first. He began to borrow from friends and relations. There is a story that his father-in-law telephoned the CIA to ask if Itkin did work for them. 'If he does, don't believe anything he says,' he added and hung up. By 1969 Itkin was in debt to the tune of $600,000. On the plus side, however, clearly he did have knowledge of the Mafia and the Teamsters Union system of fund operating. He was turned over to the FBI in 1964.

On 18 January 1967 Itkin flew into London with Tony 'Ducks' Corallo and Tommy Mancuso, with a view to the latter buying into British gambling casinos which were starting to take off in a big way. The visit was also in relation to gaming machines which Corallo was placing in Britain with Dick Kaminitsky, known as Dick Duke. But Corallo was refused entry to the United Kingdom and the mission aborted.

What he was also doing was getting out of control and making money for himself without accounting to his handler. Worse, from everyone's point of view, he was boasting about his activities. Diana Kane said, 'Herbie told just about everybody about the CIA and the FBI. He told some fellows he commuted on the train with.'

By the end of his career, Itkin – who had been involved with countless women and had now fallen in love with a divorcée, Scotty Hersch – was a liability. He was pulled off the street and into protective custody along with his first and second wives – Diana Kane had long been replaced – and their families. He was kept at a military post in New York where, said a Government official, he was allowed the use of the recreational facilities and post exchange but was not allowed to buy liquor. In December

1967 he appeared in the first of the trials in which he was to give evidence. It led to the conviction of Tony Corallo, who received 4 and a half years, and Carmine De Sapio, as well as James L. Marcus, the former city commissioner and confidant of Mayor Lindsay, who received 15 months.

Although a major figure in dozens of pending cases, described by the FBI as 'risking his neck almost every day' and being praised for his 'reckless patriotism', Itkin was not without his critics. Manhattan District Attorney Frank S. Hogan was out for his blood. In the trial of De Sapio, which resulted in a conviction for conspiracy to bribe Marcus and to extort contracts from Consolidated Edison, the court heard that Itkin had kept large sums of money from swindles, bribes and kickbacks. Now Hogan wished to prosecute him. 'They would love to get me on a perjury conviction to destroy me and all my work,' said Itkin.

A representative of Hogan's office asked:

How could the federal officials allow an informer to take that kind of money which was admittedly made from criminal deals and keep it? What do they think informers are? Some sort of bounty hunters?

Time has shown that the answer to the last question is a resounding yes.

Until the last twenty years, as a general rule judges could be regarded as safe from attack by disgruntled clients and their friends and relations in criminal cases. However, things have changed. In 1979 Judge John Wood, 63 years old and known as 'Maximum John' because of his tough sentencing in drug cases, became the first federal judge in America to be killed. Wood, a judge of eight years' standing, was shot in the back with a single dum-dum bullet as he went to get into his car in the parking lot of his apartment block in San Antonio, Texas, on 29 May 1979. He was pronounced dead on arrival at the Northeast Baptist Hospital in the city. Almost immediately the police announced that they were seeking a curly-haired man aged about twenty who had been seen driving a small red car.

However, the killer was not a twenty-year-old but Charles V. Harrelson, the son of a prison guard, and father of the actor and star of *Cheers*, Woody Harrelson. He was convicted on 14 December 1982 of being the hitman in a $250,000 contract and received life imprisonment.

Wood was in fact the third man he had been charged with killing. Described by historian John H. Davis as a Dallas-based racketeer, in 1968 Harrelson had been acquitted of the murder of a carpet salesman, but in 1973 he was convicted of killing a grain-dealer in Texas. For this he received 15 years and was paroled some eight months before the killing of Wood. By the time he came up for trial on that murder charge he was already serving sentences totalling 40 years for cocaine and weapons offences.[12] He has been described as a man of charm who at times looked out of place facing a charge of murder, but also as a man without respect for authority. He is quoted as saying:

> The Gestapo is alive and well and highly refined and doing business as usual in Washington DC. First they pick on the ones that are easy to deal with like me, but before long they'll be herding all you poor bastards into boxcars that don't go anywhere and showers without water.[13]

Certainly he was a man with considerable charm for women. Tape recordings made secretly while he was in prison have him promising three women that he loved and wished to marry them. Jo Ann Harrelson's daughter gave evidence that she had had an affair of several months' duration with her step-father.

The prosecution alleged that Harrelson had killed Wood in a contract bought by El Paso drug-dealer Jimmy Chagra, a one-time rug salesman who now had an empire stretching from Florida to Las Vegas running marijuana. He was also known as a high-rolling gambler who had once paid off a $900,000 casino debt in cash and had lost a $580,000 game of golf. Chagra had been found guilty on drug-smuggling charges and was due to appear for sentencing before 'Maximum John'.

It would seem that this option was suggested to Chagra by his El Paso lawyer brother, Joseph, who was indicted on charges of lying to a Grand Jury investigating the killing of the judge as well as making an attempt on the life of US Attorney James Kerr. Known also to be harsh on drug cases, on 21 November 1978 Kerr was shot at – six blocks from where Wood would later be killed – as he drove to work. He escaped by ducking down under the dashboard. Joseph Chagra had been recorded talking with his brother in the investigation into the BRILAB scam, had been given immunity from prosecution and allegedly had discussed the murder.[14]

Chagra's wife Elizabeth was also found guilty in the drugs conspiracy and Harrelson's third wife, Jo Ann, was found guilty of obstructing the course of justice; the prosecution had alleged that she had bought the murder weapon. But Elizabeth Chagra's conviction was overturned and a re-trial set.

Jimmy Chagra, then in his late thirties, was acquitted on the murder charge but received a total of 47 years for drug smuggling and impeding the course of justice over the Wood killing. His brother Joseph pleaded guilty to conspiracy to kill the judge and received a 10-year sentence; he was paroled in 1988.

Joseph Chagra then gave evidence against his sister-in-law Elizabeth, saying that although she had no part in the decision to have Wood killed she had delivered the pay-off of $250,000. She maintained that she thought the money was to pay off some of her husband's gambling debts, and that she did not know its destination until Joe Chagra told her. Convicted again after her re-trial, she was sentenced to 30 years in prison. Eligible for parole in 1992, she had not been released when she died of cancer in 1997.

It is a case which has rumbled on over the years. Harrelson – who always denied his involvement in the killing of Wood, saying that he had simply been trying to con Chagra out of $250,000 – has protested that his trial was unfair because the presiding judge, William Sessions (who later became director of the Federal Bureau of Investigation) had been an honorary pallbearer at Wood's funeral. Sessions had also delivered a number of eulogies over the years, including one at the naming of the San Antonio Federal Courthouse in Wood's honour. At the trial his lawyers urged the judge to recuse himself, but he declined and his decision was upheld by the 5th Circuit Appeal Court which held that the relationship between Sessions and Wood 'can at most have served to create a degree of hostility toward the actual killers'. The Court went on to say that this hostility was consistent not only with a desire to convict the guilty but to acquit the innocent.

The case was reopened in 2000 in Denver where Harrelson was being held. Now he endeavoured to overturn the conviction, alleging that the government had lied and was in collusion with his defence lawyer. Additionally he claimed that the government had also targeted a further group of conspirators as the possible killers of the judge. The group, he maintained, included one of his (Harrelson's) defence team, allegations strongly denied by his earlier lawyers.

Since the Wood case, however, there have been more killings of federal judges. In 1987 Robert Daronco was shot by Charles

Koster, a retired police officer, while he was gardening. The shooting occurred two days after he had dismissed a sexual-harassment suit brought by the daughter of the officer. Koster then killed himself.

In 1989 Judge Robert Vance was killed when a mail-bomb was sent to his home in Birmingham, Alabama. Initially it was thought that he had been the target of Colombian drug-dealers, but this was soon discounted. The same year Maryland Judge J.P. Corderman lost part of his hand when a bomb exploded in his apartment. He too was known for heavy sentencing.

In the Vance case, in which Walter Leroy Moody jnr. was charged with his murder and that of a Savannah civil-rights lawyer Robert Robinson, judges were more willing to recuse themselves. In February 1990 the entire US Court of Appeals for the 11th Circuit stood itself down in a civil suit growing out of a federal investigation of the mail-bomb murders. All three judges in the Middle District of Georgia then withdrew when a separate federal prosecution accused Moody and his wife of tampering with a witness. This did not satisfy Moody or his lawyers, who wanted the recusal of all United States judges and magistrates, and for the Senate Judiciary Committee to appoint an 'independent judicial officer'.[15] He did not manage this and Moody was convicted on 28 June 1991 in St Paul, Minnesota, on 71 federal counts. He was given seven life terms plus 400 years. The killing of the judge and the civil rights lawyer was part of a vendetta which he had waged against the court system following his release from a sentence imposed in 1972 for possessing bomb-making equipment, coupled with his belief that black people received preferential treatment over whites.

More recently District Judge Mark Luitjen had round-the-clock protection from the Texas Rangers for two months while police investigated a plot to kill him. The threat followed Luitjen's refusal to recommend that a higher court should hear an appeal of Robert E. Lee whom he had sentenced to 25 years in 1997 for the attempted murder of his wife. In that case the two would-be hitmen were convicted of attempted murder and received 15 to 25-year terms. The plan had been to make it appear that the murder took place during a burglary.

After the case it is alleged that Lee and his friend, a high-school teacher Carroll Parker, had tried to raise the money to hire a hitman to kill the judge. The prosecution claims that the plan came to nothing when the potential hitman turned out to be an undercover officer.

One of the great advantages which lawyers and judges have over the general middle-class population is that when they wish to have a rival or encumbrance eliminated there is usually a raft of people to whom they can turn for advice, help and action. Whether this raft is unsinkable is another question altogether.

For example, take Marie Elisabeth Cons-Boutboul, a 69-year-old disbarred lawyer whose daughter Darie, the champion woman jockey of France, married Jacques Perrot; at this wedding Laurent Fabius, the one-time Socialist prime minister of France, had been the best man. Perrot was found shot dead on the landing of a block of flats in the fashionable 16th *arrondissement* in Paris on 27 December 1985.

When Perrot and Darie became estranged, she had refused him access to their child. Four and a half years later, at the trial of Cons-Boutboul, the prosecution alleged that the killing had been over the custody of Perrot's young son. On the night of his death, said the prosecution, Perrot was due to have dinner with Mme Cons-Boutboul to discuss arrangements for the child, but she cancelled the engagement. She denied that there was ever any such appointment.

In 1989 the body of Bruno Dassac, a known French criminal, was found in the Channel near Le Havre; he had been shot in the head. Dassac, to his undoubted cost, had boasted of the Perrot hit and claimed £15,000 had been transferred to his account by Mme Cons-Boutboul. Isauro Figuier, a prosecution witness, said he had introduced Dassac to her when she said she wanted someone to give Perrot a beating. Charged with complicity in Dassac's killing, Mme Cons-Boutboul was acquitted.

The evidence against Mme Cons-Boutboul in the Perrot case was tenuous. No gun used in the killing was ever found. It was suggested by his friends that Perrot discovered that his mother-in-law had been disbarred after being convicted of embezzling money from one of her clients, a Catholic charity, and it was also thought that he was trying to use this as a lever to obtain access to his son. Nevertheless, on 24 March 1993 Mme Cons-Boutboul was found guilty of ordering the murder of her son-in-law and sentenced to 15 years' imprisonment.

On 14 September 1987 Judge Vincent Sherry and his wife, Margaret, were shot in their home in Biloxi. They had been missing for some days before their bodies were found by Sherry's law partner, Peter Halat. The investigation into their deaths uncovered an amazing web of intrigue both in Biloxi and in the state penitentiary at Angola, Louisiana. This led to a reassessment of the health of the so-called Dixie Mafia, which was found to be good. In fact the Dixie Mafia had always proved themselves quite capable of taking on the judiciary. In January 1980 an unfulfilled contract was taken out on the life of Superior Court Judge George A. Horkan after he had sentenced drug-dealers to terms of 8–12 years.[16]

In a convoluted way Sherry's death resulted from the imprisonment of Kirksey McCord Nix jnr. for the robbery-murder on Easter Sunday 1971 of Frank Corso, a New Orleans grocer. Nix jnr. was the son of a lawyer who had made his way up from being the janitor to the Oklahoma House of Representatives to being elected to the House. His mother, Patricia, was also a lawyer who, after divorcing Nix snr., married oilman B.B. Kerr.

Unfortunately Nix snr. – despite his rank, wealth and position as an Appellate Judge – had friends amongst the Dixie Mafia, notably Biloxi strip-club owner Mike Gillich (known as Mr Mike), a man implicitly trusted by criminals. When Nix jnr. was sent to the Keesler Air Force Base his father told him to get in touch with Gillich. There on the Strip, after he had finished his military service, he dealt in drugs, pimped and ran the badger game.

In March 1972 Nix and his companions in the killing of Corso were found guilty, but the jury voted against the death penalty and they received life 'at hard labour'. The sentence meant that they could never be paroled but could only receive a governor's pardon. In a way this was the making of Nix's criminal career.

From inside Angola prison, he began an elaborate scam on homosexuals by setting up what appeared to be a dating agency. In this enterprise, with the assistance of his girlfriend Sheri LaRa Sharpe, his new wife Kellye Dawn Nix (whom he purported to marry in prison) and the law offices of Halat and Sherry, he conned around a million dollars from lonely men.

The scheme involved the placing of an advertisement for a 'summer lover' in a local paper and, when it was answered, writing back explaining that the 'lover', Eddie, was in some serious if temporary difficulties. Could Eddie call collect and explain things? A picture of a handsome young stud was enclosed. The call came through from a rehabilitation programme for first offenders. The victim would speak to a correctional officer who explained that the lover was a decent boy at heart. Eventually the victim would put up the air fare. Then followed a series of disasters for Eddie all of which, to keep him out of prison and to get him nearer the victim, required more and more money to be sent.

What was amazing was that all the parts – Eddie, the correctional officer, policemen, social workers – were played by Nix. And, with variations and refinements, it was successfully repeated time and again. Apart from purchasing privileges in Angola, the bulk of the money was to be used to try to obtain parole. Other money was invested in a house on the Gulf Coast, a Trans-Am which Kellye Dawn was allowed to drive, and was used for allowances for both his wife and girlfriend. Nix would later state that his expenses to buy privileges in prison were $12,000 a month.

Some of the proceeds of these scams found their way into the accounts of the Biloxi law firm of Halat and Sherry. And, it appears, out of them again. But to where?

When Sherry and his wife were shot it was suggested this was because it was he who had been skimming the profits. Another suggestion was that Margaret Sherry, a City Councillor, was about to expose a major corruption scandal in Biloxi. She had consistently threatened to run as Mayor and, if successful, to shut down the Strip which, for all practical purposes, meant Gillich.

Throughout the inquiry into the death of the judge and his wife, the name of Peter Halat, his law partner and now Mayor of Biloxi, was in the frame. In the autumn of 1990, Kellye Dawn, who was now seeking to annul her marriage to Nix, pleaded guilty to one count of felony theft in exchange for agreeing to become a witness. She had been indicted on 15 counts by a Grand Jury in 1989.

When the indictment of the Grand Jury in the killing of the Sherrys was finally handed down on 21 May 1991, Halat's name was not included. He called an immediate press conference describing this as his vindication and complaining about unfair media treatment. The defendants included Nix jnr.; John Elbert Ransom, who was already serving a manslaughter sentence and who was said to have been the gunman; and Mike Gillich, at that time the unofficial head of the Dixie Mafia. In the early 1960s Gillich set up his first club with striptease and gambling. From then on his political and police contacts and hard work ensured the success of a string of near-beer and other clubs on Biloxi's Strip where Judge Sherry was happy to drink.

On 11 November 1991 Nix, Ransom and Gillich were convicted of a rolled-up conspiracy indictment which included both the scam and the contract to kill. They received consecutive sentences totalling 15 years in each case. Once again Halat said that he had been vindicated. It was never actually made clear by the prosecution why the judge and his wife had been shot.[17]

Meanwhile, back in Biloxi, Halat was by no means yet out of the wood. In October 1996 he was charged with ten counts of racketeering including murder, all connected to the death of the Sherrys. On 17 July 1997 he was convicted. Much of the evidence against him had come from Mike Gillich, who sensibly had negotiated with the government so that his 20-year sentence be reduced to one of 6 years. Two months later Halat was sentenced to a term of 18 years of which he must serve 16. This was part of a curious sentence bargain in which he undertook not to appeal his sentence but was allowed to appeal his conviction.

As might be expected, US District Judge Charles W. Pickering had a small homily for him:

> I hope that you will have a new beginning and even in prison that you will make a positive contribution to society. It won't be easy but it can be done.

Italian Mafia killings of judges and police officers who were actively working against them continued. Despite major security, judges have been singularly vulnerable not only to the Kalishnikov-bearing motorcycle pillion passenger but to the bomb. On 23 May 1992 Giovanni Falcone, who had been a major scourge of the Mafia, decided to take a short break with his wife and go home for the weekend to Palermo. They drove in a motorcade to a military airport in Rome and took the flight to Sicily. Someone in the Ministry of Justice betrayed them and, at the turn-off to Capaci, a two-ton bomb exploded. Falcone and three bodyguards died instantly; his wife, Francesca, five hours later from her injuries. Twenty other bodyguards and civilians were also injured.[18] His colleague, Paolo Borsellino, vowed to continue the fight but survived for only a few months before he too was blown up when he left his mother after a Sunday visit on 19 July that year.[19]

Drive-by shootings of lawyers have become common in South America and they are no longer so unusual in Europe. However, it is not always clear who has ordered the execution. On 18 December 1996, Neapolitan lawyer Aniello Arcella was killed as he drove home shortly after midnight. Four killers on two motorcycles overtook his car on either side and opened fire; more than 20 shots were fired. Better known as Anjo, Arcella had once defended both Luigi Giulano and Raffaele Stolder, two heads of the Camorra who started as allies and ended as enemies. He had been suspected of helping organised crime figures, including Stolder, to avoid prosecution rather more than a lawyer should.

One Californian prosecutor who survived a courtroom assassination attempt in the early years of the twentieth century was Francis J. Heney, seriously wounded during an afternoon recess of the trial of Abe Ruef. A small nondescript man with greying hair shot him while he was talking to court staff. The dubious lawyer Earl Rogers was suspected of complicity, although he was not at the time acting for Ruef, but it turned out to be a Morris Hass, a man with a conviction many years earlier who now had a wife and family and had held down a job. Hass had been called for jury service, while Heney in the *voir dire* had ruthlessly exposed his well-hidden past life to the public. Hass lost his job and, as an ex-convict, could not obtain another. As a result he shot Heney and, after he was arrested, hanged himself in his cell.[20]

As gangs have become less controlled and their members younger, the old rules have been scrapped. For a time it was believed that the young and extremely unpleasant Boston-based Intervale Gang (named after the street from which members operated) did something which the old Italian murderers such as Albert Anastasia would not have dreamed of doing: they had killed a prosecutor. Paul R. McLaughlin, a Special Assistant Attorney General assigned to prosecute gang crimes, was shot on 25 September 1995 near the railway station in commuterland West Roxbury.

In September 1996, 23 alleged Intervale members were arrested of whom half were eligible for life imprisonment if convicted. Then on 9 September 1996, in the holding cells at the federal courthouse in Boston, six members squared off against a group of United States deputy marshals whom they said had spat and thrown objects at them. Before the fighting started one had shouted, 'We'll get them like we got the one at the railroad.'

But the longer the investigation went on, the more it seemed that the claims were largely boasting. In July 1997 a Grand Jury began hearing evidence about Paul McLaughlin's murder, focusing on Jeffrey Bly, a member not of Intervale but of the Theodore Street Gang. The day after his death McLaughlin had been due to prosecute Bly on car-jacking charges for which the youth was later given 10–15 years. Bly, who was given life without parole for the murder, had remarked just before he shot McLaughlin, 'He's not my DA anymore.'

On 5 June 2000 Commonwealth Attorney Fred Capps was shot and killed in his home in Burkesville. Dying, he returned the fire and killed his attacker, a man he was due to prosecute that day. Capps was the third prosecutor to be killed in the past 20 years. In January 1982, Florida prosecutor Eugene Berry had been shot to death by Bonnie Kelly, whose husband was being prosecuted by him.

This does not mean to say there have been no threats. In the 12 months ending in 1999 there were just under 500 threats logged, and 70 federal judges and prosecutors had been assigned 24-hour security which lasted three or more days. In Texas a judge who sentenced a man who hired a hitman to kill his wife and make it appear a burglary gone wrong, spent two months of 2000 under 24-hour surveillance. The man's girlfriend, a schoolteacher no less, was arrested for trying to drum up the funds to pay another hitman – the two in the first case were in prison. Fortunately the man she chose was an undercover agent.

In January 2000 New York stockbroker Stuart Winkler received the maximum sentence of 8 and a half to 25 years for trying to arrange the murder of the charismatic Justice Leslie Crocker Snyder, who had been due to preside over his trial for a stock fraud. Advised by a lawyer friend that Ms Crocker Snyder was biased against him and that he would not get a fair trial because she favoured the prosecution, he decided to remedy things and approached his cellmate, who unsportingly went to the authorities and wore a wire in order to assist in Winkler's second prosecution.

As for the lawyer who counselled Winkler against the judge, she may find herself facing disciplinary proceedings. Winkler still faced trial on the stock fraud. While Judge Crocker Snyder will deal with his 32 co-defendants, the judge who sentenced Winkler kept his trial for herself.

In England attacks on judges are rare, but in early January 2001 Judge Ann Goddard was assaulted at the Central Criminal Court when a man on a murder charge leaped out of the dock and managed to get to the bench before he was pulled away. She received a cut above her left eye which required stitches. He was remanded for psychiatric reports.[21]

Of course, just as unhappy clients take against their and other lawyers, so sometimes do lawyers lose interest in or take against their clients. Over the decades there have been countless cases where lawyers have slept through proceedings, but in recent years attempts have been made to improve standards. A quarter of the convicts on death row in Texas in 2000 were represented by lawyers with records of professional misconduct. The lawyers had been reprimanded, placed on legal probation, suspended or banned from practising by the State Bar of Texas. Their misdemeanours included failing to appear in court, falsifying documents, failing to present key witnesses and allowing their clients to lie.[22]

The behaviour of lawyers who have slept through their clients' capital cases in America seems to have reached a new high (surely, low) with the conduct of David B. Smith of Greenboro, North Carolina, a lawyer of nearly 30 years' standing and well respected as a fearsome trial lawyer. Appointed by the court in a post-conviction death penalty phase of the trial, Mr Smith decided that his client should die and to this end deliberately missed a deadline for the filing of an appeal against sentence. An affidavit filed by Mr Smith at the State Supreme Court read, 'I decided Mr Tucker deserved to die and I would not do anything to prevent his execution.'

The client, Russell Tucker, had been sentenced to death for the shooting of a Kmart security guard, Maurice Williams, after being caught shoplifting. Mr Smith and his co-counsel Steve Allen went to see their new client on death row in Raleigh soon after their appointment in February 1998:

> At the end of the visit I decided I did not like Mr Tucker. My own beliefs against capital punishment were severely challenged as I read the trial transcripts in preparation for post-conviction relief.

Mr Smith then began to believe that Mr Tucker should be executed.

> I shared with my therapist my feelings and the consequences of my inaction but I could not bring myself to act in a professional and responsible manner.

He was jerked out of his slumbers by a letter setting the date of the execution for 7 December. '[It] made me face the fact that I had been an agent of the state, seeking to have Mr Tucker executed rather than ethically protecting his constitutional and statutory interest.' Smith filed an affidavit asking for an extension of the deadline and to be taken off the case.

The good news for Mr Tucker was that the State Supreme Court granted the request to extend the deadline. The bad news was that it did not immediately dismiss Messrs Smith and Allen from the case. The position of the Attorney General would seem to be that Tucker has neither the right to conflict-free counsel nor for that matter to 'effective assistance of counsel'.[23]

1 Interview with author, 12 October 2000.
2 Conversation with author, 10 October 2000.
3 Interview with author, 12 October 2000.
4 Ralph Haemms in 'A Very Personal Practice' in *New Law Journal*, 13 March 1987.
5 See *BNA Criminal Practice Manual*, 15 March 1995, p.125; also *San Francisco Chronicle*, 17, 18 and 19 January 1995.
6 See John Roeburt, *Get Me Giesler*, Chapter III.
7 Ovid Demaris, *The Last Mafioso*.
8 Unnamed source quoted in William Marsden, 'Lawyer was informant, RCMP confirm' in the Montreal *Gazette*, 13 April 1993.
9 Montreal *Gazette*, 5 May 1993.
10 As a rule Canadian judges of the time did not act kindly when they discovered that the Goverment had interfered with the confidentiality of the client-lawyer relationship. In 1990 all charges against three alleged drug-traffickers were dismissed in Newfoundland when it was discovered that the RCMP had been bugging the lawyers' meeting rooms, hotel bedrooms and a table lamp in a restaurant where they ate. The RCMP argued that it was fortuitous they had heard these conversations; in fact they had been investigating Vito Rizzuto. The Rizzuto Family were the target of the 1987-88 Project Scorpion which linked them to the N'drangheta group and to cocaine trafficking.
11 Even worse is finding that the prosecutor is tied into organised crime. In 1940 Detroit prosecutor Duncan McCrea was prosecuted for his part in running a $10 million baseball pool. He left his office one Spring lunchtime never to return. The fedora hat which he left behind remains as a prized memento in the District Attorney's office. See *Time*, 6 May 1940.
12 John H. Davis comments on allegations that Harrelson was one of three 'tramps' arrested in Dealey Plaza immediately after the assassination of President Kennedy. Jack White, a Fort Worth graphics expert who testified on the identity of the tramps before the House Select Committee on Assassinations in 1978, had concluded without reservation that Harrelson was the youngest tramp. He also points out that when Harrelson was arrested for the Wood murder he had a business card of Russell D. Mathews, another Dallas man who had been a close associate of Jack Ruby in the 1960s and who had documented connections to both Santos Trafficante and Carlos Marcello. *Mafia Kingfish*, p.470.
13 Teresa H. Anderson, U.P.I., 14 December 1982.
14 BRILAB (after bribery and labour) was a Justice Department nationwide sting operation begun in 1979 to 'criminally involve labor officials' suspected of being involved in illegal activities in association with leaders of organised crime. One of the targets was the New Orleans alleged racketeer Carlos Marcello.
15 Jane Okrasinski, 'Who tries a colleague's killer' in *Legal Times*, 26 November 1990.
16 Jeff Kunerth, 'The Dixie Mafia: Bad ol' boys in a Southern web of crime' in *Orlando Sentinel Times*, 16 January 1991.
17 For a full and thoroughly entertaining account of the investigation and the case see Edward Humes, *Mississippi Mud*.

Another lawyer who had a colleague killed was James L. Anding. In 1976 he purchased a contract on Joseph H. Langworthy jnr. of St Louis, whom he feared was about to file a misconduct suit against him. In 1986 Anding was convicted of manslaughter and sentenced to 10 years' imprisonment. In prison he ran a lucrative if informal legal practice. In June 1988 his conviction was overturned on the basis that a manslaughter conviction was insupportable. Anding died shortly after his release. For a full account of the case, see the articles by Ronald Lawrence in *St Louis Post-Dispatch* or a condensed version on http://www.crimemagazine.com/langworthy.htm

18 On 29 July 1993 Antonio Gioc was found in his Rome prison cell hanged from the bars by his shoelaces. He was known to have been at Palermo airport when Falcone's plane landed and was thought to have been the one who passed on the message. In the past year he had become prone to mistakes and there was speculation that he killed himself to spare his family from the reprisals which were then commonly being wrought.

19 A fortunately rare casualty in the US was the Boston lawyer John Harrison who survived, but with severe injuries, when his car was blown up during the Winter Hill wars in the city. Stephen 'The Rifleman' Flemmi was acquitted after a witness had changed his evidence.

20 See Adele Rogers St Johns, *Final Verdict*, Chapter 36.

21 In 1898 Sir Edward Parry, a Manchester County Court judge, was shot and badly injured as he sat on the bench. In 1973 a man was sentenced to nine months' imprisonment for attacking a member of the Court of Appeal. *Crowley*; *The Times*, 2 March 1973.

22 *The Times,* 11 September 2000.

23 *New Law Journal,* 8 December 2000. I remember a case where I fell out with the client so badly that he reported me to the Law Society. I asked to have my name taken off the legal aid certificate, and this was granted. The difficulty was that the client was known as being difficult and no one would take him on. The Crown Court then asked both me and the client if we would accept each other subject to the complaint and we both agreed.

# 21 Sex: Mary Ann Marxkors, Gary Alderdice and many others

NOT ALL LAWYERS who become sexually involved with their clients suffer the fate of the Chicago lawyer Benjamin E. Burr, shot in July 1919 by a 17-year-old chambermaid named Margaret Seithamier, whom he had impregnated. He had acted for both the girl's mother and elder sister Marie in divorce proceedings. What particularly annoyed both girls was not that they shared his affections but that in his watchcase there was a picture of yet another woman. Little Miss Margaret along with Marie called on him and shot him. She was charged with murder and her sister with being an accessory. Margaret had spent a restless first night in custody unable to sleep, because every time she closed her eyes she saw poor Benny on the floor and it was an opportune time for a spot of moralising.

Said Mary Bartelme, a woman police court official:

> Her case ought to be a striking lesson to all parents of the necessity of providing helpful pleasures for the children instead of leaving them to the hazards of casual encounters.

Nothing about lecherous lawyers ...

Unfortunately over the years a great many lawyers have allowed their hearts to impede their conduct of cases, as a result of which their clients have suffered. None more so than Reginald Powell, aged 29 at the time of his death, who claimed that the then 35-year-old Mary Ann Marxkors, the Kansas City public defender assigned to his case, became so emotionally involved with him that she was unable to prepare his defence properly. In March 1988 he had been convicted of stabbing two men to death while mugging them; the take was $3 and a packet of cigarettes, but Powell stayed behind and killed the men with a butterfly knife. His IQ tests were put at 65. His new lawyers claimed that Ms Marxkors insisted he should plead not guilty, when an admission might have saved him from the death penalty. Nor did she put him on the witness stand when his obvious mental impairment might have had an effect on the jurors. She was, she said, afraid that on the stand he might not seem as impaired as he was. The jury could not agree on the death penalty and so it was the judge who imposed it.

Ms Marxkors conceded that she had had intercourse with Powell three times in his cell during the trial. She had also written him a series of letters described as 'varying in tone from a junior High School romance to the smutty and obscene things you read about in *Penthouse*'. Later she would tell a reporter, 'It was my first death-penalty case and I spent a lot of time with him to gain his trust. I came to know a lot about where he came from, what his life had been. Yet, he was always caring to me.' Ms Marxkors had been in therapy herself for 15 years.

The Missouri Appeal Court, never one to be described as lily-livered, ruled that this was no reason why he should be reprieved. Mary Ann Marxkors kept in touch with Powell during his period on death row in Potosi where he was later executed.[1]

One of the more enterprising of jail breaks was that of Tim Kirk – a man with a long record including two convictions for armed robbery – on 31 March 1983. He was then serving a 65-year sentence and, following a number of attempted escapes, had been sent to Brushy Mountain prison where it was alleged he shot and killed some black inmates in a struggle for control of the prison on 8 February 1982.

His lawyer, Mary Evans, came from the upper middle-classes and had been brought up by her lawyer Baptist father, Bob Pentecost, vice-president of the University of Tennessee School of Agriculture. Regarded as something of a loner, she had recently left the firm in Knoxville where she had been working and had joined the public defender's office in London, Kentucky.

Now she had to meet Kirk at the office of Gary Salk, a psychologist, for an evaluation on whether he might qualify for an insanity or diminished responsibility defence. This lawyer was not, however, leaving the defence of her client to chance. With her in the red Toyota Celica she was driving were four rolls of shipping tape, a pair of scissors, a man's Calvin Klein sweater, a pair of men's Levi's and, most importantly, a .25 calibre pistol. When she reached Salk's office Kirk and the security guards were already there. Salk had arranged for the restraints to be removed. During the two hours of tests she waited outside the room and from time to time Kirk came out to consult with her. Then, as the psychologist marked the tests and the pair stood chatting with the guards, Kirk pulled out the gun she had passed him. She used the scissors to cut the telephone cord; the guards and Salk were taped. Kirk took $25 from the psychologist's wallet and they were off.

They were not arrested until five months later on 17 August when they were living at Daytona, Florida, and spending most of their time at the local greyhound track. She had been sent money by friends. In his absence Kirk had been found guilty of manslaughter of the prisoners at Brushy Mountain. When they were returned to Tennessee, the only real question was what would happen to Mary Evans.

She was perhaps fortunate to benefit from the mutual antipathy between Judge Buddy Scott and Attorney General Jim Ramsay. Over a period of five years Scott had cited General[2] Ramsay 20 times for contempt of court, 15 for misconduct, and had thrown him in jail twice. Ramsay would later write to the *Guinness Book of Records* asking if this was a record and if there was a category into which he fitted. He was told there was not.

Ramsay, after he had lost a motion in which the defence sought to exclude some evidence because of an illegal search, agreed to a plea bargain for which he would be roundly criticised. Mary Evans would plead guilty to aiding and abetting the kidnapping and escape, which carried a maximum sentence of three years. He also agreed to urge probation coupled with a condition that she undergo psychiatric treatment and make certain reparations, such as the loss of Dr Salk's $25 as well as the loss of the three firearms confiscated by Kirk and herself during the escape. Kirk agreed to take a further 40 years on his own sentence. It was thought that Kirk was so handsome and had such charisma that he might be acquitted on a sympathy and envy verdict but, rightly, he was prepared to sacrifice his chances for the lawyer whom he thought loved him and who had certainly sacrificed her career for him. General Ramsay did not appear at the sentencing hearings, at which it was argued by her lawyers that Mary Evans was schizophrenic and by the judge that she had read up the symptoms from a textbook.

Ramsay had come under heavy fire for his seeming liberality, the *Knoxville Journal* suggesting he had bargained away the right of a jury to decide the insanity issue and that he had cut the case in half to prevent Scott trying a high-profile case with the nation's press in the public gallery:

> It can be firmly stated that any notion of justice is better left to prayer whenever that judge and prosecutor are engaging one another in court. But that's another matter, and the citizens of Anderson County, who are abundantly aware of the feud and its detractions from the business of justice, seem to like it that way and keep re-electing the antagonists.[3]

The doctors called by the defence were clear on their diagnosis. They had a catalogue of symptoms consistent with schizophrenia including, at an early age, abuse of her Barbie dolls, burning one of them on a light-bulb. She had smashed a ceramic cat, had seen tigers jump through hoops and had visualised small blobs which she described as little one-celled animals of various colours. After a date with a young man, she dreamed fourteen nights in a row that she had stabbed him repeatedly. She felt that eyes on record albums looked at her.

When the sentencing process began, it immediately became clear that Scott was going to give the defence and their psychiatrists a hard time before he agreed to the sentence bargain. Time and again he took over the cross-examination, pointing to the textbook *Proof of Facts* in which there was a section 'Mental Disorder and Incapacity' which listed these symptoms.

Tapes of her sessions with psychiatrists were played but, despite repeated invitations, the defence did not call Mary Evans to give evidence. Time and again the judge pointed out that by her plea she had surrendered her defence of mental incapacity to commit the crime, and it was now only a question of the degree of her responsibility. He was clearly not impressed. The writing was on the wall when he began his sentencing speech:

> It was an active participation in this crime. She drove a getaway vehicle. It belonged to her. I do not believe her story about Kirk directing her to an isolated part of this county for the vehicle to be

left and picked up by someone else. I do not believe her when she stated to me in this probation report that she does not know who picked them up, where she went in North Carolina and what she did there ... she also reported that it was the happiest time of her life – according to her friend when she called.

Scott sentenced her to a term of three years in the penitentiary. Probably he was right not to have been convinced because she was still in close contact with Kirk, sending him cassettes with spoken messages after five minutes of preliminary music designed to deceive the guards. Kirk was impressed at her integrity in not giving up the names of those who had helped them. In prison she became something of a minor celebrity, with offers of marriage from around the world. She gave an interview in *The Tennessean* saying that no one was keeping watch on her medical condition and that, had she wanted, there had been plenty of opportunities for her to commit suicide. Rumours that she had been turned down for a position as prison paralegal were wrong; she had not applied.[4]

In October 1984 she went before the Parole Board saying that she had not contacted and had no intention of contacting Kirk. Now the Board recommended by a 3–2 majority that she be put on work release until her parole date in the following February. On the next cassette to Kirk, she explained in somewhat terse terms that she had only said these things to obtain her freedom. Even so Kirk should have realised that his romance was fading away through the bars. Mary Evans moved to Florida and on 24 May married the first cousin of her former husband. Not to be outdone, on 10 August 1985 Kirk married 31-year-old Mary Paris in a prison exercise yard ceremony. She had, it seems, been visiting him for the previous two years.

One of the greatest hooks criminals can use to gain control over their lawyers is sex and one of the saddest of such stories, of a lawyer who mixed with the *mafiya* to his fatal cost, is that of New Zealand-born Hong Kong lawyer Gary Alderdice and his lover Natalya Samofalova.

From 1973 he had worked as a prosecutor in Hong Kong, before resigning and switching to defence work when he became known as 'Never Plead Guilty Gary'. Within a short time he had become one of Hong Kong's leading criminal lawyers and, on an island where the shores were washed with money, this meant both substantial wealth and a position in society. And along with it also came the collapse of his second marriage to Pippa, the ex-wife of a friend and colleague. In 1994 Alderdice was taken to hospital with knife wounds in his chest following an argument at his home. Shortly afterwards Pippa left him and there were divorce proceedings.

It was then that Alderdice started making trips on the hydrofoil to Macau, then a Portuguese colony, a little under an hour away. While the horse-racing there was not up to the standard of Hong Kong's Happy Valley and Sha Tin, there was legal casino gambling. Macau had been invaded by Russian *mafiya* who were working with the local Triad organisations; it also had a whole army of Russian prostitutes mainly from the Vladivostock area, euphemistically described as hostesses and dancers, working the hotel circuit. Amongst them was the exceptionally attractive strawberry-blonde, Natalya Samofalova. Her contract had been signed in Macau and as protection for themselves, very sensibly, the local Triads had retained her work papers.

For Alderdice it was a question of love at first sight and it does seem to have been reciprocated by the girl. He took up with Samofalova in early April 1994 and the pair stayed first in his hotel room and then in a cottage at the Westin Resort until 9 May. This, it appears, is where Alderdice made his fatal mistake. Genuinely in love with her, he refused to pay her owners for her services. When her papers came up for renewal, the local Triads refused to return them to her and she was obliged to leave.

Alderdice returned to Hong Kong and, after completing some legal work, on 23 June he flew to Vladivostock where he was met by Samofalova at the airport. It was said he had taken with him approximately $150,000. The next day Samofalova's mother called at her flat, could get no reply and with the help of a neighbour prised open the steel door. Inside she found both Alderdice and her daughter (who seemed to have been tortured) dead. Later $20,000 was found in the ransacked apartment.

Immediately there were all kinds of rumours, including the most prevalent one that Alderdice had taken the money to buy his girlfriend's contract but they had been killed to demonstrate the power of the *mafiya*. In some stories all the money had been left untouched. Other versions of the reason for the killing included the KGB and involvement in the smuggling of nuclear weapons and an exotically named substance, red mercury.

Five years after the killings, in 1999, came a confession from a woman the police would initially identify only as Olga but who was thought to be a heroin-addicted prostitute, Olga Bogdacheuskaia, who had worked with Samofalova and who had flown with her from Macau. Her version of events was much more prosaic. It had been a simple case of robbery, Bogdacheuskaia and her husband having been persuaded to rob the pair. Alderdice was talking with Bogdacheuskaia and her husband in the kitchen of the apartment when he heard a scream from the living room by a 'second man'. He had rushed in and was shot in the eye. Samofalova was tied to a chair and tortured to make her reveal the whereabouts of the money, but according to Bogdacheuskaia only $2,000 was found.

Unfortunately for the police Bogdacheuskaia, already dying from her addiction, did just that four days later. Her husband subsequently denied the story and the mystery 'second man', who actually shot Alderdice and who was regarded as a street-level hood rather than a mastermind, was thought to have died in a gangland killing in the Primorye province back in 1995. It is, however, one of those stories where the suspects are conveniently dead or untouchable. This may be just another instance where fiction is more romantic than the truth, but it still serves as a warning to lawyers who find that their hearts are located around the seventh waistcoat button.[5]

It is unusual to find lawyers, let alone those with a commercial practice, actively running prostitutes; but in June 2000 Toronto lawyer Gary Patterson went to prison for 7 years for doing just that.

Convicted on 10 charges including kidnapping and uttering death threats as well as living off the proceeds of prostitution, he had been controlling a 19-year-old ex-nanny whom he was trying to persuade not to give evidence against her former pimp with whom Patterson was associated.

The young girl came from a small town outside Toronto and had become involved with Rick Downey, who persuaded her to go on the streets. She left him and went to the police when he showed her a gun. The police took her home but, with the job as nanny gone, she started working for an escort agency.

While working as an escort she met another prostitute, Penny Roberts, who tricked her into meeting Royce Briscoe and Patterson. They forced her back onto the streets to earn money for Downey's defence, and then sent her to work in a strip club in Oshawa. But she managed to get out of the club and again went to the police. Briscoe and Roberts received sentences of 4 and 3 years respectively. The girl was the third in the last decade to allege she had been kidnapped, threatened and abused by the 36-year-old Patterson.

Of course, sometimes lawyers find themselves in such financial straits that they feel obliged to moonlight as prostitutes. One such was Chicago-based Marsha Watt who found herself suspended from practice for six months; she had already completed three months' court-ordered supervision. Her offence followed her placing an advertisement offering 'sensitive executives and professional gentlemen companionship' for a modest $310 an hour. The 'sensitive gentleman' was, unfortunately, an undercover policeman who arrested her after she agreed to perform two sex acts. Previously she had worked for an Illinois Appellate judge.[6]

Another, in France, whose judicial career was ruined because of his involvement with a prostitute was the Lyons magistrate Phillipe Le Friant, who in June 1988 was struck off for 'dishonouring the magistrature'. Two years earlier, as a part-time activist for a Lyons association which helped prostitutes to start new lives, he had met Marie Arbant who had been put on the streets by her husband to work off his gambling debts. The left-wing lawyer's association with prostitutes had already earned him the nickname 'le juge des putes', and there was further trouble for him when his gun was found in the safe of a bar. He had also publicly criticised another magistrate for prosecuting a girl. For his pains he was forbidden to have anything to do with prostitutes and was sent to Brioude in the Haut-Loire where it was thought there were fewer opportunities for his reforming zeal.

In August 1987 he received a call from Marie Arbant saying that her life was in danger. He offered her a place in his home and told his superiors. In June 1988 he was barred from holding a position either as a magistrate or as a professor of law. While he worked as a delivery man and in a plastic-bag factory, and she became a water-diviner, over the next five years the pair lobbied to have the ban overturned. In 1993 President Mitterand granted an amnesty and the next year their book *The Magistrate and the Prostitute* was published.

Technically lifted or not, the ban remained in place and they continued to lobby, staging hunger strikes in protest at the unfairness of their position until, on 2 March 1999, the body of Marie Arbant was found in her flat in Saint-Etienne. She had committed suicide, having just finished another three-week hunger strike.[7]

Nor does sex have to be the full act to foul up a prosecution or a career. Telephone sex will do nicely and possibly can be credited with saving the Mexican drug-smuggler – former pickpocket and prostitute Griselda Blanco de Trujillo – from the electric chair in Florida. The sex alleged was amongst the secretaries in the State Attorney's office and Blanco's hitman.

Known as Muneca because of her doll-like looks and Blanco because of her stutter, she was another of the Black Widows whose husbands and boyfriends died at increasingly regular intervals. It was alleged that she boasted she had shot her second husband, Alberto Bravo, in the mouth. Blanco was 5'2" in height, very pretty and totally unprincipled. By the mid-1970s she was said to have several hundred people on her payroll. She ran her own gang, Los Pistoleros, full membership of which required that the aspirant had cut off the ear or finger of an enemy. The Pistoleros were said to have invented the art of killing from the back of a high-speed motorcycle. One member's speciality was to tape shut the eyes and mouth of victims, drain their blood in the bath and pack the bodies into TV packing cartons. In 1974 Blanco was indicted over 150 kilos of cocaine, and by 1979 she was the best-known cocaine smuggler in the United States.

On 11 July 1979 came what would prove to be a turning point for Blanco, the Dade County massacre in the Dadeland Mall, Miami. The machine-gunning of two victims and the subsequent shooting up of the car park as the killers fled was the culmination of a war which had been active since the previous November and which had resulted in the death of 24 Latin drug-smugglers. The Dadeland massacre happened, it would appear, because of the theft of four kilos of cocaine.

With Blanco finally sentenced to a federal prison on drug charges, in 1994 it was announced that the police were about to implicate her in three murders in the Miami area in 1992. They included the shooting of three-year-old Johnny Castro who was sitting next to the target, his father, who had offended Blanco by kicking one of her sons in the buttocks during an argument. The other two murders were of drug-dealers Alfred and Grizel Lorenzo, who were killed in their bedroom while the children watched television in another room. Their parents had been late with a drug payment.

Towards the end of 1997 it was decided that she would finally stand trial for murder. Her former gunman and lover, Jorge Ayala, had been arrested on a relatively minor robbery charge and was turned by the authorities. He would give evidence against her in exchange for no death penalty being imposed for his part in the murders he had undertaken for Blanco and a sentence of 25 years without parole. This was when the troubles began. Unfortunately the authorities had not bargained for his undoubted charm, particularly over the telephone. He met his wife Marisol by telephone in 1994 and, although this cannot have been down the line, had impregnated her during a jailhouse visit.

Ayala was moved to a state-county jail facility where things were much freer and easier, and he became a frequent caller to the Major Crimes Unit at the State Attorney's Office. The calls, which were on an almost daily basis and often lasted for hours at a time, were made 'collect' and recorded in the SAO telephone bills. When questioned, several secretaries/witness co-ordinators, who had been lacking guidance and supervision, accepted that they had received personal calls from Ayala, but none admitted telephone sex. However, the calls developed into personal relationships and, with Ayala happy to spread his telephonic favours, quarrelling broke out amongst them over who should answer. By February 1998 the women were no longer speaking to each other. The reasons given by them for the dispute varied – telephone sex, jealousy, a long-standing dislike. Allegations that they personally had taken part in telephone sex were denied, each suggesting one or more of the others had undertaken the task.

Ayala, who defined phone sex as conversations that involved masturbation, sometimes accepted that he had telephone sex, while denying it on other occasions. He agreed that he had discussed opening an escort agency with one of the girls, Raquel Navarro, and sent a number of $50 money orders to be used for lunches. He sent $150 to Navarro at Christmas 1997 to be used to repay another girl who had purchased some coloured pencils, with the remainder to be spent on radios. He also loaned her $2,000 to buy some jet-skis, and his son took some of the money to her house. He discussed obtaining a firearm for another of the girls who then spoke of blowing away a third witness co-ordinator, Sherry Rossbach, who had had her husband drop a Thanksgiving turkey dinner round to the jail for Ayala. When she was interviewed she claimed that one of the other girls had told her there had been telephone sex, the size of Ayala's penis had been discussed and she had been told that she, Rossbach, should flirt with Ayala. But this she thought beneath her.

The inquiry led to allegations by Sherry Rossbach into the conduct of the veteran, experienced prosecutor Michael Band. She claimed he had touched her breasts after a long period of sexual harassment. Vehemently denying the allegation, he resigned for the good of the department. Rossbach was reinstated after her suspension. Barbara Molina-Abad and Olga Cabrera, who was found to have forged Raquel Navarro's signature on certain subpoenas, were dismissed, as was Navarro herself.

In October 1998 it was announced that Blanco had been allowed to plead 'no contest' to three counts of second-degree murder for which she was sentenced to concurrent sentences of 20 years. Charges against a co-accused, Delio Palacios, had been dismissed earlier.[8]

The women had not read the Chicago papers, for a little earlier a similar problem had arisen in Chicago in connection with 'General' Harry Harris, the brother-in-law of the El Rukn leader Jeff Fort. Harris, who had once been in charge of the religious training of the group, began co-operating with the authorities in 1987 and part of his reward was to be allowed to have sex on the floor of the visiting room where he was being held in custody. He also tested positive for drugs while in the Metropolitan Correctional Center. This information should have been passed at once to the defending lawyers, but this was not done. Unfortunately a prosecution paralegal, Corrinda Luchetta, kept the information to herself; she also unwisely allowed herself to be taped while displaying an unhealthily close relationship with two other witnesses, Earl Hawkins and Eugene Hunter. On the tapes she discussed sex and was heard saying she would like to 'stop an elevator between floors ... and just stand someone up against the wall'. In February 1987 she was charged with obtaining and giving a box of Ex-Lax to Hunter. The Illinois Registration and Disciplinary Commission took the view that this was not simply a kind gesture to relieve constipation brought about by the prison diet. One way of smuggling drugs into prison is for the distributor to pass a condom filled with drugs while kissing the inmate. The condom is then swallowed quickly, followed by a powerful dose of laxative.[9]

1 *The Kansas City Star*, 4 February; *New York Times*, 16 February; *The Times*, 17 February 1998.
2 An honorific title given to Attorney Generals in the Southern States.
3 *Knoxville Journal*, 24 February 1983.

4 Quoted in Sandy Johnson, *Against the Law*, pp.253–5.
5 See James Morton, *Gangland International*; *Vancouver Sun*, 16 May 2000.
6 UPI, 26 March 1997.
7 *Liberation*, 4 March 1999; *Daily Telegraph*, 5 March 1999.
8 See Paul Eddy and Sara Walden, 'Natural Born Killers' in *Sunday Times Magazine*, 23 November 1997 for an account of the career of Griselda Blanco and Jorge Ayala; for an account of the troubles in the SAO see *Palm Beach Daily Business Review*, 19 June 1998; for the tribulations of Michael Band and a not wholly favourable account of Sherry Rossbach's record see Tristram Korten, 'The strange saga of a smooth-talking hit man, jealous secretaries, and a ruined prosecutor' in *Miami New Times*, 26 November 1998.
9 See Randall Sambourn, 'El Rukn Case Prosecutors Under Fire' in *National Law Journal*, 21 December 1992. See also Michael Abramowitz, 'The Gang that Couldn't Snitch Straight' in *Chicago Magazine,* August 1993; Corrinda Luchetta, 'My Side of the Story' in *Chicago*, January 1995.

# 22 Survival: How to stay out of trouble

HOW DO LAWYERS ACQUIRE ORGANISED CRIME PRACTICES, and how do they stay out of professional trouble when they have acquired them? Some, of course, never make it to that happy position in the first place.

Law students from time to time forget their position. Robert Cargo of the Polytechnic High School, Los Angeles, was apparently a well-thought-of student who won a debating prize the night after he – along with Samuel Shapiro alias Sandburg, Charles Wagner, Frank Tesciaio and George Dawson – robbed a truck. Cargo gave the game away by settling a debt with a high-value note from the robbery, telling the recipient to keep the change. He received 25 years in Leavenworth.[1]

The wheel goes around and around. Zolton Williams, regarded as one of Columbia University Law School's brightest pupils – 'intellectually curious', 'energetic' were two descriptions – was convicted in December 1998, shortly before he graduated, of smuggling tens of thousands of dollars' worth of cocaine from Jamaica. He had, it was alleged, begun his smuggling enterprise almost as soon as he entered law school.

In fact Williams had enjoyed an even better career as a criminal than as a law student. At the age of 18 he had been given 5 years' probation for a robbery during which his companion carried a gun. The records had been sealed – which meant that, officially, he had no criminal record. In his early twenties, he had a series of arrests for possession of stolen property and a weapon. These were dismissed. It was alleged that while at law school he had also run a credit-card fraud, something for which he was not charged.[2]

As for those who do qualify, Gerry Shargel explains building a clientele very simply:

> I represent an enormous number of Hassidic Jews. If you represent someone successfully whether they are Italians, Hassidic Jews or orthodontists they are bound to tell their friends. So any group that has members charged with criminal offences can be fairly expected to recommend [someone who has worked well]. The government has never quite got that concept.

What behaviour does send the lawyer over the edge and engage the wrath of the authorities? In his book *The Best Defense*, Alan Dershowitz argues that getting into bed with the client is a serious danger.

> Of course getting into bed physically can lead to all sorts of problems, principally blackmail. One solicitor recalls: 'I was taken by some clients to a strip club where there was this truly gorgeous black girl. After she'd done her turn she came over for a drink at our table and one of the clients said, "We've bought her for you." I can't say I wasn't tempted, but I wasn't drunk enough not to think of that photograph of my pink bottom.'

Not all lawyers have been so squeamish, and often the wife of an accused who has received a short sentence has shown her appreciation to her defence barrister or solicitor in a tangible way:

> There used to be a girl whose husband I'd got a short stretch for and now she worked at the Venus Rooms in Soho. I'd pop down quite often in an evening.

Perhaps the first brief was unduly squeamish, because the second never reported any problems.

One of the problems lawyers face, not when they physically get in bed with their male and female clients but when they climb into a business bed with them, is that very often the client is a great deal more streetwise and smarter than they are. The result is that this frequently causes more heartbreak for the lawyer than for the client. F. Lee Bailey, fine trial lawyer that he is, has found on two major occasions that clients and business can lead to court with himself as the defendant. In the first case he found himself a defendant in a pyramid fraud trial which lasted for several months before the judge finally agreed to sever him from the indictment and he was acquitted.

On the second occasion he advised the drug-smuggler and money launderer Claude L. Duboc that the way out of a mandatory life sentence was to plead guilty and to give up millions in cash, yachts and a home in the South of France. In a long-drawn-out plea bargain it was arranged that something in the region of $40 million was to be handed over, and the prosecution agreed that Mr Bailey should be allowed to keep $6 million of stock which Dubroc had agreed to forfeit but which was expected to rise in value. Normally the government's policy is to immediately liquidate stock seized.

Under this arrangement, however, the stock was to be applied to pay expenses on forfeited properties until they could be sold. The government's intention was that Mr Bailey should eventually return the stock, together with any profit less his agreed and approved expenses. The stock duly rose, but instead of returning the profits in the region of $20 million he announced that he was keeping this as his fee. The government maintained that the intention had been that Dubroc should have the benefit and not Mr Bailey. In January 1996 he disagreed and declined to return the disputed assets as ordered. He was then sentenced to six months on a civil contempt order and sent to the Federal Detention Center in Tallahassee where he was reunited with his former client. Dubroc had dismissed his lawyer in the January.[3]

Another way to find oneself in trouble is to cause the authorities grief in court or in the press. Then, if at all possible, reprisals will follow. Take the case of a young female lawyer asked to do a kindness to her client by taking a suit into prison so that he could wear it at his next court appearance. She did this and perfectly properly turned the suit over to the prison officers. Unfortunately, in one of the trouser pockets was a small amount of marijuana. This led to many days of inquiry before she was exonerated.

It is easy to throw up one's hands and say, 'Whenever was taking clothes into prison a part of a solicitor's work?' But if a solicitor undertaking criminal cases wants to establish a rapport with a client and his family, even to show a certain amount of compassion for the difficulties they face, then such gestures go a long way to help. There must be few solicitors who regularly practise criminal law who have not done such favours to clients and their families over the years; mostly, fortunately, without such disastrous consequences.

There are, of course, professional conduct guides published by the Law Society, and a helpline, but most of the difficult decisions arise on the spot and the unfortunate solicitor is in no position to say, 'Hang on a minute. I'll go and ring the Law Society to see if I can do it.' The best thing to say when a client asks, 'Will you do something for me?' is to reply, 'It depends on what it is' instead of 'Yes'. If I had only said that some years ago, I would not have found myself in possession of a Building Society passbook which a police search of my client had failed to reveal since it was inter-rectum at the time. If you are obliged to back down when the scope of the favour sought is revealed, you lose face with the client. You are, as Roger Ede of the Law Society says:

> Working with people whose moral code is not yours and who may consider things to be acceptable which the courts would not. Solicitors take risks day in and day out and get very little credit.

Clients, however, are often not averse to compromising those who are trying to help them.

It is easy to give dogs bad names but, it must be added, there is a fairly slippery slope down which to slide. The older, perhaps more staid, lawyers would say that the first golden rule is never to accept any invitation from a criminal client, even to lunch in the local greasy spoon.

Ralph Haemms is strict on the subject:

> It's one of the few rules I have for my staff. They must not associate with any client outside the office. The reason is simple – I think they could be compromised. I look on them as my family. I employ them as responsible people but I am responsible for them.[4]

Joe Beltrami represented the Glasgow gangleader Arthur Thompson for over 20 years:

> During that time he never called me by my first name. He knew I would have been insulted if he had done. If he saw me and my wife in the street he would take his hat off, but he would never say anything but pass the time of day.

Saiyad Mubarak Shah was one barrister who perhaps mixed too closely with his clients. He was a drinking companion of Frank

Fraser and had the misfortune to be in a club when the father of snooker player Ronnie O'Sullivan was involved in a fight which led to his being charged with murder. Shah was perhaps fortunate that he died before efforts were made to persuade him to give evidence.

Nor, however much they may entreat you to be best man and godfather, does it do the professional image too much good to be photographed at clients' weddings with your arms around men twice your size with mohair suits, Havanas in mouths, and sporting a deal of gold jewellery.

Another step on the slope is accepting presents. Even in these hard times a 'big drink' on an acquittal to supplement inadequate legal aid fees is not on; nor is the £500 private interview prior to a client signing a legal aid form. On reflection, though, £500 is perhaps not unreasonable. One very fashionable London firm is said to have asked for £15,000 cash for a substantial case before legal aid could even be contemplated.

Nor may solicitors invent a defence, something the police and TV scriptwriters suspect they do of an evening instead of the crossword. Most criminal defence lawyers regard the thought as rather insulting. If they could not dream up better stories than their clients come up with, they would consider their education wasted.

But some solicitors do help out. I had a client accused of a long firm fraud (buying goods on credit and then selling them for cash at a substantial discount before taking a world cruise) or LF as it is known in the trade. He'd been to see another solicitor before me. 'What's your name?' the solicitor had asked. 'John Smith.' 'Like that?' said the lawyer. 'LF is it?' And when my client nodded, he queried speculatively, 'Too late for a fire is it, then?'

As for the case itself, must a solicitor do exactly what the client wishes? It is clear that in an English court an advocate is free to present the case as he sees fit, and if he refuses to accept express instructions he may withdraw. So what does one do if the client says, 'I was on the robbery but let's say I was in Birmingham'? Within certain fairly complicated rules you are entitled to allow him to plead not guilty and to make the prosecution prove its case, but as a general rule it is not a good idea. The defender cannot, however, call your client or witnesses to say he was not on the raid. The experienced client will rarely put his solicitor in that position, but if he does so the safest thing is to say that now you know of his guilt he must either plead guilty or go to another solicitor. By the time he reaches that man's office he will no doubt have learned the rules of the game.

Should clients be advised to co-operate with the authorities? Those lawyers who have represented supergrasses have often found themselves held in less than admiration by their colleagues.

Professor Al Alschuler has good advice:

Should you advise a client to roll over and co-operate with the authorities? Do you ever advise your client to do himself a good turn? Isn't it malpractice not to do so? But you can always say, 'I grew up to believe you took responsibility for what you did and, besides, the boys wouldn't like it.'

Why is it that lawyers, often those who appear in seriously heavy cases, drink so much and have such a high divorce rate? The problem is worldwide. You take the blame if you fail. In your mind it's your fault. He does the extra time because of your recommendation or how you conducted the trial or the plea. 'How many jobs can you point to one person as a winner or loser?' asks one assistant district attorney. He believes that defending lawyers may actually suffer from defending organised crime figures:

Hopefully you never get over the thought that if you get, say, Gotti out on the street what's he going to do next. I think many attorneys fear this.

Sometimes the cigars, the drink, the gambling and the long nights simply get to the lawyer and the wheels come off. F. Mac Buckley, defender of Hartford, Conn., mobsters over the years and one-time boxing trainer and promoter of the welterweight champion Marlon Starling, disappeared on his way to court. On 1 March 1999 he used his cellular telephone to say he was on his way to the federal court in New Haven where he was defending in a drugs case, but he never arrived. Few would accept that the ebullient and charismatic Buckley had disappeared voluntarily. For years he had charmed juries and annoyed other lawyers with his sarcasm, use of street slang and his failure to keep appointments. He had been a commentator for ESPN on the OJ Simpson trial.

New Haven lawyer William F. Dow III commented:

> He was always late, always out of contact, no one ever knew how to reach him. That was always part of the mystery about Mac – how someone that difficult to get hold of could be so successful. The answer was that he was a great lawyer.

Stories that Buckley had been harmed by former gangland clients or their friends, had joined the federal witness programme, that he was gambling in Canada or that he had joined the IRA were rife. Then a different picture began to emerge. He had sold 50 acres of his country estate in 1995. The house had been in his wife's name since 1990, and she was the registered owner of their three cars. He no longer had negligence insurance. Clients began to tell of fees demanded in advance. On the day of his disappearance a lawyer for the State Bar's grievance committee had recommended that Buckley's licence be suspended. He had obtained a complete power of attorney from David Messenger whom he was defending on a murder charge. Messenger's assets were thought to be in excess of half a million dollars and it was feared that Buckley might have disappeared with them. The previous month there were complaints from a couple who had received £580,000 in a settlement over the death of their daughter. Now they alleged that he had forged their signatures on deposits of $144,000. Other clients complained that Buckley had taken tens of thousands of dollars and failed to appear in court. In his absence his licence was suspended. He was named on the Fox television programme 'America's Most Wanted'.

Seven weeks later, looking two stone lighter and tanned, Buckley surrendered and, charged with first-degree larceny and second-degree forgery, he was bailed on condition that he reside in a psychiatric hospital until the next hearing.[5] By the next hearing the court learned that Buckley was suffering from alcoholism and bi-polar disorder, a psychiatric condition characterised by manic and depressive episodes. The signs were that the ground was being prepared for an incapacity defence to the charges.

On 8 November 2000 Buckley was sentenced to 8 years' imprisonment, suspended after 15 months, with 4 years' probation. He had by now repaid $363,000 to two clients and 260 pages of letters in support had been presented on his behalf.[6]

Another high-profile (this time Canadian) lawyer, who found things too much was Windsor-based Don Tait. He came from a family with a drinking father who had been a professional with the Montreal Canadians, and was devoted to his mother. After her death in the 1980s it was said that a light went out in his life and he filled his loss with bigger homes, more expensive cars, jewellery and women. For a time in the 1970s he was retained by the Outlaws Motorcycle Club, and its former president remained a close friend. But the lines became blurred and he began what North Americans call 'partying' with them and living their lifestyle. Over the years he acted for members of Hell's Angels and Montreal's Rock Machine. He was also drinking heavily and on one occasion was so drunk that the judge ordered him to be taken out of court on a stretcher. He was arrested and given a conditional discharge for possessing a restricted weapon. It was then that he signed on for an alcohol rehabilitation course, and he remained sober for 17 years.

But in June 1999, at a time when he was again drinking, now up to 40 oz of vodka daily, he was charged with assaulting his girlfriend Sylvia Muldoon. His law practice, severely damaged by his drinking, now collapsed. In January 2000 he disappeared, leaving some 50 remaining clients without a lawyer and debts totalling $700,000. He was cited for contempt of court, charged with breaking his bail conditions and then with stealing Sylvia Muldoon's jewellery. As with Buckley, rumours of his whereabouts were varied including one that he was living with a biker gang again. In fact he was living in Costa Rica, still drinking and gambling. As a young reporter, Veronique Mandal watched him in his heyday destroy witnesses: '... his head at an arrogant tilt, he lithely strutted across the room, his tall, elegant, hard body once again oozing confidence.' Now she went to interview him and saw:

> Between drinks his hands have a fine tremor and he sweats profusely. He also cries easily when he talks about his past, his children, and his mother.

She was sure that his 'booming oratories' would never again be heard in a court of law.[7]

Criminal clients can, of course, be extremely useful at times of a crack-up:

> In the middle of the night I had this call from a brief I went drinking with on occasions. Could I come over straight away. He was in a

dreadful state, pissed and I should think he was pissing himself with fear as well because he must have rung me a hundred times, no, that's an exaggeration but you know what I mean, on his mobile while me and another fellow were on the way over. What he'd done is knocked someone down whilst he was out driving pissed. What could we do? We took the car off him. I wanted it cut up but the fellow with me put it on a car site out of town and the brief reported it stolen. I didn't charge him but he didn't do me no favours either.

Later he took 32 grand off a friend of mine for an appeal and he only paid the counsel fifteen hundred. When I went to see the man he'd been working for it hadn't gone through the books. The Law Society said I could go to the law but I'm not a grass. His punishment is that he's never going to know for sure whether one year from now or later I'm going to come after him.[8]

Generally, lawyers who defend career criminals see themselves as standing up to far superior forces of government:

I pride myself on being who I am. We're not on Park Avenue. We're in one room in Brooklyn. So long as we in our Western world can have lawyers who are independent it ensures our freedom in our judicial system.[9]

Philadelphian lawyer Robert Simone summed up his position:

[The government's] goal is to knock lawyers out of the box who are desperately needed for the defence. It's not every lawyer who would take a case like Stanfa's or Scarfo or Gotti because they feel they'll get in trouble.[10]

On another occasion he warmed to his theme, linking the government's attitude to the persecution of Japanese-Americans during the Second World War and the Left during the McCarthy years:

The 90s appear to be the decade to target criminal-defence lawyers who represent to the fullest of their ability individuals who are members of unpopular groups, races or nationalities.[11]

Simone's approach is very similar to that of John Gotti's lawyer, Gerald Shargel, who believes that 'People accused of being gangsters are very much in need of an aggressive, hard-fought defence, which is what I bring to the table.'[12]

There is, however, the repeated story of the London lawyer who awaits the tip-off from his contacts in the police over his imminent arrest. Against this he has taken the precaution of having a suitcase of money in his office and tickets for his flight overseas. Why then, if his clients and half the London Underworld knows of this, has no attempt been made to liberate the suitcase? Perhaps sometimes, after all, there is honour amongst thieves.

1 *Thomson's Weekly News,* 21 December 1925.
2 *New York Times,* 21 December 1998.
3 *New York Times,* 19 March 1996.
4 Ralph Haemms, 'A very personal practice' in *New Law Journal,* 23 March 1987.
5 *New York Times,* 21 March, 20 April 1999; *Boston Globe,* 18 July 1999; *Hartford Courant,* 9 November 2000.
6 He must have envied Judge Richard Gee, who was found too stressed to face a re-trial at the Old Bailey on fraud charges. He had been charged with deception during an alleged mortgage swindle during the housing boom of the 1980s. After the first trial Gee had been examined by a professor from the Maudsley Hospital in London who found that the stress of a re-trial would endanger his life. Some eight months after the Attorney General halted the proceedings, Gee was living happily in New York and still drawing his £92,000 a year salary while discussions continued between the authorities and his solicitors.
7 Veronique Mandal, 'Lost and Found: The Decline and Fall of Don Tait' in *Canadian Lawyer,* June 2000.
8 Conversation with author, 19 January 2001.
9 Jack Evseroff, conversation with author, 22 October 2000.
10 *Organised Crime Digest,* 13 April 1994.
11 Quoted by Andrew Coe, 'Mouthpieces' in *Crimebeat,* January 1993.
12 Joyce Wadler, 'Not Mob Lawyer. Just Lawyer. Uh for Gotti', in *New York Times,* 5 February 1998. Quite apart from that he thinks the clients are 'engaging. Charming and oftentimes, smart. A good number of people are undeniably boring. These people are not boring. My wife tells me that I fall in love with my clients.'

# Bibliography

Asbury, H., *Sucker's Progress* (1938) New York, Dodd, Mead & Co.

Bechofer Roberts, C.E., *The Mr A Case* (1960) London, Jarrolds.

Bishop, J., *The Murder Trial of Judge Peel* (1962) New York, Trident Press.

Boswell, C., and Thompson, L., *Advocates of Murder* (1962) New York, Collier Books.

Bowen, C., *The Elegant Oakey* (1956) New York, Oxford University Press.

Browne, D., *Sir Travers Humphreys* (1960) London, George G. Harrap & Co.

Callow, A.B. jnr., *The Tweed Ring* (1966) New York, Oxford University Press.

Campbell, R., *The Luciano Project: The Secret Wartime Collaboration of the Mafia and the US Navy* (1977) New York, McGraw-Hill.

Cohen, D., *The Encyclopedia of Unsolved Crimes* (1988) New York, Dodd, Mead & Co.

Crater, S. and Fraley, O., *The Empty Robe* (1961) Garden City, New York, Doubleday.

Crocker, W.C., *Far From Humdrum* (1967) London, Hutchinson.

Cummins, J. and Volkman, E., *Mobster* (1991) London, Futura.

Daley, R., *Prince of the City* (1981) New York, Berkley.

Danforth, H.A. and Horan, J.D., *The D.A.'s Man* (1957) New York, Crown Publishers.

Darling, Lord, *Lord Darling and His Famous Trials* (n.d.) London, Hutchinson & Co.

Davis, J.H., *Mafia Kingfish* (1989) New York, McGraw-Hill Publishing Co.

Dawson, L.H., *Hoyle's Games Modernised* (1950) London, Routledge & Kegan Paul.

Denning, Lord, *The Denning Report* (1992) London, Pimlico.

Dershowitz, A., *The Best Defense* (1983) New York, Vintage Books.

Dewey, T.E., *Twenty Against the World* (1974) New York, Doubleday & Co.

Dilnot, G. (ed.), *The Trial of the Detectives* (1928) London, Geoffrey Bles.

———*The Trial of Jim the Penman* (1930) London, Geoffrey Bles.

English, T.J., *The Westies* (1990) New York, F.P. Putnam's Sons.

Felstead, S.T., *Sir Richard Muir* (1927) London, John Lane, The Bodley Head.

Ferber, N., *I Found Out* (1939) New York, The Dial Press.

Fowler, G., *The Big Mouthpiece* (1934) New York, Ribbon Books.

———*Beau James: The Life and Times of Jimmy Walker* (1949) New York, Viking.

Fraser, F., *Mad Frank* (1994) London, Warner.

———*Mad Frank's Diary* (2000) London, Virgin Publishing.

Giradin, G.R. with Helmer, W.J., *Dillinger, The Untold Story* (1994) Bloomingdale, The University of Indiana Press.

Goodman, James, *Stories of Scottsboro* (1994) New York, Pantheon Books.

Goodman, Jonathan, *The Modern Murder Yearbook* (1994) London, Robinson Publishing.

Gosling, J., *The Ghost Squad* (1959) London, W.H. Allen.

Harlow, A.F., *Old Bowery Days* (1931) New York, D. Appleton & Co.

Hastie, R., Penrod, S.D. and Pennington, N., *Inside the Jury* (1983) Cambridge, Mass., Harvard University Press.

Honeycombe, G., *The Murders of the Black Museum 1870-1970* (1988) London, Mysterious Press.

Howe, W.F. and Hummel, A., *In Danger or Life in New York, a True History* (1886) New York, J.S. Ogilvie.

Hummel, A., *The Trial and Conviction of Jack Reynolds for the Horrible Murder of William Townsend* (1870) New York, North American News Co.

Hutter, E., *The Chillingworth Murder Case* (1963) Derby, Conn., Monarch.

Hynd, A., *Defenders of the Damned* (1960) San Diego, A.S. Barnes.

Ianni, F., *A Family Business –Kinship and Social Control in Organised Crime* (1972) New York, Russell Sage Foundation.

Johnson, S., *Against the Law* (1986) New York, Bantam Books.

Juxon, J., *Lewis & Lewis* (1983) London, Collins.

Katcher, L., *The Big Bank-Roll* (1958) London, Gollancz.

Katz, L., *Uncle Frank: The Biography of Frank Costello* (1973) New York, Drake.

Keeler, C. and Meadley, R., *Sex Scandals* (1985) London, Xanadu.

Kennedy, L., *The Airman and the Carpenter* (1985) New York, Viking.

Kobler, J., *The Life and World of Al Capone* (1971) London, Coronet Books.

Lacey, R., *Little Man* (1991) Boston, Little, Brown.

Lang, G., *Mr Justice Avory* (1935) London, Herbert Jenkins.

Langford, G., *The Murder of Stanford White* (1962) London, Gollancz.

Lewis, A.H., *The Worlds of Chippy Patterson* (1960) London, Victor Gollancz.

Lief, M.S., Caldwell, M. and Bycel, B., *Ladies and Gentlemen of the Jury* (1998) New York, Scribner.

Littleton, M., *My Partner-in-Law* (1957) New York, Farrar, Straus & Cudahy.

Lockwood, B. and Mendenhall, H.H., *Operation Greylord: Brocton Lockwood's Story* (1989) Carbondale, Southern Illinois University Press.

Lynch, D.T., *Boss Tweed* (1927) New York, Boni & Liverwright.

———*Criminals and Politicians* (1932) New York, Macmillan & Co.

———*The Wild Seventies*, Port Washington, London, Kennikat Press.

Mark, R., *In the Office of Constable* (1978) London, Collins.

Mitgang, S., *The Man who Rode the Tiger; The Life and Times of Judge Samuel Seabury* (1963) New York, J.B. Lippincott Company.

Morton, J., *Gangland* (1992) London, Warner Books.
———*Gangland International* (1999) London, Warner Books.
———*East End Gangland* (2000) London, Little, Brown.
Mustain, G. and Capeci, J., *Murder Machine* (1992) New York, Dutton.
Nasaw, D., *The Chief* (2000) New York, Houghton Miflin.
Osborne, T.M., *Within Prison Walls* (1914) New York, D. Appleton & Co.
Pannick, D., *Judges* (1987) Oxford, Oxford University Press.
Parris, J., *Scapegoat* (1991) London, Duckworth.
Peterson, V., *Barbarians in Our Midst: A History of Chicago Crime and Politics* (1952) Boston, Little, Brown.
———*Captive City* (1969) New York, Lyle Stuart.
Ragano, F. and Rabb, S., *Mob Lawyer* (1994) New York, Charles Scribner's Sons.
Read, L., *Nipper* (1991) London, Macdonalds.
Read, P.P., *The Train Robbers* (1988) London, W.H. Allen.
Reynolds, Q., *Courtroom* (1961) New York, Popular Library.
Rockaway, R.A., *But – he was good to his mother* (1993) Hewlett, New York, Gefen Books.
Roeburt, J., *Get Me Giesler* (1962) New York, Belmont Books.
Rothstein, C., *Now I'll Tell* (1934) New York, The Vanguard Press.
Rovere, R., *Howe & Hummel* (1986) London, Arlington Books.
Schatzberg, R., *Black Organized Crime in Harlem: 1920–1930* (1993) New York, Garland Publishing.
Sharpe, M.C., *Chicago May* (1928) New York, The Macaulay Company.
Smith, N., *Catch and Kill Your Own* (1995) Sydney, Ironbark.
St Johns, A.R., *Final Verdict* (1963) London, Jonathan Cape.
Stone, I., *Clarence Darrow for the Defense* (1941) New York, Doubleday & Co.
Sullivan, A.M., *The Last Sergeant* (1952) London, Macdonald.
Thomas, D., *Honour Among Thieves* (1991) London, Weidenfeld & Nicholson.
Train, A., *My Day in Court* (1939) New York, Charles Scribner's Sons.
Tuohy, J. and Warden, R., *Greylord: Justice, Chicago Style* (1989) New York, G.P. Putnam's Sons.
Turkus, B.B. and Feder, S., *Murder, Inc.* (1951) New York, Farrar, Straus and Young.
Van Every, E., *Sins of New York* (1930) New York, Frederick A. Stokes.

Wain, J. (ed.), *The Journals of James Boswell* (1992) London, Mandarin.

Whittington-Egan, R., *Oscar Slater* (2001) Edinburgh, Mainstream.

Willensee, C.W., *Behind the Green Lights* (1931) New York, A.A. Knopf; (1933) London, John Long.

– – –*A Cop Remembers* (1933) New York, E.P. Dutton & Co.

Wolf, G. and DiMona, J., *Frank Costello: Prime Minister of the Underworld* (1975) London, Futura.

## Articles etc:

Michael Abramowitz, 'The Gang that Couldn't Snitch Straight' in *Chicago Magazine*, August 1993.

Andrew Anthony, 'Crime and Passion: Sleeping with the Enemy' in *The Observer Review*, 14 September 1997.

A. Arthur, 'Captain Arthur's Own Story' in *Empire News*, 22, 29 November and 6, 13, 20 December 1925.

Frederic Dannen, 'Defending the Mafia' in *The New Yorker*, 21 February 1994.

J. Richard 'Dixie' Davis, 'Things I couldn't tell till now' in *Colliers*, 22, 29 July and 5, 12, 19 August 1939.

Ernest Havemann, 'The Great Trotting Scandal' in *Life*, 16 November 1953.

Anne Keegan, 'Sting in Cook County' in *Reader's Digest,* 9–16 June 1990.

John Lombardi, 'The Goodfather' in *New York Magazine*, 8 August 1998.

Jayant Mammen Mathew, 'Mob's Angel' in *The Week*, 15 August 1999.

Pennsylvania Crime Commission, *Report on Organized Crime*, Office of the Attorney General, Commonwealth of Pennsylvania, 1970.

President's Commission on Organized Crime, April 1986.

Charles Poletti, *Reminiscences*, Columbia Oral History Project 47, 1948.

Royal Commission of Inquiry into Drug Trafficking, February 1983, Australian Government Publishing Service, Canberra.

Randall Sambourn, 'El Rukn Case Prosecutors Under Fire' in *National Law Journal*, 21 December 1992.

Lester Velie, 'When Lawyers Plot the Crime' in *Reader's Digest*, April 1957.

# Index